THE NEW BASIC BLACK

THE NEW BASIC BLACK

Home Training for Modern Times

Revised Edition

KAREN GRIGSBY BATES

& KAREN ELYSE HUDSON

Illustrations by Deborah A. Porter

Doubleday

NEW YORK • LONDON • TORONTO • SYDNEY • AUCKLAND

PUBLISHED BY DOUBLEDAY
a division of Random House, Inc.

DOUBLEDAY and the portrayal of an anchor with a dolphin
are registered trademarks of Random House, Inc.

A previous edition of this book was published in 1996 by Doubleday under the title *Basic Black: Home Training for Modern Times*

Book design by Debbie Glasserman

Library of Congress Cataloging-in-Publication Data is on file with the Library of Congress.

ISBN 0-385-51626-6

PRINTED IN THE UNITED STATES OF AMERICA

1 3 5 7 9 10 8 6 4 2

For
our mothers
and grandmothers

A Note About the New Edition

Life has changed a lot since we wrote the original *Basic Black.* Technology has evolved by leaps and bounds. Time, a short commodity even then, is now more precious than ever. And global events have shown us that lives can be altered, even ended, in the blink of an eye on what outwardly looks like a perfect day.

So much change in such a short period of time! Yet despite the warp-speed changes in the past several years, some things remain classics: love of family, loyalty to friends, commitment to community, pride in culture, protection of children, and preservation of traditions. Those things remain perennially precious and will be cherished throughout generations.

We believe the information in the new Part VII, Looking Forward, will provide you with knowledge and resources that will enable you to move forward in your life and live it in the way that is best for you and your loved ones. Knowledge is power—and protection. So whether it's readying yourself for travel, using the new technology to stay in touch with family members, shielding yourself from identity theft, or striving to be the best you can, we want you to be as prepared as possible.

We *still* believe our mothers—and your mother—were right. Continue the traditions upon which we were all raised, and pass them on to your children.

Karen Grigsby Bates
Karen Elyse Hudson
May 2005

HOME TRAINING:
Our Definition

home training *(hōm trān'ing) n. colloq., African American.* 1. The education, instruction, or discipline of a person in accepted mores or values. 2. Possessing behavior that is reflective of proper rearing. 3. Correct breeding. *Synonyms:* good manners; proper breeding; polite behavior. *Antonyms:* rude; impolite; without culture or refinement

Contents

III. Life Lessons
The Complete Seminar 109

26. Pride and Joy 259

V. Function at the Junction
Party All the Time 277

27. The Honor of Your Presence 279

28. Hostess with the Mostest 292

VI. Milestones
Important Stops on the Road of Life 343

VII. Looking Forward
Life in the New Millennium 433

Introduction

We're often asked why we chose to write an etiquette book for our community, and many thoughts come to mind. To begin with, our culture is unique and filled with tradition that has not been addressed, to our knowledge, in other etiquette books. We take pride in this heritage. While manners in general are colorless and span class, age, and environmental and geographic differences, nothing beats good old "home training." No one can teach us the way our grandmothers, mothers, and aunts have taught us for centuries. From fathers and grandfathers, boys, too, learned lessons that endured. In that spirit, we offer you a guide for modern living, not a mandate.

Now that women are working outside the home in greater numbers, our family structure has changed. Today's household may be traditional, it may be headed by a single parent, or it may even involve "babies raising babies." Gone are the days when families sat down to dinner together each and every night. Gone, too, are the days when everyone looked out for each other. Those were the days of knowing that your mother would have been told about one of your lapses in manners long before you ever returned home from school.

Remember those evenings when you'd get home, do your homework and chores, and eagerly await dinner? At the dinner table you learned from listening as elders spoke; you learned to listen (because you'd better not interrupt when your dad was asking your sister why he got a note from her teacher); you learned to speak clearly when you were asked about your day;

you learned to share and not blow bubbles in your milk. And the lessons extended to the kitchen. As you became old enough to participate in setting the table, you also learned which dishes should arrive covered, which tablecloth was used for holidays, and which glasses were for milk, lemonade, or Dad's favorite beverage.

You also learned, by example, the importance of sharing as a family. You may have dreaded that evening when you knew you couldn't leave the table before you finished those lima beans, but you genuinely anticipated your brother's birthday because you knew it meant having his favorites—Chinese food and chocolate cake. You developed family traditions that were special to your family. They were extra special because they may not have been mirrored anywhere else.

It was a kinder, gentler time. We took extra care to be courteous and helpful to one another in light of legally imposed second-class status. Youngsters knew not to talk back to elders, and there was a widespread respect for codes of conduct nurtured by the matriarchs and patriarchs of our families. Today, instead of tailor-made family traditions, too many of us—by necessity—are living a *microwave lifestyle.* We're too busy to sit down to dinner together more than once a week, and the manners we once absorbed, unconsciously, have been displaced.

As we move into the corporate workplace, as we become members of country clubs, as we take advantage of educational opportunities from preschool through college and graduate school, we begin to walk on other playing fields. We have progressed from being barred from joining certain organizations to not only being active members but assuming leadership roles. Mentors have been few and far between. Often we have been left in the position of being invited to play a new game without the benefit of the new rule book. It's one thing to have your children travel across town in an attempt to gain a better education or to broaden their experiences; it's quite another when a new friend invites them to a bar mitzvah. Nowhere in the freshman guide to an Ivy League school does it explain what to wear or what to expect at a tea given for the women in your dorm.

Make no doubt about it, this is a book for you brothers too. Although you may not be into planning a wedding or hosting a two-year-old's birthday party by your lonesome, you do entertain, you do travel, you have a family, you work, and by all means, you are black in America. Enjoy the information offered, share the tips with your friends, and remember that our lives are more complete when we arm ourselves with whatever information will make life easier. The book is for everyone, but we thought we'd single out some messages just for you. You'll find them under the "And Brother, Remember" sections scattered throughout the book.

It's a new world out there, and we look at this book as a reference that can be consulted at those times when you're not quite sure how to respond to a particular situation. It's all about being comfortable—comfortable in unfamiliar situations, comfortable as you host a business dinner, comfortable as you attend a wedding at a church or mosque that differs in custom from yours. Manners and etiquette are, simply put, about being comfortable and being confident enough to make others feel comfortable, too.

Most people think of etiquette in its traditional forms: how to set a formal dinner table; how to extend an invitation; the correct procession for a bridal party; the dreaded "which fork goes with what?" In our world, etiquette is so much more. It's how to react in the workplace when a racial joke is told in your presence. It's how to conduct yourself when a controversial vote or action has taken place and everyday life in the workplace takes on a new level of discomfort. Before you know it, a single word from you or a coworker can precipitate an ever-widening gap in understanding. Without a doubt, it's also about how to plan a funeral for a loved one. Let's face it: no matter how fancy the hospital was where you were born, no matter how integrated your school was, no matter if you're head of a Fortune 500 company—*you die black.* We return to the churches we were raised in, we look for a soloist from our community, we make that first call to the same mortuary where your aunt set up a pre-need account some thirty years earlier. When asked by our white colleagues to give them an example of what we mean by cultural differences in etiquette, we have frequently cited the ritual of funerals. Instead of going into long-drawn-out explanations, we just say, "For one thing, we feed people!"

Historically, our rituals, ceremonies, and family traditions have shown tremendous respect for the dignity of the family. To us, no one will die if you use the wrong fork, but each of us will lose a little piece of ourselves if we choose to live our lives without a genuine respect for morality, character, kindness, and, of course, other people.

We don't expect you to read this book from cover to cover, but chapter by chapter as the need arises. With this book we hope to increase the comfort level in our community, to arm you with the same information everyone else has, and to take the mystery out of conventional etiquette. Hasn't your mother ever told you, "It's better to have it and not need it than to need it and not have it"? And the older you get, the more you realize that *your mother was right!* We know you understand.

The Two Karens

Part I

YOUR MOTHER WAS RIGHT!

Remembering the Good Advice You Got "Back When"

A refresher course on the basics of everyday black life

elementary courtesies

supporting our community

pride in our heritage

friendship

living within your means

church life

Chapter 1

IT GOES WITHOUT SAYING

If you're going to play the game properly,
you'd better know every rule.

Barbara Jordan

Here's where we run through the basics. And basics are the foundation upon which good home training is built. You know what the basics are; you learned them in Sunday school. Or at the knees of your mother, grandmother, and aunts. And though the hectic pace of daily life sometimes threatens to hide that foundation, you know that if you reach deeply enough, you'll find the basics right there when you need them.

Manners transcend social status, race, and gender. Courtesy and consideration help to make the unbearable parts of life a little more bearable. And you probably know, from having met one (or better, being one yourself), that a person who is considerate of others is welcome almost anywhere.

All major religions have a simple phrase that distills what good manners are: doing unto others as you would like others to do unto you. This Golden Rule applies to friendships, workplace relationships, romances, and family interaction—virtually all human relationships.

The basics of good manners (besides the above) include the very things that, in another age, were referred to in our culture as "home training." We're sure you remember them. They include the following:

Respect for Elders

- Standing (if sitting) when being introduced
- Offering to pull up a chair or help put on a coat
- Offering a seat when on public transportation
- Speaking respectfully (saving one's slang for one's peers)
- Offering to serve as an extra pair of arms and legs:

  "May I bring you some dessert, Aunt Emma? Let me tell you what's on the buffet table."

  "Would you like me to reach that for you? Those cereal boxes are always stacked up so high!"

  "Excuse me, but you dropped your change purse."

CP Time

We all know what CP time is. But when we let our personal clocks dominate Greenwich mean time, all kinds of trouble happens. (We've been told this is not endemic to "colored people"—a Jewish friend assures us there's JPT, an Italian IPT, etc.) If you're going to be late meeting a personal friend, try to call so she's not kept waiting. *Definitely* call ahead as soon as you know you won't arrive at a business or professional appointment on time. (Here's where cellular phones can be a blessing: "I'm calling from my car; a big accident up the road has tied things up for miles. I'm afraid I'm going to be at least twenty minutes late; would you check to see if he'd still like me to come, or should we reschedule?")

The same should apply to an appointment with a doctor, lawyer, or hairstylist: call and let them know you've been delayed for reasons beyond your control, ask if it will still be convenient for you to come, or, if not, if you can reschedule the appointment. People often don't mind trying to accommodate you if they feel you've shown them a little consideration. For someone who owns his own business or who bills by the hour, time is literally money. And this works two ways: doctors should not keep their patients waiting, either.

Note: Do not have a chronic excuse. If you're *always* late for a haircut because of "heavy traffic" or some other excuse, sooner or later your stylist will simply factor in your habitual late time and make you wait. If you always overbook your patients or clients, sooner or later they vote with their feet and move elsewhere.

Excuses, Excuses, Excuses

Sometimes excuses are unavoidable: your child becomes sick at the last moment; you get a flat tire; your plane leaves late. In those cases, you explain briefly what's delayed you or forced your deadline back: "Janet, I'm so sorry. We were planning to come to your party tonight, but Courtney has a sore throat and a temperature. I hope we haven't inconvenienced you too much."

For work, you need to indicate that you're aware the delay may cause problems and will try to clear things up as soon as possible: "Mr. Sanders, my mother-in-law died this morning, and I'm afraid I'm going to be gone for the rest of the week. I plan to take the Jeffrey account with me and I hope to have my recommendations to you by next Tuesday."

Never invent an illness or death as an excuse for not completing an assignment or meeting a deadline. If you're not ill but don't wish to go to a social engagement you've already agreed to attend, think of an excuse that doesn't require you to "gift" your family (or yourself) with a dire fate you'd like to avoid in real life. Remember what the old folks say: what goes around comes around.

Public vs. Private Manners

Don't make the mistake of being more courteous to strangers or people upon whom you wish to make a good impression than you are to your own family and close friends. The same rules of consideration apply: there is no such thing as second-class manners (or if there is, we don't want to know about it). Everyone in your life should be treated as if it's vitally important that he or she thinks well of you.

And Brother, Remember

It may be your sister, your wife, your girlfriend, or a casual buddy at work; when you honor and appreciate your relationships with women, you'll be surprised at what you receive in return.

Race and Good Behavior

"Act your age, not your color" used to be how some folks reminded others that the world expected lesser standards of us because of our race. When we behaved poorly, we were "acting like . . ." well, *you know*. And when we behaved well, we were considered a "credit to our race." Both phrases assumed that black people were one big population, one lumpen stereotype.

Good behavior, like manners, transcends race, gender, and even age. Reflecting well on oneself should be the rule of thumb.

Respect for Other Cultures

Variety *is* the spice of life, and the patchwork of different cultures and ethnicities is part of what makes America such a vibrant country. As we continue to evolve into what sociologist Marshall McLuhan called a global village, our exposure to and comfort level with other cultures increase. And we learn that what is acceptable in one circumstance may be offensive in another. In some Asian cultures, for example, a recipient wouldn't think of opening her present in front of the giver; in the Western world, we consider it important to open a gift when it's given to us. It's always a good idea to ask if you're not sure: "Mai Lee, when we go to your sister's wedding next Saturday, how should we dress?" "Robin, do women have to have their heads covered to visit your mosque?" The key here is to be as sensitive to another culture's traditions as we would want others to be to ours.

Welcoming People into Your Home

From the first time we came to these shores, even in the dark, lean times, we have been a hospitable people. So honor that tradition. When folks stop by to see you, tell them you're glad they've come to visit. Offer them refreshments. Warn them if you have pets they may be afraid of or allergic to: "Do you mind cats? We'd be happy to put KitKat in our bedroom while you're here." You want your guests to feel comfortable, and people are always more comfortable outside their own environment when they know what the rules are. If you don't smoke and don't want others to do it, either, a lack of ashtrays is usually enough of a hint to the astute guest. If someone doesn't catch the hint, feel free to let him know it's okay to smoke outside, but not in your home: "Oh, Jay, we don't smoke here. You can use our patio/balcony/sunporch if you need to, though."

When "No" Is All You Need to Say

Some things need no explanation, just a blunt, clearly understood "*no.*" Never feel you have to explain why you'd prefer not to:

- Accept an alcoholic drink
- Indulge in drugs
- Consider an improper sexual overture
- Participate in anything you consider illegal, immoral, or unethical

Making Things Right When You've Offended

They're the faux pas from hell, and they happen to all of us at one time or another: You've spoken badly about a woman who's turned out to be the listener's best friend. Your child, while tearing through someone else's house, bumps a table and a vase smashes. Your date mortifies you at a dinner party by drinking too much and making a pest of himself for the rest of the evening.

A sincere apology goes a long way toward easing bruised feelings. If you've spoken badly about a person who turns out to be a dear friend of (or worse, related to!) your listener, 'fess up: "Oh, gee, that's your sister? Me and my big mouth! I'm *really* sorry. Maybe we were both having a bad day when we met, but we did not get along."

If you or someone with you has broken a host's belongings, point it out, immediately offer to make repairs or replacements, and ask where the item was purchased: "Oh, Marcy, I am sorry! That was a beautiful vase. If you'll tell me where it came from, I'll call tomorrow and see if it can be replaced." (Your host may decline the offer, but she will appreciate the fact that you've made it.) In the case of irreplaceable objects, such as antiques, make profuse apologies and an offer to make amends for the appraised value of the item (even if you may have to pay it off in installments).

And if your inebriated date makes a fool of himself and puts a dent in everyone's evening, apologize to your hostess. And make your date (who, we hope, will be smart enough to figure this out on his own) send the hostess a written apology the next day. (Flowers wouldn't hurt, either.)

Can You Hear Me?

Unlike stereos, people don't come with dials or knobs you can use to turn down their volume. For the habitual shouter (and some people aren't aware that they are being loud), it's best to quietly take him aside and tell him he's decibels above everyone else: "Aaron, do you think you could speak just a little more softly? We can't hear the news at the other end of the room." Most people appreciate the hint.

Lateness of the Hour

Most of us don't lead lives of leisure. If invitations specify that dinner is from 8 to 11 P.M., don't inconvenience your host by staying on until 1 A.M. (The exception, of course, is when the host urges you to stay.) If the social event is held on a workday, it's especially important to leave promptly. If you arrive late to a social event, you should still leave when everyone else does.

Keeping Up with Social Mores; New Places

If you've got out-of-town guests who want to go club-hopping and you grab the Yellow Pages to look up "Nightclubs," you might want to think about updating your personal resource file. Keeping track of new restaurants, clubs, museum exhibitions, and so on doesn't take much time, and saves you from hectic, last-minute scrambling when you're trying to entertain your guests—or when you and your friends are looking for something to amuse yourselves. Snip interesting possibilities and keep them in a folder or shoe box so they're handy when you need to browse through them.

Table Manners

You remember these basics, we're sure: Elbows off the table. Squelch the urge to stretch past someone to retrieve what you want (your older relatives might have called this the "boardinghouse reach"), and ask that the desired item be *passed*, please. Resist the urge to place your napkin anywhere but in your lap: don't wear it like a bib (unless you're under two, or you're eating lobster in a restaurant) and by all means, don't tuck it into your belt! Ladies should remember to discreetly blot their lipstick, to lessen the chance of leaving hard-to-remove stains on a hostess's napkins and glassware.

When There's Only You, or a Very Few

Don't assume the burden for the race—although, in all likelihood, it will be handed to you from time to time anyway. Try to be patient with people who want to know how "all black people think." Emphasize that your opinions are your own and that you haven't polled the community at large: "I can't speak for all of us, but here's how I feel about raising standards in public schools." Recognize that for the culturally deprived, you are a new experience and that some lessons may have to be taught as well as learned: "Jean, I don't mind you asking about my hair, but I'd prefer that you not touch it."

Try to keep a sense of humor about the brave new world the noninitiated are entering. It's entirely possible that small children who have never seen black people may stare or even ask to touch you. Follow your instincts; children are often avidly curious, and you may make an impression on them that will last for a lifetime: "See, Shana, my cheek feels just like yours, but it's brown, just like chocolate milk."

Racial slights may occur, and when they do, certainly you shouldn't feel obliged to suffer in silence in the interest of racial harmony. People need to know they've offended you, and why—but they'll absorb the fact that they've made a major error if you can point it out *calmly*: "Jack, my mother never allowed that word in her presence, and I'd just as soon not hear it, either. Black people simply are not described that way." The civilized person will promptly apologize. (The uncivilized person may not, in which case you may feel free to remove yourself from his presence and seek more amiable company.)

Calling people racist is usually counterproductive. Pointing out racist behavior, however, can curb those tendencies in the future: "Mr. Jennings, I'm sure some people find that pretty amusing, but I think that kind of humor is racist—and totally unlike you." (What's Mr. Jennings going to do when you've pointed out his boorish behavior so politely? Protest that he is indeed a racist and tells these jokes all the time?) By condemning the remark and observing this behavior as atypical of the speaker, you've left the speaker with room for an apology: "Oh my God, Michelle, I don't know what got into me. You're right—that's not my kind of joke, and you won't hear it from me again." (For more on this, see chapter 23, "Plantation Life.")

It's also important to pick and choose when to point out such offensive behavior. Like the boy who cried "wolf!" the accusation of racism is much more potent when the occasion truly merits it.

Pledging Allegiance; the National Anthem

African Americans' relationship to the Pledge of Allegiance and the national anthem has been constantly evolving since the 1960s. Regardless of our political or religious beliefs, the Pledge of Allegiance and national anthem are for some as revered in American society as "Lift Ev'ry Voice" is. Many of our relatives fought and died on behalf of the United States in several wars so we could have the privilege of freedom.

When the Pledge of Allegiance is recited, no matter where you are, stop and stand at attention. This is done everywhere, from elementary schools to community meetings, and it's an unbendable rule. If you think "and liberty and justice for all" stretches things a bit, simply stand silently at attention. If you choose to recite the pledge, do it clearly and in time with those around you. When our national anthem is played, stand and sing it. (If you don't know the words, learn them.)

"Lift Ev'ry Voice and Sing"

Black Americans often feel we have two national anthems: "The Star-Spangled Banner" and "Lift Ev'ry Voice and Sing," which is popularly referred to as the Negro National Anthem. Whenever this song is played, stand at attention and sing. If you don't know the words, which eloquently trace our history in America, learn them. (See chapter 2, "Lift Ev'ry Voice.")

Prayers

Sometimes in large gatherings, you'll be asked to bow your head "for a moment of prayer" or for an invocation or benediction. Whether or not you believe in God, bow your head and remain silent for the duration of the prayer. Do not, under any circumstances, talk, fidget, or otherwise interrupt others around you who might want to pray. (But you knew this, didn't you?)

Chapter 2

LIFT EV'RY VOICE

For I am my mother's daughter,
and the dreams of Africa still beat in my heart.
They will not let me rest while there is a single
Negro boy or girl without a chance
to prove his worth.

Mary McLeod Bethune

Home training, as we know it, is much more than simple table manners and party etiquette. For generations our relatives have instilled in us a sense of pride, heritage, and empowerment. We had many lessons to learn, and each new generation has been faced with a new set of challenges and standards. Above all, we were taught to be proud of our heritage, to prepare ourselves by getting an education, to look out for one another, to hold family in the highest esteem, and, finally, to "open your eyes and watch your back." When we as a people "lift ev'ry voice . . . till earth and heaven ring," we have quite a legacy to sing about.

Pride, Heritage, and Grace

For centuries African Americans have contributed to the growth and development of our country. Knowledge of the history of blacks cannot help but instill pride and commitment in all who have been fortunate enough to have had access to the information. We must learn to record the history that each of our families has to share, to preserve the treasured photographs and artifacts, to disseminate the information to others. The young person who falters as he learns how to cross the street will pay much more attention when he is taught that a black man invented the traffic signal. The teenager who resides in a public housing project may find inspiration to solve the urban housing crisis when he learns an African American designed his building. And the young lady who thinks her entire social life depends on having her own telephone can be reassured by stories of the grace and elegance of her great-grandmother, who had no modern conveniences. We have accomplished so very much with so little.

Family Values

We African Americans have held our families together with love and a sense of deeply ingrained values that have transcended slavery, hard times, and evolving definitions of family.

Along the way, we have learned some simple truths: Protect and take care of the children. Look after and respect the elders. Take time to listen to each other. "Be there" for your parents, your siblings, and your extended family. Be supportive of each other's dreams. Recognize the fears. It's a sharing of the good times as well as the bad times. It's not giving up on each other. It's sharing. Be it a tiny apartment, a single room, or a mansion—home is what you make it. (P.S. Extend a hand to those in need—even if they aren't blood relatives.)

The Children Really Are the Future

Recognizing the significance of the adage "It takes a village to raise a child" is half the battle. All children deserve to be armed with the necessary tools to face the challenges that they will meet. Think in terms of the information you would share with young people in an effort to raise them to be outstanding members of their community. As we seek to inspire them to become the persons they aspire to be, there are a few lessons we don't readily think of. It's not enough to teach them which fork to use or how to address their teachers. We must also give them a love of reading; the gift of being a good listener; as broad an education as possible; and exposure to the history and culture of their ancestors. We must also embrace the passion in young people and teach them to understand both civil rights and politics in this country. By doing so, we are passing the torch to a new generation, helping to ensure that the flame continues to burn brightly.

Passing the Torch

As we learned from the elders that preceded us, today each of us has a responsibility to the next generation, and they to their successors. Speaking during the turbulent 1960s, veteran civil rights activist H. Claude Hudson shared a message that remains equally relevant today.

> *The burden of carrying on this struggle today belongs to our young people, who must not feel that all the battles have been won. Though the problems they face may differ in number and kind from those my generation faced, American Negroes must continue to be vigilant, courageous, and persistent in the fight for full freedom and equality. My generation has opened doors with dignity, courage, and determination. It is the task of our young people to keep them open and to forge ahead.*

Heroes and Role Models

All of us can be inspired by role models. From legendary heroes of the past who broke ground in various fields to the neighborhood teacher who fights for better books, we can find these models in many places. Although we appreciate advancements in all fields, we should look beyond the obvious athletes and entertainers and find our own examples of pride and accomplishment. The youngster who doesn't know about Ronald McNair or Mae Jemison may not truly believe that he or she can be an astronaut. Committed young lawyers may not realize there is a role for them in civil rights litigation if their only point of reference is Clarence Thomas and not Thurgood Marshall. Young men need to see fathers who are role models, and how scientists are making a difference in finding medical cures. Enlist your friends, neighbors, church groups, and club members to take part in career days at school; clip articles about African Americans who are making a difference and *make* their voices heard.

Education

Education has always been important to African Americans. When we were slaves, we risked death to learn to read and write. Later, as freedmen, we made enormous sacrifices so our children would, with education, live better lives and help to uplift their brethren. Being eager to learn, and serious about education, is as much a birthright for us as it is for any American. Revering education isn't "acting white"—it's acting smart.

Read, Listen, Observe

Perhaps an elder in your family pointed this out to you when you were tiny, but it bears repeating: all learning isn't found in books, and learning doesn't stop just because we stop going to school. The truly intelligent person, whether he has a third-grade education or was fortunate enough to earn a Ph.D., never stops in his quest for knowledge. A lot of the most important parts of our education take place outside the classroom. So try to keep up with current events, read at least one newspaper daily, read any and all books and magazines you can get your hands on, and pay attention to what's going on around you. Take advantage of cultural events and exhibitions that visit your city, plan excursions to museums (check your newspaper listings; often there is a day each month or week when admission is free). When you hear that an interesting person will be lecturing in your city, call a friend and go together. The more information we have at hand, the better prepared we are for the challenges that lie ahead.

As You Visit Other Cities

As you, your friends, and your family visit cities across the country, make a point of reading about local black history, visit sites of civil rights deeds, look for "hidden tours" not offered by the local chamber of commerce. Often small companies have a wealth of information about regional history. From underground railroads to little-known museums and recipes of yesteryear, a trip to another city can actually transport you to another place and time.

Black History Month

True, February is the shortest month of the year, and it is the only month when institutions across the country choose to celebrate the accomplishments of African Americans. Participate in Black History Month activities in your community. These will take place at your place of work, your child's school, city facilities, academic institutions, churches, and businesses. Have you ever noticed that every black film you've ever seen shows up at one time or another during Black History Month? Bookstores fill their windows with African American literature, and African American experts on black achievers grow hoarse from public speaking. We can lobby for television and newspapers to highlight African American achievements throughout the year. Speakers can request to make presentations in a month other than February, and schools can teach black history year round. Blacks have contributed to history on a daily basis, and information can be shared on a daily basis.

Families and Extended Families

As independent and self-sufficient as we may be in our everyday life, at one time or another we will need each other. Historically, blacks have benefited from the hospitality and comfort of extended families. It's a give-and-take proposition. One day you'll welcome a newcomer at work and offer much-appreciated guidance in navigating the minefields of a corporate workplace (where for years you've been the only one, or one of a few); and the following year your teenager may be going three thousand miles away to school and your coworker's family will be the only name she knows other than that of her unfriendly roommate. When Thanksgiving comes and she can't make it home, you and she both will welcome the hospitality of her new "family." Sometimes it's simply a matter of a friendly face in an unfamiliar surrounding, sometimes it's a shoulder to cry on or someone to try out your speech on.

Sharing and Mentoring

Sharing of information and mentoring those who have chosen paths similar to those you have trod will be as rewarding to you as it is to those who will benefit from your generosity. Anything that helps us be better informed, and prepared, will benefit our community in general.

Historically Speaking

Too often events in our history are forgotten because they have not been recorded. The stories of grandparents and great-grandparents are themselves history lessons. Record those histories, either on a tape recorder or in writing. Once history has been recorded, it cannot be forgotten. To ensure that our history is recorded correctly, we must emphasize the importance of recording oral histories or writing it *ourselves*, rather than leaving this important task to others' interpretation and *possible* distribution to those less informed.

Economic Empowerment

Economic empowerment comes down to this: *support black businesses.* In using black-owned and -operated businesses, you reinvest in your own community and help to strengthen and stabilize our neighborhoods. From the mom-and-pop store on the corner to the financial institution that will use your deposits to ensure home loans within the community, with each dollar we further secure our position and help realize the dreams of private practitioners in medicine, law, and business. It's not just the beauty shops, it's the bookstores. It's the restaurants that make you feel good when you've had a bad day, and the private school that nurtures our children.

It's Your Right and Privilege

Throughout our history, African Americans have fought and died for the right to vote. Their blood, sweat, and tears—reinforced by constitutional amendments and key voting rights legislation—have ensured our right to vote. It would exhibit a woeful lack of home training to disregard their sacrifices and achievements.

Participate in the electoral process. Disenchantment with the political system does not negate your ability to affect and empower your community. Each and every vote counts. You may believe that on a federal level it's a no-win situation, but failure to vote in a presidential election also means you lose the opportunity to influence your local elections and the propositions and ballot measures that will affect your daily life. When you feel passionately about a candidate or an issue, work for them. The donation of time or money can be invaluable in a close race. Do your homework, learn about the candidates and ballot measures—*do not let the media make your decisions for you.*

Media and the Portrayal of African Americans

Just as the media have the strength to influence elections, they also have the ability to portray African Americans in a less-than-favorable light. When people treat you in an inappropriate manner because of the stereotypes that have become ingrained in their subconscious, it becomes quite apparent that we can easily be misunderstood. Generalities abound, and we do have a course of action if we deem it necessary. If you witness an egregious lack of judgment and racial inappropriateness, you can call or write the offending station or newspaper. A simple postcard campaign can affect programming and future decisions. You are not being asked to be the "media police," but do be cognizant of what is being distributed. This is also true of the books and films that are being used as part of the curriculum at your child or grandchild's school. Alert others, take a stand.

Giving Something Back

When time and energy permit, identify an organization that shares some of your goals and that would allow you to give something of yourself to those less fortunate. Much of the change that we as a people dream of depends on vast amounts of money and man hours. Once again, it's being appreciative of what you've been given.

You may possess skills that you take for granted. Your organizational skills as a mother, your telephone skills that come from your sales job, your confidence as a mediator from your days as president of the ladies' auxiliary, or your ability to canvass neighbors door-to-door may be just the talent an organization or group needs to make meaningful change in our society. Certainly everyone doesn't have time or money at each step of their life, but *do what you can, when you can.*

That Fifteen Minutes of Fame

Just because a television camera is in your face and someone has shoved a microphone up to your mouth, there's no reason to lose your mind. We're not sure when our people started telling all their business on nationally televised talk shows, but there must be times you look at them and think, "I know that child's grandmother must not be living—either that, or they simply have *no* home training." Accept the media attention that comes with success, but do not brag. When asked about an unfolding event such as a trial in process, a police beating, a family misunderstanding, or the highs and lows of your local politician, *think before you speak.*

Celebrate the Accomplishments of Others

Don't wait for a retirement or an unexpected tragedy to tell others how much you admire them. With the joys of success often comes a group of people waiting for you to fail. We don't know why a scandalous story in a tabloid is more interesting than completing an exciting project or raising a delightful child. Take a moment every once in a while to call your friends or family members and let them know how terrific they are. You can brighten an otherwise dismal day with a phone call to a friend just to let her know you think she's a talented photographer and everyone loves the photos she took of your son. And nothing beats opening a short note from a friend or acquaintance who was thrilled to read you'd just received an important appointment or promotion. A stay-at-home mother is rarely complimented on her volunteer efforts, her great baking, or her polite child. Again, it's the personal touch that counts.

What's That? A Chip?

Through no fault of any of ours, some are born to a more comfortable life than others. But everyone has crosses to bear, challenges to face. Accept the cards that are dealt you and make the most of them. Identify opportunities, be a good friend to others, take a moment to reflect before you take the path of least resistance, and cease to think the whole world owes you something.

Allowing a chip to remain on your shoulder, for whatever reason, could hinder your becoming all that you hope to be.

Roads to Travel

We still have a long way to go. Live your life to the fullest, take time to care about others, and no matter where you go, or how lofty the goals attained, give something back to your community.

"Lift Ev'ry Voice and Sing"

Written by James Weldon Johnson, with music by his brother, composer J. Rosamond Johnson, this inspirational song is often referred to as the Negro National Anthem. The words are a testimony to the struggles, as well as the achievements, of African Americans past, present, and future.

Lift ev'ry voice and sing,
Till earth and heaven ring,
Ring with the harmonies of Liberty;
Let our rejoicing rise
High as the list'ning skies,
Let it resound loud as the rolling sea.
Sing a song full of the faith that the dark past has taught us;
Sing a song full of the hope that the present has brought us;
Facing the rising sun of our new day begun,
Let us march on till victory is won.

Stony the road we trod,
Bitter the chast'ning rod,
Felt in the days when hope unborn had died;
Yet with a steady beat,
Have not our weary feet
Come to the place for which our fathers sighed?
We have come over a way that with tears has been watered;
We have come, treading our path thro' the blood of the slaughtered,
Out from the gloomy past. Till now we stand at last
Where the white gleam of our bright star is cast.

God of our weary years,
God of our silent tears,
Thou who hast brought us thus far on the way;
Thou who hast by Thy might,
Led us into the light,

Keep us forever in the path, we pray.
Lest our feet stray from the places, our God, where we met Thee,
Lest our hearts, drunk with the wine of the world, we forget Thee;
Shadowed beneath Thy hand, may we forever stand,
True to our God, True to our native land.

Chapter 3

BE A FRIEND

No person is your friend (or kin)
who demands your silence, or denies your
right to grow and be perceived as
fully blossomed as you were intended.

Alice Walker

For those of us who are fortunate enough to have wonderful families, siblings and other family members can be among your best friends. And for those of us who are sure the saying "You can't choose your relatives but you can choose your friends" was written just for them, friends are and will always be an integral part of our well-being. Being a friend, and having a friend, gives us an unsurpassed strength in both good and bad times.

A friend is someone with whom you can be "the real you," someone who understands the give-and-take of friendship. It is often said that a friend is a present you give yourself. Friends come in all sizes, shapes, and colors. They're the little boy who pulled your hair in elementary school, the girl next door who walked to school with you, the roommate you got by accident, the coworker who took you under her wing, the guy who saved you from a life of misery with someone you had no business dating, the pen pal from across the water, someone who shares your love of genealogy or argues the same issues at a meeting.

Friends who belong to the same club or organization are often easier to identify, but friendship can spring up among people vastly different in personality, political views, or lifestyles. Old friends may offer comfort, while new friends may energize you and allow you to look at life with a different perspective. We're always pleasantly surprised at that special, unexpected moment when an acquaintance becomes a friend.

Time brings about a change. Friendships change and grow just as you do. Over the years, circumstances may not allow you to talk on the phone all day as you did as a teenager, but we can adapt to the changes. Do not judge your friend because he or she has "changed" and may not be available to you the same way as before. As we wade through life and go from student to employee, spouse to parent, experiencing the challenges along the way, we must stick by our friends and accept them for who they are and for who they have become. There may be times when time and distance separate true friends, but the lack of day-to-day contact will not lessen your friendship. Friends will always be there when you need them even if you haven't seen them in years. It's during times of celebration, and crisis, that we realize who our true friends are. Friends celebrate the good times, and more important, they are there for the life-changing experiences. As you and your friends go through the trials and tribulations of life, remember how important it is for you to be a friend. It will always be the little things that are most remembered.

Listening

A friend is always there to listen, and listens with a different ear than the average person. When a friend tells you about her impending divorce and how dreadful her husband is, if you are a good friend, you listen but do not offer unsolicited advice. As you listen to the words, you must also listen to what is not being said. The friend who says she is not lonely and really "loves being alone" may or may not be telling you the truth. Listen with your heart *and* your head as well as your ears.

And Brother, Remember

Being There for Your Best Friend

Men often play ball together, go fishing, share breakfasts, and generally "hang out," but they're hesitant to talk openly about their hopes and fears. If you think your friend is troubled and would like to talk, make it easy on him and let him know that you realize something is bothering him and you're there if he'd like to talk.

When Your Best Friend Is a Woman

When your best friend is a woman, by all means show her the same consideration you show your spouse or current love, but do not be disrespectful of your wife or girlfriend. Do not use your friend as a convenient escape from your spouse and the problems you may be having.

Giving and Receiving Compliments

Often it's harder to accept compliments than to give them. We forget to compliment friends because we assume they know how we feel, and we have difficulty accepting compliments because we feel uncomfortable about being singled out. You should compliment both friends and acquaintances freely, and with sincerity: a compliment loses its significance if it's tossed around indiscriminately and fails to show genuine feeling.

Nothing beats an unexpected compliment when you're feeling as if the whole world is against you while walking down the street, showing up for a party, or going off to face the wolves at the morning office meeting. Instantly, a smile emerges when someone tells you that your new hairstyle is flattering or raves about the spectacular report you gave at yesterday's meeting.

Although they may sometimes be embarrassing, compliments should be accepted with a simple "thank you." There is no need to feel that you must reciprocate with a similar compliment. But knowing how good a compliment makes *you* feel and what a boost it can be to *your* confidence, remember to reciprocate freely when appropriate.

Being the Same with Family and Friends

Don't take your family for granted. Frequently, our behavior suggests that "family will understand" and therefore we are not as kind and considerate as we should be. Under no circumstances should you treat your friends with more respect than you do your family. Do not assume that you must be on time for friends and not for family. Remembering birthdays, offering assistance during illness, and keeping promises are not reserved for friends. You don't, for instance, cancel going to a family dinner at the last minute because you received a last-minute "better offer" from a friend.

Remembering Birthdays and Significant Events

Celebrating birthdays is among our favorite activities when it comes to friends. We remember our friends on their birthdays as a way of demonstrating how glad we are that they were born. Again, it's the little things. Acknowledging significant events does not mean you have to indulge in purchasing extravagant gifts or throwing "the best party in town." Your remembrance can be as simple as a phone call, a handwritten note, a card, or lunch. Some of the events you should consider remembering/observing:

- Birthdays
- Funerals
- Engagements and weddings
- Births and christenings
- Anniversaries
- Graduations
- New jobs
- Promotions
- Opening a business
- Creative accomplishments (selling a painting or publication of a book)
- Anniversary of the death of someone who had been very special to your friend. (Don't let her think she's the only one who remembers.)
- Moving

Anticipating Needs

Friends don't wait for others to request help; instead they anticipate needs. The friend with the flu may not have the energy to cook for her kids and would love you to take them out to eat or bring over a casserole. When studying for the bar exam, a care package of aspirin, with his or her favorite coffee or tea, chocolate chip cookies, and some fried chicken might be just the medicine after an all-nighter spent studying. A friend with a recently rescheduled late meeting may not want to impose by asking you to pick up her daughter from dance class, but you know she would gladly accept if offered. And when death strikes a friend's family, an offer to notify others, help prepare an obituary, locate a soloist for the funeral, or drop off paper plates, cups, and napkins may be made quietly and unobtrusively. Anticipating needs isn't always about the crisis of the moment. Friends who slip into the kitchen to wash dishes while you're serving after-dinner drinks are hailed as lifesavers.

Friends anticipate needs by putting themselves in your shoes. Even though you may feel uncomfortable about accepting their generosity, accept it graciously with the knowledge that you will reciprocate when the need arises. Friendship is not a matter of keeping score, it's a give-and-take. There's no reason to feel that you have to be superwoman and totally in control. Friends will accept your offers more readily if they believe they will have an opportunity to help you out one day. On the other hand, never abuse the friendship by assuming someone will always be there to bail you out of situations that could have been avoided if you'd planned better or taken others into consideration.

Borrowing and Returning Items

"Neither a borrower nor a lender be" is an admonition we've all heard at one time or another. There's nothing wrong with borrowing and lending—just be sure to follow the rules.

Never borrow anything that is irreplaceable or has extreme sentimental value. None of us has the resources to be fully prepared for every situation. While you may be fortunate enough to be able to entertain fifty friends without borrowing a glass, unexpected events often require you to ask to borrow that missing "something." If your mother-in-law's seventy-fifth birthday is coming up and you forgot to order enough serving pieces for the party to be held in your home, it is perfectly acceptable to call a friend and ask to borrow a platter or two. The appropriateness of the request is measured by the depth of your friendship. While you may feel that you can borrow anything from a friend, it would be inappropriate to ask to borrow anything expensive from a casual friend or neighbor. Extra chairs or an onion can easily be secured from a neighbor, but a request to borrow that silver tea service is only made, if at all, of your dearest friends. Some things to remember:

- Be prepared to be a lender if you are a borrower.
- Make arrangements to pick up and deliver items yourself. Do not expect the lender to bring them to you or excuse the fact that they have not been returned in a timely manner.
- Ask if the lender needs to use the items in the next few days, in which case you should return them immediately. (It's not that you wouldn't return them in a timely manner, but she may be preparing for her own party the next day and there you are, still in dreamland, recovering from your event the night before.)
- Return all items clean and in good condition. Don't even think about using someone's tablecloth without washing it before you return it—even if it wasn't freshly laundered when you borrowed it. (If the cloth requires special cleaning, ask your friend if there is a particular place where she has it cleaned and take it there.)
- If you lend an item to a friend, don't put undue pressure on her by repeatedly saying, "I'll just die if anything happens to it"; if it's that precious, don't lend it.
- Never lend an item to another person if it doesn't belong to you. It is *not* yours to lend.
- When lending a book, make sure that your name is on the inside in case the borrower forgets where she got it. If you've already read the book,

you may not be in a hurry to get it back, but if you're intending to read it, ask your friend to return it within a specified time.

Borrowing Money

Money has always been a touchy subject when it comes to borrowing and lending. There are times in all of our lives when circumstances prove to be overwhelming and financial aid may be needed. If you find yourself needing to borrow money, in order to preserve your relationship with the lender, try to follow these guidelines:

See if you can borrow from a financial institution first; if you can't, then consider asking a friend. Don't ask someone to loan you money who may be putting themselves in the hole by doing so. And don't assume that people who "should" be able to afford to help you out can: some folks put a lot of energy into *looking* prosperous when reality is considerably different. Only ask for as much as you need (you need to get your engine overhauled, but you can wait for that paint job), and prepare some schedule for repayment.

If you're given the loan, make sure you make your repayments when you promise to—in full and on time. If you promise to return the entire amount by a certain time, do: "I need $1,000 for a month; I can give it back to you on the thirtieth" should not mean the lender receives $200 on the thirtieth and the rest in drips and drops over the next several months. And if something happens to delay repayment (you lose your job or must take off from work for a few weeks without pay), immediately notify the lender and modify your payment schedule.

Finally, good home training means if *you* lend someone money, you don't forever remind him how much you've done for him and what a prince you are for having made the loan. And you certainly don't make the loan recipient feel guilty or awkward for having requested assistance.

Please Don't Ask . . .
Dos and Don'ts of Asking for Favors

Immediate relatives may be the obvious choice, and fair game, for *almost* any request. This may not hold true, however, for even the closest friends. Be reasonable, considerate of the time and circumstances of others, and flexible. Some dos:

- *Do* ask for favors when someone's welfare is in jeopardy. Don't feel uncomfortable when asking a friend to pick up your child from school when you've had an automobile accident and will never get there.
- *Do* ask for directions from the airport to your hostess's home. This is

much more considerate than assuming (especially in a city like New York) that it's convenient for the hostess to pick you up. If it's convenient (or the path of least resistance, such as in Los Angeles), your hostess may offer to get you. Let it be her decision.

- *Do* offer favors with the same enthusiasm as you ask for them.
- *Do* appreciate any favors performed for you, and remember to thank your friend.
- When asking, convey your desire to reciprocate.
- If you've asked a friend to pick up lunch, your dry cleaning, or a sale item when you can't make it to the mall, give her sufficient money to cover expenses. If she offers to cover the cost until she returns, thank her and reimburse her as soon as you see each other. When requesting the favor, consider parking costs, selling price including tax, and any other extraneous expense. Be sure your friend is not saddled with additional costs that are your responsibility, not hers.
- Reciprocate.

The don'ts are a little easier to identify:

- *Don't* even *think* about asking to borrow large sums of money.
- *Don't* ask a friend to lie for you.
- *Don't* ask to borrow your friend's new dress and wear it among your mutual friends before she has an opportunity to wear it herself.
- *Don't* ask to be invited to your friend's work event because you think it's a good place to catch eligible men.
- *Don't* ask to be in your friend's wedding.
- *Don't ever* ask to charge something on someone else's credit card.
- *Don't* take an extra guest (no matter how special) to a dinner party without calling ahead and obtaining permission from your hostess.
- *Don't* ask a friend to do anything illegal, immoral, or just plain stupid.
- *Don't* request a friend to do anything that would jeopardize her marriage, job, chance for advancement, family relations, or your friendship (no matter how desperate you are).
- *Don't* ask friends to intercede on someone else's behalf when they don't know the person or are unfamiliar with the situation.
- *Don't* expect your friend, simply because she is a member of an organization that accepts new members by invitation only, to submit your name for membership just because you asked.
- *Don't* ask to be invited to *anything*.

Reciprocity

From the beginning we've said manners are about doing unto others as you would have them do unto you. This is especially true when it comes to appreciating and reciprocating kindness afforded you. Do not, for a moment, think reciprocity is a matter of keeping up with the Joneses—or even with your friend. True friendship is not measured by "she took me to an expensive place so I have to take her somewhere even more expensive to show I care." Reciprocity is simply taking the time to demonstrate your appreciation of a kindness. This ranges from offering to drive sometime rather than always being picked up for those shopping excursions, to being there for a friend whose mom just died, because you fondly remember how comforting it was to have her by your side when your sister died. People most often think to return a dinner invitation when they've recently dined at someone's home. The issue also arises when you are presented with an unexpected holiday or birthday gift from a new friend or coworker (see chapter 23, "Plantation Life") and ponder whether you should run out and buy a comparable gift. Reciprocity should never be extended out of obligation but rather out of a heartfelt desire to do something nice for someone else. Some guidelines:

- An at-home dinner is usually reciprocated by a dinner in your home. If dinner is inconvenient for you, consider a weekend brunch with homemade goodies.
- An invitation to the theater may be reciprocated in kind, or you could offer to treat to a pretheater dinner. If you cannot afford theater tickets, think of another cultural event that your friend would enjoy. Taking time to research available events and trying to find something your friend would like is much more important than trying to impress her with something you can't afford.
- *Do not* get into a gift exchange with someone you would not normally have on your gift list. That's not to say you shouldn't occasionally buy a friend a gift because she's been especially helpful—just be careful not to add so many people to your Christmas list that being included is no longer special.
- *Do not* try to lump all friends together and "pay back" everyone at once by throwing one big bash. Chances are the members of the group are not compatible and your guests will feel uncomfortable. Haven't you ever been invited to join a friend, thinking it was just the two of you, and been surprised to find four or five people who all knew each other but with whom you had little, if anything, in common?

Volunteer Time

Being a friend is being a friend to those in need, not just your good buddies. When making a commitment to volunteer time or expertise, consider it a *binding* commitment. Keeping your word when you've made a volunteer commitment is no less important just because you aren't being paid for your time. The gratification that comes with making a contribution to your community often results in unexpected dividends. You may meet new friends who share similar interests, be exposed to people and places beyond your everyday existence, and in many cases, gain more from the experience than those you are expected to assist.

Saying You're Sorry

Apologies should be timely and heartfelt. Even the smallest indiscretions cannot be ignored. You may realize, immediately, the need to accept fault and extend apologies to a casual acquaintance, new friend, or coworker. Sometimes we are so eager to maintain a relationship that we feel is important (with a wealthy person, someone with A+ contacts, or anyone else you feel compelled to impress) that we jump through hoops trying to get them to forgive, yet we neglect to extend an apology to people who mean a lot to us.

Too often, unfeeling friends mistakenly believe that an unfriendly, hurtful incident has been forgotten just because the victim has continued to treat the other warmly. Under no circumstances should you assume that a friend will "understand" and that no apology is needed. "Love is never having to say you're sorry" was not a motto embraced by anyone we know.

"Sorry" can be said very simply in person, with a phone call, a handwritten note, or flowers. Keep it short, don't make a big deal out of it, and above all let your friend know you appreciate the relationship and didn't mean to say or do anything inappropriate.

By all means, treat children in your life with the same respect you give an adult. It is important for them to know that their feelings matter to you.

> *Dear Philip,*
> *I'm sorry I didn't make it to your basketball game. I looked forward to it all week and was really disappointed when my boss insisted I stay for a late meeting. I would have called you as soon as I found out, but there was no way to reach you at school. I'd love to hear about the game and your winning basket. I'll call later in the week—I think there's a hot fudge sundae in our future.*
>
> *Love,*
> *Auntie Karen*

It is unacceptable to think that because it's "only a child," you have the right to be inconsiderate on a regular basis and simply brush it off with a weak "I'm sorry." If children don't learn the art of apologizing from you, who will teach them?

Keeping Secrets

Sharing secrets with a friend is a sure sign that you trust each other's discretion when it comes to upholding confidences. A friend's secret should be handled as gingerly as you would a ticking time bomb (or even your very *own* secret). If it's a secret, it's a secret—not a secret to everyone *but* your best friend and your spouse. If someone confides in you, you have a responsibility not to betray that trust. If you are confiding in another, be sure to inform your friend that your juicy tidbit of news is, in fact, a secret not to be shared with others. Don't assume she automatically understands that the information is for her ears only.

Asking Friends to Perform Professional Services Free of Charge

If your friend is in business for herself or is an independent contractor, don't ask her to waive her fee. Her time and expertise are at a premium, and the work is probably her primary source of income. A friend may offer you her services, in which case you may accept if it will not be a long, complicated, or terribly costly favor; but do something to recognize the value of her time and skill, even if your recognition isn't monetary (flowers, books, tickets to a play, etc.). If you feel uncomfortable about accepting her offer, or if you are unable to afford the services, ask if you can barter. *Do not* ask a doctor or lawyer to a dinner party and proceed to play twenty questions or drop hints that would prompt your friend to offer her services out of a sense of obligation.

House-Sitting

House-sitting is usually advantageous to both the homeowner and the sitter. If you accept the responsibility of "sitting" for a friend, do not abuse the relationship. In exchange for a place to stay, you agree to perform certain services. These often include checking the mail and recording messages, watering the plants and feeding the goldfish. It does *not* include giving a party for everyone you've ever met and feeding them from the family freezer. Treat the home as if it were your own and leave it in a clean and orderly fashion for the homeowner's return. Some basic dos and don'ts:

- *Do* stay at the home. The purpose is to deter burglars. That's not to say you may never leave, only that you shouldn't leave for several days at a time and assume the home is secure.
- *Do not* give an extra key to a friend and allow him or her unrestricted access to the home.
- *Don't* play loud music or otherwise disturb the neighbors.
- *Do not* entertain without the homeowner's knowledge.
- If there is a housekeeper, do not expect her to wash and iron *your* clothes.
- If you are given the use of the family car, do not drive it unnecessarily. Leave it in the same condition you found it, and with a full tank of gas.
- Stock the refrigerator with fresh juice and sweet rolls on the morning you expect your host to return. If she plans to return in the early evening, you might leave the makings for a quick dinner.
- *Do not* assume the food left in the refrigerator was put there for your personal use.
- If you break an item, save the pieces and discuss the incident as soon as your host returns.
- *Do not* allow persons unknown to you into the home or divulge any confidential information about the homeowner.
- Treat the home as if it were your own.

Keeping in Touch Across the Miles

When a friend moves across town or across the country, you will both feel the loss. Your pledges to stay in touch will frequently fall victim to the everyday demands that make us wonder where the weeks, the months, and the years have gone. Staying in touch requires a conscious effort on your part. Some ideas that have worked for us:

- Make a phone date at a particular time each Saturday morning.
- Write once a month (each week sounds good but is often unrealistic). Don't resort to the annual Christmas letter as your only form of communication.
- Develop a checklist when your friend is overwhelmed and you have some extra time. Include questions that will let you know how she's doing and make it something fun to receive and return. ("Cydney, answer yes or no: 1. Did you meet any new, exciting men this week? 2. Do you know how to spell v-a-c-a-t-i-o-n or are you working too hard? 3. Have you calmed down since you found out your daughter wants to go three thousand miles away for ninth grade?")

- Fax short notes to each other.
- Remember special occasions (birthdays, anniversaries, etc.) just as you would if you saw each other all the time.
- Use e-mail. Short notes sent over the Internet are an instant, timesaving method of sharing experiences and daily ups and downs.
- When you run into members of your friend's family, ask to be remembered to her: "Please give Faith my best and let her know I asked about her."

When a Friend's Mother Comes to Town

If your good friend's mother is visiting your city, plan to offer to take her out for an evening or afternoon, or ask whether there is something she'd like to see or do that you can treat her to. Even if your friend lives in the same city, her mother may appreciate being treated as if her company is enjoyed for its own sake, and not just because she's so-and-so's mother.

Friendship vs. Business: When There's Only Time for One

Sometimes your obligations or commitments crunch you from both ends. Perhaps your best friend's son is making his debut as a budding musician in the kindergarten follies on the same weekend you've been assigned to travel for business. Or a close friend has broken up with a longtime beau and calls to unload when you have one hour to finish a project.

If business obligations aren't pressing and your friend has an emergency, you may be able to reschedule your deadline or trip. Often, though, it's work that's less flexible. In that case, you have to bite the bullet and gently explain that you promise to get back to her as soon as you've fulfilled your professional responsibilities: "Shelley, I wouldn't miss Teddy's concert for anything but a good reason—but this is my project, the client picked this weekend, and I have to go. Please tell Teddy I'll call as soon as I get back to ask if he'll come to dinner at my house and maybe give me a little recap of the piece he played." Or "Deanna, I know you're hurting and I hate that this has happened to you, but I have to have this report on the boss's desk before he leaves tonight. Can you meet me for dinner this evening? Let's go somewhere quiet and talk."

When Your Best Friend Is a Man

When your most prized girlfriend is actually a guy, most of the best-friend rules still apply. You should be careful, though, especially if you both have significant others, not to give any appearance that would indicate your friendship is a romantic one. He can escort you to events when you need a partner of the opposite sex (or he does), but you should try to make sure you're not hurting his girlfriend's (or wife's!) feelings. Be specific about why he's needed: "Brenda, I've got to go to the annual partners' dinner; would you mind if Ron took me?"

Convert Rice, Not Friends

If you've changed religions, found a perfect self-realization philosophy, or otherwise had a life-changing experience, share the news with your friends—but don't pressure them to see the same light you've discovered. They may be perfectly happy with their lives as they are and resent being told, over and over, how much better things could be if they'd just listen to you. If someone expresses an interest in knowing more about your experience, feel free to hold forth. If you're not encouraged to share your views, however, that may be a subtle hint that you've said enough.

Chapter 4

BEST FOOT FORWARD

Little powder, little paint make you
look like what you ain't.

Della Givens Williams

Remember the 1963 March on Washington? On a sweltering August day, more than a quarter million people, most of them black, marched for equality through the baking streets of Washington, D.C., where they assembled on the Mall to listen to speeches from some of America's most prominent citizens. Although it was near a hundred degrees and the humidity was unbearable, the marchers did not wear gym shorts, tank tops, and sneakers. The men wore jackets and ties and straw fedoras. The ladies wore Sunday-best dresses, shade-providing hats, and high heels. Small children wore suits and frilly dresses. This had happened throughout the civil rights movement, when protest marchers unfailingly wore their best—even as they faced police dogs, fire hoses, and hostile, rock-throwing crowds.

Why did they do it? "Oh, it showed we were serious," one veteran marcher remembers. "We took ourselves and our purpose seriously. And we wanted others to take us seriously, too."

Since some of the goals of the civil rights movement have been realized, we no longer need, thank God, to dress for demonstrations. But the veteran marcher's point is well taken: you may be treated better and taken more seriously if your grooming and dress indicate you take yourself seriously, too. Waiters may give you better tables, salespeople may move to wait on you more quickly, and so forth.

Being Clean and Neat

Your mother really *was* right: God forbid you're ever in an auto accident, but if you are, and if the paramedics hustle you into the ER, you *do* want to have clean undies . . . And even if you're blessed enough to lead an accident-free life, you should still make sure the basics are covered whenever you leave the house:

- Is your hair neatly combed?
- Did you brush your teeth and use a swish of mouthwash?
- Are your nails scrubbed clean? Nicely manicured?
- Are the heels of the shoes you're wearing even and not run-down? Are your shoes polished?
- Do your socks match? Are your stockings run-free?
- If you're wearing makeup, is it applied evenly and neatly (no lipstick on teeth, no running mascara, etc.)?
- Are your shirttails tucked in? Is your tie straight? Are you sure your slip isn't hanging?

A Little Dab'll Do Ya

Perfume is a personal indulgence, your individual signature that follows wherever you go. Whether you're wearing the most expensive perfume in the world or a drugstore favorite, the same rule applies: don't wear too much of a good thing. A beautiful scent becomes noxious when great waves of it assault others before you even get into the room. (And if everyone laid it on thick, the clash of scents would clear out the room in no time.)

Remember, too, that more and more people are discovering that they are allergic to perfume or to a specific ingredient of some perfumes. The allergies range from watering eyes and sneezing to violent headaches, and you can imagine how miserable someone can become, and quickly, if there's too much Eau de Bucks wafting their way. Some folks have other conditions, such as pregnancy, that may make strong scent intolerable. So be considerate—wear enough for you, not the room.

Some other ground rules to remember about the art of wearing perfume:

- Use less on hot days, as your elevated body heat may make the scent more intense—especially if you're fond of scented body oils or something else that isn't alcohol-based.
- In summer, you might consider switching to a lighter version of your

favorite scent: body lotion, an eau de cologne (which has more alcohol than perfume or eau de toilette), or after-bath splash.

- If you ride public transportation, as a courtesy to other riders, consider applying perfume *after* you get to work, as tight quarters tend to make scents—especially aggressive ones—more noticeable.
- Apply perfume on your pulse points (behind the ears, knees, in crook of elbow) or spray yourself lightly with eau de toilette, but don't bathe in it. Your scent should be a pleasant surprise to those who are closest to you (your dinner partner, someone you're dancing with, a friend you hug)—not a billboard advertisement to everyone in sight.

Finally, perfume is a wonderful present—but only if it's a perfume the recipient really wants. If you know that your best friend has worn and loved the same scent for five years, it's probably safe to give her something from that line as a present. (In fact, she may have longed for scented body lotion or shower gel, but wouldn't break down and buy it for herself.) If you don't know, or aren't sure, don't guess about what another person might wear. Instead, give her a gift certificate to a perfume store or a top-quality department store that carries a good selection of perfumes and let her pick her own favorite.

Beauty Shop Etiquette

Statistics tell us that black women spend more time and money on their hair than anyone else in America! Which means, of course, that we spend more time in the beauty shop. Whether it's the local Kitchen Beautician or the La-De-Dah Salon, the basics still apply:

- Arrive on time.
- Have some idea of what you want done before you walk in the door. (If you want a trim, not a cut, be firm. Color but no blond streaks? Speak up.)
- If you want to experiment, remember that the outcome isn't guaranteed.
- Don't expect miracles: the stylist is a stylist, not a magician.
- Tip properly (15 to 20 percent of the total bill for the stylist in big cities, a couple of dollars each if someone else shampoos you; same for the manicurist).
- Don't gossip in a voice that carries; you know that business about there being only four hundred of us in the whole world—and you never know who knows the person you're discussing.

Putting on Makeup in Public

Don't do your makeup in public. That's one of the reasons ladies' rooms were invented. If you're at the table—whether in a restaurant or someone's home—excuse yourself and patch up in private, where you can take as long as you like.

There are a few places where this rule can be fudged: if you're in your car or on a train or airplane, putting on lipstick quickly isn't so bad—but if you have to do much more (mascara, blush, eyeliner, and definitely hair combing), do it in the bathroom, in private. Some things should remain blessed mysteries.

All That Glitters . . . Rules for Jewels

Love jewelry? Have a lot? Good for you—but don't wear it all at once! Who hasn't seen a woman laden down like a Christmas tree with all her favorite pieces? With jewelry, real or faux, if you think you might be wearing a bit too much, you probably are.

One famous beauty developed a solution to this dilemma: she'd get dressed, put on whatever accessories she wanted, including jewelry, inspect herself in the mirror—then remove one piece of jewelry. And this woman was known for her streamlined elegance.

If you have a gorgeous pair of earrings, you may not want to call attention away from them by adding a necklace so close to your face. Perhaps a bracelet is the only addition you'll need.

In the old days, there were a great many formal rules about how and when to wear what kinds of jewels. Much of that has gone by the wayside now, and many of us do wear diamonds before five (OK if they're stud earrings—save the chandeliers and diamond bibs for evening) and mix our metals (watches and bracelets that combine gold and silver are currently hugely popular). It used to be that women did not wear watches to formal events, since these affairs were considered strictly social and a lady was deemed not to need to consult her watch at social occasions (since her escort could always consult his for her). Now dress watches for women are a jewelry staple. Common sense dictates that the watch with a strap or simple band goes with you to work or church, and the watch with the solid gold band and the diamond numerals goes to the theater and out to dinner.

Men's jewelry choices are usually less extensive: a watch, perhaps a wedding ring, maybe a bracelet, are pretty much it. It's becoming more common for men to wear an earring in one ear (usually a small stud or a tiny hoop),

although many who do so do not wear this particular piece of jewelry to work. The multiple-chain, gold-knuckle-initials, pinkie-ring look belongs in the movies.

Pierced Ears and Miscellaneous Punctures

Some baby girls—especially those who have parents or grandparents from the Caribbean—have their ears pierced soon after birth, and wear tiny gold hoops or pearl studs well before they're able to walk. Others have their ears pierced when they're older. And some people refrain from piercing their ears at all. Whether or not you do this is up to you.

Two holes (one in each ear) used to be standard. Three (two in one ear, one in the other) or four are not uncommon. After that, additional holes get to be superfluous. For men, one hole was considered standard, but two—one in each ear—are starting to gain favor, especially among young, trend-conscious men.

Some people even pierce one nostril—an operation best left to a doctor. Pierced noses are usually decorated with a very small stud (gold or a precious stone) or a small hoop. If you opt to do this, check your pierced nostril daily—and be especially careful to discreetly inspect it after blowing your nose or sneezing.

Your body *can* be pierced almost anywhere, as fetish magazines cheerfully illustrate for us, but we think piercing your nose is about as adventurous as most of us need to get.

Oh, Those Legs!

Stockings are a part of our wardrobes we all silently curse, but we have to have them. While the rules for when stockings must be worn have relaxed considerably in the last few generations (for instance, you don't have to wear them to shop downtown anymore, especially since, in many cities, "downtown" has given way to suburban malls), there are still times and places when you must, *must* pull them on:

- Any church ceremony, unless it's very, very informal. (For instance, some churches encourage casual dress in the summer.)
- Business meetings
- Funerals and memorial services

Stockings for these occasions should be sheer, flesh-colored (which can range from ivory to espresso, depending on your color), or neutral-toned (cream, navy, black, etc.). For festive occasions, you might want a stocking with a little sheen to it, or even one made of a delicate lace pattern, provided it doesn't clash with your dress or shoes.

Other than the occasions above, stockings are now considered a fashion accessory, used to enhance or tastefully contrast with your chosen outfit. The only rule might be to consider the type of outfit you want to pair with the stockings: more casual stockings, like opaque tights, go with casual clothes (a short knit jumper or suede culottes), delicate stockings (very sheer, lace, other delicate patterns) go with dressier clothes. Novelty stockings (fishnets, seamed) should be considered carefully before they're paired with anything. (Fishnets with black leather might be popular in the music industry, but outside in the real world they give nonperformers that oldest-profession look. You're grown. You decide.)

Can Pants Really Take You Everywhere?

We probably wouldn't choose to wear pants to funerals, since some people are still very conservative about this and we don't want to offend, but we suspect that, with a very few other exceptions, pants probably can take you anywhere as long as they're part of a well-cut suit and are accessorized properly.

Be aware that some professions, such as law and banking, still frown on their female employees wearing pants. They may not forbid it outright, but the women who adhere to the corporate dress code may be promoted faster and farther. And there are still private clubs with dress codes that forbid women to wear pants anywhere on the premises, except maybe the golf course and tennis courts. In some parts of the country, evening pants are perfectly acceptable to wear to black-tie events, while in other places, pants—even glamorous ones—are frowned upon as evening wear. (And they aren't appropriate for white-tie events, ever.) If you're in doubt, ask someone whether pants will be acceptable in the environment you're planning to wear them.

Chapter 5

KEEPING UP WITH THE JONESES

Know the difference between substance and style. Too many of us think success is a Saks Fifth Avenue charge card or a "bad" set of wheels. Now, these are things to enjoy but they are not life goals.

Marian Wright Edelman

Sometimes we can have too much of a good thing. Our economic advances have afforded us the opportunity to go a little overboard and lose our perspective. It's about "mo' better" cars, bigger and better homes, elaborate parties, and enough clothes to outfit a small country.

Wretched Excess

We have worked hard to achieve financial stability, and we deserve to spend our money any way we like. The problem arises when we cease to find enjoyment in the possessions we have acquired, and the game switches to outdoing our friends and neighbors. Life is not about keeping up with the Joneses, nor is it about who has the most material possessions.

The Bajillion-Dollar Birthday Party

Has it been a while since you attended a child's birthday party that was simply cake and ice cream? When children are at the age to be on "the birthday circuit," parents are required to buy presents by the truckload, dress the kids in adorable outfits to attend the weekly party, and spend an inordinate amount of time trying to take notes on what everyone else is doing so they can outdo them. We don't presume there is a true competition, only that the parents who are "able" want only the best for their child. But when a three-year-old has a pony, clown, face painter, petting zoo, make-your-own-T-shirt area, and videographer, plus pizza, popcorn, hot dogs, cake, and favors, what will she have to look forward to for her fifth birthday? Or her tenth, or better yet, her sixteenth? There are no rules that say you have to have a birthday party every year. You can be very creative and make your child feel just as loved with family traditions that simply call for the child being allowed to choose his or her favorite meal, type of cake, and video for the family to watch together. Some parents allow their children to invite one friend for each year of their age. Eight guests at an eighth-birthday party seems quite reasonable.

Pot nor Window: Living Within Your Means

The easy accessibility of credit and the need to impress your boss, neighbors, or friends can lead to trouble. Sometimes you're the family member who "made good" and has chosen to help the family out financially or with special treats. When circumstances change for the worse, you may not want to admit to family members that you are struggling somewhat and so you continue to shower them with gifts. It's always good to pay yourself first, and save for a rainy day. When it's a matter of choosing between the newest, sleekest car on the road (when your three-year-old one works just fine) and your child's education, education wins hands down. If it's too hard to swallow, and you're not ready to admit you won't be keeping up with the Joneses this year, just play like you've become an eccentric.

When You Make Much More Money Than Your Friend

First off, unequal incomes could be a temporary situation, so don't get too excited. Aside from that, you'll be a lot happier and so will your less fortunate friend if you follow these simple guidelines:

- Never hold your success over anyone's head.
- Certainly you should offer to treat on occasion if you have cash to spare, but don't *always* treat.
- Let your friend pay sometimes so he or she won't feel like the poor relation.
- If you regularly go dutch, either choose a less expensive place than you would normally or offer to treat on the occasions that you select something fancy. It's a give-and-take proposition, like all good relationships.

- If something comes up that you would really like to experience with your friend, like a terrific new play, offer to purchase the tickets for you both. If your friend protests, just let her know that her company means more to you than the price of the tickets. Convey to her (and act like you mean it!) that you would enjoy the event much more if she was there to share it with you.
- If you're the recipient of the tickets, graciously thank your hostess and perhaps offer to pay for parking or intermission beverages.
- A gracious friend does not expect equality in reciprocity, only in sincere friendship.

When the Label Means More to You Than the Clothes

You've got your own style and need not define yourself with someone else's initials. If you genuinely admire a designer's work and can't stay away from that outfit that's caught your eye, by all means purchase it. But if your interest in this season's latest trends is simply to show off your fashionability as you continue to attempt to keep up with the Joneses, remember, you can't wear that label by itself.

Chapter 6

PRAISE BE!

My hope for my children must be that they respond to the still, small voice of God in their own hearts.

Andrew Young

Church has been an integral part of our community since slavery. Back in those dark days, it was often the religious community that lifted our flagging spirits that the oppressor's yoke tried to crush daily. It also served as an ad hoc community center, dispensing advice, assistance, and even, under pain of death, education. Although it was illegal to teach slaves to read or write in Southern states, black ministers, many of whom were literate, often risked their lives to share their knowledge with their congregants by teaching them simple reading and writing skills. And the moving melodies of slave spirituals often held covert meanings that could mean the difference between life and death, freedom and servitude.

In this century, churches played an important part in the antilynching movement and later served as a mobilization base for the civil rights movement. Activist ministers such as Vernon Johns, C. T. Vivian, and, of course, Martin Luther King, Jr., were pivotal in galvanizing and organizing black citizens to press for their own liberation. And still later, linchpins of the black power movement, such as Stokely Carmichael and James Forman, clearly were influenced by the ringing cadence of the civil rights ministers, even as they rejected the ministers' philosophy of nonviolence. The first black American to make a viable run for the presidency, Jesse L. Jackson, is a minister.

Today our religious institutions, be they churches, mosques, or temples, remain at the center of many parts of our community, and, as in the old days, they serve as much more than a place of Sunday worship. Social programs, day-care centers, and services for the elderly and indigent are frequently administered by churches in our neighborhoods, and religious life remains an important part of who we are as a people. And in a society that is no longer as segregated as it was, the church is an important magnet for black coalescence: often parishioners who work in overwhelmingly white environments or who are the "only ones" on their block, joyfully return to church each week as a way to stay in touch and water their thirsty cultural roots. In many communities, church is still the hub of local social life.

Whether you are one of the devoted or an occasional visitor to your place of worship, we'd like to remind you of some of the things you probably absorbed as you leaned against your mother, grandmother, or aunt when you sat in Sunday service years ago.

Getting to the Church on Time

Do make every effort to get to church on time or even a few minutes early. In some churches, late arrivals will only be seated at specific intervals (while the congregation is singing, for instance) so the service is not disrupted.

Order of Service

Each denomination adheres to its own order of service and etiquette for parishioners. Usually, you'll be given a program for the day's service when you enter church; the program will indicate the order of service and will sometimes note when you are to stand, kneel, or remain seated. Ministers may also indicate what you are to do at a particular point in the service: "Let us stand and say the Lord's Prayer." Out of respect you should stand, sit, or kneel when the people around you do (unless you have a physical condition that precludes this, in which case you'd remain seated as you follow the service), but you may be silent and not mouth the words if they don't reflect your beliefs. If the program or minister does not give you an indication, you may want to observe the people around you for clues, or quietly ask a worshiper seated next to you.

Making a Joyful Noise

Many churches have Bibles, hymnals, and study guides positioned in special holders in the pews in front of you or stored beneath the pew itself. The minister will often indicate the passage that will be read or the number of the hymn that will be sung, or it may be contained in the program. Some churches reproduce Scripture and lyrics in the program itself for the ease of congregants.

Read or sing along with the congregation at the instruction of the minister. If you are uncertain of the material being used, an usher or nearby congregant is usually glad to help you find your place. If you see a visitor struggling to find his place or keep up with the service, don't hesitate to help him catch up by indicating—either by turning the pages or sharing your own hymnal or prayer book—where you are in the service.

Respecting Ministers

As we noted earlier, a significant amount of our social and political evolution as black Americans is directly attributable to our ministers. Most important, ministers are accorded respect for their role as spiritual leaders. In our community, we traditionally refer to our ministers, whether they've been called to preach or have received graduate degrees from divinity schools, as "Reverend," "Pastor," or "Doctor" as a sign of respect.

Women in the Clergy

While there has been some opposition to installing women as full-fledged pastors in some denominations, the pastorate continues to attract larger and larger numbers of women each year. If you have a minister who is female, you should accord her all the respect and deference you'd give any man in the position. And yes, she would be addressed as "Reverend Weems" or "Pastor Weems" or "Dr. Weems," not "Mrs. Weems."

Children in Church

The practice of having children attend "regular" church services varies from congregation to congregation. Some churches welcome small children as part of the general population. Others provide day-care and Sunday school services and prefer that small children be introduced to church this way, in doses they can absorb (physically as well as spiritually), while the adults in their family worship nearby. Use your discretion: If you think your children are old enough or have a great enough attention span to sit through the service, you should feel free to have them join you. If you're not sure, or have an infant or toddler, be considerate of the other parishioners and seat yourself near an aisle or toward the back, so you can slip out and calm a fretful little one if that becomes necessary. (Some ministers don't mind being interrupted by a baby's cooing or babble, but others become visibly irritated when they have to speak over the wailing of an infant.)

Joining a Church

During many church services, it's traditional for the pastor to issue an open invitation for anyone at the service to come forward and join the church. If you've been considering this for some time and decide you want to make the commitment to become a church member, you may simply follow the minister's instructions: "At this time, we'd like to invite anyone who may wish to become a member of Mount Olive to come to the altar . . . please don't be shy. All are welcome; won't you come?" After telling the minister your name, you may be introduced to the entire congregation and welcomed: "I'm so pleased to present the newest members of our Mount Olive family, Myrtle and Henry Lockwood. Those of you who are joining us during fellowship hour following service, please take a moment to introduce yourselves to them."

Some churches request that you take religious instruction before you join. In that case, the minister or priest has several meetings with you to discuss your spiritual philosophy, the history of the religion and/or church you are about to join, and so forth. Large churches where one-on-one religious instruction would be impractical often hold classes at specific times of the year so people can fulfill this requirement.

Passing the Plate

Monetary contributions are the financial lifeblood of the church; they provide support for the physical structure (heat, mortgage, etc.), the pastor's salary, and many of the programs that the church sponsors. Church members may have envelopes used for their weekly contributions, or they may drop money or checks directly in the collection plate. Members of many churches are encouraged to tithe, that is, contribute 10 percent of their annual income to the church. This is done in myriad ways, through weekly or monthly payments, or some other arrangement mutually agreed upon between the parishioner and the church's financial board or deacons.

If you are a visitor, you may place your money directly in the plate; try to have the amount you'd planned to give readily accessible so you don't have to hold up everyone in your row, or you may write a check to the church. The collection plate, by the way, is not the place to search for change.

Some churches have more than one collection each service, for specific purposes. In addition to the main collection, there may be a separate collection for the missionary fund, the building fund, community outreach programs, or for other things. If you only have enough for one contribution, make it to the main collection. If you can donate a token amount to the second collection, do. If you can't, don't fret; you have given what you were able.

And remember that church is not a pay-per-view event: even if you don't have a dime to drop in the plate, you're still welcome and you shouldn't hesitate to attend services. Sometimes the times that leave us financially pinched are also the times when we most need a spiritual uplift, so don't cheat yourself out of this comfort. And if you can't contribute, don't feel you have to leave the service when collection is taken.

Other Kinds of Contributions

While money is always welcome to help support your place of worship, there are other ways to give what are called in-kind contributions. You can always offer to donate flowers to the altar, help to edit, type, or print the church program or newsletter, or provide coffee and cake for after-church social hour.

Church Committees

Money is important, but it's not the only thing that keeps a church going. The loyalty and dedication of the congregation can make a critical difference between a church that is lively, involved, and a valued asset to its members and its community and a church that is doing little more than taking up space. Some of the most dynamic congregations are fueled by people who join church committees and contribute their effort and expertise in this important way.

If you're a member of a church committee, be a member in more than name. If you agree to sit on the development board, make an honest effort at fund-raising. If you decide you'd like to teach Sunday school, make sure you're there every Sunday so your students aren't disappointed and the other teachers don't have to scramble to cover for you. Remember that committees aren't dictatorships, and vow to work with your fellow committee members harmoniously, even though you may think things can be accomplished faster, cheaper, or better if everyone just shut up and did it your way.

Special Notices

Most churches have a place in their bulletins that mention members of the congregation who are ill or otherwise shut-in or who have died. If you have a family member or friend whom you'd like remembered, call the church office well before Sunday and ask that they be included in the roster of those for whom good wishes and special prayers are offered during the service. The same procedure would work if there are announcements you would like to have read: "Troop 104, which meets here on Wednesday evenings, wishes to remind us that its car-wash fund-raiser will be held next Saturday morning. Please plan to bring your dirty cars by, as these children are trying hard to earn enough money to represent us at the Explorer Scout Jamboree in Denver this summer."

Recognizing Visitors

Many congregations ask that visitors to their church rise and identify themselves so they can be welcomed. This can be done several ways: If you're visiting a church member, he or she may forward your name to whoever is responsible for reading visitors' names, and you merely stand when your name is called: "We're so pleased to have Mrs. Sadie West's nephew, Mr. Carleton Jamieson, with us today from New York City." In other churches, all visitors are simply asked to stand together at the same time. They may or may not be asked to identify themselves: "I'm Maura Edmonds, and I'm visiting my friend Gail Jackson." Or "We're the Thompsons, from this city." If you're shy, and the idea of making yourself so publicly obvious gives you the shakes, you don't have to stand.

If you are part of a delegation from, for example, another church, one among you may be asked to give what's commonly referred to as the Visitor Response. This is a brief statement identifying the group and its relationship, if any, to the church it is visiting: "Good morning; I'm Rabbi Stephen Jay Wolff of Temple Beth Shalom, and we're pleased to share worship with our sister church, Zion AME. We bring you greetings from our entire temple, and hope you'll visit us anytime you like, but especially next Saturday, when we have our annual Open House." Or "We're the Wellmon family and we're in Memphis for our thirty-eighth family reunion. Many of our Memphis relatives grew up in Zion, so we're happy to be 'home' with you this morning."

Communion

Whether or not you take holy communion depends on you and your denomination. Some churches, such as the Roman Catholic and Episcopal ones, insist that you be confirmed before taking communion. Other denominations offer communion to anyone who wants to take it, as a gesture of spiritual hospitality.

If you are invited to take communion, it's up to you whether or not you do. Usually an usher will indicate when congregants in each row should rise and go to the altar. If you'd prefer to skip communion, simply remain seated. If communion is passed, as it is in many Protestant churches, the plates of wafers and grape juice (symbolic of Christ's body and blood) will be sent down each row. If you don't want to take communion, quietly pass the plate to the person next to you.

Dressing for Church

While some of the rules for church dress have relaxed considerably over the past several years (for instance, Catholic women no longer have to cover their heads), it's still best to dress respectfully and if you have to err, err on the conservative side: better you show up in a suit and tie when everyone else is in an open-neck shirt and sport jacket than the other way around.

Female congregants in many black churches are justifiably celebrated for their chic, imaginative hats. But that beauty of a brim—especially if it's *broad*-brimmed—might win more friends if the people behind you can see the minister, too. If you're the proud possessor of a huge hat, try to seat yourself so the people behind you don't have to crane their necks to see around you. Whatever you wear, make sure you're well groomed, and consistent with the mores of your church. (For more information, see chapter 14, "Glad Rags.")

Feeling the Spirit

The character of churches varies from congregation to congregation; some are quite conservative, while others are exuberant and truly believe that making a joyful noise is the best way to honor God. In many Holiness, Evangelical, and Apostolic churches, it is not unusual for members to be inspired to move in the aisles; this can range from a quiet little shuffle-step to a flurry of fast footwork. Or members may be possessed by the Spirit to speak in tongues, an ecstatic language that may or may not be intelligible to outside observers. But it doesn't matter, as participants feel that God is speaking directly to them and through them, and no translation is needed. If you're a visitor and you've never seen someone speak in tongues, you might become nervous or alarmed, and wonder whether the person before you is suffering some strange medical condition. Don't worry; after a time, the person who's been "touched by God" comes out of his trance, perhaps a little sweaty and a lot exhausted, but exhilarated that he's felt the Spirit.

Finally, be open to the customs of the church you're visiting. If the congregants are demonstrative and do, indeed, make a joyful noise, feel free

SUNDAY BEST

to join them. If the church is very reserved, tone yourself down accordingly—or don't, but realize that some people may find your individual exuberance unsettling.

Beyond the Traditional Christian Church

Although our initial introduction to religion in this country was through the Christian church, many of us have now chosen other paths. Islam is growing in popularity, as is Buddhism, and there are even larger numbers of black Jews, many the descendants of Ethiopian Jews who have settled in the United States. In addition, relationships with religious institutions different from our own are beginning to be explored, as a way to broaden our definition of community, to forge new alliances, and to confirm that, whatever one's denomination or religion, we all share a transcendent belief in the existence of a higher spirit.

Research shows that those of us who may have grown up in the church and later parted ways with organized religion are returning in record numbers. Some of us have chosen not to return to the religious institutions of our youth, but have embraced a different spiritual community. Several so-called New Age religions incorporate different aspects of several traditional religions—the gospel music of Christianity and the contemplative spirituality of Buddhism, for example—to form a new kind of church that is nondenominational, inclusive, and, unlike many of the churches of our youth, integrated. Today, where and how one worships is less important than the ongoing spiritual nourishment many receive from being an active part of a religious community.

More of us than ever are visiting religious institutions other than the ones we're most familiar with. You might be curious about another religion, or you may have a friend or colleague who invites you to worship with her, or you may be considering changing your religion. Whatever the reason, if you're going to visit a house of worship decidedly different from your own, it's mannerly to do a little research ahead of time:

- *Ask someone about the proper etiquette for attending their religious services.* If covered heads are a must, you should know this ahead of time. Same for long sleeves, the removal of shoes, and other customs.
- *Observe what goes on about you.* If the congregants kneel or even prostrate themselves, you should do the same unless this is physically impossible.
- *Honor each institution's cultural imperatives.* Even if you stand foursquare for women's rights, a religious service that traditionally seats the sexes separately is not the place for you to begin your lecture on why you find this personally unacceptable. If the notion of gender-segregated seating is that offensive to you, it might be better for you to skip the service.
- *Call the specific religious institution you're planning to visit,* explain you'll be visiting, and ask for guidance on dress, the service, etc. Most places will be happy to help you out.

Part II

COMMUNICATING

The Drum and Beyond

The fine art of introductions

how we speak to others

gossip

using the telephone, fax, e-mail, pagers, and cellular phones

writing letters, notes, and cards

showing appreciation to others

Chapter 7

MEETING AND GREETING

"How do you do?"
"Oh, I does jes' fine, thank you kindly!"

Early Negro vaudeville act

There are some basics involved in introductions, and we've absorbed many of them from the time we were small. Who doesn't remember an older family member instructing us to "stand up straight and look people in the eye" when we were being introduced? You've probably been introducing friends, relations, and business associates for years now, so this chapter may be a refresher course for you.

Ground Rules

While introductions have become more casual over the years—several decades ago, for instance, "nice girls" never spoke to men who hadn't been formally introduced to them by a third party—some of the basics still apply. There is still a formula for most introductions, and the essential formula has one person being introduced to another; the person being presented is always mentioned last:

- Children are introduced to adults. "Aunt Hattie, this is Marva's youngest son, Isaac."
- A man is introduced to a woman. "Mrs. Styles, I'd like you to meet Mr. Burroughs."
- Younger people are presented to older people. "Dr. Sloan, may I introduce my friend Lisa Wright?"
- Guests are introduced to the host or hostess. "Deborah, I'd like you to meet Larry and Pamela Morse. Larry, Pam, this is Deborah Norton."

When introducing people, the more prominent person takes precedence. This doesn't mean that the person who is receiving the introduction is more worthy than the one to whom he or she is being introduced, but it does mean that if he or she holds an office or position, the other person is presented to him, in deference to his office. Here are some examples:

> "Reverend Worth, I'd like you to meet Sarah McCabe. We were roommates at Spelman."

But if Sarah McCabe were, for instance, very elderly, you would do it this way:

> "Miss McCabe, I'd like you to meet our pastor, Reverend Steven Worth. Reverend Worth, Miss McCabe taught me Latin when I was a freshman at Spelman."

> "Mayor Whitfield, may I introduce Jean Samuels? Jean, this is our mayor, John Whitfield."

> "Professor Michaels, I'd like you to meet Sonya Washington. Sonya, this is Professor Jacob Michaels, dean of students."

Remember when introducing your relatives to another person that, unless your relative is elderly, he or she should be presented to the nonrelative:

> "Mrs. Williams, I'd like you to meet my father, Harry Banks. Dad, this is my department head, Mrs. Frances Williams."

> "Dr. Carter, I don't believe you've met my parents, David and Amelia Blake. Mama, Daddy, this is Dr. William Carter, Sylvia's father."

Notice that we put each introduction in context, so people can "place" each other a little. It's not essential for your minister to know that the young

woman you're introducing is an old friend from college, but it's nice if you can remember to include it. And it helps people who haven't met before to ease into a conversation. They don't have to start with, "So how do *you* know Sarah?"

First Names Only?

Everyone in the above examples was introduced by his or her full name. Many things about modern life have become more casual, but automatic use of only a first name shouldn't be one of them. (Do you *want* perfect strangers calling you by your first name?)

If first names are being used all around (a party, picnic, or something equally informal and social), go with the flow. If you're not sure, use the person's formal name ("Nice to meet you, Dr. Green") unless you're urged not to ("Oh, please call me Harold").

If you have a professional relationship with someone, he or she is addressed by title ("Dr. Talmadge, my wrist hurts when I turn it this way") unless he's also a good friend ("George, my wrist is killing me whenever I turn it this way"). You should both address each other similarly (Dr. Talmadge/Mrs. Hudson or George/Marilyn; *never* Dr. Talmadge/Marilyn).

Calling You Out Your Name

When your name is mispronounced, given incorrectly, or otherwise mangled during introductions, it's best to set it straight right away, or the mistake can take on a life of its own, kind of the way a sentence does in the children's game of telephone. It's best to nip name mistakes and unwanted nicknames in the bud by speaking up immediately: "Nice to meet you, and it's *Karen,* not Kathy, Bates." Or "Hello. I'm *Jeffrey* Spann; I'm introduced as Jeffie a lot, but I haven't been called that since I was three."

If your name is unusual or difficult to spell or pronounce, offer to help people with it the first time you're introduced: "My name is Nola Ehelene. That's A-*hell-ayne.* It's Hawaiian." Or if someone's trying to write your name in his address book: "I'm Sediqui Matthews: S-E-D-I-Q-U-I."

In-Laws . . . and Out-Laws

This is relatively straightforward: you can introduce your in-laws as your in-laws or as your spouse's parents. And remember that, as when introducing any family member, the relative (even by marriage) is presented to the other person:

> "Sheila, I'd like you to meet Aaron's mother, Paula Cleaver. Paula, this is Sheila Jackson. She's in my walking group."
>
> "Sheila, I want to introduce you to my mother-in-law, Paula Cleaver. Mom, Sheila and I are in that walking group I told you about."

Former in-laws (sometimes facetiously referred to as out-laws) should be introduced by name if the person you're introducing them to has no idea you were ever married or to whom. If the person *does* know (or knows of) your ex-husband, simply refer to your former in-laws as (ex-husband's name)'s mother and father: "This is Steve's mom and dad, Ophelia and Steven Maynard." No need to get into a drawn-out explanation of why they're no longer in-laws.

Group Introductions

Let's imagine that six of you come out of a movie theater and you run into a friend: "Jeanette, I'd like you to meet Don and Brenda Norris, Lou Weston and Nedra Phillips, Mike Thomas and Linda Swift. Everybody, this is Jeanette Reese."

You're giving a dinner and a guest arrives who knows no one. Introduce him to a few of your friends and see that he's included in the conversation. Unless he's horribly shy, he will not be afraid to introduce himself to other people as they come over. And if you have a guest of honor, you should remember to point him out to others as they arrive, and ask that they greet him and introduce themselves to him.

Introducing Yourself

Sometimes you find yourself in a situation where no one has introduced you. Maybe it's a really huge party. Or it's one of those open-house things where the hosts know everyone but not everyone knows everyone else. In that case, try not to be shy; introduce yourself to the people nearest you (it doesn't hurt to give your relationship to the host, either): "Hi, I'm Pat Simms. The Mitchells and I are neighbors."

Introducing a Third Party

If you're with one person and run into someone else you know, introduce them to each other, even if you're sure they'll never meet again. It's awkward—and rude—to leave the first person standing by, unacknowledged.

Forgetting Names

Scientists say we lose several thousand brain cells every day, so it's no news flash that sometimes a name or two gets sloughed off in the process. If you're being introduced and your introducer obviously can't remember your name, help him out: "Hi, I'm Jason West. Brenda and I are coworkers at Party Planners." If you're the one who's blanking, and the people you're introducing don't, for some reason, come to your rescue, 'fess up: "Okay, I'm mortified to admit it, but I cannot, for the life of me, remember your name." An honest admission is better than a lot of lame groping.

When People Forget Your Name Consistently —Maybe on Purpose

Sometimes a person is afflicted with a really bad memory, but sometimes the "amnesia" is the result of something more sinister. Maybe your boyfriend's mother keeps "forgetting" your name because she'd rather her favorite son date someone else. Perhaps a person you've seen socially several times just cannot be bothered. Whatever the reason, such episodes of forgetfulness are rude. They're telegraphing to the person being "forgotten" that he is not significant enough to be remembered.

So address this problem directly. Remind the person that you've met several times. *Pointedly.* "Oh yes, Mrs. Grace and I have met several times. I must have one of those names that's impossible to remember." Or "Actually, we've been introduced more than once. The last time was at St. Philip's annual fund-raiser, and the time before that was at the Eastern Star tea." We suspect their memories will, miraculously, improve the next time you meet.

When Your Names Are Different

You're a married couple, but your last names are different. If the person you're introducing your spouse to knows your name, be sure to emphasize your spouse's, so he's not called by your surname all night: "Mrs. Matthews, this is my husband, Charles Bonner." If you're introducing a couple with two different last names, make sure both names are included: "Mrs. Matthews, I'd like you to meet Lois Greene and her husband, Charles Bonner."

Shaking Hands

When you're introduced to anyone, always extend your hand and shake firmly. A brief, firm shake is always appreciated. We all shudder at the mention of the "jellyfish" handshake, the limp, slithery grip sometimes mistakenly referred to as a "lady's handshake." Neither do you want the opposite end of the spectrum, the shake so firm it literally crunches the bones of your hand. (Some men mistakenly think this is a "real man's" shake.) And don't pump up and down, either. What we're aiming for here is acknowledging someone's presence, not ripping his arm from the socket.

The rules for initiating the handshake are similar to the ones for introductions. A woman properly offers her hand to a man first. An elderly person offers to shake a younger person's hand. And a person with a title or an office extends his hand to the person who is being introduced.

As we noted earlier, those rules can be bent if an alternative is practical and polite: for example, a young pastor might wait for his elderly parishioner to extend her hand first, in deference to her age and gender.

Introducing Children

Your children should always be introduced to friends and business associates who visit your home. It helps children if, as with adults, you can place the new face in some kind of context: "Mr. Sargent, this is our son Jamie. Jamie, Mr. Sargent works with Daddy at the post office." Children who are old enough to talk in sentences should be able to say, "Hello, Mr. Sargent," and answer, "Thank you," when the guest tells them it's a pleasure to meet them. Practice shaking hands, too, so they'll know how to respond (and with which hand) when a guest offers to shake.

Standing When Being Introduced

A man always stands when being introduced to a woman. He may or may not stand when being introduced to another man, depending on that man's age and status. (An employee would stand when being introduced to a company's board member, for example.) Both men and women usually stand when being introduced to elderly people. Children should stand when being introduced to any adult.

When a woman enters a room for the first of what may be several times, men are expected to stand the first time; after that, they don't need to get up again.

Special Circumstances

Sometimes you'll find yourself being introduced to a person who is disabled on the hand or arm usually extended in greeting. Offer your hand anyway and let the other person decide how he wants to take it. A person we know who, as the result of polio, lost the use of his right hand usually shakes with his left. Other people simply smile and nod and ask that you forgive their not being able to shake your hand. This is an individual preference, and it's best to let the person with the disability lead, or use your common sense.

If you're handicapped by a disability that's evident (such as a missing hand, a broken arm) or more subtle (perhaps you have severe arthritis, and it's painful to shake), nod when you're introduced and say something like "Pleased to meet you. Forgive me for not shaking your hand, but it's hard to do with my arthritis." People will understand.

Introductions Across the Miles

Sometimes the most appreciated introductions occur when you aren't even in the room. Perhaps a good friend is moving from your town to another part of the country or state. Or a colleague would like a business contact in a city he's unfamiliar with. A call or letter of introduction from you is a big help in getting your friend or colleague started in a new place.

Traditionally, this was always done by letter, but a telephone call can work just as well: "Michael, this is Ed Flowers. Joan and I have close friends who are moving to Stamford at the end of the month. They have children almost the same age as yours, and I was hoping they could call you if they have questions about local schools, finding a new pediatrician, shopping, and things like that. Their names are Glenn and Dina Edwards."

If you want to send a letter, it should contain information on how or when to best reach the newcomers, and a request to pass on your friends' number. (See chapter 11, "Write On.")

More than anything, introductions help to make us all a little less strange to each other in a world that sometimes seems full of nothing but strangers.

Chapter 8

STRICTLY SPEAKING

Speak the truth to the people
Talk sense to the people
Free them with reason
Free them with honesty.

Mari Evans

The Art of Conversation

Conversations take up a large part of our waking day, and learning to converse well is an art. Our conversations range from mindless babble on the bus with someone we've never seen before and most likely will never see again to intimate conversations with our partners. The way we speak to our longtime coworkers is certainly different from the way we speak to a salesperson, and our words are chosen quite differently when watching a sports event or participating in a church service. The ability to carry on a conversation, simply and politely, is a skill that will enable you to express your ideas in all areas of your life.

The tone of your voice, your body language, your ability to make eye contact, knowledge of the information you wish to impart, and the desire to listen are all factors in a successful conversation.

Listening Is a Gift

Conversations involve listening as well as speaking. While you think you may be imparting absolute brilliance to your boss, unless you have mastered the gift of listening (to someone other than yourself!), you may miss critical information that will further your understanding of the subject at hand. The best conversations are a give-and-take process, much like the best friendships. You must listen to, and hear, what those you are conversing with are saying. Without listening, you are simply "talking"—not having a conversation. And even those of us who genuinely enjoy hearing ourselves speak would like the person we're speaking to to listen. Think back to the last time someone made you feel like you were "the only person in the room" and take note. It's an incredible compliment to be considered "a wonderful listener." And the better you listen when others speak, the more often you will be listened to.

Familiarity

Do not, under any circumstances, believe that you have a right to address people by their first names when you have not been introduced to them as such. If you are introduced to Mrs. Williams, then address her as "Mrs. Williams," not as "Stacy," even though others in the group have done so. Mrs. Williams may ask you to call her Stacy, at which point you may. A well-bred young man once remarked to the oldest woman in the room that he felt uncomfortable referring to an older woman as anything other than "Mrs." because that's the way his mother raised him—to respect his elders. The matriarch suggested that, although she admired his manners, it was even more gracious to call a woman whatever she felt most comfortable with.

Our society's tendency to become increasingly more casual and familiar does not grant you the right to refer to your physician by her first name, to call someone's mother's home and say, "Sadie, is LuLu home?" or to refer to your child's teacher by her first name. Frequent abusers of this concept are those in customer service industries. Bank employees should refer to customers as "Mr." or "Mrs." unless they are specifically requested to do otherwise. The same is true for telemarketers, retail salespeople, and others who interact with the public. It is best to err on the side of formality than be too familiar.

Addressing Members of the Clergy

Traditional etiquette calls for Protestant ministers who hold doctoral degrees to be addressed as "Dr. Livingston" and those without doctoral degrees to be addressed simply as "Mr. Livingston." Priests of the Roman Catholic church are addressed as "Father Mahoney," or they may ask you to call them by a given name, such as "Father Bill." A rabbi is referred to as "Dr. Wolf" or "Rabbi Wolf" if he holds a scholastic degree and as "Rabbi Wolf" if he does not. It is a sign of respect to check the proper terminology for religions you are unfamiliar with. In our community, ministers are commonly referred to as "Reverend" or "Doctor." Those who have been elevated to bishop are addressed accordingly.

Speaking to Retail Clerks and Service Workers

Show clerks, waiters, salespeople, repair persons, and all service people the same respect you would show to your dear friends.

Calling People What They Want to Be Called

You've just arrived for a long-awaited visit to your hometown for a high school reunion. You glance across the room and see your old classmate from French class and move to greet him. Upon closer inspection, you notice the name on his name tag doesn't match your memory: "Since when did you become François Lamé? Last time I checked, you were still Frank Lame." François, thrilled to see you, goes on to explain that he is now an award-winning float designer with his own business and goes by "François Lamé." It would be rude to call him Frank all evening and question his sanity. Rather, accept his decision and call him François as he has requested. This also applies to people who adopt Afrocentric names or those who feel they have outgrown their childhood nicknames. When the Jerrys become Jamals, the Sallys become Saras, and the "Wump" says she will answer only to Winnie or Winifred, respect their wishes.

Homosexuals

Male homosexuals are commonly known as gay, and female homosexuals are known as lesbians. Slang terms for homosexuality should never be used, even if gays or lesbians use such terms themselves.

Raising Your Voice

Unless your child has run out into the street in front of a speeding car or is about to run his hand over an open flame, we can't see the value in raising your voice—ever. It may feel good when you yell at that friend or family member who has disappointed you (yet again), but it will not help your case. If anything, raising your voice will make the listener stop listening. No one at that meeting will hear your ideas with any more enthusiasm because you raised your voice. There's a big difference between cheering your child's Little League game and voicing your opinion of the coach's bad judgment over the roar of the crowd. Once you raise your voice, you risk losing your composure completely—not a position we recommend.

Interrupting Others

People who find it necessary to regularly interrupt others in the middle of a thought are just plain rude. *Don't do it.* If you find yourself being interrupted, wait a few moments, then continue where you left off and make your point. Just as it is rude to interrupt others, it is equally tasteless to point out the intrusion to the offender.

Casual Profanity

In our perfect world, profanity would not be used. But, given that we live in a world that is far more grounded in reality, we know that profanity *will* be used by some people, though not by all. If you must use casual profanity, only a few situations in which to do so are acceptable. We don't suggest the use of profanity in mixed company. The girls can "let loose" among themselves in the privacy of a home; so can the guys when they're together and no women are present. Never use profanity in the presence of children, older people, in a business or work situation, at church, or around people you don't know very well. If you think you can't survive without profanity, listen to someone you admire and you'll be surprised how often he or she gets along quite well without it.

Jack Sprat

Just because Jack Sprat could eat no fat—and you're a firm believer—doesn't mean you must become the food police. Although a genuine interest in a friend's health and welfare may be warranted, it is not your place to reprimand someone's food choices. Personal choices, whether vegetarian or pure sugar, are not yours to publicly pass judgment on: "Do you really think you should be eating those french fries? A lettuce leaf would be so much better for you." (Don't even *think* it!)

Race and Conversation

Remember growing up and hearing that you should steer clear of certain conversations? Politics, religion, race? The reality is, we will all be engaged in conversations from A to Z, involving all areas of our lives. Undoubtedly, the subject of race will creep into conversations between friends and acquaintances. How we handle these conversations is often dictated by whether we are talking within the "safe" confines of our own race or are part of an integrated gathering. Unfortunately, situations will arise where the issue of race becomes contentious. Rarely do people enter into these conversations without preconceived notions, and a single conversation will not sway either party one way or another. If you find yourself in such a position, listen to the others, state your position clearly and concisely, and move on. You have no obligation to "educate" the world, but you do have every right to state your opinion in a polite manner.

When People Act As If You're Invisible

At times, when you work or socialize in an integrated environment, the majority feel so comfortable with you, or are so busy listening to themselves talk, that they forget you are there. This unfortunate lapse in memory may result in an exchange of words or ideas that would not have been shared had they been cognizant of your presence. It may be a general reference to race with an inappropriate term, or perhaps an observation about how "they've" been acting ever since that uppity Negro got elected mayor.

There's no need to fade into the woodwork to avoid confrontation. Rather, in a soft, controlled voice, interrupt the conversation and simply state that you are offended by their remarks, make your beliefs known if you choose, and ask them to please change the subject.

Responding at all to such a lack of home training is a judgment call. If you feel you will lose control, get up and walk away rather than make a scene. After you've had time to think about it, you may feel the need to take one of the offenders aside and speak to him or her privately. This, too, is acceptable, but be tactful.

Excuse Me, I'm Speaking to You

You're giving an important presentation at work and reality sets in: no one is listening. Address the problem with humor rather than lashing out at your audience. You might interject a silly anecdote that has absolutely no relevance to what you're speaking about. No doubt you will get their attention. Assure the listeners the end is near and sum up your most significant points. Better to get across the most important ideas than alienate what may be a future audience. Besides, it's not nice to point out other people's shortcomings—and not listening to a speaker is unquestionably rude. The situation is a little harder to gauge when you're pouring out your heart to a friend or love interest, and one look in his eyes lets you know he hasn't heard a thing you've said. You're entitled to feel disappointed, but choose another opportunity to discuss the subject, and the problem of his inattentiveness. When you're close to someone, be it friend, spouse, or relative, you may already know that there's a better chance of being "heard" when he or she *wants* to listen.

Sometimes you have to time your conversations to coincide with another's attitude.

Knowing What to Say in Uncomfortable Situations

- *When people talk too much.* There's not much you can do about this other than *attempt* to get a word in edgewise. Hopefully, the offender will realize that a conversation is much more interesting when more than one person is participating.
- *When people tell the same story over and over and over.* "Have I told you about the time . . ." Those famous words never seem to wait for a reply. Like the person who talks too much, some people have an inflated sense of just how interesting their lives are and feel a need to repeat the same stories over and over. Disinterest, plain and simple, is your best defense.
- *When people continually brag about their children and themselves.* While we welcome the joyous news of the latest achievements, we frown on those who continually brag about the accomplishments of their "smartest kid who ever lived" or how much bigger and better their house is. Resist the impulse to play one-upmanship and certainly don't respond and give them the satisfaction of thinking you want to hear more. We're reminded of the matriarch who was told once too often that her granddaughter's current beau held a Ph.D. Finally, she remarked to the young lady (out of earshot of the scholar) that Ph.D. simply stood for "piled high and deep."
- *When people ask a rude question.* When someone blindsides you and asks, "How much do you make?" simply let her know you don't discuss such things. Be tactful but firm. Feign ignorance or memory loss or let her know that topics like family finances are private.
- *When people are too boring for words.* Picture yourself on a five-hour cross-country flight seated next to the most boring person in captivity. It is quite easy to extricate oneself from a boring conversation when you are in a public place with someone you do not know. Open a book, pretend to be sleepy, or beg off conversation due to your heavy workload. A little more tricky is the boring dinner partner. Listen, try to engage others in the conversation, or direct your attention to another guest. In a large party, that ever-present buffet table can be a tactful escape.
- *When people need to admit they are wrong.* If you're wrong, you're wrong. Admit it quickly, and with humor. No high drama required, just a sincere admission that you've made a mistake.

- *When people complain, complain, complain.* There's always someone in your life whose day is not complete without complaining about every little thing. Hard to believe, but some people can even find something negative about a beautiful sunset. There's not a lot you can do about chronic complainers, but they can spoil everyone's day.

Best Not Mentioned

Some subjects and questions are simply inappropriate at any time.

- *Don't* ask about people's health unless they've recently been ill and you're wondering if they are feeling better. Ask how they're feeling and let them know you're interested in their well-being, not just being nosy. When asked how you are, it's best to say, "Fine" or "Better, thank you," and leave it at that.
- *Don't* ask what specifically is wrong with people who are ill or what kind of medication they are taking. You might find out more than you want to know.
- *Don't* tell people they don't look well. If they aren't feeling well, you certainly have confirmed their suspicions that they look as bad as they feel. If they feel great, your comment can make them feel ill faster than the speed of light.
- *Don't* ask people why they're not married or why they don't have children. In addition to the fact that it's none of your business, it's a personal matter that may be painful to discuss.
- *Don't* give unsolicited advice. This is another judgment call. Advice not asked for can be a source of resentment. If you think the advice is critical to your friend's well-being, it may be worth the risk. Put yourself in his or her position and weigh the consequences. If you're not a close friend, don't even think about it.
- *Don't* talk about your health all the time. While *you* may be obsessed about the current state of your health, even your closest friends don't want to hear about every little detail every day.
- *Don't* ask how old someone is. Again, revelations are matters of personal choice. Some people relish their youth, while others applaud their own longevity. If your childhood playmate has suddenly become six years younger than she was the last time you celebrated your joint birthday, so be it. It's a good idea not to ask if someone has had plastic surgery, either. It's like age: some people boast about it, and some shun public knowledge.
- *Don't* correct a person who has mispronounced a word or used it incorrectly.

Chapter 9

I HEARD IT THROUGH THE GRAPEVINE

If people gossip to *you,*
they will also gossip about *you.*

West African proverb

Marvin Gaye and wise old folks always cautioned us about gossip: only believe half of what you see, and as for what you hear, if it's second- or thirdhand, just assume it's tainted information. Gossip has a life of its own; as it gets carried along, it changes shape and direction until what might have been a casual observation ("I saw Laura yesterday; she was coming out of Harvard Tower") turns into something entirely different, often to the detriment of the person being discussed ("You know, almost all the offices in the Tower are devoted to mental health services; I didn't know Laura was seeing a psychiatrist"). While we all profess to hate gossip, it's a very human thing to do, and no one, even the most saintly among us, is totally immune to the urge to tell what we think we know. Remember your home training, and suppress the urge. *Don't* gossip.

When You're the Conduit of Gossip

Sometimes you contribute unknowingly to gossip's passage and transport, since people love to put two and two together and will add your neutral comment to information they may think they already know. If you talk about other people, even talk you consider harmless, make sure you have your facts correct so you don't at least compound the error.

It's always tempting to indulge in gossip about others—it's a habit that transcends gender (no matter what men say to the contrary), race, and nationality—but it's a temptation that should be resisted, since the end result can be devastating for the person who is being gossiped about. Hurt feelings, severed romantic relationships, and ruined careers have all been traced back to wagging tongues.

When You Know Whom They're Talking About

It's happened to everyone at some point: you overhear a couple of people talking about someone, and it becomes distressingly clear to you that the subject of the gossip is a neighbor, friend, or relative. While you don't want to appear rude by injecting yourself into someone else's conversation, you feel honor bound to set them straight about the subject of their gossip.

Perhaps the best way is to be straightforward: "Excuse me, but I couldn't help overhearing your conversation, and I thought I should let you know that Dawn is a very close friend and that she has never, ever behaved that way—and I've known her for fifteen years." Gossips are usually quick to stop the conversation—at least in your presence—and may even offer an apology.

When They're Talking About You

Maybe you're in a stall in the ladies' room when it becomes apparent that the women who are combing their hair at the sink are talking about someone you know really well—you!—and to add insult to injury, they've gotten their facts wrong. Or you hear your name mentioned by someone you don't know at a crowded reception, and listen (partly horrified, partly amused) as the latest twist in your love life is shared with another perfect stranger.

Probably the best thing to do in this case is identify yourself and let the gossipers know you'd really appreciate it if they'd stick to what they know: "Excuse me, but I happen to know that divorce didn't happen exactly that way because you're talking about *my* divorce. I don't believe we've met; I'm Marissa Johnson." Or "I'm glad the story of how I met Kofi is a favorite, but I'd really rather my private life wasn't discussed in public."

When You Know Your Friend Is Dating a Dog

Your best girlfriend is walking on clouds because she's found Mr. Right. Unfortunately, you've known him to be less than fabulous. Maybe he's married and it just slipped his mind to mention it. Or he has at least two other "serious" relationships you know about—despite the fact that he's declared undying, monogamous love to your friend.

Chances are, she will find this out in fairly short order for herself. Although you may be tempted to inform your friend of the true nature of Mr. Right before she discovers it on her own, she may not appreciate your intervention, however well intentioned. Keep silent. Be supportive of her. And if you get the chance, let Mr. Right know you're familiar with the other side of him as well, which might be enough to make him straighten up.

Seeing Your Girlfriend's Husband on a "Date"

You're out to dinner with friends, and as you walk to the ladies' room, you realize you've run smack into a dear friend's husband—and he's having what appears to be an intimate conversation with a woman who is definitely *not* his wife. After the initial shock subsides (yours *and* his) you'll have to decide how to handle it.

It's always possible that things aren't as they seem: perhaps your friend's husband is entertaining a business client or having a completely innocent dinner with a colleague or a visiting friend from college or is himself being pitched by someone who is trying to close a deal.

But if your common sense tells you otherwise, if dinner looks a little too cozy to be strictly business, if he seems more uncomfortable than a business dinner should make him, perhaps your suspicions are on target. In that case, don't tell your girlfriend (who may or may not suspect what's going on), but do let the husband know you've seen him: "Hi, Frank! Imagine running into you here." If he hesitates to introduce you to his dinner companion (a worrisome sign), introduce yourself: "Hi, I'm Alana Whittaker, nice to meet you. Frank, say hi to Amy for me; remind her we're supposed to go to aerobics together on Wednesday." You've shown Frank that he hasn't escaped undetected, you've established that he does have a wife or significant other, and you've indicated that you'll be talking to Amy soon—and Frank can't be sure aerobics class is the *only* thing on the agenda. Any discomfort that needs to be felt should be felt by him—and will, you hope, serve as the impetus to nipping his extracurricular activity in the bud.

Things Better Left Unsaid

Most of us, at one time or another, have let slip some question or observation that has hurt another person. It's impossible to avoid doing this all the time, but to cut down on these incidents as much as possible, try to refrain from making comments about:

- Someone's health—especially if you're not certain of it. "You look awful—are you sure there's nothing seriously wrong? Maybe you should see a doctor." Maybe she *has* seen a doctor and the news isn't good—and she doesn't want to discuss it.

- Someone's choice of a date. "Look, I know you think you really like him, but he's a major sleaze. I heard that . . ." What you heard but cannot verify is not going to do anything but anger your friend, especially if she becomes truly attached to the date you can't stand.
- Someone's in-laws. "How are they treating you? I know they were crazy about his first wife; they still see her frequently." This is information a new bride probably isn't going to find very reassuring.
- Someone's business, especially if you're a competitor. "I hear they're going to go into Chapter 11 sometime soon . . . too bad." If this is true, it will be public knowledge soon enough. If it isn't, it could have ruinous consequences that might, ironically, end up becoming a self-fulfilling prophecy.
- Someone's sexuality. "Do you think he's not married because he's gay?" "How would gay guys do it, anyway?" Imagine how annoyed you'd be if the situation was reversed and *he* was speculating about *your* bedroom preferences . . .

Chapter 10

REACH OUT AND TOUCH SOMEONE

When I get home I have two messages. The first one's from Vanessa. "Girl, Angela called and told me you're going to Jamaica! How come you didn't tell me? Way to go, girl."

Terry McMillan, *How Stella Got Her Groove Back*

Nowadays, most households have an answering machine. This little tool makes life easier and more complicated—sometimes at the same time. (Thank goodness videophones are still a few years from widely being used!) Telephones, answering machines, pagers, and cellular phones are both the bane and the boon of modern life. Almost everyone has at least one of them, and their convenience is undeniable. They may be part of the new technology, but good old-fashioned manners still apply. And they'll probably *still* apply whenever the technological advancement to replace our current, can't-do-without-them machines comes along, too.

Answering the Telephone

Always answer with "hello," not "yup," "yo," "what's up," or other slang of the moment. You can never be entirely sure (even when you think you are) who's on the other end; a simple "hello" covers everyone.

Answering the Telephone in Someone Else's Home

This is almost as simple: "Hello, Markham residence" or just "Markham residence" is enough. If the person being called is busy or unavailable, identify yourself and offer to take a message: "This is Debbie, her cousin. Would you like to leave a message?" If the family indicates it would like to know who is on the line, ask the caller if you may tell the family who's calling: "They're out in the garage; may I tell them who's calling?" Don't ask, "Who's calling?" Since the caller didn't call to speak with you (and may not even know you), he may well consider his identity none of your business.

When the Housekeeper or Caregiver Answers the Telephone

If you have someone who works in your home regularly and you want her to answer the telephone, tell her how you'd like her to do this. "Markham residence" or "Good morning, Markham residence" are two traditional options. Or, for security's sake, you may just prefer that she answer "hello." It's up to you.

Let It Ring!

Nothing is more annoying than to race across a room to answer a ringing phone only to have it stop once you've reached it. When you call someone, always let the phone ring enough times—at least a half dozen—so that the party has a chance to answer. If you know the person you're calling has only one phone, or is elderly or disabled, be considerate and add some extra rings.

Keeping Track of Calls in the Office

Many people like to keep their phone messages in a central place; some even keep "call sheets," ledgers that indicate who called and when. You can strike through a name or number when you've returned a call so that, at a glance, you know which calls are still outstanding. If your office days are usually hectic, you may want to reserve a specific block of time during the day (many people do this first thing in the morning; others prefer day's end) to return calls.

Returning Calls in a Timely Manner

One of the advantages of using a call sheet is that it reminds you how long an interval has passed between when you were called and when you return a call. Savvy executives tell us they always try to return calls within twenty-four hours. Even if you can't have an extended conversation for a couple of days because of pressing deadlines, callers appreciate it if you can call and indicate when you might be getting back to them: "Leslie, I've got to get this report to my department head by tomorrow morning, but I promise to call you before I leave the office tomorrow."

Calling People Who Work at Home

Many people who work at home complain that home office workers don't get the same respect their corporate counterparts do. Callers who are telephoning people who work in home offices should remember a few things:

- Keep business calls businesslike. Don't rattle on about things other than the job at hand.
- Don't call because *you* need amusing. You may be at loose ends, but the person you're calling is actually trying to get some work done.
- Don't ask for favors you wouldn't ask of a colleague who is not in a home office. People who work at home are doing just that: they are not free to run errands or baby-sit for you, accept your deliveries, or fix lunch because you happen to drop in on your way to somewhere else.

Answering the Telephone in Someone Else's Home Office

Act as you would if you were answering a colleague's phone in your own office: "Marcy DeVeaux's line, this is Anita." Or "The DeVeaux Group, this is Anita."

Call Waiting

It's the service we love to hate, but, by now, many American households use some kind of call-interrupt system. If you're making an important call and don't wish to be interrupted, disable call waiting. (Check the front of your telephone directory or call your phone company for instructions on how to activate this option.) This effectively blocks a second call from coming in.

If you can't disable call waiting (you don't have the disabling service or you've answered an incoming call and a second call comes through), here's what you need to do:

1. Apologize to your first caller and put him on hold for a few seconds.
2. Click on the second call, identify the caller, and promise to call back when the first call is finished.

3. Click back to your first call and finish the conversation.
4. Return the second call promptly, as promised.

As always, there are exceptions. Medical emergencies or other true crises must be handled immediately, in which case you explain briefly to the first caller why you must hang up, and promise to call back when things are calmer: "Margaret, that was Gene's school. He slipped in gym and I have to meet them at the emergency room." Or "Tyson, the baby-sitter just called; we've got to figure out why the smoke detector's going off. I'll call you back later."

Work priorities may also be a legitimate excuse. If you're expecting a work-related call you must take, let your first caller know she may be preempted: "Janet, my editor may call from San Francisco with some last-minute changes, and if she does, I'll have to take that call." Your caller can decide whether she'd like to continue or call you later.

A considerate caller will always offer to let the person at the other end answer the line ("It's okay; I'll hold while you get that") or ring off, if necessary ("Oops! There's your other line. I'll talk to you later").

Never, ever hang up from a first call just because a call you'd rather take comes in. This all but announces you think caller number two is a more important human being. Wouldn't you find that annoying if it were done to you?

Answering Machines

Sure, you hate reaching them, but could you live without yours? These machines can be less onerous if some simple rules are followed:

- Make your message short and to the point. Telling the caller which number he's reached (and/or whom) is enough: "Hi, you've reached 555-1212, the Thompson residence. If you'd like to leave a message for Sharon, Michael, Nate, or D.J., wait for the tone."
- If you let young children record the message, make sure they can be easily understood: "This is D. J. Thompson. If you want to leave a message for my mom, my dad, or my brother, Nate, wait for the tone."
- Stay away from cutesy, risqué, or otherwise iffy messages: "Hi, this is Zena. Jimmy and I are out celebrating our first two weeks of married bliss, so we can't come to the phone right now" is more than anyone—including your boss, minister, and people who've never met you—needs to know.
- If your machine has a time limit, let your callers know. "This is Marcy.

You have forty-five seconds to leave me a message after the tone." Or "This is Marcy; leave me a message of any length after the tone."

Callers should remember to:

- Make your messages brief and to the point: "Jan, it's Cynthia. Sam and I decided to have a last-minute chili cook-off tomorrow night at six. We hope you can come. Call us. Our number is . . ."
- Save your personal messages until you actually get the person you're trying to reach.
    Do: "This is Nikki Adams. Could you please call as soon as you can? My number is . . ."
    Don't: "This is Nikki Adams, and I hear you've been seeing my boyfriend, Stewart . . ."
- Do the same for sad messages, if possible.
    Do: "Fred, call when you get in; it's important."
    Don't: "Fred, Mom called. Grandmom died. We don't know when the funeral's going to be yet, but we're all planning to fly out for it. Call me."
- However, if you wish, you can leave happy news on the answering machine.
    "Sue, we've been trying to reach you all week—you're going to be an aunt! Call us!"
    "Mike: Zack got into Morehouse! We know he has a thousand questions for his favorite uncle about your alma mater!"
- *Never, ever leave confidential information of any kind on an answering machine.* Even if you know the person you're calling lives alone, you cannot know if he is always alone when he listens to his messages. Medical or legal information or news involving finances should be delivered when the person you're trying to reach picks up the telephone. This is also true when communicating via answering services, fax machines, and voice mail.

Answering Services

Some people prefer to have a live person, rather than a machine, take their messages, so they hire a service with operators.
If you reach an answering service:

- Identify yourself, spell your name for the operator if necessary, and leave a brief message and your number.

- Do not quiz the operator as to the caller's whereabouts: it's not part of her job to serve as the FBI for you.
- Even if you know the operator well, don't tie her up with chitchat. She has other calls to take.

If you use an answering service:

- Check your messages at least once daily and always identify yourself: "This is Jeanine Taylor; I'm checking for messages."
- Have a pen and paper ready so the operator is not kept waiting and doesn't have to repeat the message.
- Always thank the operator, by name, if you know the voice: "Thanks, Terry. Talk with you tomorrow."

Voice Mail

Voice mail is the electronic equivalent of the answering machine. Messages go to a central number that the voice mailbox owner can pick up at will, via a remote call. The same rules apply for answering machines (be precise, no cutesy messages, etc.) with one other rule: *remember to clear your mailbox regularly.* It's very annoying to a caller who wants to leave a message to receive a recording indicating the message box is full and no additional messages will be taken.

Services and Machines When You're Away

Perhaps you're on vacation or a business trip or have some other reason to be away from home for a few days or longer. Some people choose to change the tape on the answering machine to say they won't be available for a few days. Others simply call in once a day to check messages. This is probably best, if you can do it, as it doesn't announce your absence. If you can't check daily (maybe you're overseas, and the long-distance calls are expensive; or you're at a retreat where there are no phones), you might want to leave a neutral message: "This is Lisa Wright. I may not be able to return your call immediately, but I promise to get back to you if you'll leave your name and number."

Answering Machine Messages and Security

If you're a woman living alone or an elderly person, you may not, for security reasons, want the message on your machine to indicate that you live by yourself. In that case, you could ask a male friend to record your message, perhaps omitting your name: "This is 555-1212. Please leave a message at the sound of the tone." Or you could indicate, via your message, that "we" can't answer the phone at the moment, leaving doubt as to whether you really live by yourself: "Hi, this is 555-1212. We can't come to the phone right now, but if you'll leave a message . . ."

Children Answering the Telephone

Children old enough to write can be taught to answer the telephone. They should be prepared to take a name and number. For safety's sake, they should be taught never to give out any information other than the fact that their parent cannot come to the telephone at that moment.

Don't: "My mommy's not home now. Do you want to leave a message?"
Do: "My mom can't come to the phone right now, but I can give her a message for you."

"Sorry, Wrong Number"

If you think you have the right number, tell the person who picked up the phone the number you're trying to reach: "Oh, I was trying to reach Joe Payne, at 555-1212." If he tells you you've reached an incorrect number, apologize before you hang up: "I'm sorry to have bothered you." You may hang up without apologizing if you reach an answering machine.

Obscene Phone Calls

Hang up immediately if you receive an obscene call. If the calls persist, tell the caller you will notify both the telephone company and the police—especially if the obscenity is accompanied by violent talk. Let your answering machine screen your calls; you can give the tape to the police if necessary. Caller ID machines are available in many states and can be useful in indicating where the calls are originating. If the calls continue, the telephone company may offer to attach one of these to your phone to trace the calls. A final solution would be to change your number. It's annoying to have to do this, but it's worth your peace of mind.

Public Telephones

Public phones are a communal convenience and should be used for short periods of time only. If you're by a bank of phones and there's no one waiting to use them, feel free to monopolize the one you're on. If, however, there is only one telephone, or a very few phones, and certainly if there is a line of people waiting for a phone, some basic courtesies apply:

- Make your call short.
- Do not make multiple calls if others are waiting. (It's a public phone, not your portable office.)
- Don't give the public phone number as a callback, thereby blocking others' ability to use the phone while you wait to receive calls.
- If you have a medical or other emergency, you can explain to others if they're waiting, or ask someone who is on the phone to hang up and call 911 for you.
- Try not to touch the mouthpiece directly or "spray" or splutter into it.

Cellular Telephones (Car and Handheld)

Technology has kept pace with our busy lives and made cellular telephones commonplace, especially in urban areas. Once the toy of the wealthy, cellular phones now come in a wide price range, and can offer a sense of safety and security. It's great to have a phone at hand when your car breaks down in an unfamiliar neighborhood or when you're running late for an appointment. But there are times when this modern convenience *shouldn't* be used: Don't engage in idle chatter on your cell phone while eating alone in a restaurant. Try not to leave your phone on when you're dining publicly, meeting in someone's office, or walking down the street. (A television executive once said she assumed that people who had to have their cellular phones on at lunch to receive calls "couldn't afford to have someone answer their phone and take messages.") Basically, you should refrain from making or receiving calls anywhere people can reasonably expect some peace and quiet. (Some unsuitable venues: libraries, hospitals, concerts, religious services, and lectures. Use your common sense.)

And it goes without saying that, unless you have a hands-free mechanism for your phone, always pull over to the side of the street or get off the highway before making a call. As a result of too many chat-induced accidents (some quite serious), several states are considering legislation that prohibits talking and driving.

Speakerphones

Speakerphones are common in offices where hands-free telephoning or conference calls are common. Home telephones, especially those equipped with built-in answering machines, now offer hands-free speaking via a speakerphone feature, which has its pros and cons. It's often disconcerting to the person on the other end of the line because she thinks you are being impersonal, or even arrogant. ("I don't make speakerphone calls," one executive insists, "and I don't take them. I think speakerphones are rude.")

The obvious exception to the no-speakerphone rule would be people with physical handicaps. Whether it's something temporary, such as a broken wrist, chronic (perhaps a pinched nerve that makes holding a receiver uncomfortable), or permanent (the loss or paralysis of a limb), callers with physical disabilities should do what's most comfortable for them. If the disability is temporary, you might explain why you've put your caller on the speaker: "I'm sorry, but I broke my collarbone last week, so I'm using the speakerphone until the pins are taken out." If your disability is permanent, it's up to you whether or not you choose to explain why you're not using a handset.

And of course you should keep in mind that you never know who is in the room with the person you're calling, so anything sensitive, confidential, or in questionable taste shouldn't be broadcast over the speaker.

Using Someone Else's Telephone

Sometimes you're visiting someone and must ask to use the phone. For local calls, the same rules would apply as for public telephones. For long-distance calls, some additional things to remember:

- Always use your phone card, or ask the operator to charge the call to your number.
- If this isn't possible, time your call, ask the operator for an estimate of the charges, and leave a check for that amount, with a brief note that explains the date, time, and destination of the call: "Al: I called Charlotte, N.C. (704-555-1212) on 8/22 for 10 minutes. $5 attached. Please let me know if I owe more. Gina."
- If you need to have someone call you at someone else's number, always get the permission of the person who owns the phone first.
- If you need to give a number that's not your own to call forwarding, be sure to ask if this is all right *before* you have the calls forwarded.

Time Zone Differences

Because our country is so effectively linked together with efficient telephone service, we sometimes forget about the changes in time zones. If you're returning a call outside your area code and aren't sure about which part of the country you're calling, consult the front of your telephone book. Don't forget to check the current time for the geographic area you are trying to reach. (Californians routinely complain about being awakened by East Coast callers who neglect to note the three-hour time difference. And East Coast people don't appreciate late-night calls from West Coast callers who forget that a call made in, say, Oregon at 9 P.M. is, to someone in Boston, midnight.)

Pagers/Beepers

Not all that long ago, the only people sporting pagers were those who had to be found on a moment's notice, often for life-and-death reasons. Physicians and news personnel were the main users of this particular gadget. Today doctors still carry pagers—but so do people who've never seen the inside of medical school. We may give them to our children to keep track of their whereabouts, to our spouses to await critical family updates; we may even keep them ourselves so our families can reach us when an emergency arises. Employees have begun wearing beepers in order to receive personal calls that are not allowed in the workplace, because beepers allow you to be notified that someone is trying to reach you, and you may call back at your leisure.

While pagers are a convenience, they're not meant to be a nuisance—or a fashion statement. Carry yours in an inconspicuous place, preferably so that the casual passerby does not know you have it. Most beepers are equipped with both sound and vibration features; we believe the well-mannered person will only use the vibration mode. That way, only you know that you're being paged.

Beepers are not designed to intrude on the lives of others, so be sure always to be mindful of those around you: don't allow your beeper to interrupt movies, plays, the quiet of a library, office, or classroom environment.

E-Mail

As we begin to travel the cyber-highway, corresponding by electronic means, or e-mail, as it's commonly called, has become the "fast food" way of communicating. Although nothing on the Internet is totally private, you have the luxury of sending a personal message to an individual "mailbox" that may only be accessed with a password. The transmissions are instantaneous, and we are able to communicate with friends and associates worldwide. Unlike faxes, which are sent to a telephone number you dial, e-mail is transmitted to an electronic address which you "address" while on-line. Its convenience and speed have made e-mail popular quickly: now we generally see telephone books and business cards that have space for e-mail addresses, along with telephone numbers, fax numbers, cellular numbers, and "snail mail," or postal street addresses.

Never, under any circumstances, use vulgar language in e-mail or write anything suggestive. Besides being bad manners, this is against the rules of many on-line services that transmit e-mail, and using profanity or vulgarity can result in your being unplugged from your service. While the issue of freedom of speech on the Internet (what cyberspace is commonly called) is currently being argued, most commercial on-line services do have specific and stringent rules about what's not allowed on-line and are, so far, legally permitted to monitor and, if necessary, delete mail they receive complaints about or otherwise deem offensive.

Believe it or not, there is a protocol attached to driving on the information highway. Recognizing this, several Internet guides have at least a small section devoted to "netiquette." Try to scan one or two so you'll know the basic courtesies your cyber-colleagues practice—and expect of you.

Fax Machines

Facsimile, or fax, machines are an instantaneous way to send written information that may otherwise take days by traditional mail. The ease of fax transmissions has proved to be a convenience that shouldn't be taken lightly.

Unless the fax machine you're sending to is in the privacy of the recipient's home, remember that your communication will probably be received at a central station and may possibly be read by any- and everyone. Correspondence sent by fax should be written with the same care as regular letters. Writing "confidential" on the cover sheet is no guarantee that your transmission will be kept in strict confidence, so the same rules for other modern forms of communication apply: no vulgarity, profanity, private matters, or sensitive medical or legal information should be sent in this manner. And documents that require a legal signature must be followed up via a "hard," or real-paper, copy that is delivered via mail or messenger.

Giving Out Phone Numbers

This is one of those "it goes without saying" things, but of course you check with another person before giving her number (or fax number or e-mail address) to a third party. And remember that cell-phone numbers are often given out reluctantly, if at all, by the people who own them because of the expense involved. (You're charged for a cell call both when you initiate the call *and* when someone calls you.)

Chapter 11

WRITE ON

May 15, 1943
Dear Lance,
Your letter was like sweet music. I could just about hear you talking to me as I read it . . .
Much love,
Pop

Anita Richmond Bunkley,
Wild Embers

True letter writers are becoming an endangered species, which is ironic, considering how most of us treasure receiving a "real" letter. Isn't it nice, when sorting through the bills and junk mail at the end of the day, to find a card, note, or letter from a friend? But if we don't write letters, there's no incentive for others to write to *us*, is there? A handy supply of attractive stationery is sometimes enough inspiration to encourage you to write more often. Even if you're just dashing off a few lines, the person you've written to will appreciate the effort. And you might even find you've started a letter-writing trend among your friends.

An Integrated System

Years ago, the size, weight, and color of your stationery were dictated by your gender, the occasion, and even the locale from which you were writing. But that rather complicated way of communicating has given way to a more streamlined approach to paper. Today we assemble our stationery wardrobes based on the practicalities of our daily lives and our personal tastes. You probably would choose a different kind or size of paper to dash off a note to a friend than you would to send a short letter to your local politician, but the unifying element might be the color (maybe pale blue with blue ink for your signature) or your monogram or your name in a distinctive typeface. The only rule is that your paper reflect you. (If you're the sporty, athletic type, for instance, a frilly typescript wouldn't be representative of your true self, but something bolder might be.)

Just Your Type

For purists, there are two kinds of typesetting: engraving and everything else. Engraving produces a product that is crisp and precise. It's the perfect counterpoint to an elegant paper stock and is always properly used for the most formal occasions (wedding invitations, for example). But engraving is expensive (each piece of paper literally has letters carved into it and ink transferred via a steel die, a sort of template that is created just for you). Modern technology has developed some options that are more affordable and are almost as attractive as engraving.

Embossing raises the print by pushing back-to-front. It can be inked or left uninked (usually referred to as blind embossing) and is often used for monograms and letterheads. *Thermography* is the process of producing a raised print impression via heat application. It is widely used for personal stationery, informal correspondence, and many kinds of notes. *Printing* or *flat printing* is the process of applying ink to paper. You choose a paper weight, color, and size, and pick a typeface from a sample book. The printer then sets the type and runs the paper through a press. The end product looks quite finished. Printing is used for everything from business and personal stationery to memo paper, business cards, and informal invitations. *Laser printing* is something many people do at home, with a good software program, good paper stock, and a laser printer. In many instances, it produces a product that is indistinguishable from a professionally printed job.

Popular Papers

While you can choose anything for your stationery needs, some basic types of paper have proved popular:

- Letter paper, for business and personal correspondence
- Notepaper, when a brief line or two is enough
- Correspondence cards, made of a stiff paper that is perfect for short notes or informal invitations
- Household notepads, for to-do lists and short notes for domestic things: "To the paper carrier: Please do not deliver from August 9 to 22. Thank you."

- Postcards, for brief correspondence that isn't confidential: "Save the date: Big Sisters' Annual Luncheon on Saturday, October 14, at Café Jackson."

Afrocentric Touches

In addition to the typeface, color, weight, and size of your paper, you may want to consider Afrocentric accents to make your selection even more individual. A batiklike border, textured paper with lots of natural fiber, and symbols such as cowrie shells, Adinkra symbols, or African masks are all striking additions that celebrate our ancestral heritage.

Folding and Stuffing an Envelope

Business letters should be folded in equal thirds: bring the bottom third up beyond the middle and fold; then fold the top third over the bottom third. Place the letter in the envelope with the folds facing the flap. This way, the recipient will pull out a letter that faces him and open the top first.

Personal letters are folded according to size. Letter paper is folded as described for business paper. Small letter paper (the traditional "half-sheet" is an example) should be folded in half and placed in the envelope with the fold at the bottom. Correspondence cards are put in envelopes with the front of the card facing the flap, right-side up.

Return addresses are normally placed in the upper left-hand corner of the front of the envelope. An alternative is to place the return address on the back flap. (Printed envelopes almost always place the address here.)

Business Cards

"Do you have a card?" is probably the second most frequently asked question when you're in a group of people. (The other, we'd guess, is "What do you do?") And it's always wise to have a cache of business cards to hand out when they're requested in appropriate circumstances.

If your company decides you need business cards, it will have them made for you. If you're self-employed, you can have cards made with your business's name, address, and telephone and fax numbers. Even if you don't have a paid job but do volunteer work for which others need to reach you, a card with your telephone and/or fax number would be useful. (People without business addresses may decide, on a case-by-case basis, whether they'd like to handwrite their address on the card.)

Social Cards

Social cards are the alter ego of the business card and are used in nonbusiness situations. A descendant of the old-fashioned calling card, social cards are used when you want to give people you meet a way to reach you and you don't want to scribble on a ripped-off corner of a miscellaneous piece of paper.

Choose a typeface you like. Have your name centered on the card. If you are a traditionalist and want to indicate your marital status, you'd list yourself the traditional way. A married woman who uses her husband's name would be "*Mrs. Mark Austin Williams.*" A married woman who has retained her name, or who uses a hyphenated name, would have her cards printed as "*Jill Marie Thompson*" or "*Jill Thompson-Williams.*" Single women may prefer to list themselves by their names only ("*Stella Marie Brown*") or with an honorific ("*Miss Stella Marie Brown*").

Seals, Stamps, and Other Extras

Sealing Wax

As an added flourish, some people like to customize their letters and notes with sealing wax. This colored wax (red, dark green, deep blue, and gold are popular colors) is melted with the aid of a lighted match and applied to the flap of an envelope drop by drop. (Some wax sticks have a wick similar to a candle's, to aid this process.) While the wax is still soft, an impression is made with a carved metal seal. Seals can be bought in stationery stores, or custom-ordered, like stationery dies. Initials or simple designs are often used. A neatly applied wax seal looks very impressive on an envelope. And, like the reason it was used historically, a seal keeps an envelope closed until it's opened by the intended recipient.

Commemorative Stamps

Several years ago, the post office began to issue postage stamps that honored the achievements of Americans from many different communities. The Black Heritage series features black Americans in science, education, the arts, and politics. We love being able to place stamps with W. E. B. Du Bois, Duke Ellington, and pilot Bessie Coleman on our correspondence as a cultural affirmation. Ask at your post office branch about these stamps.

Decorative Seals

Often charities solicit funds via letter and, as an inducement, add decorative seals. The Easter Seal Society has done this for years each spring. The TB Society's Christmas Seals are a holiday tradition in some families. Boys

Town, AIDS organizations, and other nonprofit groups continue to raise part of their funds this way. Using these stamps helps to publicize their cause.

If decorative stamps have been sent to you without solicitation, the law allows you to return them, throw them away, or use them on your envelopes. If you do choose to use them, make sure they don't obscure U.S. regulation postal stamps, or any information critical to the post office. It's best to position these as you would a wax seal, at the base of the envelope flap.

Stickers and Stamps

Once thought the province of kindergartners and bureaucrats, colorful stickers and rubber stamps have exploded in popularity among the general population, too. Use them to customize an informal invitation or letters to friends. (Some stamps are quite intricate, almost works of art in themselves.) Avoid using them on formal correspondence (wedding invitations, condolence letters), business correspondence (unless you own or sell stickers or stamps), and anything where a casual, lighthearted touch would be inappropriate.

Bookplates

If you lend your books and they have a hard time finding their way back to you, you ought to consider investing in bookplates. These are paper labels that you glue onto the inside front cover of your books (many now have gummed backs). Bookplates can contain something as simple as your name or initials, or they might have a favorite emblem or picture above the space for your name. Most have the words "Ex Libris" on them, which means "from the library of." You can buy bookplates in stationery stores and bookstores, order them through catalogs, or have them custom-made at the printer.

Season's Greetings

The Christmas holidays may be the only time some of us receive more "real" mail than bills! All the nonwriters we know seem to manage to squeeze out a few lines during the season to check in, say hello, and catch us up on all the news that's happened during the year.

Christmas cards send greetings to fellow Christians; they celebrate Christ's birth or the Christmas season. They can be religious or secular in tone, serious or humorous. Many families now have a favorite snapshot of themselves made into a card that is sent to friends. (You'll probably want to do this a couple of months early, since last-minute printing can be more expensive.)

Kwanzaa cards should be sent to arrive sometime during the week of December 26 to January 1; they traditionally make some reference to at least one of the Seven Principles of Kwanzaa: Unity, Self-determination, Collec-

tive work and responsibility, Cooperative economics, Purpose, Creativity, and Faith.

Cards to people of non-Christian faiths should not have Christmas-like emblems or sentiments (no Christmas trees, Nativity scenes, wishes for a Merry Christmas, etc.), since they're not really appropriate for those who don't subscribe to Christian beliefs. You can, though, send cards that use winter as their theme (a snowy field, for instance) or are faced with striking photos. Have the inside greeting wish the recipient "Happy Holidays" or "Season's Greetings" or "Peace on Earth."

Holiday cards to business associates should, to be safe, follow the rules for cards to people of non-Christian faiths. Your company name might be printed below the greeting, on the inside. And you can always add a few lines of your own, to personalize the card.

Christmas newsletters pop up every year, and they seem to get longer and longer! This is a controversial area, and people seem to have no neutral feelings about these things: they love 'em or hate 'em. If you *do* decide to send a holiday newsletter, try to keep it relatively brief: two pages should be the maximum; four pages is stretching things. Hit the highlights of the year.

Stay away from bragging—unless you're bragging about a new family addition: "January made us first-time grandparents, when we welcomed Jeanne Marie Tolbert, Richard and Leslie's first child." Don't list a compendium of what you've bought, where you've vacationed, or how much money you've spent since last time we heard from you. (One of our favorite newsletters, in fact, did the opposite: the writers, who really did seem to have had a horrible year, started out by saying, *"You'll want to read this letter, because when you finish, you'll realize your year wasn't as bad as you thought!"* It was a funny, tongue-in-cheek way of telling us everybody's got problems, but we'll live through them to greet another year.)

New Year's cards are preferred by some people as a way of getting around the Christmas card dilemma. These cards can have virtually any kind of theme, although many center around the notion of new beginnings. The inside greeting can wish the recipient something as simple as a Happy New Year, good luck and prosperity, or, simply, peace. Mail New Year's cards at the beginning of the Christmas holidays so they arrive by the first of the year.

Printed Names

Unless they are specifically bought for business, holiday cards are considered personal communications, and personal communications should be signed. Although printed signatures are not considered proper, they're certainly practical, and many people, especially those with long lists, choose this option. If you do choose this option, be sure that the cards you send to relatives and close friends have a slash placed through the printed name, and your name penned in above it:

Marie and Family

Marie and Gene Washington
Brooks, Caroline, and Erin

(Come visit us this year)

Letters That Shouldn't Be Written

It's fine to write a letter to someone who has hurt or angered you *as long as you don't mail it.* Words that are committed to paper have a way of never being able to be retrieved, and once that angry letter is dropped in the mail, you can't pull it back. Write your letter. Sit on it for twenty-four hours. Read it again. Then put—or throw—it away. And if you still need to communicate your anger or hurt, call the person who's hurt you and tell her how you feel, calmly and directly.

Here is a sample letter that shouldn't be sent:

> *Linda:*
>
> *I hung up on you last night because I was so angry to discover that you'd been dating Derek when you know I'm serious about him. I know it takes two, and that he will have to answer for accepting your invitation to spend the weekend at your parents' beach house. But he didn't have to be placed in that position in the first place, and you bear the responsibility for that.*
>
> *This is not "just" a disagreement over a man. I'll get over Derek and move on. But I will not so easily get over what I consider a betrayal by a woman who I counted among my closest friends. Please don't call me anytime soon. I'm much too upset to speak with you in any rational way. I'll call you when I feel we can both talk about this calmly.*
>
> *Maya*

Business Letters

Business letters should be written in block form, with the recipient's name and address on the upper left-hand part of the page and your signature on the lower left-hand side. The "block" in between should describe in the first paragraph why you're writing and conclude with a thank-you for the reader's time and attention. The closure should always read "Sincerely," "Sincerely yours," "Yours truly," or, if you have a cordial relationship with the recipient, "With best regards." *Never* close a business letter with "Affectionately," "Peace," or (horrors!) "Love."

Sample Business Letter

> *Ms. Marcy A. DeVeaux*
> *The DeVeaux Group*
> *West Hills Plaza Bldg., Suite 340*
> *Glendale, CA 95521*
>
> *Dear Ms. DeVeaux:*
>
> *I'm a lawyer who practices civil rights and criminal law. Lately, my firm has handled a number of high-profile, controversial*

cases. A mutual friend, Ken Miller, suggested that your firm might be interested in talking with us.

My partners and I are seeking to place a public relations firm on monthly retainer to handle requests for interviews from the media and outside speaking engagements from several different communities. If this work would appeal to you, I'd be interested in talking with you further at your convenience.

Thank you for your time. I'll look forward to hearing from you soon.

Sincerely,

Carlton Denton
Managing Partner
Law Offices of Willie P. Jefferson, Jr.

Correspondence Samples

Moving Announcement

We've Moved!
Jack and Carolyn Griffin *finally* found an apartment!
2050 S. Wacker, Apt. 3115
Chicago, IL 60600
New telephone number: (312) 555-1212

or

NEW ADDRESS for:
Jack and Carolyn Griffin
2050 S. Wacker, Apt. 3115
Chicago, IL 60600
(312) 555-1212
after January 1st

Letter of Congratulations

Janet Clayton
Editor, Editorial Pages
Los Angeles Times
Times Mirror Square
Los Angeles, CA 90053

Dear Janet:
Just heard about your elevation to editor of the entire editorial page. Good for you—and good for the *Times!* I hope you'll enjoy your new job. Maybe when you dig out from under that pile that I know is on your desk, we can lift a glass of champagne to celebrate.

All the best,

Susan H. Payne

Letter of Reference

To Whom It May Concern:

Jacqueline Velasquez has worked for Ebb Tide Productions for over five years. She came to us as an administrative assistant, but her industriousness, initiative, and cheerful demeanor quickly earned her successively more responsibility. As of this writing, Jackie heads our Community Affairs department, and has four people reporting to her. She has been responsible for an annual budget of over $500,000.

While we would miss Jackie terribly if she decides to leave, we would never begrudge her the potential to expand her horizons yet further. Please do not hesitate to call if you have additional questions; I'd be happy to answer them.

Sincerely,

LeRoy Talbott
Senior Vice-President

Proposing Someone for Membership in a Club

Mrs. Sadie Worthington
President
Ladies' Circle
1801 R Street NW
Washington, DC 20009

Dear Mrs. Worthington:

At our December meeting, you asked for current members to submit proposals for potential members by the end of this month. To that end, I would be grateful if the Circle would consider my friend Anna Terry as a member for the new calendar year.

Anna has been a dear friend since she moved to Washington nearly forty years ago. Our children grew up with each other. I have known her to be a tireless community volunteer, always providing leadership and a pair of extra hands for the PTA (she served as president of Nannie Burroughs Elementary for five years), the Girl Scouts, and the Ladies' Auxiliary at Children's Hospital.

I think Anna's commitment to our community, her evident belief in the value of volunteer work, her demonstrated willingness to be a hard worker, and her warm friendships with several current club members all indicate she would be an asset to our club.

Thank you for considering Anna. If you have other questions, please don't hesitate to contact me.

With warm regards,

Lucille Banks

Resigning from a Club or Organization

Belinda Armstrong
Vice-President, Programs
The Writers' Cooperative
612 Adams Place
Los Angeles, CA 90001

Dear Belinda:

Due to an overloaded schedule and the continued health problems of my oldest child, Marcus, I feel I must, with regret, resign my board membership in the Writers' Co-op.

I'll be happy to participate when possible, but although the doctor says Marc will recover fully, he predicts the process will be lengthy and consume both time and energy. I feel my first obligation in this case is to my family, and I'm sure you understand.

It's been good getting to know you this past year. Let's try to keep in touch. And if there are small things I can do for the Co-op this year, I'd be happy to try.

Sincerely,

Leila Nickens

Changing Your Place of Worship

The Right Rev. James E. Wilkins
St. Paul's Episcopal Church
1200 Market Street
Philadelphia, PA 19101

Dear Bishop Wilkins:

As you know, my husband, Michael, has been looking to change jobs for almost a year now. We are thankful that he finally found one he seems to love—but the new job is in Baltimore! So we're torn between our joy that Mike's long search is ended and our sorrow at having to leave Philadelphia.

We are especially sorry that this will mean our resignation from St. Paul's. We've enjoyed the ten years our family has spent here, and hope we'll be able to return "home" to St. Paul's frequently to see you all.

Thank you for all the help and comfort you've been to us while we've been part of the St. Paul's family. Our best to you all in the coming year.

Warmly,

Monica Lewis-Brown

Letter of Introduction (Social)

Dear Mike and Leslie:

We want you to know that some close friends of ours, Glenn and Dina Edwards, are moving to Stamford at the end of the month. They have two small children who are almost the same age as yours, and we know they have questions about finding a new pediatrician, the local schools, shopping, etc. We've really enjoyed getting to know Glenn and Dina since we've been in Atlanta, and we think you'll like them a lot, too. May we give them your number? It's always nice to see a friendly face in a strange town. And if you'd like to contact them, feel free to call (555-1212) until the 21st. After that, they'll be at the GuestHaus Apartments on High Ridge Road.

Thanks lots! We're looking forward to seeing all you Barkleys this summer, when we take the kids to New York.

All the best,
Ed and Joan

Letter of Introduction (Business)

Mitchell Wright
CEO
The New Order Foundation
430 E. 68th St.
New York, NY 10022

Dear Mitchell:

I know you're always keeping an eye out for sharp young talent, and recently I ran across someone I think may fit that description.

Malcolm Hayes worked with us as a summer intern from June to late August. He's a graduate of Howard University and Law School. He seems passionately interested in community economic development and, in fact, is working as a short-term employee for the Urban Planning Committee of the Mayor's Office. This is a six-month project that seeks to identify and give seed money to community-based businesses in the Watts area.

I don't know what your current needs are at the foundation, but I thought you should know about this young man. We were all very impressed with him—in fact, we would like to have hired him ourselves, but we're still recovering from the closure of two field offices, and don't anticipate hiring anyone anytime soon. Given that, we're hoping to introduce him to a few people who might hire him or, failing that, introduce him to someone else who might. May I have him call you when he's in New York next month?

Thanks for your help on this. My best to your colleagues; I still chuckle at the time we had when we all—finally—closed the Petersen account!

With best regards,

Harvey G. Samuels

Letter to a Local Elected Official

Gilbert Lindsay
Councilman, 9th District
Los Angeles City Hall
25 Temple Street
Los Angeles, CA 90000

Dear Councilman Lindsay:

As you're aware, a small child was badly injured in Leimert Park last week when yet another motorist ran a stop sign at the intersection of 39th and Degnan. We members of the Leimert Park Homeowners' Association have been requesting a stoplight to replace the stop sign for two years now and would like to emphasize once more that the time to do this is now.

To date, five people, three of them children, have been seriously hurt while attempting to cross this intersection. We have had little response from the police and transportation departments and hope that you will add your weight to our request. We have the traffic reports and pedestrian traffic statistics to support this request and would be happy to share them with you and your staff.

Thank you for your prompt attention to this matter. We would greatly like to avoid having any of your constituents injured or killed in this dangerous spot.

Sincerely,

Michael W. Terry, Jr.
President
Leimert Park Homeowners' Assn.

Chapter 12

THANKS BE TO YOU

Gratitude is what shows whether [or not] a gift is appreciated.

Hausa proverb

Showing your appreciation is important in all of your relationships. From the time you're old enough to write Grandma to thank her for the sweater she sent you for Christmas, to the heartfelt thanks offered to a close friend who was there for you in your moment of need—nothing replaces a sincere thank-you.

Ways to Say Thank You

There are many ways to say thank you. Appreciation may be shown verbally, by written note, by giving of your time (such as offering to paint a friend's room), or with flowers or some other gift. (When you receive a gift in person and open it in the presence of the giver, it is perfectly appropriate to thank him at the time, and a written note is not necessary.)

The most common vehicles for saying thank you are:

- Telephone call. Telephone calls should be made immediately (or as soon as possible) after you've been shown a kindness.
- Informal notes with the sentiment handwritten. (See chapter 11, "Write On.")

- Preprinted thank-you cards. If you select a store-bought card, be sure to include a handwritten personal note—don't just sign your name.
- Flowers. For example, if a party is being given in your honor, you may choose to send your host cut flowers or a floral arrangement. Do not send, or take, the flowers on the day of the event. Your host or hostess may already have arranged for floral decorations, and your gift of thanks may not fit in with her color scheme or decor. Do not place him or her in the position of seeming to act unappreciative when your flowers are put away until after the party. Send the flowers either earlier in the week of the event or after the event.
- Gifts. If you choose to say thanks with a gift, try to select one that is well suited to the recipient and to the occasion. (A nice gift for someone who helped you prepare for an exam might be a silver bookmark.)

When You *Must* Send a Thank-You Note

In our perfect world, most thanks would be acknowledged with handwritten notes. Understanding that no one has all day to write notes, these guidelines will serve you well when you're unsure of whether or not you should send a handwritten note. Be sure and write them:

- Anytime someone sends you something and wasn't present when you received it
- Whenever an older person does something nice for you
- Whenever someone hosts you in their home for the first time. (Close friends do not expect a note every time you go by for dinner—but even a close friend would appreciate a note when you're visiting from out of town and he or she has you over for dinner.)
- When your children are too young to write an appropriate note themselves
- Anytime it just seems like what you "*ought*" to do
- For a wedding gift

When You Should Receive a Note—and Don't

If you send someone a present and you don't receive an acknowledgment of the gift, you're entirely within your rights to call or write and see if it reached its destination: "Gloria: Did you get a package from Crate & Barrel in the past month? I'm trying to find out if they sent it on time. Please let me know. All the best, Imani." It's possible that your gift—or the thank-you note—was lost en route.

Acknowledging Gifts You Hate

Just because you really don't like a gift you received does not give you license to ignore writing a thank-you note. Keep the note short and simple and *never* mention your dislike of the item.

Sample Thank-You Note

> *Dear Aunt Lucille,*
> *Thank you for the unusual quilt. John and I can't wait to show it to our friends. We would have given up getting your thoughtful gift (in a minute) if we'd been able to have you at our wedding instead. I was really looking forward to your getting to know John. We really missed you. Every time we look at the quilt it will make us think of you. Hope to see you soon.*
> *Love,*
> *Cheryl*

Gifts Received from a Group of People

If you've received a gift from a group of coworkers, teammates, or club members, send a group thank-you note in care of the person responsible for selecting the gift. You may consider purchasing a colorful card that has space for you to add a handwritten sentiment—something that can be posted on the organization's bulletin board or passed around. If the gift was from a few people, let's say three or four, each individual should be sent a personal note of thanks. The gift may have been a gift of thoughtfulness (unpacking all of your moving boxes) or something more tangible. Separate thank-you notes may seem like a chore, but they cared enough about you to extend themselves—it's the least you can do.

Thanks for the Money

When thanking someone for a gift of money, do not mention the amount given in your note. Instead, let them know how you plan to spend (or spent!) the money and how much you appreciated it:

> *Dear Grandpa,*
> *Thanks for the unexpected check. You must have been reading my mind, and knew that I was a little short when it came time to pay for the school ski trip. I washed enough cars the*

last few months while saving for the trip to make me think I had earned enough money to host the entire class. The trip is next week, and without your kindness I would have never been able to participate. Thanks for helping to make my dream come true.

Just me,
Clarence

P.S. I'll call you as soon as I get back with all the details.

Saying Thank You When You've Been a Houseguest

Even though you may have taken a "hostess gift," following your visit you must still acknowledge the kindness extended to you. This may be done with a thank-you note or with a gift and a short note. Suggested ways to thank your host(s):

- While you're still visiting, you may treat the household to dinner or a special event, such as a concert or a trip to the local amusement park.
- For a family that enjoys spending time together, it may be a game, popcorn maker, ice cream sundae–making set, or a video everyone can watch.
- You may have noticed something the household needs or might enjoy, such as:

  Coffee, tea, or jam sets
  Guest towels or soap
  Cocktail napkins
  Candles
  Candy or a fruit basket

When a Note Isn't Necessary

- When you've received a thank-you present for something nice you've done for someone
- When the gift comes from a good friend with whom you exchange gifts regularly (although it's still nice if you do)
- When the "present" is an unsolicited gift from a business or other commercial entity

Part III

LIFE LESSONS

The Complete Seminar

Setting your own rules and regulations

clothes make the man—and woman

when to use which fork and glass

how to eat difficult foods

eating and ordering in restaurants

the artful gift-giver

how to tip, and how much

travel at home and abroad

being a good neighbor

joining and participating in clubs and organizations

life at work

Chapter 13

MY HOUSE, MY RULES

Repeat after me, Bernetha:
"In my mother's house, there is God . . ."

Lorraine Hansberry, A *Raisin in the Sun,* 1965

You know that when you visit other people's homes, you abide by their household rules: If they leave their shoes at the door, Japanese style, then you do the same. If they don't eat meat, you don't look around for the rest of the meal when several vegetable dishes are passed at dinner.

The same is true when others visit you. If you don't allow your children to "skate" through the house in their socks, you can politely but firmly tell visitors' children what the rules are and let them know that everybody—residents and visitors alike—abides by them.

The bottom line is, our home environment is one of the few things in life over which any of us has some measure of control; it doesn't matter if people agree with the house rules or not. A good guest will abide by them anyway. And it goes without saying that you don't need to feel obligated to ask people who don't respect the house rules to come back.

Sharing the Rule Book

Sometimes we'd like to tell people what the rules are, but we thrash around for a way to explain them that doesn't offend. Below are some examples:

- *They smoke and you don't.* "Nancy, we don't smoke in the house, but you can use the yard (or balcony or front porch or whatever) if you need to." (You're not forbidding her to smoke; you've given her an option of doing it elsewhere.)

- *They don't say grace and you do.* Bow your head in a moment of silence before everyone begins to eat.
- *Men wear their hats in the house.* Offer to take the hat and hang it up for them. If they don't get the hint, then tell them you don't wear hats in the house.
- *You're more strict with your kids than they are with theirs.* Your guests' children are mountain climbing across the back of your sofa? They've encouraged your children to join them in jumping from the top of the bunk beds? Engaging in a toilet-flushing contest? Ask your children to explain the rules to the visiting children in your presence, to make sure that everyone understands what the deal is: "Nathan, can you tell Leslie and Brandon why we don't jump from the bunk beds? And why I don't let you slide on the kitchen tile." And be up front about what the penalties are if they disobey: "I don't want to do this, but if I see you all trying to slide down the banister again, I'm going to have to have everyone sit down and do something quiet, like read a book."
- *You remove your shoes before walking through the house and they don't.* "Sam, we don't wear our street shoes in the house. If you're not comfortable in your socks, we have paper slippers for visitors."
- *You're worried that they might be carrying guns, drugs, or other dangerous and unacceptable substances.* Now is not the time to mince words: "Jesse, I know you believe in self-protection, but we don't allow guns in our house. If you don't want to leave it locked in your trunk, I can put it somewhere safe here while you visit." Or "Simon, I know how you feel, but drugs are illegal and we don't allow them in our house. Please leave them somewhere else when you come to visit."

When Grown Children Move Back In

Time for that "it's my way or the highway" philosophy. If you don't want your grown children creeping in at 4 A.M. after a fabulous night out, inform them that they'll need to make arrangements to stay with a friend—or in a hotel—when they don't want to come home till dawn's early light.

If his beloved comes to visit for the weekend, but you're uncomfortable with unmarried couples sleeping together, firmly inform your son that his company is welcome, but she will be sleeping in the guest room. If he feels he's too adult to tolerate such an arrangement, encourage him to make reservations somewhere. (Conversely, when you visit him, don't fuss if his girlfriend stays over; you're under his roof, and you agree to abide by his rules while you're there.)

If you don't want your grown child to act as if your home is a Holiday Inn, encourage him to do his own laundry, pick up after himself, and appear for meals when the rest of the household sits down to eat. (If he misses a meal, he can find his way to a burger joint or cook for—and clean up after—himself.)

Hiring Household Employees

Perhaps you have someone come in once a week to help you with household chores, such as dusting, mopping, and changing the beds. Or you have a gardener who cuts your lawn. Or an aide who comes half a day every day to "do" for your aged parent. Here are some things you should consider when hiring him or her:

- Who was her last employer; can she provide references?
- Will she provide a Social Security number (mandatory for tax purposes)?
- If she's not an American citizen, does she have a valid residency card or work permit (commonly referred to in the U.S. as a "green card")?
- If being able to drive is part of her job, does she have a driver's license? Does she have her own car? Is she insured?

Common Courtesies with Household Help

Historically speaking, we've spent generations working for Miss Anne. Now that some of us are in the position to afford household help, it is incumbent upon us not to repeat Miss Anne's mistakes. Address your help as courteously as you would anyone else. When you hire her, ask what she'd prefer to be called ("My name is Teresa, but everyone calls me Tessie"). Give plenty of warning if you're going on vacation and won't need her for a week or two, because if you don't pay for vacation time this could seriously affect her income. If she comes on a regular day each week and you need to switch days, ask if this is convenient. If you pay a certain amount each day (common for nannies who don't live in), make sure you pay extra if she works extra hours.

If she lives with you and is paid for a certain number of hours each week, do not simply assume she is available just because she's under your roof; her time off is her time off. If she volunteers to spend some of it doing something for you, pay her accordingly.

If she's sick, give her enough time off, without docking her pay, to allow her to get better and return to you in good health. If she has a family emergency—the death of a close family member, a serious illness—try to be accommodating.

When Your Help Doesn't Speak English

In many parts of the country (the Southwest, parts of the West Coast, southern Florida), household help may speak English as a second language or barely speak English at all. If this is true in your home, it's essential that all emergency instructions, such as how to reach you at work and the phone numbers for the Poison Control Center and pediatrician if you have children, be listed both in English and in your help's language. Develop a procedure for what to do when packages or items are delivered that require a signature (in some parts of the country delivery staff are now bilingual or carry an instruction sheet in both Spanish and English).

When Things Are Missing or Broken

Sometimes in the course of doing her job, your housekeeper may inadvertently damage one of your possessions. Depending on how shy she is, she may have a hard time presenting you with the damaged goods; stories of employers from hell circulate among domestic staff, and she may be wondering if that broken cake stand will cost her a job. Emphasize to her that you'd rather *know* when something is broken so you can replace it, assure her that accidents do happen, and let her know you'd rather find out from her directly that you'll have to replace something than discover at the last moment, when you desperately need it, that your cake stand is in three pieces.

Your Children and Household Employees

Children should always show your household help respect. Ask her how she'd like your children to address her: "We think it's important for the children to show respect to adults by addressing them by their last names. Do you mind if they call you Miss Luzon? Or Miss Tessie?" If you have live-in help, children should always knock before entering their rooms, and be very clear that this is the housekeeper's personal space. Requests should be prefaced with "please," and the children should always remember to say "Thank you," just as they are expected to do with the rest of the family. It's important for the child to remember that the employee works for his parents and that she is not his—the child's—personal servant. (He shouldn't, for instance, leave his bed unmade because "Jean will do it for me"; his toys and clothes shouldn't be left in heaps all over the room because "Jean will take care of it.")

Hanging Out on the Front Porch

Whether or not this is done varies according to which part of the country you're in. In some apartment-filled parts of the Northeast, people visit indoors, even in warm weather. In the South and Midwest and in much of rural America, friends and neighbors relax and visit on the front porch—especially if it's deep, shady, and has comfy seats. Having cold drinks on a hot day on the front porch is a cherished ritual; many of us have fond memories of childhood birthday parties held on the front porch, or rainy summer afternoons spent with jacks, game boards, dolls, and tanks.

Some things, however, should be saved for the backyard: sunbathing, barbecuing, real meals (as opposed to snacks), and anything raucous, so you don't disturb your neighbors.

Alcohol

If you choose not to serve alcoholic beverages for religious or health reasons, don't apologize. If someone asks for something stronger, simply say, "What we have is out already. We don't drink alcohol." No explanations necessary.

If you're serving alcohol, but you feel that one of your guests has had enough—or too much—cut him off. (See chapter 29, "Let the Party Begin," for more advice on how to handle this.) If one of your guests has a problem with alcohol and is in recovery, you should let him know ahead of time that you'd love to have him, but you are having champagne at your brunch. If he feels the prospect of mimosas will be a needless temptation, he can see you another time. (If the guest of honor is in recovery, skip the alcohol entirely.)

Anywhere but Here: Uncomfortable Situations

Sometimes things happen in the open that should be kept in the privacy of the participants' home, turning all of us into unwilling spectators. To avoid feeling as if you've stepped into a real-life version of *Who's Afraid of Virginia Woolf?* leave the room if a huge argument you know you shouldn't hear erupts. And if you're the person who's erupting, take it somewhere more private—the bathroom, a hallway—to keep *your* business *your* business.

What if you open the door to a room and flash upon a man vigorously enjoying the company of a woman not his wife? Best to excuse yourself, shut the door quietly, and not discuss what you've seen. If the occupants of that room are underage—adolescents—it's your duty to get them up, get them clothed, and inform their parents of what's gone on under your roof.

You're at a party and go to get your coat. While you're there, you see guest A pay guest B for what looks like a little plastic bag filled with something illegal. Definitely exit and, depending on how well you know the host, inform him before you go that there might be commercial activity that would make him unhappy: "Allan, I don't know how you feel about marijuana, but I thought you might want to know that someone is selling it in your bedroom."

Chapter 14

GLAD RAGS

God created black people, and black people created style.

George C. Wolfe, *The Colored Museum*

If, as the old adage goes, "clothes make the man" (or woman), it follows that the *wrong* clothes can probably make a lasting unfavorable impression. If you've ever been to a fancy party and seen a lone guest stroll in wearing a T-shirt and jeans, or watched someone attend a funeral in clothes that are more appropriate for a cocktail party, you know what we mean. This chapter will discuss some of the dos and don'ts of what's basic and appropriate.

Sparkle Plenty

It should go without saying, but let's say it anyway: the time of day dictates what kind of clothes you'll choose to wear in public. Just as you wouldn't wear high heels to the gym, it's inappropriate to wear party clothes to business meetings or evening wear to an afternoon event. A good rule of thumb might be this: it's always better to err on the conservative side. A little black dress won't steer you wrong at an afternoon tea, whereas a little dress paved with sequins could make it look as if you dropped into the wrong party.

Hats are appropriate almost anytime before three o'clock. If the invitation indicates that the wedding or party begins at four-thirty, a bare head is better. After five, cocktail hats (which are much smaller, more frivolous, and may or may not have veils) are sometimes worn.

Wearing Age-Appropriate Clothes

It's hard to say which is more unnerving: a teenager wearing clothes that are sophisticated beyond her years or a woman well past middle age who dresses like a teenager. Let's just say that gracious living involves keeping in mind who and how old we are and dressing to enhance the charms of that particular age. Style is as much a matter of adapting fashion to your personal taste as it is about being fashionable.

APPROPRIATE CASUAL DRESS FOR TEENAGER

APPROPRIATE CASUAL DRESS FOR ADULT

Excuse Me, Is It After Labor Day?

The traditional rules for seasonal dressing were made from an East Coast perspective, although most of the country followed them. But the rules were geared to seasons that varied greatly from weather in places such as Dallas, New Orleans, Los Angeles, Phoenix, and Miami. So the old dictate prohibiting white after Labor Day was fine for New York but began to feel a bit forced in places where the autumn temperature still hovered in the eighties.

In recent years people have begun to rely more on common sense than the old rules and have adapted the wisdom of seasonally appropriate dress to the practical aspects of where they live. A woman in Dallas may continue to wear linen after Labor Day, but the colors may be darker. Another may choose to wear white—but an off-white cream color, in wool. About the only old rule that still stands involves shoes: white shoes should be placed in the closet after Labor Day.

When the Invitation Says . . .

Casual: "Casual" usually means that dress is fairly relaxed. An invitation to an office picnic that says "casual" probably means that shorts (but not short-shorts!) and T-shirts are fine for both men and women. An invitation to a casual dinner or party might indicate that women are welcome to wear pants, skirts, anything that's comfortably chic, and men might wear jackets, but not ties.

Semiformal: Strictly speaking, a semiformal event calls for black tie for men and a very dressy dress for women. Invitations that truly require semiformal dress usually say "black tie" at the bottom of the invitation. For men, this means a black tuxedo with a starched formal white shirt (the plainer the better—no ruffles, please) with a regular or wing collar, a black bow tie, an evening vest or cummerbund, and patent-leather or highly polished black shoes. In some parts of the country white dinner jackets are worn in warm-weather months. (Some invitations state semiformal when they really want men to wear dark suits; if you're in doubt, ask.) "Black tie optional" appears more and more, to the confusion of many of us. Translated, it means the host would prefer men to wear black tie, but dark suits are appropriate, too.

Women invited to semiformal events wear dresses or suits suitable for a cocktail party. A brocade dinner suit, for instance, or a plain sheath with a very fancy jacket or evening shawl would work. Pants are appropriate for semiformal events if they are clearly dressy: flowing chiffon pants and velvet trousers are two examples. Women may even wear a feminized version of a tuxedo, an alternative that is becoming increasingly popular. In this case, the stiff white shirt is replaced by a soft silk one, a satin tank top, a lace camisole, or a fancy vest of brocade, velvet, or sequins that is cut high enough that a shirt underneath is not necessary.

Formal: This is at the top of the formality food chain. When the invitation says "formal," it means something very specific: white tie, white pique vest, stiff white shirt with wing collar, black trousers, and formal tailcoat. Because so few occasions demand a truly formal dress code (very fancy evening weddings, cotillions, the opening of the opera or the symphony in some cities, certain benefits), this kind of ritual wear is usually rented. "Formal" for women means a long gown and your fanciest jewelry. Pants are not appropriate for women at white-tie events.

Nothing: If the invitation gives no indication of what you're expected to wear, you are left to guess, and to rely on your common sense. Formal clothes don't, as a rule, go to picnics, and shorts and T-shirts don't show up at the ballet. You can always call the person who sent the invitation to ask for guidance: "Jeanine, how did you want people to dress for your Christmas party?" The point of the dress-code invitation is to provide guidance to potential guests, not strangle them with a hard-and-fast set of rules. Again, in the real world, we adapt to circumstances.

When You Absolutely Must Wear a Long Gown

If you're going to a white-tie event, a long gown is the only appropriate choice. Because so few women need these on a regular basis, a small industry has grown up in recent years in gown rentals. Check the Yellow Pages for a business near you that rents formal clothes to women. Many shops provide chic, current fashions that can be rented for a fraction of their purchase price. If you only need a long gown once every couple of years, this might be a practical alternative to buying one that would sit in the closet, unworn (and perhaps slowly going out of style), until you need it the next time. If you choose to buy a long gown, look for classic styles and colors that will remain fashionable for more than a few seasons. ("Timeless" is the look we're going for.)

Fashion and the Woman Executive

Dress for today's female executive is much less rigid than it was twenty years ago, when women first started to appear in executive suites. Many have abandoned so-called power suits altogether and now wear dresses to the office, or pantsuits in businesses where pants are appropriate. There are still some rules that should be considered, though.

Save overtly sexy clothes for another environment. If you can't help but look alluring in a plain navy dress, so be it. But if you look alluring because the plain navy dress has a plunging neckline and midthigh hemline, you may be sending your colleagues a message you don't intend to send.

If you think a garment might be inappropriate, it probably is, and you're better off wearing something else. Go with your gut. (Sure, that black leather suit with the gold medallion buttons looks fabulous on you, but unless your client makes motorcycles, best to save it for a hot date.)

Our Man in the Conservative Office

Would you *really* want your mortician to greet you wearing a purple double-breasted suit? What would it say to you if your banker appeared in a nipped-waist, houndstooth check number? That's why some businesses have decided that the way their employees dress may well affect clients' confidence in the business. For men who work in these kinds of establishments (such as law firms, mortuaries, and almost any business that handles money) there is a code—spoken or tacitly understood—that is quite specific. It requires dark suits, conservatively cut, white or pale (usually blue) shirts—sometimes monogrammed—and ties that are not too gaudy or cutting-edge in width or fabric. Shoes are dark and highly shined. Socks are equally low-key. Jewelry is minimal: a watch and perhaps a wedding or school ring; bracelets, neck chains, and earrings stay at home in the jewelry box and come out on weekends.

MONOGRAM PLACEMENT OPTIONS

Casual Fridays

Wearing casual clothes to the office used to be an eagerly anticipated perk. Then some offices got casual on a daily basis. Check with your boss to see how casual things get in your office and to determine what's acceptable.

Some offices (entertainment, some editorial offices, advertising, and other creative kinds of businesses) have become jeans-casual every day or just Fridays, while others (law, banking, brokerage firms) remain comparatively formal.

Wedding Attire for Guests

For weddings, six o'clock is the magic hour, the time that divides daytime and evening. Weddings held before six can be quite formal but never require white tie or tuxedo. After six, those clothes are necessary for a proper formal wedding, although in some instances, dark suits will work just fine for men. Traditionally, the rules for "who wore what when" were very strict, but the pressures of modern life have changed to reflect more closely how people in what we call the "real world" would dress for the same occasion. We've included both, so you can make your own decision.

- *At an informal wedding during the day*

  Traditional: Dark business suits and ties for men, dresses or suits (the kind you'd normally wear to church) for women. Women may or may not wear hats.

  Real world: Dark suits or, in summer, light summer suits for men, dresses or suits for women. Hats optional.
- *At a formal wedding during the day*

  Traditional: For men, gray cutaways with black-and-gray striped trousers, dove-gray waistcoat. Wing collar and ascot. Black leather shoes and black socks. Women wear dresses or suits of a fairly dressy material, such as silk.

  Real world: Dark suits for men; "dressy" dresses and/or suits for women. Hats optional.
- *At an informal evening wedding*

  Traditional: Male guests wear dark suits. Women wear dresses (appropriate for a cocktail party or an evening at the theater) in a suitably dressy fabric, and no hats.

  Real world: The same.
- *At a formal evening wedding*

  Traditional: Male guests wear black tie or (much more rarely) white tie and tails. Women wear evening suits or long dresses if the invitation says white tie.

  Real world: Men wear black tie or dark suits. Women wear long dresses or very dressy short dresses in glamorous fabrics, and evening accessories (peau de soie or jeweled handbags, etc.).

(For more on wedding attire, see chapter 34, "To Love, Honor, and Cherish.")

Dressing for Funerals

For a funeral your common sense will be your best guide. Black is still the most common mourning color used in this country, although white is frequently worn in warm weather. If you are not a member of the funeral party, you can wear any dark or neutral color (navy, brown, taupe, gray). Men should stick to dark suits, plain shirts, and sober ties, and women to conservatively cut dresses or suits (no thigh-high slits, no plunging necklines) in dark or neutral colors or muted prints. Jewelry should be minimal—or at least conservative enough so it doesn't make noise or cause a commotion. Stockings are a must. Hats and gloves are optional. And sunglasses should not be worn indoors, period.

Children, if they attend, should be dressed in something they find comfortable.

Hats and Gloves

Look around you in church on any Sunday, and you'll probably notice that there is a generational split among the congregation. Older ladies who grew up in a time when no well-dressed woman would even *consider* attending church without a hat still wear them proudly. Younger women tend to view them as an occasional fashion indulgence, although many are starting to follow in the footsteps of their mothers, aunts, and grandmothers. If you like to wear hats, please remember to remove yours when you're in a public place, such as the theater or the movies, where the person behind you might not be able to see.

Gloves worn purely for propriety's sake (as opposed to wearing them for the practical reason of keeping your fingers from freezing) are even more scarce than hats these days, but it's always a delight to see a woman who wears gloves well.

During the day, gloves are worn with suits or dresses to complete a look. In cool months, they may be made of fine kid, and can range from wrist-length to midarm, depending on the sleeve length of the garment you're wearing. During warm-weather months, gloves made of white cotton or a cotton blend are often worn.

Men should remove the right glove when shaking hands. Women may keep theirs on with one exception: custom dictates that you remove your glove before shaking hands with the Pope.

Men and Hats

If everything you place on your head counts as a hat, it's probably safe to say that more men than ever are wearing hats, but they're usually billed caps that advertise something: a sports team, a movie crew, a beer company. And they're often worn backward. Which doesn't make the habit proper, just popular.

Male cap wearers should remember, regardless of the style or position, to remove caps as soon as they come indoors, whether they're in a private home or a shopping mall.

Male *hat* wearers, on the other hand, are a dying breed. If you're one of the few who still feel incomplete without a chic chapeau, remember to remove it when you come indoors. It's still considered polite for gentlemen to remove their hats in elevators, although almost none do anymore. And should you decide to tip your hat to a woman as you pass, we guarantee she'll be charmed. The exceptions for hats that aren't removed are hats worn for religious or traditional cultural reasons, such as the kuufi, a Muslim prayer cap that resembles a skullcap; the crowned, brimless hat that is worn throughout much of sub-Saharan Africa; and the crocheted beret-type hat that Rastafarians use to cover their dreadlocks.

Exercise Wear Is for the Gym

Although it's become more common—especially in parts of the country where dress is more informal—for people to walk around, *après* exercise, in their exercise clothes, we hope you'll resist the urge. Save the muscle-baring tank tops, the thong leotards, and the jogging bras in bright colors for the gym or your weekend run through the neighborhood.

Cruise and Vacation Wear

A few decades ago dress for cruises and vacations was actually a separate fashion category. (Remember Bermuda shorts? Hawaiian shirts?) The increasing informality of daily life and frequent travel have pretty much blurred the distinction for most of us. (See chapter 20, "Ease on Down the Road," for suggestions on how to dress comfortably and appropriately when traveling.)

When It's Too Hot to Think

In many parts of the United States, summer bears a more-than-passing resemblance to a sauna. Dress codes may become more relaxed, and we all cast about for an appropriate way to stay cool without baring too much. In our efforts to beat the heat, we should remember a few things:

- Even though it's hot enough to swim, beachwear doesn't belong on the streets or in the office.
- Skimpy tops and gauzy cover-ups are no-nos. So are tank tops for men.
- Tone down the perfume and aftershave in hot weather, as a little goes a long, long way. Consider switching to a lighter version of the scent you like—an eau de toilette or cologne, perhaps.
- If your office allows women to wear sandals and no stockings in warm months, make sure that you have a regular pedicure and that the sandals are functional and appropriate for your office clothes. (No flip-flops, high-heeled mules, or sandals encrusted with rhinestones, please.)

Coats That Can Take You Anywhere

A trench coat is a wardrobe staple for many fashion-conscious men and women because it covers so many needs. It works as a raincoat for casual or business occasions. If you travel between climates, the lining can be buttoned in or out to adapt to the temperature. It even serves as an evening coat in a pinch. Make sure the coat you buy fits well, is conservatively cut, and is a neutral color (the most popular is a putty-colored tan, followed by black, gray, and olive). Women sometimes choose a silk raincoat in a dark color as the alternative to a trench. Either will work over a dressy dress for an evening out.

Furs

Once a longed-for luxury, fur hats, coats, and jackets are now a controversy. Whether or not you wear a fur is a totally personal decision. Remember, though, that there is a fair amount of strong feeling against the wearing of animal skins, so be prepared for some possible confrontation by animal rights activists along the way. If you wear your fur to a public place, such as a restaurant or the theater, be aware that, because of changing insurance policies, some places no longer accept liability for checking furs. In this case, simply bring your coat to your seat and drape it over the back of your chair. (Or you can use it as a "liner" for your theater seat.)

Chapter 15
AT TABLE

On the white damask tablecloth, blue Willow bowls were laden with the Thanksgiving feast. In the corner, a turn-of-the-century breakfront cabinet gleamed with crystal and china reserved for very special occasions—more special than Thanksgiving.

Florence Ladd, *Sarah's Psalm*

If you take an informal poll of men and women on the street and ask "What is etiquette?" you can almost bet that the bulk of your answers will have something to do with using the right fork, knowing which glass the red wine goes in, and so on. Years ago, the rules for dinner etiquette were fairly rigid. But etiquette is nothing if not the evolution of custom, coupled with courtesy, to assure the comfort of your guests and friends. So this chapter gives guidelines to help demystify that fork-spoon-wineglass stuff, and when you know the basics, you can relax and enjoy dinner just as your host intended.

Table Settings

Chances are, by the time you were old enough to walk around the table unassisted, you were helping to set it for a meal. The smallest children got to place the napkins. Older ones carefully aligned the forks, knives, and spoons under an adult's supervision. And a Big Person put the breakables—plates and glasses—down last.

Depending on what time of day you eat and how formal the occasion, that's still pretty much the way it goes.

Breakfast

The first meal of the day is usually the simplest. There is usually a plate, perhaps topped by a cereal bowl. A fork is to the left of the plate, with a folded napkin to the left of the fork. And a knife is to the plate's right (with the sharp edge facing plateward, or left, *always*), and a spoon is next to the knife. If you have cereal, a larger spoon is to the left of the teaspoon. Your juice glass is at the "one o'clock" position above the plate, and your coffee or tea cup is to the right of the juice glass.

Lunch

Let's start from left to right: salad fork, if you're serving salad; fork; luncheon plate; knife (blade facing inward); spoon; soupspoon, if soup is being served. The salad plate is placed on top of the luncheon plate, or, if soup is being served, the soup bowl, on a small plate, sits on top of the luncheon plate. The water glass is at the "one o'clock" position, with, for example, the glass for iced tea or lemonade to the right of it. If bread is served, the bread plate is at the "eleven o'clock" position vis-à-vis the luncheon plate.

Dinner

Dinner, unless it's formal, looks basically like the place settings for lunch. There may be a couple of additions: Wineglasses are placed to the right of the water glass. If you're serving more than one kind of wine (not usual for an informal dinner), the glasses should be placed in the order in which the wine will be drunk. Example: Water goes in the glass closest to you, white wine next, and red wine last. If there is a champagne flute, it will go to the *rear* of the wineglasses, since champagne is served last. Directly above the dinner plate, at the "twelve o'clock" position, you should place the dessert utensils: the dessert fork's handle faces left; the dessert spoon is above it, with handle facing right.

Formal Dinner

Formal dinners make everyone—even experienced diners—quake! But the same basic rules apply: work from the outside in. Starting from the left, the salad fork will be first, then the dinner fork. (*Note: In formal meals that are served European style, the salad is served after the main course, so the salad fork is placed to the right of the dinner fork.*) The dinner plate (perhaps placed on top of a charger, or service plate, that is usually of silver or porcelain, and is used for decorative, not eating, purposes) is next. Then, directly to the right of it is your knife, followed by a steak or fish knife if the menu demands it; to the right of that will be your soupspoon. (The spoon's bowl will be shaped according to the type of soup being served: round for cream or clear soups, such as consommé, oval for other kinds of soup. Remember: since these are oversized spoons, you should sip from the spoon's side; don't attemp to jam the entire bowl into your mouth.) There will not be a teaspoon at a formal setting, as this will be brought out with the coffee and tea cups after the meal.

Your wine and water glasses, in order of use, will be placed at the "one o'clock" position on the right. Directly opposite them, at the "eleven o'clock" position, will be a bread plate, with a butter knife placed across the top of the plate, or slightly angled to the right, blade facing toward you. Individual pepper shakers and salt cellars (pepper on the left, salt on the right) may finish off the setting. The napkin will be placed across the top of the plate and should be put in your lap before the first course is served.

We didn't mention dessert plates or utensils here because frequently in formal dinners the dessert fork and spoon are brought out on the dessert plates when dessert is passed. If this is not the case, the fork and spoon are positioned directly above the dinner plate (fork handle left, spoon above it, with handle facing right) and below the salt and pepper.

The Buffet

Buffets have turned into one of the most popular methods of entertaining, because like a good black dress or suit, they can be dressed up or down, depending on the need. A buffet meal allows the host to spend more time with his guests, is often expansive enough that one or two last-minute addi-

CREAM AND CLEAR SOUPSPOONS

FORMAL TABLE SETTING

tions don't cause a complete collapse of best-laid plans, and allows people to circulate and get to know each other a bit better.

Setting up the buffet table requires a little thought as to how you want the pattern of your guest traffic to flow. Ideally, you want people to start at one end of the table and work their way to the other. A frequently used pattern, which is probably popular because it draws on common sense, has a guest start at one end picking up her plate, then moving on to the main dish(es). The side dishes are next, then salad, bread, and condiments. Finally, she can fill her glass with the beverages offered (hosts often opt to set up a separate table for drinks; more on this later) and pick up her silverware before leaving the buffet table to find a seat.

If it's a large party and you have a large table, sometimes double buffet lines are formed that are mirror images of each other. For instance, if the side of the table you're on starts with plates on the left, the opposite side of the table would begin with plates on the right, so guests don't bump into each other.

If space allows, many hosts prefer to confine drinks to a separate table. This can be done in the room where the buffet is being offered, or in a corner of the room where people actually sit to eat, depending on the layout of the rooms you plan to use.

Desserts can be placed on the buffet table, once it's cleared, with coffee and tea, or they can be arranged on a side table if one is available. (In that case, coffee and tea would probably still be served at the cleared buffet table.)

THINGS TO REMEMBER WHEN SERVING A BUFFET

- If your main dish is something to which some people may be allergic—shellfish, for example—make sure your side dishes are plentiful and filling, as these may be the main course for those guests who can't eat the entrée.
- You don't have to have a table large enough to accommodate all of the guests, but some part of a hard surface—an end table, low bookcase, tray table, your coffee table—is appreciated by most people, as it's hard to balance a plate and a full glass on your lap.
- If you can, provide a small folding table for older people, who may not feel comfortable eating from their laps or perched over an end table.
- When you lay out your flatware, it's often useful to wrap a large napkin around the end of it, so guests can carry their utensils and napkin in one neat package to their seats.

Tea for Two—or Twenty

Years ago, an afternoon tea was the preferred way ladies entertained. Whether it was steaming tea served in fine china cups or tall glasses of cool, iced tea in the shade of a front porch, the ritual was eagerly looked forward to as a welcome pause in a day filled with domestic chores and responsibilities.

The English, who have elevated tea to an art, would fall over at the idea of tea being made with (gasp!) tea bags. (Charles, the Prince of Wales, once joked that "America is where they always give one tea from a bag.") Proper tea to them is loose tea that has been measured into a pot that's first been warmed by rinsing with heated water, then emptied and filled with boiling water. The tea is then allowed to steep to the desired strength, and the person pouring holds a small strainer beneath the spout of the teapot, to keep (most of) the leaves from falling into the guest's cup. (See chapter 30, "Parties and Celebrations.")

Because the teapot is usually prepared in the kitchen, and because so many premium teas can now be bought in bags, your guests probably won't complain if they don't find those telltale flecks of tea floating in their cups. But if you're a purist, loose tea is the way to go.

Whatever the reason, more people are taking—and giving—tea(s). In some places, commercial teas (in a restaurant, hotel, or tea shop) have even begun to take the place of a working luncheon between businesswomen. In others, it's a pleasant, relaxed alternative to drinks after work.

If you'd like to give a tea at home, there are some things you'll need to have or borrow:

- Teapot or tea urn (sometimes called a samovar)
- If you use an urn, a small bowl (traditionally called a waste pot) to catch any tea overflow
- Pot of hot water, for use if guests want less-strong tea
- Pitcher of milk
- Saucer of lemon slices and a small fork so they can be picked up
- Bowl of sugar, with a sugar spoon. (If you have lump sugar, you should offer a small spoon or tongs to grasp the lumps.)
- A tray large enough to hold the things mentioned above
- Cups and saucers
- Teaspoons
- Luncheon-sized napkins

Although it didn't show up in traditional teas, in deference to modern tastes, you may want to have some sugar substitute on hand, as well as honey and an assortment of herbal teas (perhaps in a pretty basket) for noncaffeine drinkers.

Set up your tea table with the tea service at one end, closest to the person who will be pouring tea. It's an honor to be asked to do this, so don't hesitate to ask a good friend to perform this duty for you while you see to your guests' other needs. The pourer pours the tea, adds whatever the guest requests (sugar, etc.), and hands the guest the cup. A teaspoon will be handed to your guest with her cup.

Farther down the table, your guest will find a tea saucer or tea plate (a small, salad-sized plate with an indentation in one corner for the cup); she can use this to hold the small sandwiches, cakes, and perhaps fruit you've set out for her. And you should supply napkins (anything marked "luncheon-sized" will work; use cloth or top-quality paper).

Tea and Alcohol

Hard alcohol is never served at tea, but sometimes a glass of sherry is offered. If you'd like to offer this option to your guests, place the sherry at a separate table with small glasses (anything that holds just a few ounces and is dainty-looking will do), and let the guests who'd like sherry serve themselves. Champagne is starting to show up as an alternative—or complement—to sherry.

When "Tea" Is Really Coffee

In some parts of the country, people have "coffees" instead of teas, or they include coffee at their teas. Coffee can be served at the other end of the tea table, if the table is large enough, or at a separate table altogether. To set up a coffee table, you'll need:

- Coffeepot or urn
- Insulated carafe (for decaf)
- Small bowl to catch the overflow
- Small pot of hot water
- Pitcher of cream
- Bowl of sugar with a sugar spoon
- A tray large enough to hold the things mentioned above

Again, in deference to modern palates—and dietary restrictions—try to have packets of artificial sweetener available, as well as some nondairy creamer for the lactose-intolerant.

We prefer to brew a pot of good decaf ahead of time, knowing that many people do request it, and place it in an attractive thermal carafe. (For coffee-service illustration, see chapter 30, "Parties and Celebrations.")

Tea Food

Sometimes referred to as "ladies' food," probably because of the size and delicacy of the fare, tea food has always been finger food, and traditionally has been light enough to not interfere with the flavor of the tea—or kill a real meal that might follow a few hours later. Some traditional tea foods are:

- *Sandwiches,* open-faced or closed, on thin crustless bread (thinly sliced cucumber on buttered white bread; smoked salmon and cream cheese; watercress and cream cheese; shrimp, crab, or chicken salad)
- *Sweet breads or pastries* (date-nut bread spread with cream cheese; scones; banana-nut bread; apple-cinnamon bread)
- *Cakes and cookies* (finger-sized brownies; pound cake; tiny fruit tarts; lemon bars)

In short, anything that can be eaten with one hand (the other is holding a teacup, remember?) is fine for the tea table. You can even add a down-home twist by serving fried chicken drumettes, individual quiches made with greens, or tiny sweet potato tarts.

Standard Serving Pieces and Utensils

If you're serving family or guests at home, you'll need to have some basics on hand:

Bread basket. Used for serving bread or rolls. It can be made from something as simple as wood or as elaborate as woven silver wire. It is usually lined with several thicknesses of napkins to keep heated bread warm.

Casserole, open. This is a serving dish a few inches deep used for side dishes (macaroni and cheese, for example) or a main dish. Usually made of tempered glass or pottery.

Casserole, covered. Often used for one-dish meals (chicken potpie, red beans and rice) and side dishes that lose heat quickly.

Gravy boat and ladle. A vessel that has a spout on one or both sides, to make pouring gravy easier and less messy. The ladle is a deep spoon, often with a spouted side, for the same purpose.

Meat platter. A platter for arranging meat or poultry. Made of porcelain, pottery, sometimes even silver. Usually accompanied by a *meat fork*, a large fork used to lift meat from the platter.

Salad bowl. A deep bowl, often of glass or wood, used to serve salad. Accompanied by *salad tongs* or *salad servers* (an oversized fork and spoon used to grasp salad).

Soup tureen. A large, covered bowl, often of porcelain or pottery; it usually has a cutout so a *ladle* (made of the same material as the tureen, or of silver or other metal) can be inserted. Often accompanied by a matching platter beneath. Used for soups and some stews (gumbo, black bean soup, Brunswick stew).

Vegetable bowl. A wide, fairly shallow bowl traditionally used to serve vegetables (black-eyed peas, corn, brussels sprouts). Often made of porcelain or tempered glass. Can be made of fine china. Usually accompanied by a *slotted spoon*, a perforated spoon that allows the vegetables to rise from the bowl minus most of their juices.

China and Crystal

When you were growing up, there were probably two sets of dishes in your household: the "everyday" dishes the family used for meals and the "good dishes" of fine china that were saved for company and special occasions. The latter were often locked away in a china cabinet or kept safe in a special closet until they were needed. The same went for glasses: delicate stemware was saved for special occasions, and the sturdier, cheaper glasses were placed on the table for daily use.

Many modern families mix it up: perhaps they use the "good dishes" Aunt Lucy left to them more often than just holidays and fancy occasions, or they mix their silver with the pottery plates they use every day. There are no rules, and if you'll scan design magazines, you'll see that some of the most sophisticated tables mix and match patterns and materials regularly. Don't hesitate to combine your flea-market finds with your wedding china, or use your grandmother's cut-glass pitcher to serve juice at Sunday brunch, poured into cute glasses you picked up for a song at a discount housewares store. Or place your batik napkins on top of your mother's cutwork cotton tablecloth. Your table should reflect you and your tastes.

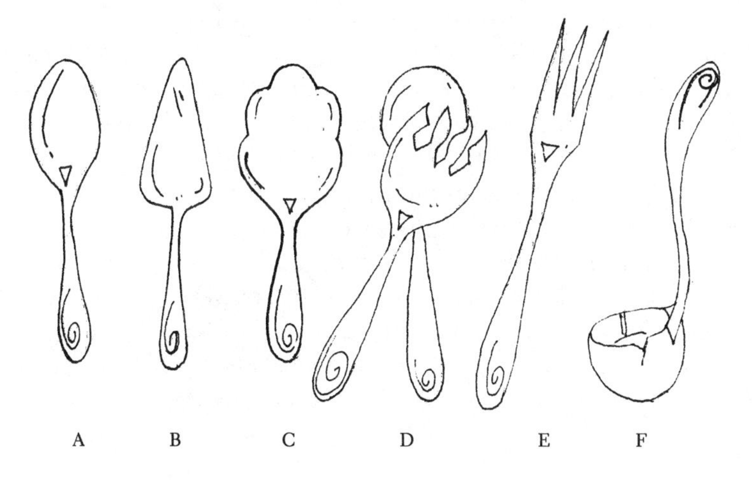

From left to right: A, serving spoon; B, cake server; C, pie server; D, salad tongs; E, meat fork; F, gravy ladle.

Basic Flatware Wardrobe

If you've seen "four-piece place settings for four" advertised, you've probably figured out that the "four pieces" the advertisement is referring to are the basics upon which your flatware wardrobe is built: dinner fork, salad fork, teaspoon, and knife. A five-piece place setting for four would include a soupspoon as well. Stainless-steel flatware usually comes in this grouping, and you can enlarge your collection by adding serving pieces, if you buy your stainless by the place setting. Most stainless is low-maintenance and can be washed in the dishwasher; a brief polish will remove any water spots that might be left. The introduction of high-polish stainless steel (often referred to by its weight, 18/8) makes it a modern, sophisticated, and less costly alternative to sterling or silver plate.

Silver-plate and sterling-silver flatware are often (in the case of the latter, virtually *only*) sold by the piece or place setting (as opposed to service for four, eight, or twelve), as these can be rather pricey. Several decades back, before sterling (solid) silver became a market commodity, many brides received sterling flatware as a wedding gift. Today the cost of sterling has increased so much that the price of one teaspoon can often equal what one of your grandmother's place settings cost back when she married! No wonder, then, that many people who are looking for fancy flatware also consider good-quality silver plate. Silver plate is base metal (nickel, brass, steel) that has been plated, often several times, with sterling silver. It is less fragile—and less costly—than sterling because its core is not precious metal.

To care for silver plate or sterling, keep it encased in a box lined in a tarnish-retarding cloth. Use it often, so it gets the little nicks and scars silver collectors affectionately refer to as the "patina" good silver acquires over time. And polish it regularly with a good silver polish. It's preferable to wash silver by hand; if you *must* use the dishwasher, don't stick your knives in, since the high temperatures used during the washing and drying cycles can separate the silver handles from their steel blades. And never allow silver to come into contact with other base (nonprecious) metals in the dishwasher; it can become pitted and scarred. Always wash any silver that's been on the table, even if it looks clean; minute flecks of leftover salt and other materials can scar silver if not rinsed away in a reasonable amount of time. (That's why silver salt cellars usually have enameled interiors or glass liners.)

Odd but Useful: Serving Pieces with Specific Purposes

Remember the Owl and the Pussycat who went to sea "in a beautiful pea-green boat"? In that children's poem, after they were married (by the "Turkey who lives on the hill") they "dined on mince and slices of quince, / which they ate with a runcible spoon."

A runcible spoon is one of those odd but useful things. It's actually got a spoonlike bowl, with two fork tines, one with a curving edge. Just right, we suppose, for eating quince. We'll have to take poet Edward Lear's word for it.

But there are other utensils, far less odd than the runcible spoon, that you've probably come across, and may again, in your eating adventures:

Escargot tongs. Small tongs with loops or open circles on each end. They hold snail, or escargot, shells so the diner can use a small pick to reach inside and grasp the snail. A corresponding dish with small indentations holds the shells upright.

Fish knives. Knives with wide blades, suitable for breaking the delicate skin of cooked fish.

Fruit knives. Short and sharp. Their handles are often silver or are made of more exotic material, such as mother-of-pearl, ivory (usually in antique knives), or rare wood. They're used for paring and cutting fresh fruit that is served at or after a dessert course.

Grape scissors. Small scissors (often silver) that can be used to separate a small cluster from a bunch of grapes.

Shellfish crackers. These look like nutcrackers and serve basically the same purpose: grasp the claw of a lobster or crab firmly, place the cracker around it, and exert pressure until the shell cracks (you may have to do this in a couple of places). Then use a shellfish fork or pick to take the meat out of the claw or leg.

Shellfish forks. Small, two-pronged forks used to spear oysters or shrimp or pry lobster meat out of its shell.

From Paper to Silver: When to Use What

Common sense is probably the best guide here. But we have some suggested guidelines for when to use the following:

Paper plates, plastic cups and utensils: Children's birthday parties; picnics in the park; potluck barbecues. Poolside parties. Tailgate picnics. Postfuneral repasts if they are very large and/or held in a facility (perhaps a church hall or outdoors, after the service) where washing dishes will be difficult or impossible.

Real plates, real glasses, cloth napkins: Buffets, sit-down dinners, teas. Almost anything that requires handling more than casual food—especially if your guests will be balancing plates on their laps. (Have you ever had your dinner cascade into your lap because the paper plate that held it got soggy?)

ODD BUT USEFUL UTENSILS

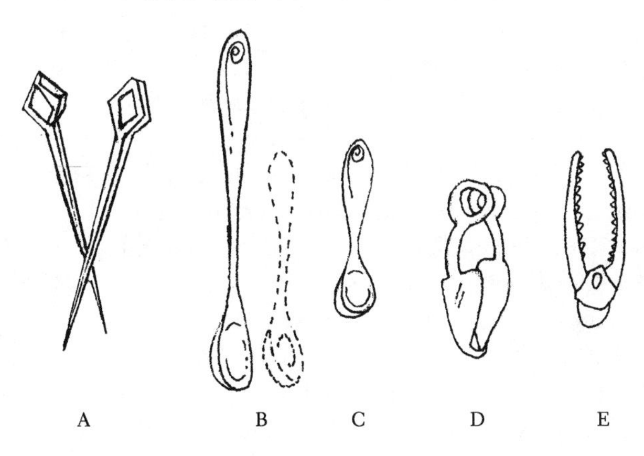

From left to right: A, *kabob skewers;* B, *iced tea spoon;* C, *jelly spoon;* D, *escargot tongs;* E, *claw crackers.*

Best china, crystal, flatware: Your best occasions. Special birthdays, anniversaries, and holidays. Meals celebrating something momentous. To honor a dear friend. Just because you love it and don't use it enough.

Glossary of Table Accessories

Chargers. Decorative plates that are used as underliners for dinner plates. They are also called service plates. You usually see chargers at the most formal dinners, where your best china and flatware are pulled out. Recently, we've begun to see more informal versions of chargers, made of pottery, stoneware, and lacquered wood.

Linen, damask. Fine fabrics usually reserved for dressier tables. They may be white, ivory, or even pastel. If cloth napkins are used at a formal dinner, they should match the tablecloths.

Place mats. Usually rectangular, but sometimes other shapes (square or even round). They're placed beneath the table setting and serve as an ornamental—and protective—barrier between the hot plate and tabletop. The materials for place mats can be as varied as the occasions on which they're being used: Colored paper place mats are often used outdoors, in the backyard, or at the children's table. Mats made of bright cotton fabrics (even woven or quilted) might be used at an informal lunch. Plain linen place mats for a more formal dinner. Beautiful mats of fine damask, or even cotton with embroidered Battenburg lace, for more formal occasions.

Runner. Goes lengthwise down the center of the table and may be used with place mats or alone. Like place mats, runners may be made of plain or fancy materials (from gingham to tapestry). They usually go just to the table's edge, or hang over the edge several inches at either end. Sometimes they are finished with a tassel or fringe.

Trivets. Used to protect your tabletop from the heat of serving dishes and other warm things, such as bread plates. Trivets can be made of something simple and functional—cork, wood, wrought iron (on rubber or felt feet, to prevent scarring), tile, or thick, woven strips of cloth—or they can be fancy: carved silver or marble or granite.

Place cards. Cards that indicate where the host would like you to sit at the dinner table. They may be simple table tents for an informal meal, or, for more dressy occasions, they may come as fine stationery (with gilt or marbled edges) that has been carefully hand-lettered. Place cards are usually held up by place-card holders. These can be as simple as a crab apple with a gash in it to hold the place card, or as ornate as a miniature sterling pineapple whose gold spiked top keeps a fancy place card upright. If there is a seating arrangement indicated, you can be sure that the host has gone to considerable trouble figuring out who might most enjoy sitting next to whom. Never, *ever* switch place cards at dinner; this is considered the height of rudeness, a mortal guest offense.

Menu cards. Sometimes used at very formal place settings, these cards denote the progression of the meal. They may be prettily written on fine paper or placed in a silver or porcelain frame. Often these are given to each diner at the end of the meal as a souvenir of her evening with the host.

Candles add a festive glow to almost any gathering. Use *votive* candles in simple holders of glass, wood, or metal for an outdoor meal, or line them up on a bookcase or mantelpiece (away from anything overhanging or flammable) to make a room sparkle. Candleholders are properly referred to as *candlesticks* and can be as simple as a stick that holds one candle (with or without a stem) or several at once. These latter are called *candelabra.* Candelabra are reserved for more formal dinners and are placed in the middle of the table between diners, to either side of each diner. Candle arrangements should provide an enhancing glow to dinner, but they should never prevent diners from looking across the table and making eye contact with each other. (On state dinner occasions, especially in Europe, the stems of candelabra are sometimes tall enough to allow diners to see each other, and the candles tower overhead. So far, we've not encountered that particular arrangement at dinner.)

Salt cellars. Small, shallow bowls, usually only a couple of inches across, made of fine silver or crystal. They appear directly above the dinner plate and dessert utensils at a formal dinner and are occasionally accompanied by a *pepper shaker* or *pepper mill,* or sometimes the pepper is served in a cellar as well. Salt cellars may or may not be elevated by feet. If made of silver (or, rarely, gold or gold-over-silver), they are virtually always lined, with either glass or enamel, to prevent the salt from corroding the silver. The tiny spoons used with salt cellars may or may not be silver (and should be washed after every meal, to remove all traces of salt), horn, tortoiseshell, or ivory.

Finger bowls. Small, shallow bowls, almost always crystal, that are placed before each diner; a plate that will be used for dessert is underneath the bowl. The diner quickly dips his fingertips in the bowl, then blots them on his napkin. The bowl is then placed to the upper left of the dessert plate. The plate on which the bowl rested will be used as a liner plate when dessert is served. Finger bowls have pretty much gone the way of the dinosaur, except in very elite social circles.

Clearing the Table: What Stays, What Goes?

At a sit-down dinner: The plates and glasses no longer needed are removed, as are any serving dishes (if you've served family style and dishes were passed). All eating utensils are taken to the kitchen, too—except for dessert forks and spoons, if they were part of the original setting.

At a formal dinner: Plates, utensils, and glasses are removed course by course, when they are no longer needed.

At a buffet: Main-course items and any remaining utensils used for serving or eating them are removed. So are extra unused plates and, if served on the same table, glasses. This allows the host room to place dessert, coffee and tea cups.

Remember the old rule you were taught as a child: as you serve, lower dishes from the diner's left; when you clear, raise dishes from her right.

Chapter 16

FINGER-LICKIN' GOOD

The most important people I know
is the least highfalutin'. They don't come into my place like they is
visitin' a mu-zeem and lookin' down their noses
at chitlins an' tripe.

Princess Pamela,
Princess Pamela's Soul Food Cookbook

Have you ever lost your appetite because you had a plateful of terrific-looking food in front of you and you hadn't a clue as to how to eat it? Unusual foods such as artichokes may seem daunting, but deciding whether it's appropriate to pick up the fried chicken with your fingers (at your boss's home) may be just as unsettling. For the most part, it's a matter of common sense. Better to know the accepted way to eat certain foods than to be embarrassed and feel uncomfortable. Even though you were dying to pick up those egg rolls with your fingers, you (and as it turned out, no one else) thought that just because you were eating at a fancy Chinese restaurant, your friend's aunt would have been mortified if you had.

For starters, *don't* salt and pepper your food, or liberally sprinkle on Tabasco sauce, without first tasting what's on your plate. In addition to possibly being disappointed in the resulting taste, it is an insult to your hostess or chef to season food prior to tasting it. Otherwise, follow these simple guidelines:

Artichokes (whole). Begin at the outside and pull off one leaf at a time. With your fingers, dip the leaves into the sauce or butter that is provided. Place the leaf between your teeth and pull forward. Place finished leaf neatly on the side of your plate. When all of the leaves have been removed, scrape away the inedible thistle part with a knife. Place on side of plate with "used" leaves. Cut the remaining part, the "heart," into bite-sized pieces and with a knife and fork dip into sauce and enjoy.

Asparagus. If the asparagus are cooked al dente (still firm) with sauce across the tips, it's fine to pick up each spear with your fingers; if you're uncomfortable eating them with your fingers, use your knife and fork. If limp or in a sauce, cut with a knife and fork and eat. Leave the hard ends, if there are any, on your plate.

Bacon. If crisp, break each strip (with your fork) into pieces, then pick up and eat with your fingers. If limp, eat with a knife and fork.

Barbecue. There are no hard-and-fast rules with this: let your common sense—and the region the barbecue's from—be your guide. Certainly an informal setting, such as your backyard or a picnic, means you may use your fingers for barbecue with a bone (ribs, chicken) or that's rigid (links). If the barbecue is minced or shredded meat off the bone (which is how it's served in the Carolinas), is unwieldy (a big chunk of fish or a steak), it's better to use a knife and fork. And a knife and fork are appropriate in more formal settings (an elegant soul-food restaurant, a fancy party).

Bread. Do not pick up an entire piece of bread and continuously bite pieces from it. Break the bread into pieces, as needed, and pick up a piece with fingers and eat. If olive oil or balsamic vinegar rather than butter is served with the bread, pour a small amount onto your bread plate, dipping small pieces into oil and eating.

Butter and jam. If butter has been served to you on a butter plate, presliced, use your knife (or butter knife if provided) and place a pat or two on your bread plate. If the butter is served as a whole cube or in individual ramekins, take a small amount and place on your bread plate. Butter individual bite-sized pieces of bread one at a time as you eat them. Do not butter all of your bread at once. The exceptions to this are biscuits and toast, which are buttered at one time while they are still warm.

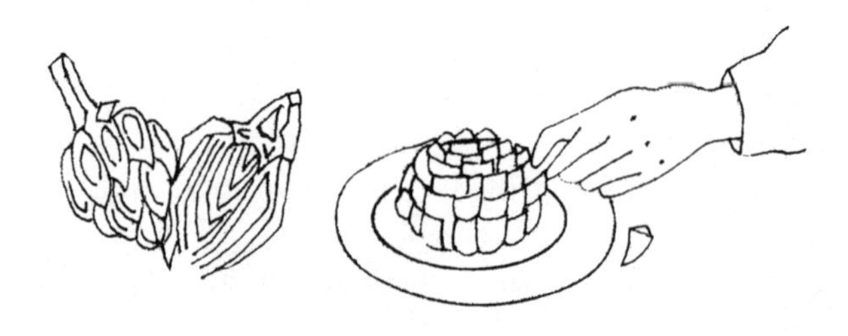

THE CORRECT WAY TO EAT AN ARTICHOKE

Spoon a small amount of jam onto your bread plate and spread it on your bread with your butter knife (or regular knife if no butter knife is provided). If a bread plate is not provided, place all bread and condiments on the side of your salad or entrée plate.

Cherry tomatoes. If they're served in a salad, cut them and eat them with a knife and fork. If they're passed in a relish bowl (with celery stalks, pickles, and olives), you may eat them with your fingers, one by one, as you would grapes. And as with grapes, try to put the whole little tomato in your mouth, to avoid squirting the person next to you.

Chicken wings. Wings are finger food, fried or not, and are meant to be eaten with your fingers.

Club sandwiches. Take the toothpick out and eat as you would a normal sandwich. If the sandwich is too big for your mouth, separate and eat the two sides as an open-face sandwich with either your fingers or a knife and fork.

Condiments. Place your choices on your bread or salad plate. Never eat directly from the condiment dish (spoon the ketchup onto the plate and then spread on your food with your knife). Olives can be picked up and eaten with your fingers.

Corn on the cob. At formal dinners, corn is cut from the cob and meant to be eaten with a fork. Otherwise, pick up the corn with your hands. There's no need to attack the corn—just eat it neatly. If you desire butter and/or salt, put it on small sections of the corn as you eat.

Crabs. Smaller, East Coast crabs, such as *Maryland blue crabs,* can be cracked with a hammer. Remove the "bib" on the underside, pull out the lungs, and pick through the delicate meat (there won't be much of it). Crack the legs and suck the meat out. *Alaskan King crab legs* should be cracked, and the meat removed with a shellfish pick. *Dungeness crab,* the huge West Coast variety, is cracked, opened from the back, and the rich, meaty flesh is taken out with fingers and forks. *Soft-shell crabs:* These are seasonal delicacies and are eaten "shell" and all. Cut them down the middle, then into pieces. If you want, you can cut off the legs and eat them separately. Leave any inedible parts at the side of your plate.

Crudités. Often served with dipping sauces, the first thing to remember is to *never* dip a vegetable into the sauce, take a bite, and then redip the same piece. If served as a relish at the lunch or dinner table, place them on the edge of any plate in front of you.

Dessert. When dessert arrives in a stemmed glass on a service plate, your spoon is placed on the service plate between bites, and never left in the glass.

Egg rolls. While eating egg rolls with chopsticks or a knife and fork is always acceptable, it is perfectly all right to pick up with fingers in an informal setting. If sauce is provided, dip an individual piece into the sauce and eat. Do not redip in a communal sauce dish and never pour sauce over egg rolls.

Foods from afar. "When in Rome . . ." check how everyone else is handling their food, or if uncomfortable, ask.

French fries. If served with a hamburger or other sandwich, certainly pick them up with your fingers. If served with an entrée, eat with a fork.

Fresh fruit. For *melons*, if they are served in bite-sized pieces, eat with a fork. If served as a half or quarter melon (cantaloupe), spoon into bite-sized pieces to eat. *Cherries* are eaten with your fingers. In your mouth clean the pit as much as possible, then remove the pit from your mouth by placing your cupped, almost closed hand over your mouth, removing and placing the pit on side of plate. *Grapes:* Never pull grapes off the stem one at a time to eat. Pull off a "branch" or cut off with fruit scissors. Seedless grapes aren't a problem, but for grapes with seeds, dispose of the seeds just as you would cherry pits.

Gumbo. Like a stew, gumbo requires more than one utensil. You may be given a soupspoon, seafood fork, shellfish cracker, and a knife—or perhaps only a spoon. Hopefully a bowl will be placed on the table for the disposal of shells. If not, put them on your plate, under the soup bowl. (This is also true for bouillabaisse.)

Hors d'oeuvres. If hot, let them cool or they will burn your mouth. When a toothpick is offered, spear the item and eat. Dispose of the toothpick in a receptacle provided for that purpose, put in a napkin until you can find a wastebasket, or place on the side of your plate. *Never* put a used toothpick back on the serving tray.

Lobster. Slowly crack at all points to diffuse it from squirting. Hold claw in one hand, twist the nutcracker on claws, and pull out meat. Tail meat is pulled out one side at a time. A large bowl is normally provided for disposal of the shells.

Olives. Eat with fingers. If the olives have pits, bite off meat but don't clean the stone. Remove stone from mouth with fingers or push into spoon with tongue. If in salad, eat with fork.

Pigs' feet. It's often said that in the old days, our folks used "everything on the pig 'cept the squeal." Pigs' feet are still considered a delicacy in many households. They're boiled and brought to the table split lengthwise or whole. Use your knife and fork to peel back the skin, then divide the foot into several sections, pick up the section with your fingers, and suck the meat out as best you can. The skin can be eaten with a knife and fork. (And you *will* need wet-wipes afterward!)

Pizza. Small wedges may be eaten with fingers, or cut into bite-sized pieces and eat with a fork.

Salad. If served on a salad plate, use your salad fork. If served as an entrée on a large plate, use the fork intended for entrées. Cut large pieces of greens with fork, or a knife and fork if you're having trouble. Cut only one bite at a time. Don't cut up all of your salad at once.

Salt. Salt served in a salt cellar is meant to be served with a tiny spoon, picked up with the tip of your knife, or pinched with your fingers and sprinkled on your food.

Seafood on the half shell. Water pollution has made this chancier, but if you have a good source with pristine seafood, it's a pleasure worth investigating. In an informal setting, it's fine to use the bottom shell of clams and oysters as a cup and "slurp" down the mollusk with its juice. In less casual settings, when the shellfish arrives with a seafood fork, take the hint and use the fork to separate the tender seafood from the tough muscle that attaches it to the shell. If the bivalves are served as part of a cooked dish—paella, gumbo, steamed mussels, etc.—remove the "meat" with your fork or spoon and place the empty shells on the side of your plate, or in a discard bowl, if one is offered.

Shellfish. If shrimp, and served as a first course, hopefully each shrimp can be eaten in one bite. If too big, grasp cup it's being served in and cut shrimp with fork. Never spear a shrimp and take a bite, then redip into sauce.

Shish kebob. If small and served as an hors d'oeuvre, eat directly from the skewer. If served as an entrée, lift the skewer with your fork beginning with the bottom and slide meat and/or vegetables off skewer and onto plate.

Soup. Consommé is served in a handled cup. You may use either a small spoon to eat, or you can drink directly from the cup. Always spoon soup away from you. When you are finished, do not leave the spoon in the bowl. Place spoon under bowl on plate.

French onion soup is slightly more challenging than regular soups. You are usually served a soupspoon as well as a knife and fork to eat the cheese and bread. Cut through the cheese and croutons so cheese doesn't drag as you eat the soup. If you want, you can twist the cheese around the bowl of your spoon and cut off with fork at the edge of the bowl.

Spaghetti. There's a method of eating spaghetti for everyone. You may either (1) cut spaghetti and eat with fork; (2) take a few strands at a time and curl around fork; or (3) with fork in one hand and a large spoon in the other hand, twirl until no dangling strands remain.

Tacos. Tacos and tortillas are meant to be eaten with your hands. Any food that falls out of the tortillas is to be eaten with a fork.

Variety meats. These used to be eaten more frequently in this country than they are today, but many restaurants and non-American households still enjoy them. *Brains:* These are about the consistency of scrambled eggs and should be eaten with a knife and fork. *Chitterlings:* Cut with a knife and fork, especially if they're liberally sprinkled with hot sauce or vinegar. *Headcheese:* Again, knife and fork, discreetly remove inedible gristle with your fork and leave at the side of your plate. *Kidneys:* Knife and fork. *Tripe:* Knife and fork.

Chapter 17

EATING OUT

A man hath no better thing under the sun than to eat, and to drink, and to be merry.

Ecclesiastes

Most of us enjoy a meal out now and then. In the past twenty years, a combination of less time, more—and more affordable—restaurants, and an interest in various cuisines has made the restaurant industry one of the country's most successful. According to industry analysts, black Americans are right in the forefront of this trend. Whether it's a chili dog grabbed on the run between school and choir practice, a romantic dinner à deux to celebrate an anniversary or Valentine's Day, or a bridal shower held at a favorite brunch spot, eating out is a treat that we indulge in often. The experience is enhanced even more when you know how to do it with style.

Reservations

Some restaurants demand that potential diners reserve their places in advance. If you've decided you want to try a restaurant that maintains this policy, call a few days ahead (several days ahead for a weekend reservation) and let the person who's taking reservations know what day you'd like to come, what time you'd prefer, and how many are in your party. If you know the restaurant well and want to sit in a specific part of it, ask when you make reservations: "This is John Bass. I'd like to see if you have space for four at eight o'clock on Saturday night. And if there's room on the terrace, we'd like to sit there, please."

If the restaurant is well known for its food or clientele, or is a new and especially "hot" one, the further ahead you can make a reservation, the better off you'll be. Many places like this can't take mere mortals for at least a couple of weeks, although they have been known to bend the rules for celebrities and other public figures. (From the restaurant's perspective, it's logical: a scattering of celebrities helps to make a hot place even more desirable.)

Being on Time

It's important to places that take reservations—especially restaurants that are hard to get into—that diners arrive on time. If your reservation is for 8 P.M., try to get there on time or even a little early. Like airlines, many restaurants have started to overbook tables as defense against customers who neglect to show up or cancel. If you don't want your table to be given away, let the restaurant know if you're running late, and give them an estimated time of arrival: "This is John Bass; my reservation is for eight o'clock tonight, and I'm sorry, but we won't be able to get there until 8:15." Restaurants are deeply appreciative when you warn them that you won't be there exactly on time but would still like your table to be held for you. Some places take your phone number when you make reservations, and will confirm, twenty-four hours ahead of time, your intent to keep the reservation.

Most restaurants will give you a bit of a grace period—usually about fifteen minutes—and then it's simply up to the reservations booker or maître d'. If you're a regular, they will probably wait considerably longer before your table is given to someone else. If you're a first-timer, or if the restaurant is especially sought-after, you may find you've lost your table if you're even five minutes late.

When One of You Is Going to Be Late

If the restaurant will seat the incomplete party (and be forewarned—some won't), take your seats and at least order drinks and hors d'oeuvres. The latecomer will have to catch up with you when she arrives. If she's familiar with the menu, she may tell someone what she'd like to have and ask that she be ordered for: "I'll be there by 8:30, for sure. Could someone order me the pasta with shrimp and garlic?" And of course she'll pay for her meal if anything happens to prevent her from joining you: "Lisa, I'm so sorry I'm not going to get there after all; tell me what my part of the bill is and who I owe for dinner, and I'll take care of it first thing in the morning."

If You're the Late Arrival

Call ahead to the restaurant and tell the person who takes reservations that you're part of a party but have been unavoidably detained. Ask that they be notified of your predicament and request that they be seated without you. Some restaurants won't seat an incomplete party; in that case, tell the staff person someone will order for you—and pay for your meal if you ultimately don't get there—or that you'll join them for drinks only, but emphasize that, for the restaurant's purposes, the party is complete.

Canceling a Reservation

Last-minute glitches occur: One of you is stuck in a meeting that should have lasted only two hours. The baby-sitter doesn't show up. You come down with a twenty-four-hour bug—just when you finally managed to get a table at that glamorous soul-food restaurant it took a month to get into! You'll be remembered fondly if you call as soon as you know you can't go, explaining that, because of unforeseen circumstances, you have to cancel: "This is John Bass. I'm truly sorry, but I just found out I won't be able to keep my reservation for four at eight tonight." If you have an alternate date, you might try to see if they can fit you in before you hang up.

Deciding Where to Eat

If you eat out with a friend or group of people regularly, you've probably figured out a way to decide where you're eating out on any given night: "It's Naomi's turn to choose, right, since Vicki did it last time?" Or perhaps you reach a consensus based on cuisine ("Thai next Tuesday? Where should we go?") or by consulting local restaurant guides and working your way through an agreed-upon list. However you do it, remember that some among you may have dietary restrictions, so make sure the menu has something all of you can eat: "Gayle's allergic to shellfish; does the seafood place we're going to have chicken or steak on the menu?"

If one person is treating another, she may ask the person being treated if there is a place she's especially fond of, or a type of food she loves or would like to try. If you're offered this choice as a guest, do feel free to make suggestions—but remember to be considerate of your host's budget. You could give general guidelines ("Well, you know I love Creole food; are there any places you like that we could try?") or something specific ("It's not fancy, but Chez Allard has the best crawfish étouffée. Can we go there?"), as long as it's not outrageous. (The happy exception here is when your host wants to go all out for a special reason, and tells you so: "Nikki, it's not every day they make me floor manager of Gleason's. Let's do it up: what's the best Italian restaurant you can think of?")

When You're on Time and the Restaurant Isn't

You've moved heaven and earth to get into Le Fuss Box, because "everybody" swears the food is wonderful and the celebrities make your eyes pop. You confirm your reservation, arrive on time—and proceed to cool your heels in the bar for forty-five minutes while you starve.

A good restaurant will apologize for the inconvenience, and many properly sweeten the experience with free drinks or hors d'oeuvres to compensate for the wait.

If the restaurant is having a bad night, bear with it. The downside of eating someplace hot and trendy is it takes a while for the kinks to get worked out in a new system. If, however, the place is well established and just arrogant (it happens), inquire of the maître d' how much longer the wait will be. If the wait has soured your enthusiasm for dinner, ask for your coats and leave. There's no reason you should pay for the privilege of being abused.

Bad Table, Bad Service for "Certain People"

Maybe the person you spoke to when you made your reservations by phone was quite cordial—but considerably less so when you showed up in person to claim your table. The partially filled restaurant suddenly requires that you wait for a half hour before a table can be found for you—and then it's behind the kitchen door, next to a service station or opposite a bathroom. Service is proper but with a distinctly frosty edge.

Hmmmm . . . Some restaurants haven't quite gotten the word that segregation's over and second-class service for "colored" is a thing of the past. (One large restaurant chain lost a huge class-action suit to black plaintiffs and is discovering just how expensive the wrong attitude can be.) The feeling may be so subtle it's hard for you to put a finger on—or so blatant you're tempted to leave and call the NAACP—but a nagging sense of déjà vu tells you you're not just being paranoid.

If you feel you've been given a poor table, or are receiving poor service because you look different from the other diners, speak up. When you're offered the offensive table, tell the maître d' firmly, "I'm sorry; this isn't acceptable. We'd rather sit somewhere over there, please." If you're told they're all reserved, simply smile and insist "I'm sure you'll work something out," and remain standing until you get a better table. If the matter isn't resolved to your satisfaction, you may choose to leave and take your business elsewhere.

If your waiter is rude or indifferent, ask for the manager or maître d' and explain the problem: "Perhaps our waiter is simply having a bad day, but his attitude is ruining our meal. Could you send someone else over, or change our table?" Use your judgment as to how pointed you want to be. Some black diners have gotten excellent results simply by asking point-blank: "Does your restaurant not want black clients? We're getting that impression from your staff, but we thought we should check with you directly." Service usually improves considerably after that. If it doesn't, find out who owns the restaurant and write a letter outlining your treatment. Businesses like restaurants live—and die—by customer satisfaction, and will usually try to make amends, if only out of their own self-interest.

Ordering and Speaking to Waiters

Your waiter will come over, probably take drink orders, and leave you to scan the menus for at least a few moments. If you have questions about how a dish is cooked, what comes with it, and so forth, address him politely and directly: "Excuse me, but could you tell me whether the grilled chicken is boneless?"

When the waiter goes around the table to order, if you don't know what you want, it's fine to ask him to skip you and return to you after everyone else has ordered. If, as a table, you know you need more time, simply ask him to give you a few more minutes.

Verbal Daily Specials

Many restaurants have at least one or two special dishes that change from day to day, depending on the availability of the ingredients and other factors. If the waiter reads you a long list of specials and does not include the prices, ask before you order. Sometimes the specials are considerably more costly than the dishes on the menu, and you should know how much you're spending before you spend it.

If you'd like to modify a dish (regular or special) for dietary or other reasons, ask if this can be done. Some restaurants are happy to do this; others do it and charge for any substitutions or changes; and some flatly refuse to do it at all. Ask your waiter if substitutions are allowed—"Could I have two vegetables with those lamb chops, instead of potatoes and a vegetable?"—and if there is an additional cost. (This is usually, but not always, noted on the menu.)

Splitting Plates

If the portions are huge and you know you'll never be able to eat that slab of prime rib all by yourself, you can request to split the plate with a fellow diner. Most restaurants charge a small fee for this service—from two to five dollars—but will perform it if you ask.

Children's Plates

Since so many families now eat out, many restaurants are responding to the changing market with menus designed especially for children. These menus may be smaller portions of the adult fare. Or they may be pint-sized plates with things designed to tempt little gourmets (individual pizzas, drumsticks, french fries and salad, burgers and dogs with the works). Keep in mind that children's plates are for *children*—not dieters who only want to eat a little bit. Or diners wanting a cheap meal on the sly. Or kids over the age limit (usually twelve) whose parents are trying to save a dime here and there.

All-You-Can-Eat Buffets

A few people with infinite capacity for consumption interpret "all you can eat" literally, but most restaurants serving buffets mean for you to enjoy all you *care* to eat, not all you are physically able to cram into yourself before you become sick. Buffets are a good place to try new foods without having to commit to an entire plate of them. Or for people who are fond of one kind of food—breakfast fixings, for instance, or seafood platters—to indulge (within reason) to their hearts' content. Don't feed people you haven't paid for (if there are six of you at the table, there should be six people paying for buffet service) and don't shovel buffet contents into your own personal doggie bag. "Toting privileges" do not apply here.

Ordering Family Style

"Family style" is an option that is appearing in more and more restaurants, at least in part because it's a cost-efficient way for a group of people to enjoy sharing a meal together. A family-style menu will feature a group of foods (two spit-roasted chickens, corn on the cob, rice, salad, dessert, for example) that will feed an estimated number (usually four to eight) for a fixed price. If you are all agreed on a certain kind of dinner (ribs, chicken, grilled fish), this is an ideal, and very reasonable, way for you to enjoy it.

Fixed Price vs. à la Carte

À la carte (literally, "according to the [menu] card") is the most expensive way you can eat—but the trade-off is, you get exactly what you want. If you want to design your own meal, à la carte is the way to go, but be prepared to pay for the privilege. If, on the other hand, you chose a prix fixe, or fixed price, meal, you may enjoy many of the elements of an à la carte meal for as much as one-third less. Prix fixe meals may offer you some latitude within certain categories (you might choose a Caesar salad or mixed greens, sauteed fish fillets or broiled chicken, baked or mashed potato, and have a choice of several different desserts); they usually do not allow for substitutions or changes beyond the ones offered in each group of foods.

Ordering from the Middle of the Menu

Considerate guests order neither the cheapest thing on the menu (unless you really *want* broiled chicken) or the most expensive (save that lobster Jones for another day), but stay within the medium (or middle) range of choices. The same goes for wine. Again, the exception is when the host urges you to go for broke.

Ordering Wine

Wine with dinner is one of the great pleasures of civilized life. If you're eating out and you're interested in ordering wine, ask if there is a separate wine list. Don't be afraid to canvass your table for suggestions, or ask the waiter. Or in more formal restaurants, the wine steward, who is also called the sommelier, will be happy to suggest one or two appropriate wines if you tell him what you and your companions are having and the general price range you'd like to stay within: "We're both having the sole. Can you suggest a moderately priced white wine, not too dry, that would go well with our meal?"

When the bottle arrives, the waiter will show you the label, so you can be sure you've received what you ordered. He will then uncork the wine and pour a little into your glass. You may take a sip and nod approval (this ritual is more symbolic than anything else, as most corks now fit tightly and air seepage into the bottle, which results in a vinegary taste, is a rarity). Don't sniff the cork—it won't tell you a thing. If you want, you may rub the cork to make sure it's wet (a wet cork means the wine has been stored properly). And never send the wine back unless something is genuinely wrong with it (strong chemical smell, vinegary taste, full of muddy sediment, etc.). Even wine professionals say they send wine back very, very rarely, and doing so without good reason just marks you as a showoff, not a connoisseur.

What Do I Do With . . . ?

The heated towel you're presented when you eat at a sushi bar: This is the Japanese equivalent of the finger bowl, a little ritual that cleanses and refreshes the diner before the last part of the meal. Just wipe your hands with the warm, moist towel (you can press it against your lips, too, if you want to) and leave it on the sushi bar above your tray. The chef or his assistant will pick it up and dispose of it.

The wet-wipes that come with some meals: If you've ever cracked steamed crabs, tackled a plateful of ribs, or peeled a mountain of spiced shrimp, you know that most restaurants that serve these foods provide grateful diners with a pile of premoistened, packaged paper towelettes. Remove the towelette from the foil packet, wipe your hands and mouth, then place the soiled towelette and the foil packet with the discarded bones, shells, or whatever so the staff can remove everything at once. In some places, the tables are covered with paper and you can simply make a pile of the inedibles as you eat. Less casual restaurants will provide you with a plate or bowl for the discards.

Chopsticks, when you've finished with the meal: Leave them angled across the plate at the "four o'clock" position, as you would your knife and fork, so the waiter can take the plate away without dropping the utensils.

Dropped and Dirty Utensils and Other Mishaps

If your fork drops between courses, or your napkin, simply ask for another. If you've been given a water glass with someone's lipstick imprint on it, quietly point it out to the waiter and request a clean replacement. Some restaurants serve bread without a bread plate; if you feel you couldn't eat bread without one, just ask for a bread plate. Restaurants are usually happy to oblige any reasonable request their diners might have.

It happens rarely, but it does happen: You find a hair in your dish. Or a little insect crawls across the butter. Ugh. Just signal the waiter, hand him the offending dish, and explain you'd prefer a fresh plate. Health codes for restaurants are *very* stringent, and any restaurant worth its salt will bend over backward to make sure you have a pristine plate the second time around.

Splitting the Bill

Many times, when a group of friends goes out, everyone is responsible for her own meal. Few restaurants today have the time or patience to run separate tabs for each member in your party; instead, group diners routinely split the bill, including the tip, among themselves and pay the proper amount at the end of the meal.

If you're with a group that's splitting the bill, it's important that you all agree that the bill be split evenly, so there's no interminable haggling about who had what and what the cost differential is. Ostensibly, part of the reason for eating out together is to enjoy each other's company—and the glow from a fine evening of food and fellowship can dissipate pretty quickly when you're arguing over who had a glass of wine and who had the iced tea.

If you're splitting the bill, when it arrives:

- Have one person check it for general accuracy.
- Figure out the proper tip (in many places, an automatic surcharge is tacked onto groups of six or more; this can run anywhere from 15 to 20 percent).
- Add the tip to the amount of the total bill and divide by the number of diners present.
- Collect the money and make sure it's all accounted for before the waiter is paid.

If one of you wants to pay by credit card, she should be handed everyone else's cash. She will then present her card and sign for the meal at the agreed-upon price. In some states, restaurants will split the bill among up to three or four diners paying by credit card.

When someone balks at paying the bill ("I don't believe in tipping more than 10 percent" or "I didn't have dessert, and I don't want to pay the extra six dollars"), quietly reach into your pocket and make up the difference—and make a note to never include that person in group dining again, as she obviously has an incompatible philosophy regarding how you pay for eating out when you're splitting the check.

If you're the dissenting bill-splitter, pay for the dessert you didn't eat anyway, as the sharing of the meal, not the meal itself, was the point of the outing. If you stated your philosophy up front, when you all decided to eat out together, and everyone's fine with it, that's one thing. It's another thing completely to do this at the last minute and expect someone else to cover the shortfall you've caused by not contributing your share. Bite the bullet this time—and resolve not to eat out with people who don't have the same philosophy about splitting the bill that you do.

How to Pay Whom

If the bill says "pay cashier," as it does in many casual restaurants, leave the money intended for your waiter's tip on the table and bring the bill to the cashier to be paid. Unless the bill is otherwise marked, you'll usually be expected to pay your waiter for the meal.

Hogging the Table When Others Are Waiting

Many restaurants have multiple seatings for dinner. So, if you have an earlier seating, it's altogether possible that your table has been reserved for other diners later in the evening. While the length of time between table turnover is usually generous, it's considerate, if the restaurant is crowded and you're aware that there are people backed up waiting to get to their tables, to finish your meal and leave. This doesn't mean that you should hastily bolt down your meal so the next diner can be served, and you certainly shouldn't be hurried along by your waiter. But it's rude to scan the bar area crowded with hungry diners waiting for tables—and then lean back and order a second espresso.

In the Wee, Small Hours of the Morning

You've had a wonderful dinner and the evening has been memorable. But the restaurant closes at 11 P.M.; it's 10:55, the waiters are pointedly sweeping up near you, setting the tables for tomorrow's luncheon, and generally all but telling you it's time to go home. Be considerate of the staff, gather your things, and leave. You can move on to another spot that serves coffee and cordials until the wee hours and let the restaurant staff go home to grab some sleep.

Doggie Bags, Pros and Cons

We're going to go out on a limb and assume that very few dogs actually get the delicacies that are packaged—allegedly for them—by the restaurant for clients to take home. There seem to be two schools of thought about this: Some people belong to the "it's mine, I paid for it, and I can take it home if I want to" school. Others feel that doggie bags are a little gauche: there you are, dressed to the nines, swinging a little tinfoil packet of leftovers.

We fall someplace in between. If you're eating at a restaurant that's famous for its gigantic portions, by all means ask for a take-out container if there is a considerable amount of food left (enough for at least one meal or very healthy snack), and you don't want it to go to waste. If you're at a fancier establishment, the portions are usually more manageable, and it's considered a little, well, *tacky* to take home that last bite you couldn't fit in.

Dining Dos and Don'ts

- *Don't* snap your fingers at the waiter or call him "garçon" or "boy." Ever.
- *Don't* send a dish back unless it really is inedible (maybe the kitchen inadvertently added far too much salt, or the chicken is bloody in the middle and needs to be cooked more) or it contains something you specifically asked be omitted. (If you're allergic to cheese and your omlette arrives dripping with Cheddar, you'll need to say something—or starve.)
- *Do* ask your waiter for suggestions of dishes that have proved especially popular.
- *Do* tell your waiter or wine steward if you have a general price range you'd like to stay within if you've decided to order wine: "We'd love a suggestion for a bottle of red wine that's in the neighborhood of thirty dollars or so; we're all having lamb."
- *Do* make sure, if you're using a credit card with a credit limit, that you haven't reached or exceeded your limit *before* you decide to plunk it down to pay for your meal.
- *Don't* engage in a wrestling match for the check—or sit on your hands when the check arrives. "Let me" is sufficient. If the other diner insists, thank her and make a mental note to pick up the check the next time.
- *Don't* table-hop when you're with someone, even if you know nearly everyone in the dining room. It's fine to chat in the bar if you're waiting for your dinner companion to join you, but working the room in the middle of a meal is plain tacky.
- *Do* tell the maître d', as you leave, if your waiter was especially wonderful, so he can receive credit due him for helping to make your evening more pleasant. Conversely, if the waiter was rude, surly, or indifferent, this should be mentioned as well, so he can be encouraged to improve.

Chapter 18

GIFTS FROM ME TO YOU

It is more blessed to give than to receive.

Acts 20:35

Gifts are treats that should be given freely and warmly, not out of a sense of obligation. Sure, sometimes it's the politically correct thing to do—or you need to keep peace at home or with your in-laws—but even then you can make it an enjoyable experience for you the giver, as much as for the recipient.

Thoughtfulness and the Personal Touch

Take the time to think about the gift you'd like to give. You know when your friend or partner's birthday is each year, that Christmas is coming, and that Mother's Day always falls on the second Sunday of May. Take the hint, plan ahead. For those you are close to, keep them in mind throughout the year as you shop, because that perfect gift may turn up at the most unexpected moment. Gifts can convey the underlying message that you took the time to select something that you thought the recipient would enjoy, or that you actually forgot the occasion and settled for whatever you could find at the corner store. It's not the cost of the gift, but rather the thought, and the joy with which it is given. And frequently gifts are not tangible items that can be ordered from your favorite catalog. Remember, as with all the lessons of home training, it's the thoughtfulness and the personal touch that make your gift a standout.

Gifts of Time and Thoughtfulness

Gifts are not relegated to holidays or special occasions. Gifts of time and thoughtfulness are welcome treats at any time of the year. Some of these may include baby-sitting, grocery shopping, running errands, and reading to those with limited eyesight. A simple flower from your garden can bring a smile to a weary neighbor. Staying with your grandchildren while your daughter and her husband get away for the weekend, picking up your elderly aunt's medicine each week, or taking your girlfriend's teenage daughter for a day at the mall are all gifts that will be appreciated.

When Flowers Say It All

Flowers are a delightful gift anytime, anywhere, as far as we're concerned. With the exception of those with allergies to flowers, those who may have medical restrictions, and those who detest floral gifts, flowers can bring sunshine to an otherwise dreadful day. With the convenience of ordering flowers by phone, or on-line with your computer, those with little time or creative thought may resort to ordering flowers sight unseen for every occasion. Don't for a minute think that's what we had in mind. Something gets lost in the translation when the same "sweetheart bouquet" shows up on the doorstep each and every holiday. Keep in mind that the price of fresh flowers escalates the closer you get to major holidays such as Valentine's Day, Easter, Mother's Day, Thanksgiving, and Christmas.

From My Hand to Yours

Handmade and homemade gifts exhibit your talents while showing the recipients that you care enough to exert time and energy in an effort to please them. Some examples of "gifts by hand":

- Kitchen goodies (your special cookies, coconut cake, etc.)
- Quilts
- Photographs or videos of the children
- Scrapbook of special moments together or career highlights
- Collage of special places you've visited together
- Painted boxes

Gifts to or from Several People

- Plants or tree for the garden
- "Goodie basket" that can be shared with a group (muffins, popcorn, fruit, nuts)
- A "set" of something, given in pieces by a number of people (flatware; everyday dishware; collector's edition of books)
- A restaurant outing

For an individual giving to a group, such as employees: matching T-shirts, monogrammed baseball caps, individual books on each person's hobby.

Exchanging or Returning Gifts

If you receive more than one of the same item, and it's not personalized, it may be exchanged or returned. Unless you are very close to the giver, it is not necessary to discuss the exchange with the giver. Do, however, thank the giver for the original gift. While the practice of "recycling" gifts that are not to your liking (passing them on to others as a gift you selected for them) may have become somewhat acceptable in our hurried world of no time and no money, think carefully before you follow suit. While it is certainly acceptable to share a gift with a college student whose taste may be more in keeping with the four-inch skirt you received from Cousin Susie, it is not acceptable to pass on personalized gifts. Heaven forbid the guest of honor at a retirement party opens a lovely fountain pen from you, in front of the crowd, only to notice it has your initials engraved on it.

When People Ask What You Want

It may be easy to inform your significant other that jewelry would make you incredibly happy, but this is certainly inappropriate in the workplace. If asked, you may make a "wish list" of gift choices in various price ranges. Since it's the thought that counts, you can always tell the giver that whatever she'd like to give you would make you happy.

When Is Money Appropriate?

Although extra money can always come in handy, it is inappropriate to ask for it, and often inappropriate to give it. When celebrating an honored occasion with members of another culture, be sure to check whether money is expected, or would be offensive. Times when money would be a natural gift:

- Bar or bat mitzvah
- Wedding
- Graduation
- Retirement (especially when the retiree dreams of a long-awaited trip)
- Students who are away at school
- Holiday tips for personal services and service workers
- When a young person has saved for something special and is a little short of the purchase price (bike, guitar, camp, etc.)
- Unexpected tragedy that requires immediate expenses

When Someone Wants to Give You What She Wants You to Have

Although you'd appreciate any gift, sometimes those close to you ignore your desires and decide what you really need is a kitchen appliance. Accept gratefully, and let them know at another time that you'd be happier if they followed your wishes. Conversely, do not assume that just because you love chocolate, you'll ignore your friend's allergy because you know that she'd feel better if she just learned to love chocolate the way you do!

Personal Shoppers and Gift Buyers

Personal shoppers have often been referred to as lifesavers. If shopping is not in your vocabulary or your time schedule, establish a relationship with a department store or gift boutique personal shopper. In the high-tech age in which we live, on-line computer stores even offer services that will keep track of the important occasions in your life and remind you of the upcoming event with suggested gifts that you may order, and have delivered, without leaving your computer.

Traditions and Collections

Family traditions and unique collections are always wonderful ideas for gifts. If your friend collects elephants, fountain pens, or unusual socks, it's fun to keep a lookout for special items throughout the year that you can keep for one's birthday. Your mother may collect Christmas plates, which you can't stand, but she'll be thrilled when you surprise her with additions to her collection.

Engraving

Use proper names when having gift items personalized. If you insist on using pet names on special items, have the engraving done on an area of the gift that will not be seen by others. If the nickname is on the back of a watch and won't be visible to anyone but the two of you, go for it. Remember, engraved gifts cannot be returned.

Wrapping and Presentation

A wonderful moment of gift giving can be spoiled by running in with the gift, unwrapped, in the store's brown bag with the excuse that you ran out of time. Taking care with the presentation of the gift is much like setting a beautiful table. The packaging sets the tone. The wrapping need not be fancy, but it should not be an afterthought. With so many decorated bags with matching tissue paper available, there's no excuse for those sloppy wrapping chores you detest. Department store gift-wrapping services are always acceptable, but perhaps you want to be a little more creative. You may choose to wrap a gift box in the recipient's favorite color, favorite comic

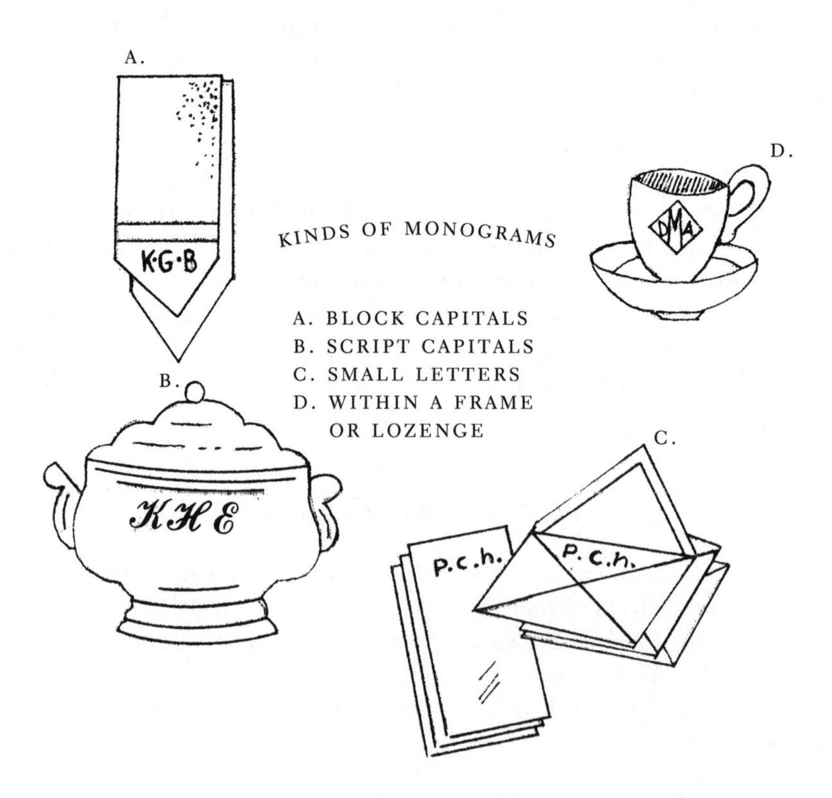

strip, or a color Xerox of special photos. And you may choose to secure your wrapping with cord, seals, dried flowers, or simply ribbon and a pretty bow. Smaller items may be tied to the box of larger items as part of the decoration. Picture a gift box, holding a teapot, tied with a cluster of tea bags.

Hand-Delivered or Sent from the Store?

If the gift is not for a close friend, or you'd like to surprise her, you may choose to have it sent from the store. If you are trying to time the delivery for a particular day, alert the store in ample time. You may want to send a token of thanks to a colleague or casual friend. If you would rather not deliver it yourself, you may be more comfortable having it hand-delivered by a service or even an anonymous friend. If the gift is perishable, it may be advisable to check with the recipient's secretary or someone else who can assure you the recipient will be in town to receive it in a timely manner.

When a Gift Is Sent and You Don't Know Whether It Was Received

If you requested a gift be sent from the store where you purchased it, and you have already been billed for the item, ask for proof of delivery. If you mailed the gift directly to the recipient, ask her about it in a way that does not make her feel guilty about not having responded: "I've been away and I was afraid the gift I sent may not have reached you." If a gift was delivered to someone's office, often you can call that person's secretary and ask if it was actually received. The secretary may have signed for the package and the recipient has yet to see it because she's been away on vacation for the last two weeks.

Should You Reward Children for Doing Things They Should Be Doing Anyway?

Be careful when you begin to reward children with gifts for good grades, perfect attendance, or doing well in extracurricular activities. You may run into trouble when they begin to feel that they will always be rewarded materially, and they may even start to negotiate with you. This is not to say children should not be rewarded, on occasion, for a job well done. Make it a surprise when you feel it's appropriate. Don't set a precedent that time and circumstances may preclude.

Books as Gifts

You can never go wrong when you give a book as a gift. Identify the recipient's hobbies, interests, places he loves, or books that have sentimental or historical significance. Coffee-table art books are always a welcome addition to a home (particularly when you know they love the book and wouldn't dare buy it themselves). Cookbooks are often a favorite, as are books signed by the author.

Some of Our Favorite Gifts

- Magazine subscriptions. (When there's a hard-to-find magazine in someone's town or city, purchase it the next time you see it or write to the publisher for subscription information.)
- Gift certificates for "pamper yourself" activities (haircut, massage, manicure, day at the spa)
- Fruit of the Month Club
- Anything personalized
- Unusual or old silver serving pieces found at estate sales, flea markets, or the swap meet
- Odd gourmet utensils
- Food goodies—anything homemade from the kitchen
- Picture frames
- Fountain pens, ink, sealing wax

Gift Ideas to Spark Your Imagination

Hostess Gifts for . . .

- Barbecue or cook-out: barbecue spices, special barbecue sauce; exotic-wood chips; a book on the art of grilling; barbecue mitts or long-handled tools
- Brunch: fancy jams or jellies; premium, whole-bean (or all-purpose grind) coffee; a deluxe box of hot cocoa; champagne; a basket of fresh fruit; home-baked bread
- Card party: interesting playing cards (African American images, interesting sites); a notebook for tallying scores; personalized pencils; fancy snacks; mixed nuts; coasters
- Formal dinner party: flowers, sent the day *before* or shortly *after* the

party; a guest book; chocolate cordials or chocolate-dipped fresh fruit; champagne
- Informal dinner party: wine or sparkling cider; pretty guest soaps; cookbook or gourmet gadget
- Ladies' lunch: beautiful guest towels; guest soaps; mints; potpourri; bath treats for the hostess
- Potluck party: inexpensive serving pieces; game for the family; chips and dip in a dish the hostess may keep
- Tea party: guest book; book about tea or tea parties; silver tea strainer; unusual or hard-to-find tea; potpourri; cloth cocktail napkins; small spoons for tea; sugar spoons; unusual shapes or hard-to-find paper lace doilies; tea cozy
- Sports day at a friend's home (swimming, tennis, badminton, paddle tennis): soft drinks; chips and salsa; fresh cans of tennis balls; sunscreen; sports towel

On the Occasion of a Birth or an Adoption

- Silver cup or spoon, engraved
- Personalized baby blanket
- Gift certificate for a diaper service
- Baby-sitting services
- Photo album or scrapbook
- If it's an older child being adopted: something personalized with new name, frame for photo of "adoption day," certificate for family outing to amusement park or restaurant; camera or camcorder (if you're Grandma and Grandpa!); book on the traditions and cultures of the new member of the family who is ethnically different from the adopters or recently arrived from a foreign country.

Christening, Baptism, or Confirmation

- Savings account in child's name
- For first child, perhaps a family Bible with family history and christening date inscribed
- Bible
- Gold or silver cross on a chain
- Rosary beads
- Book of Common Prayer
- Bookmark for Bible
- Book of Bible stories (depending on age)

Naming Ceremony

- Black-history book
- Anything personalized with new name
- Photos of ceremony
- Hand-lettered scroll with history and significance of name and how and why the name was chosen

Children's Birthday

The verdict is out on whether or not you take a gift for the birthday boy's siblings when you attend a party at their home. While often it is appropriate to let a younger child know that he, too, is being remembered, it is also a time for siblings to understand that when it's a sister's or brother's birthday, then it's that person's special day. They may appreciate their own birthday if they realize it's theirs alone to be recognized. When attending a party for children who don't live in the same city as you do, or for other reasons you see infrequently, it is quite appropriate to bring something to each child, or a family gift such as a game, in addition to the individual gift for the birthday girl. Be mindful of the age of the recipient, and whether it's a "significant" birthday, such as five, thirteen, sixteen, or eighteen. In the Hispanic culture the age of fifteen is celebrated as a major milestone. There are many items to consider in addition to the usual toys. Younger children may enjoy the latest video, a game, or a small pet (with the parents' permission, of course). Older children and teenagers may appreciate a gift certificate to a favorite clothing or music store, a gift certificate to the local amusement park, or tickets to a sports event or concert they've been coveting. Gift certificates (rather than just giving money) ensure a gift from a particular location and allow children the freedom and the experience of shopping for themselves. Be creative, and they'll remember the thoughtfulness.

Birthdays

Birthdays give us a chance to celebrate the fact that friends or family members were born and to let them know how much we appreciate them. If a close friend is having a birthday, chances are she's hinted at what she may desire. That hint may have come last Christmas when she was admiring items from the "after-Christmas sale" and was never meant to be "dropped" for your benefit. It's those times that you can feel comfortable purchasing a gift you know she'll like (and your life is so much easier when you don't have to think of something). Sometimes you realize he admires something special and has bought it for friends but wouldn't dare splurge on himself. Some suggestions:

- Take your friend or family member out for a special treat, just the two of you. This is especially appreciated by mothers and fathers who no longer get any time alone with their grown children. It may be breakfast, brunch, lunch and an afternoon of shopping, or dinner and a movie or the theater. Whatever you plan will be special because you're doing something together.
- Flowers and balloons are good for out-of-town birthday remembrances as well as the coworker across the hall. In fact, flowers and balloons are a pleasant surprise at any time.
- Basket of unusual coffees for the true coffee lover who can't begin the day without it—or tea for the person who believes we'd all be more civilized if we slowed down and had tea every afternoon
- Anything home-baked
- Stationery (preferably personalized)
- Jewelry or clothing item that signifies the recipient's sorority or fraternity
- Subscription to favorite magazine, or a black magazine the recipient may not know about
- Gift certificate to a local black bookstore
- Whatever she or he collects (boxes, elephants, frogs, 45 rpm records, teacups or mugs, handmade pottery, to name a few)

GIFT BASKET

Significant Birthdays

Those "big ones" do roll around with increasing frequency. From twenty-one to thirty, then each successive "decade" birthday, sixty-five, seventy-five, and one hundred are truly to be recognized as milestones. If the recipient is "tripping" about getting to be "that" age, don't make a big deal out of it, but do treat the birthday celebration or gift with more significance.

- Jewelry (one of our personal favorites)
- Dinner for two—which does *not* necessarily include you—at a favorite restaurant. (Remember to include tip when making arrangements.)
- A day trip somewhere. If it's a close friend, you can always "kidnap" her for a day at the beach, to the city to see a special exhibition, or simply a "girls' day out." Be sure and let her family know ahead of time what your plans are and your expected time of departure and return.
- Leather-bound journal
- Watch
- Coffee-table book
- Silver key chain
- Collector's-edition CD, album, or video
- Anything that addresses the recipient's year of birth
- A photographer hired to document the "big event"

Recital

- Book on the specialty being performed (if a violin recital, perhaps a biography on the performer's favorite violinist)
- For a vocal recital, hard-to-find sheet music
- A journal to write about the day, and the recitals to come

Special Accomplishment of a Child

If you and your child (or someone else's) set a goal for him or her to reach and it is attained, it should be rewarded. This can be as simple as treating to hot fudge sundaes or a gift certificate to the local fast-food restaurant, ice cream shop, movie theater, or bookstore. Once again, you can't go wrong with a balloon bouquet that's delivered directly to the child. In addition to preset goals, consider recognizing the youngster for volunteer efforts and community involvement. Also consider recognizing winners in essay contests, art contests, and sports and musical competitions. Even an unexpected card or note of congratulations can spur a young person to continue to achieve.

Debutante

While debutantes are busy with activities for months preceding the big event, family members and other guests often choose to mark the occasion with a special gift. These might include:

- An etiquette book
- Jewelry
- Personalized stationery
- Manicure and/or pedicure prior to the event
- Diary or journal
- Flowers
- Lace handkerchief

Graduation

Graduations, or culminations, are significant accomplishments to be recognized. If you are sent a graduation announcement from someone you are not particularly close to, you have no obligation to send a gift. If you have been invited to the actual ceremony, you should either take a gift or send one if you are unable to attend. Some suggestions for high school and college graduates:

- This is a time when money is particularly appropriate and appreciated.
- Pen and pencil set
- Leather-bound diary or journal
- Savings account in recipient's name
- Something he or she will need for college life or that first job
- Luggage or briefcase
- Something informational about the city he or she is moving to (Zagat's or other restaurant survey, guide books to landmarks and other points of interest, distance to nearest airport or major city)
- Subscription at new address to hometown newspaper or magazine
- Silver bookmark
- Dictionary
- Gift certificate for computer classes
- Personalized notepaper
- Prepaid telephone card

Gifts for the Teacher

Students become particularly close to their teachers and take special pride in pleasing them. The gift should be modest but thoughtful. Do not get into a competition with the other parents trying to one-up each other. To put that smile on Teacher's face:

- Tote bag
- Unusual bookmark
- Note cards
- Anything relating to the teacher's hobby or special interest
- T-shirt "greeting card" designed and illustrated by the child
- Personalized Post-it notes
- Flowers and balloons
- Plant for the teacher's desk

For the Ill or Someone Confined to Home

Always check for allergies, medications, and the use of oxygen before selecting gifts that may not be able to be used. For example, if the patient has AIDS, cut flowers may not be allowed.

- Flowering plant (if the doctor has approved flowers being near)
- Electric teakettle or "hot pot" that can be kept in the vicinity of the patient's room (so the patient will not have to go up and down stairs to have hot water)
- Note cards and stamps
- Offer to cook dinner for his or her family one or two times a week while the patient recuperates. (Just make extra when you do your regular cooking and let them know ahead of time which nights they can count on you for.)
- Books on tape
- Assorted magazines
- Offer to run errands
- "Pamper yourself" basket
- Special hand or body lotion
- Assorted teas with a cup or mug
- Basket of prepared foods that can easily be microwaved
- Fruit basket

Also see chapter 35, "And This, Too, Shall Pass."

Someone in Nursing Home or Senior Citizens' Home

Be sure to check on any food restrictions before taking a basket of goodies.

- Framed photos of family and friends
- Anything familiar that would make his or her surroundings more like home
- Something that can be shared with others (video, goodie basket, game, music tapes)
- Robe
- Books on tape with Walkman
- Socks or slippers
- Disposable camera for photographing friends and activities at the facility. When all the shots have been taken, retrieve the camera, have the photos developed, and return them in a little photo album.

Retirement

When thinking of gifts for the retiree, remember that he or she may be paring down his or her lifestyle and has no room (or desire) for any added clutter. The family home may soon become an apartment or condominium, and the sufficient income and regular paycheck may now be replaced with waiting by the mailbox for that single "fixed income" check to be delivered. Try to put yourself in another's situation, and project what you would appreciate. Some suggestions:

- An autograph book signed by guests at the retirement party (or coworkers if there will be no party) and presented to the retiree before the end of the party
- Computer lessons or equipment
- Video of retirement wishes from family and friends
- Contribution to a group gift of a vacation or cruise
- Dinner for two at the retiree's favorite restaurant. (You may decide lunch would be better if the person feels less comfortable being out at night.)
- Album highlighting special times and accomplishments during career (photos, news clippings, company newsletters, letters of congratulations, remembrances from coworkers)
- A disposable camera for each table at a sit-down party so guests can record the antics and participants at their table
- Anything related to his or her hobby (gardening, mystery books, horses, cooking, etc.)

Some of today's retirees continue to work. Don't offer a gift that makes a vital person moving on to the next stage of his life feel like he's been "put out to pasture."

Farewell or Going-Away Party

This type of party may be given by neighbors or coworkers for the friend who's recently been transferred to another city, or by family members for the student going away to school or leaving home to take a promising job. Whatever the reason for the departure, this gives the person going away a chance to say good-bye to all of his good friends at one time. Although it is not mandatory for you to take a gift to a farewell party, it will always be appreciated and bring back memories for the recipient long after he has left. Some suggestions:

- Video of friends wishing him and his family well
- Subscription to hometown newspaper or magazine
- Luggage
- Photo album of special moments your families have spent together
- Address book already filled in with the addresses and telephone numbers of the friends, neighbors, and coworkers he will be leaving behind
- Magazines and books highlighting his or her new city
- Prepaid telephone cards
- Memento of the hometown or longtime residence he or she is leaving. (It can be a very "touristy" or folksy item like a T-shirt from the local basketball team, a mug from the neighborhood diner, a menu from the restaurant where the two of you ate for your weekly lunch dates, or a photo of the church he or she will no longer attend.)

When There Is a New Job or Promotion to Celebrate

While this type of celebration often goes unrecognized, we believe that it's important to congratulate our friends and family members on their successes. A gift need not be expensive; it may simply be a note of congratulations or a gag gift—it's the acknowledgment of the occasion that counts. When stumped for an idea, consider:

- Personalized notepads
- Anything for her desk
- Plant for her office
- Goodie basket of "comfort foods" for those rough days ahead
- Cake decorated with "Congratulations" and appropriate theme of

workplace. (Your teenager may consider it "no big deal" that he's been promoted to chief "hamburger turner," but he'd surely appreciate a cake heralding his new position and how proud you are of him.)

- Don't do anything to embarrass your friend in her new position, but if appropriate, we're sure she'd love to receive a delivery of flowers, balloons, or chocolates at work. (No strippers or singing telegrams, please.)
- Gag gifts for "de-stressing" from all the new responsibilities
- Baseball cap embroidered with new job title

New House or First Home

You've watched your friend fret over whether she would get the loan for her dream home, and today is finally moving day. If she's staying close to her former home, or has found a home in the suburbs, there are gifts that can make the transition easier:

- Return address stickers with the new address
- Guest book
- Indoor plant or tree
- Bucket of household cleaning supplies
- Flat of flowers or plants for the garden
- Rosebush to be planted in the garden. (You may consider adding a rosebush for each significant gift-giving event—which can be planted to commemorate that moment in time. It may be a wedding anniversary, a birthday, or the anniversary of the day her mom died.)
- Recipes or cookbooks
- Gift certificate to local housewares store
- Basket of assorted batteries and lightbulbs. Throw an extension cord in for good measure.
- Offer your services for a day of unpacking and lining shelves and drawers.
- Assorted paper goods for those first few days (or weeks) when they don't know where anything they own is
- A list of "the best of everything" in the new neighborhood. This might include the best dry cleaner, tailor, meat market, fried fish place, bakery, hardware store, fresh vegetable dealer, and florist. If they have pets, add the local veterinarian. Be sure to include emergency numbers for the fire and police stations in the area. When you put your mind to it, you can think of scores of services to include. You can list the black bookstores, the best place to get videos or CDs, the local black financial institutions and other businesses, the best shuttle service to the airport—it's endless. You may even rediscover some services and places you'd forgotten about.

- When the moving van has arrived and there's much work being done, take hot coffee, cold juice or sodas, or fruit and sandwiches.
- Offer to bring over dinner for the family (a casserole and a salad would be great) while they're still in a state of flux.
- Assorted paper goods and sodas, bottled water, and coffee that can be offered by the new neighbors to those on her block who stop by to say "welcome." Better bring something like popcorn or cookies, too. The neighbors won't be expecting anything, but the new kid on the block would certainly feel more comfortable if she had something on hand to offer them. You know what they say about black folks and how they can't let you step through the door without asking you if you'd like something to drink.

MOTHER'S DAY

Although we often resent the forced celebration of certain industry-driven gift-giving holidays, we don't think anyone bemoans Mother's Day. Whatever you do for, or give, your mother, grandmother, godmother, aunts, or sisters and sisters-in-law will be appreciated. If you're tired of giving the same ol' unimaginative gift each year, take note:

- Prepare dinner for your mom at her house so she can be at home and relax. Don't even *think* about leaving her kitchen anything less than spotless!
- Airline, bus, or train ticket to visit you
- Handmade cards from all of her children (no matter how old they are) and grandchildren timed to arrive each day during the week preceding Mother's Day
- If she's been dying for you to go to church with her, just go (*with* a smile on your face).
- Framed photographs of children and/or grandchildren
- Surprise her by showing up early Sunday morning and having breakfast ready when she awakens (that is, if she still lets you have a key to her house).
- Lace handkerchief
- Have an old picture of her mother (your grandmother) restored and copied for her. Place in a frame that matches your mom's bedroom.
- Prepaid telephone cards
- Gift certificate for a day with you. (Make a date for a time when you won't be working—she may choose a Sunday and ask to start the day with you joining her at church.)
- "Pamper yourself" basket

- Anything she really wants and won't, or can't, buy for herself
- Theater tickets (or, if she prefers, tickets to hear a local jazz or blues band)
- A day at the spa
- Audiocassettes of the grandchildren singing and reciting poetry
- Arrange to take her to lunch or dinner on a day before or after Mother's Day when restaurants aren't so crowded and you won't be rushed. (This, by the way, does not let you off the hook if you live in the same area. Still visit your mom and take her a card on Mother's Day.)

Don't forget to mail cards and gifts to mothers "across the miles" in plenty of time to be received by Mother's Day. And don't forget stepmothers, your close friend's mother, women who treated you as though you were their own, and older women who are special to you whom you would like to recognize.

Father's Day

For as long as we can remember, mothers have received candy and flowers on Mother's Day and fathers have received ties. Dads have much more to look forward to these days.

- A feast of peanut butter and jelly sandwiches, or better yet, hot dogs, prepared by the youngsters in the family
- Handmade cards (appreciated by fathers just as they are by mothers)
- Books on tape
- Tickets to a sports event (preferably with you)
- Camera
- A weekend away fishing or playing golf
- Tools, if he's the tinkering type
- Photos of children and grandchildren
- Handwritten letters of appreciation and love from children
- Transistor radio or Walkman
- Classic recording of favorite musical artist
- A quiet day to himself. (Maybe next week Mom can take the kids somewhere and give Dad "his" day.)
- Anything for his car or truck
- If you share his love of sports, bring over a deli platter of cold cuts or some barbecue, along with his favorite beverage, and enjoy the day together in front of the television set.
- And there's always the shirt and tie.

Wedding Gifts

See chapter 34, "To Love, Honor, and Cherish."

Anniversary or the Renewal of Wedding Vows

From the first year of marriage to the silver and golden years, anniversaries celebrate a couple's life together. If you're invited to an anniversary party, choose your gift carefully. It should be something both the husband and the wife would enjoy.

- Photo frame (always good for displaying those special moments)
- Scrapbook filled with old pictures that document their time together
- Video of friends who were attendants at original wedding, and still have stories to tell
- Theater tickets
- Gift certificate for dinner for two at their favorite restaurant
- Vase
- Coffee-table book
- Newspaper retrospective that covers the years they've been married
- Family tree (complete with photographs, nicknames, and place of birth)

Grandparents' Day

Often grandparents do not see their grandchildren as frequently as they would like because hundreds or thousands of miles separate them. Near or far, grandparents love to hear from their grandchildren. (Don't forget surrogate grandparents.)

- Audiocassette with messages from children and grandchildren
- Tape recorder with requests for grandparents to record stories for their descendants. (The children or grandchildren may send the first tape with a message regarding why the grandparents' legacy is so important to them.)
- Easy-to-use cameras
- A ticket to visit the grandchildren for a special event. (Grandparents' Day at school? Maybe the grandchild's upcoming birthday, recital, track meet, or basketball game.)
- Anything the grandchildren made themselves
- Artwork by the grandchildren
- Prepaid telephone cards
- Videocassette recorder, with hands-on help setting it up, instructions

for use, and a gift certificate for a video and popcorn at the local video rental establishment. They may rediscover their favorite movies of yesteryear!

- A contract drawn up by the grandchildren pledging a note or phone call every two weeks, and extracting a promise from the grandparents that they will answer any and all letters written to them by the grandchildren. (If the grandchildren are too young to write, or the grandparents have difficulty responding, provide a tape recorder and tapes and they can "talk" to each other through regular "cassette letters."

Tree-Trimming Party

Christmas is a time for gathering together with friends—old and new—for parties and sharing of special memories. Tree-trimming parties offer an informal, hassle-free way of getting together. If invited to a tree-trimming party, consider taking:

- An ornament for the tree (the traditional gift)
- Book of holiday traditions
- Holiday mugs with the makings for hot cider or hot chocolate
- Disposable cameras to record the evening's festivities
- Tape or CD of holiday music
- Homemade "sweet treat"
- Holiday paper cocktail napkins or guest towels

Kwanzaa Party

- Homemade or handmade gifts
- Books on black culture and history
- Afrocentric greeting cards, tea towels, framed quotes, etc.

Secret Stash

You're always covered if you keep a "secret stash" of gifts. If you're a mom with kids on the birthday circuit, we're sure you've already discovered that purchasing gifts ahead of time can be a lifesaver. You never know when the mood or circumstance will strike and you'll need a small gift to give right away. We suggest you not prewrap the gifts just in case you forget what you wrapped or you decide to enclose a special note. If you insist on prewrapping your gifts, particularly children's birthday gifts, be sure to note the box's contents on a removable label. We suggest these small items for your secret stash:

- Bookmarks
- Note cards
- Small inspirational books
- CDs or tapes of favorite tunes from "your era"
- Pocket- or purse-sized telephone/address books
- Candles
- Sealing wax with stamp that is an image rather than an initial
- Small decorative boxes
- Handkerchiefs (men or women)
- Small picture frames
- Decorative pen for the purse

As you can see, we suspect your unexpected gift-giving needs will involve women more often than men. If you get caught without a gift for a gentleman, a bottle of wine or a subscription to a men's magazine is always appreciated. Don't give anything on a moment's notice that you wouldn't normally give as a gift if you'd thought about it for a longer time.

Chapter 19

TIPS AND GRATUITIES

Men may not get all they pay for in this world,
but they certainly pay for all they get.

Frederick Douglass

Tipping is an acknowledgment of service well done. Although you are not *required* to tip anyone, and certainly not expected to tip for poor performance, it is customary to offer a financial reward to those in service industries. This is especially appreciated by those whose base salary is intentionally low because it is expected that tips will be received. While some services, by tradition, require tipping for each time the service is performed, others are only remembered during the holiday season. Tipping and gratuities may also vary by geographic region. If you are traveling away from home, it might serve you well to inquire about the customary tipping percentage at local restaurants.

Personal Services

Hairdresser	15%–20% of total bill
Assistant who shampoos or tints your hair	$2–$3 for shampoo; $3–$5 for color
Manicurist/Pedicurist	15%
Masseuse	15%
Barber	10%–15%
Facial	15%

Stylist as owner	By tradition, an owner-stylist is not tipped because he/she receives a portion of all stylists' charges. Given today's financial climate, however, it is appropriate to tip even the owner-stylist 10%–15%.
Waxing; miscellany	15%

At Home

Hairdresser	Use your judgment. Add to the usual 15%–20% of the bill if the stylist performed extra services, went out of his/her way to accommodate you, is losing other business during the time spent with you.
Delivery person (take-out food; flowers; etc.)	$1–$2 per delivery. Consider tipping a bit more for extra service (bad weather, out of delivery range).

Away from Home

Skycap	$1–$2 per bag, possibly $5 for three if he was especially helpful
Taxi	15%–20% of total ride, 20% if driver was very helpful or courteous
Hired car	If sent from a company to squire you, no tip is expected; it is included in your monthly statement. If hired by you, whatever you desire.
Washroom attendant	$1 if attendant is on duty. $2 for extra service (sewing button, etc.)
Checked items in coatroom	$1–$2 per item
Musicians for special requests	$1–$5 depending on formality of setting

Hotels and Resorts

Bellman bringing bags	$2–$3 per bag
Housekeeper bringing iron and ironing board	$2–$3
Maid service	Up to $3 a day for single occupant Up to $5 a day for two occupants
Manicurist	20%
Masseuse	15%–20% of the bill
Messenger delivering fax or package	$2–$5
Parking valet bringing car around	$2–$5
Valet returning cleaning	$2–$3
Waiter bringing or taking away room service	$2–$3
Doorman	$1–$2 if he flags a cab or takes your packages for you
Person who brings towels, chairs, or umbrellas to you at the pool	$2–$3

Valet Parking

Public place	$1–$5 depending on how formal the location is
House party or hosted event	Even though your host has paid a flat fee for parking services, you are still expected to tip the valets unless your host has taken care of gratuities, in which case the valet should let you know and decline the tip.

Holiday Tipping

Holiday tipping is expected in many areas and is a once-a-year appreciation for some service workers and an addition to the regular tips for others.

U.S. mail carrier	It is illegal to tip a federal employee (home-baked cookies or brownies would be nice)
Gardener	One week's pay
Trash collectors	Whatever you choose, depending on your relationship with them

	and if they are city or private employees
Housekeeper	One week's pay if employed less than a year; two weeks' pay, or more, if longtime employee
Hairstylist; masseuse; waxer; manicurist/pedicurist	If you use the service once a week, it should equal the amount of a single visit.
Dry cleaner/laundry	Candy or something to share
Personal shopper	Small gift, not money
Newspaper carrier	$20
Doorman	$25–$50
Building manager or superintendent	$50–$100
Handyman/in-house fix-it person	$20–$35
Garage (rented space)	Half of one month's rent if you go in and out frequently
Maître d' at favorite restaurant	$50
Waitress who regularly waits on you	$25–$50
Elevator operator	$20–$50
Baby-sitter	$25–$50 and/or a gift
Nanny	One week's pay and one week off
Kennel operator	Food item that can be shared

Restaurants

The tip is based on the pretax total and need not include the liquor. The standard amount in most large cities is 15%–20%. Some things to consider:

- Frequently, when there are six or more diners, a flat 20% is automatically added to the bill. Usually this is mentioned on the menu. If you are making reservations, you might inquire if this is the policy. You don't want to add a tip on top of a flat rate!
- If you charge your meal, you may want to leave the tip in cash so that the waiter does not have to wait for the charge company to pay the restaurant.
- For exceptional service, you may consider tipping the captain, maître d', or chef (for exemplary food).

Do Not Tip . . .

- Employees of private clubs
- Hospital staff members
- Employees of the federal government
- Service workers (plumber, electrician, etc.) except in the case of off-hour duty for emergency or special favor

Chapter 20

EASE ON DOWN THE ROAD

The right to travel is a Constitutional right. And there's nothing in that document that says you have to be muzzled before you can pack your bag.

Paul Robeson

Travel used to be a privilege that was reserved for members of the leisure class, but no more. With the deregulation of airlines, the construction of superhighways, and our general interest in exploring new places, it's harder and harder for us to stay home. While the manner in which we travel may have changed considerably (for better or worse, people are much more casual about everything regarding travel), the courtesies that make traveling a pleasure have not. They just need to be exercised a little more often. And not just for long-distance travel, either: whether we're going crosstown by taxi or cross-country by plane, the trip is much more pleasant when we pack our manners.

Common Courtesies

Some things go without saying: If there's a line for tickets, you wait your turn. If you arrive at the airport gate late, don't expect everyone to stop what they're doing to assist you just because *you're* in a hurry. Parents who are trying to juggle a wailing baby while searching through their bags for tickets should be offered a hand. Staff members who work on trains, planes, buses, and at auto rental agencies should be addressed with the same courtesy you expect them to show you. And driving is *not* the place to work out your aggressions when you've had a bad day.

City Buses, Subways, Light-Rail Trains

If you're waiting and there's a bench, try not to take up more than your fair share of space. Don't sprawl across the bench or heap your packages around you to discourage others from sitting near you. Offer to get up if someone who is elderly, handicapped, or pregnant needs a seat. Remember to stand aside and allow exiting passengers to leave before you attempt to board.

If you're taking the bus, when you enter, greet the driver and have your fare ready. If he can't make change (many bus lines require exact change), don't berate him for following company rules. And move aside so others who *do* have change don't have to wait. Remember not to sit in the seats reserved for people with disabilities, and always offer your seat to a person who might need it more.

Keep your personal stereo personal (no earphone leakage, please!) and boom boxes turned off, so you don't intrude on the privacy of other passengers.

Taxis

Traditionally, people stand at the curb and raise their arms to signal taxi drivers they'd like to be picked up. In cities where taxis are scarce, you may need to seek out a local hotel (which will usually have a taxi stand) or call for a taxi.

Taxi Etiquette

Remember that a taxi's interior is, for all practical purposes, your driver's office. Exit with everything you brought with you, including your tissues, gum wrappers, and stray papers. If you're using a cellular telephone, remember that you are not alone, and refrain from discussing confidential or extremely personal information. And even if you've fallen madly in love on the ride uptown, keep it PG (not R!) until there's just the two of you.

When Taxis Pass You By . . .

It's an unpleasant fact of urban life, but many taxi drivers now refuse to pick up black passengers—especially men—and will often resist taking you home if you live in the inner city. Sadly, driving a taxi can be hazardous, and drivers frequently complain of being robbed and assaulted. Black men, no matter how neatly dressed or harmless, seem to be especially penalized by drivers, and are the most likely among us to be left standing for a taxi.

Be aware that the law does not allow drivers to discriminate against their passengers. There isn't much you can do about a driver who passes you by—even if he stops a half-block away to pick up another passenger who just happens not to be black—but take his license plate number and medallion number, if you can get it, and complain to the local Taxi Commission.

. . . or Refuse to Take You Where You Want to Go

If you have already been picked up and, after giving the driver your destination, he refuses to take you there ("I don't go to Harlem/the South Side/Liberty City/East St. Louis . . ."), let the driver know you will be making a formal complaint.

Many drivers would like to avoid being hauled into taxi court to explain why they refused your fare; it goes in their record, and they lose money while they're sitting in court (and the cab company notices if too many instances are brought to its attention). The sooner more of us actually follow through with making complaints, the sooner cab companies will realize such discrimination is financially undesirable as well as morally unacceptable.

Sharing a Taxi

If you're entering a taxi with a group of people and you are all going in the same general direction, you may want to share the fare. Most people, as they exit, give their share of the fare to the person who will be getting out last. (At his stop, the meter reads $2.55 and your fellow rider gives you $3.00, which you add to the total you'll owe when you reach your destination.) This is a sensible arrangement, as the person who is going farthest is usually familiar with the general cost of the ride.

If you are sharing a taxi with someone and you both are going to the same destination, the bill, plus tip, is split evenly. The tip is usually 15 percent, more if a driver has been particularly helpful (carrying your bags to the lobby door, etc.), less if he has been rude or a dangerous driver. (See chapter 19, "Tips and Gratuities.")

Car Pooling

As more and more Americans become energy-conscious, the car pool becomes more and more common. A car pool is basically a shared ride. Whether you do it daily with neighbors who all work near you or only occasionally (for sports events, meetings, or an evening out), some of the same rules apply:

Be on time, whether you're the driver or a passenger. If you have several people riding together, it's especially important to stay on schedule, because one late person can throw everyone off.

Be prepared to share the driving and expenses. Unless it's agreed for some reason that one person will always drive, car-pool members usually rotate driving. Each driver pays for gas when it's his or her turn. If there are other expenses, such as tolls or parking, they are paid by the person who drives that day or week. Or if one person always drives, everyone splits the expenses evenly.

Parking Spaces

In regular parking lots or garages, always stay between the lines so the maximum number of cars can fit into the allotted area. It's pretty annoying to swing into a space you think you've found only to discover that someone has parked well over the line and into your intended spot. One person doing it causes a domino effect for everyone coming after him. Often this is accidental, but occasionally someone does it on purpose: a thoughtless person with a new car or a very expensive one sometimes parks it catty-corner to prevent anyone else from parking nearby. Be warned that many parking garages now automatically charge double for this greedy arrogance, and they should.

Handicapped Parking

Handicapped spaces exist for a reason; if you're handicapped and have a handicapped sticker or tag, display it prominently when you park. If you aren't handicapped, don't even consider parking in a handicapped slot ("There weren't any more spaces" and "I was only going to be there for a minute" are not acceptable excuses). If you're chauffeuring someone who is physically disabled, remember that the tag must be with the person in order for you to park in this reserved space. Remember that the handicapped tag applies *only* to the person to whom it was issued, not the car in which it's hanging. If you're driving for a handicapped person, it's legitimate to use a handicapped space; it's not okay to do this if you're driving a handicapped person's car and he or she isn't in it. The fines for this violation are very steep.

One More for the Road

Don't even *think* about driving if you've had too much to drink or are so tired you're worried about falling asleep on the way home. If you're with a companion and he is willing and able to drive, give the keys to him. If not, leave the car in the lot and ask someone to call a taxi for you. You'll be safer, and so will everyone else.

Women Traveling Alone

If you're a woman traveling by herself, whether for business or pleasure, there are certain things you can do to enhance your personal safety:

- Use luggage tags that are covered, or have only your telephone number or business card on them. Strangers should not know where you live.
- Before you give your address (say, at an airline or car rental counter) check to see that no one else is within earshot.
- If you're checking into a hotel, tell the reservations clerk you'd like a room near the elevator, not at the end of the hall.
- Request a room that cannot easily be reached from the outside; stay away from first-floor rooms with sliding doors or top-floor rooms with balconies that can be reached from the roof.
- *Always* request that hotel staff identify themselves before you open the door. Use the peephole. (Staff are instructed to stand back from the door so you can see them easily.) And double-check with the front desk if anything seems off.

Traveling with Children

The biggest problem when traveling with children, especially small ones, is keeping them both comfortable and amused. Dress your child in clothes that will be easy to remove for trips to the bathroom. Bring a favorite blanket or teddy for him to curl up with while he naps. Have a "snack sack" of crackers, fruit, and other favorite nibbles, as he may become hungry before the meal is served on a plane or before you stop for a meal if you're driving.

Children in a car need "stretch time" during long rides, so plan to stop at regular intervals to potty and to allow them to get out and walk for a bit. Maybe offer to switch seats (if you're not driving and they're old enough to be out of a car seat) for part of the ride. If possible, bring some travel-sized games for children old enough to become engrossed in them.

On planes, very small children may have trouble with the change in air pressure during takeoffs and landings. If you can get them to swallow or yawn as the plane takes off or descends, a lot of the inner-ear discomfort they often suffer is significantly reduced. Offer babies a bottle during takeoff; give toddlers juice boxes or sips from a portable cup. And encourage older children to yawn frequently or chew gum to lessen the pressure on their ears. If you know or suspect your child might have problems with airsickness, ask your pediatrician to recommend something she can take to prevent nausea and vomiting.

Whether he's with you or on his own, your child should always have identification sewn or marked on the inside of his clothes when he travels. In case you become separated, include his name, telephone number, and the name of someone at his destination on a tag that's pinned to his pocket or strung around his neck and carried inside his shirt. Don't personalize a child's outer luggage with his first name (a growing trend), as a friendly child will respond with delight to an adult who seems to know him. If your child is traveling alone, check with the airline well ahead of time to see what their rules are. On domestic flights, children a certain age or older are allowed to fly only on nonstop flights and only for a certain length of time (usually flights of four hours and under).

If your child is very small and cannot walk the long distances sometimes required in airline terminals, use a courtesy phone to request a cart ride from one end of the terminal to the other. Or invest in an "umbrella"-type stroller that will allow you to roll him down long corridors, yet is narrow enough to negotiate the aisles of the plane. Most of these fit in the overhead luggage compartments.

Remember that cabin crew are *not* ad hoc baby-sitters. They will be happy to warm a bottle for you or give you an airsick bag so you can dispose of a used diaper, but they're generally too busy with their other chores to amuse your child or keep an eye out for him while you use the bathroom. Yes, it's a sad fact of life, but most parents have learned that traveling alone with a child means you don't eat much, you don't sleep at all—unless he does—and you learn to use the bathroom with one hand while you balance the li'l darlin' with your other.

Traveling Abroad

Not that long ago, travel to other countries was considered exotic, something only extremely wealthy people could afford. Very few black folks—besides the brothers who got to see the world courtesy of Uncle Sam—had the wherewithal to make the trip. Today many more Americans travel abroad every year, and our folks are no exception.

Passports and Visas

If you leave the United States for another country, you'll need to take a passport. This document identifies you and provides certain information for foreign immigration officials: it contains, among other things, your date and place of birth and a recent photograph. If you don't already have a passport, you will have to apply for one. Be sure to leave plenty of time for this, as the process can take several weeks, sometimes even months.

If you need a visa (a paper that asserts how long you plan to visit a country, and for what purpose), you will have to apply at the consulate of the country you're planning to visit. Many countries no longer require visas, but if the one you're traveling to does, you may have to write to New York or Washington, where most countries maintain staffs for processing visas. This, too, should be done as far ahead as possible. Some travelers have discovered this the hard way when they had to cancel long-planned trips because they waited until the last minute to apply for their passports and visas.

Diasporan Delusions

From a black American's perspective, it's perfectly logical to hail black- and brown-skinned folk we meet abroad as members of the same club, but be forewarned: many people of color in foreign countries don't automatically subscribe to the "one-drop" rule, and you could find yourself rebuffed. In many cultures, "black" is meant literally, and if you're a black American who does not look, literally, very dark, you could be dismissed (albeit indulgently) as being a little tetched. ("Black?" one West African friend hooted at an American visitor, "you're not black, my brother—*this* [touches own skin] is black!") And, sadly, in many cultures, "black" is still considered pejorative and might be considered a fighting word, not an inclusionary phrase.

The Ugly (African) American

You've saved and saved and you're finally setting foot on the motherland! A few words of advice:

- "Please" and "thank you" go a long, long way. If you can say it in the local language, so much the better. The effort is always appreciated.
- Don't lecture foreigners on what's wrong with their country when you're visiting it. How would *you* like it if a Nigerian said, "What's really wrong with you people is . . ."
- Do not assume everything can be bought or had for a price. Even in so-called Third World countries, not everyone will clamor to run your errands, launder your underwear, or deliver your packages just because you wave a fistful of bills at them.
- Never consciously take advantage of another person's poverty. Bartering for merchandise is one thing; exploiting the current economy ("What was he gonna do? That three dollars will probably feed his family for a week") is something you should try your best to avoid.

- Always ask permission to take photos before you actually do; while you may consider the locals picturesque, they may find your interest patronizing and offensive, or the process of photographing culturally taboo or intimidating.
- Always indicate an interest in the customs and culture of the place you're visiting. If you're perceived to be genuinely interested in and respectful of the people around you, you'll learn and be shown much more than the culturally clueless tourist could have dreamed of seeing.

The Traveler's Checklist

- ❑ Passport and/or visa
- ❑ Health card documenting all inoculations
- ❑ Copy of birth certificate. (In case your passport is lost, this speeds the replacement process.)
- ❑ Prescription medication, and an Rx in case refills are necessary
- ❑ Extra eyeglasses or contact lenses, and an Rx in case they're lost
- ❑ Camera and an adequate supply of film
- ❑ Insured traveler's checks. Keep the registration stubs in a place separate from the checks.
- ❑ Cash. You may need a few dollars for tips or taxis when you arrive home.

Air Travel

Dressing for Your Flight

As recently as thirty years ago, airplane travelers dressed for the occasion. Today almost anything goes, or seems to. But let common sense and good taste be your guide. With airplane seats getting smaller and smaller and the space *between* seats decreasing every couple of months, there's little incentive for the grand dressing that airplane travelers used to do as a matter of course. But there's a huge difference between being comfortable and, to use an old folks' phrase, "looking a mess."

Try to dress neatly. Leave your fashionably ripped jeans, cutoffs, and micro-minis for another time. Make sure you are freshly showered and aren't wearing too much perfume or aftershave: at close quarters, too little soap and too much perfume can become a real problem.

Wear clothes that are comfortable and warm, as plane cabins tend to become cool once they've reached cruising altitude. Remember that increased altitude can cause your feet to swell: if you have this tendency, be sure your shoes will stretch to accommodate any swelling that does occur. Soft shoes that can be slipped off and on are useful, and some people travel with their own pair of slippers.

Luggage: Carry or Check?

Current domestic airline regulations allow passengers to bring one bag each aboard the plane, provided this bag fits beneath the passenger's seat or in the overhead luggage compartment. If ever the old folks' expression "If it don't fit, don't force it" was appropriate, it is here. A too-large bag crammed into the overhead is not only inconsiderate to fellow travelers who have to share the space, it's dangerous. Unexpected turbulence, even a tiny bump, can pop open the overhead bins, spilling the contents on unsuspecting travelers below. Don't risk injuring yourself or anyone else: check the heavy bags, and bring with you only those things you need to keep near you during the flight.

Foreign flight has more restrictions; suitcases must be under a certain size, and a fee is always charged for extra weight or luggage.

As a safety precaution, United States airports are becoming as strict as their European counterparts. *Never* leave a bag unattended, as it may be whisked away to be scanned by the bomb squad. Be prepared to have all your carry-on bags inspected, not only by X-ray scan but by hand, too, if something appears suspicious on film. Always have your ticket handy, to prove you are a legitimate traveler, as well as a piece of photo identification (a driver's

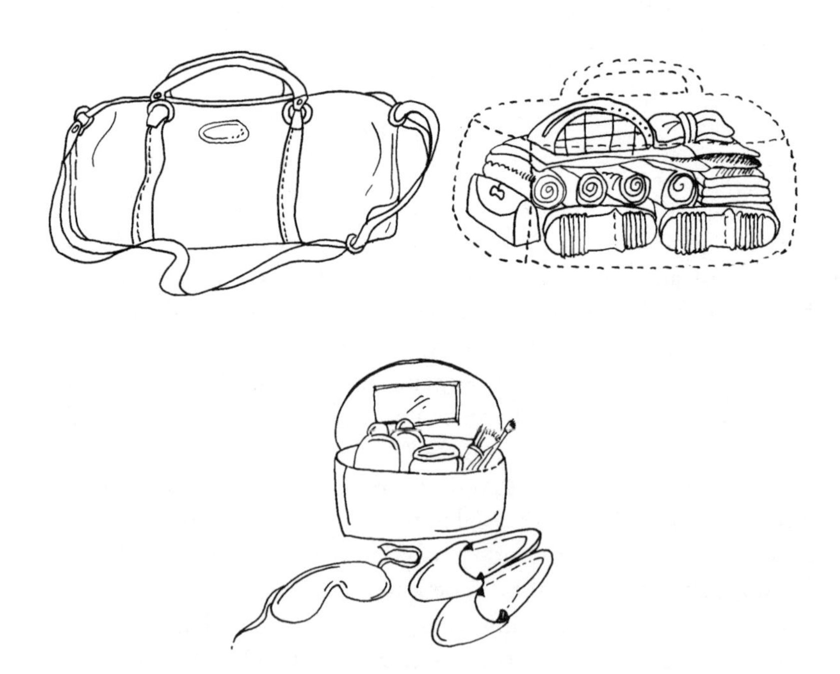

WELL-PACKED SUITCASE AND TOILETRIES CASE

license is fine) that may be used to confirm that you are, indeed, the person to whom the ticket was issued.

Curbside Checking, Assistance with Baggage

If you arrive at the airport with at least a half hour to spare, you can probably check your bags at the curb and avoid lugging them to the check-in counter in the terminal. Make sure all your bags have identification on them and look around for a skycap. Tip your skycap one to two dollars for each bag you check, more if you have a particularly unwieldy piece of luggage (a trunk, golf clubs, or a cello case, for instance).

Baggage Insurance

Be aware that the airlines' insurance for lost bags is often less than the value of the suitcase itself—let alone the cherished possessions you packed inside. If you're worried about being able to replace that designer dress, buy additional insurance before you leave. And pack any irreplaceable jewelry (your grandmother's pearl stickpin, your good watch) in a carry-on bag.

Special Needs on Airplanes

If you have special dietary needs, a call to the airline up to forty-eight hours ahead of time will usually end in some accommodation. Virtually all airlines that serve food offer no-salt, low-fat meals, children's plates, even kosher fare. When the meal service begins, a flight attendant will probably ask you to identify yourself via your seat buzzer so your special-order plate can be brought to you. (You may also bring your own box lunch; you may not bring alcoholic beverages, though.)

If you travel with a wheelchair or are otherwise disabled, or if you're traveling with very small children, you are allowed to board the airplane early, like first-class passengers, no matter where your seats are. A flight attendant will assist disabled persons to their seats, and, if you request one, a wheelchair will be waiting for you when you reach your destination. Because of airline safety regulations, if you have a physical disability, you will be seated somewhere other than next to the window seats that, in a crisis, serve as emergency exits.

Air Phones

Today most domestic and several foreign airlines offer telephone service while you're aloft. Sometimes the telephones are located in a specific area of the plane (for instance, in the back near the lavatories). In other planes, there is a phone in each row of seats, or at each seat, just above the folding tray. You will need to have a credit card or a telephone credit card to make a call. And as with cellular phones, remember that you don't want to have an intensely private telephone call or discuss anything sensitive in an environment where everyone can eavesdrop. These phones are wonderful conveniences, however, allowing you to call ahead to let the person who's meeting you know you'll be late or where you'll meet her.

Other Flight Basics

When you're boarding, find your seat quickly and take it. If you have an aisle seat, be prepared to rise and let your seatmates in and out. Don't apply or remove nail polish; besides being flammable, the fumes from polish and polish remover make many people queasy. Personal grooming should be done, quickly, in the bathroom.

If a movie is being shown during the day, try to cooperate and lower your shade if you don't need the light. If you play a personal stereo (which, to conform to FAA regulations, flight crew will ask you to turn off for takeoffs and landings), make sure it's not so loud that others are bothered by it, even though you're wearing earphones.

Remember that flight crew are not your personal servants or assistants: they have an entire cabin of passengers to look after, and their first concern is for your safety.

If you work with a laptop computer while you fly, try to turn down or disable its sound mechanism, so the little bells and chimes don't annoy your seatmates.

Train Travel

Making a Reservation

To find out if you can get to where you need to go by train, call Amtrak, at 800-USA-RAIL. Be sure to tell the reservations agent your point of departure and where you're going, as well as on what day. She will tell you what is available and give you fare information. Some cities have Amtrak offices; look in the telephone book to see if there's one near you. If not, contact your travel agent and inform her of your reservations; you may pay for your ticket through the agent.

Some train stations have completely done away with ticket agents, replacing them with a kind of self-service machine that gives you a ticket when you insert your credit card. This works if you don't need much assistance and if you're not planning to travel first-class. (First-class bookings should go through your travel agent.)

Meals on the Train

If you haven't been on a train in a long while and are anticipating the wonderful sit-down meals you remembered as a child, a word of advice: do what we all did before integration and pack a lunch. Most train meals now consist of the kind of food you can pick up in your corner convenience store: preassembled sandwiches, microwaved hot dogs and burgers, soft drinks, and chips. If you're traveling for a short time and can stand to wait, eat at your destination. If you have a longer ride ahead of you, pack enough to tide you over (a real sandwich, fruit, and cheese) until you can get a real meal.

Train Travel Abroad

Train travel in many foreign countries is much more extensive than here at home. This is partly because air travel in many places is still quite costly and also because the network of railroads from country to country, especially on continents with many nations closely packed together, is highly developed and well maintained. Some countries, like France and Japan, have trains that travel at superfast speeds.

Remember that when traveling by train outside the U.S., you may cross the borders of several countries before your journey is done. Keeping your passport close by is a must; you'll be asked to show it when you buy your tickets. It's quite possible that at points along the trip, officials from countries whose borders you're crossing will ask to see it, too. Your passport may even be taken to a central part of the train for processing, with everyone else's papers, but it will be returned to you before you exit the train.

Long-Distance Bus Travel

The options for long-distance bus travel, like train travel, have diminished greatly over the past couple of decades.

If you want to order a ticket on an interstate bus, you should call the bus company (check the Yellow Pages under "Buses, Interstate Travel") and ask if it has a route that stops near where you want to go. A company representative can quote you schedules and prices over the telephone. To pick up a ticket, you will have to travel to the bus station, or ask if tickets can be ordered through your travel agent.

Arrive in plenty of time to catch your bus. There is usually overhead space for carry-on bags, but large suitcases and parcels must be checked in the luggage compartment beneath the bus. Note where your luggage is placed so you can help the driver retrieve it when you reach your destination. Your driver will collect your ticket before you leave.

Modern buses have a small lavatory on board, but the bus may also make a few "comfort stops," especially on very long trips, to allow passengers to stretch their legs, find a quick bite at a roadside cafeteria, and use the bathroom. Be sure to return on time, or you could be left behind.

Charters

The chartered bus is still a popular way to travel for groups interested in seeing our country—or someone else's. Charters are often retained by a group of people who have something in common (membership in a church, fraternity, union, etc.) and who want to travel together, partly to enjoy each other's fellowship and partly to take advantage of the discounts groups are often offered.

If you're a charter traveler, observe the same courtesies as you would for any interstate travel: use your own allotment of space and not your neighbor's; don't hold up an entire bus while you window-shop or have a second cup of coffee. Charters often take on the aura of traveling parties, so be prepared for a livelier trip than one you'd make with a collection of total strangers.

Tour Buses

If you're new to a city and you'd like to get a comprehensive view and some of its flavor, a guided tour by bus may be just the thing. You'll get to see any major attractions, such as monuments and sites of historic interest, and a bus tour usually gives you some idea of how the city is laid out. Ask at the front desk of your hotel about available bus tours, or call the local visitor's bureau. Many cities that do large amounts of tourist business (New Orleans, for instance, Savannah, Paris, Nairobi, Hong Kong) have several different bus lines to recommend, with tours that vary from a couple of hours to a full day.

Ships and Cruises

Some people feel that a cruise is an expensive way to go nowhere fast; others wouldn't trade the experience of nonstop pampering while making new friends and eating several wonderful meals a day. Airplane travel has usurped the popularity of the vacation cruise. But perhaps because life continues to become even more hectic, more people are deciding to try the relaxed travel that cruising offers.

Unlike the earlier part of this century, when cruising was for the moneyed leisure class, today's cruises come in lengths and price ranges for everyone.

How to Book Passage

Call your travel agent, or you can contact the cruise line directly. To do this, look under "Cruise Lines" in the Yellow Pages or for cruise advertisements featuring your line in travel magazines or the travel section of your local paper.

Space on Board

Unless you're traveling on an ultra-luxury liner, chances are your closet space on board will be fairly tight. It's best to remember this when packing, since your cabin is often the only place you'll have to stow your suitcases.

What's Covered During the Trip?

One pleasant surprise about taking a cruise is you don't pay for meals, the nightlife, and sports activities separately; that's covered in the cost of your passage. In fact, you hardly ever use money during the journey. Instead, when you initially arrive on board, you establish a line of credit with the ship's banker and you sign for extras, such as drinks, massages, and any on-board shopping you might do. At the end of the trip, you're presented with a bill and can pay via credit card or cash. If a ship is a popular one, and frequently booked to occupancy, you'd do better to schedule some things—such as massages, manicures, facials, personal training sessions—before you actually take the trip or immediately after you arrive. Check with the purser as to how this should be done.

Greeting the Captain and Staff

You'll probably encounter the captain several times a day as he walks the deck, making sure things are, well, shipshape. Be sure to say hello, and if you're enjoying the trip so far, let him know. At some point during your journey, you may be asked to sit at the captain's table, which is considered a great honor. Be sure to arrive on time and thank him afterward for having extended the courtesy.

You'll find the ship's staff to be uniformly pleasant and courteous. In fact, their entire job is devoted to keeping you comfortable and happy. And if you meet a staff member who is especially kind and helpful, praise him to his boss (the maître d' should know if he has a fabulous waiter; the activities director would be thrilled to know your aerobics class was one of the best ever).

Dressing for a Cruise

On all but the most luxurious ships, dress during the day is very casual: shorts, T-shirts, and sandals are favorites if the weather is warm enough. Most large ships have at least one pool, so plan to bring a swimsuit. And a cover-up (a sarong or oversized tunic for women; a casual shirt that buttons for men) will get you into the casual bars and restaurants that are closest to the pool.

Except for dinner the final night (often referred to as the Captain's Dinner), evening dress can be fairly casual, too. Men may wear jackets without ties (although many prefer ties, especially older men) with a nice pair of trousers. Women favor sundresses (in warm climates) or loose, flowing pants with tunics. Dress for the ship's nightclubs and more formal restaurants may be more fancy; check with the social director.

Traditionally, the final dinner of the trip is when guests put on their finery. On very grand ships, guests may dress in long gown and black tie; on other ships, a suit and fancy dress are enough. (Check with your cruise director.) Photos of you and your tablemates are often taken and are presented to you before you leave.

Tips on Board

The one big surprise for many first-time ship travelers is tipping, which can come to a substantial amount. All the ship's employees will try their best to make your trip as pleasant as possible; a tip at the end of the trip is a good way to say "thank you." It *does* add up—sometimes to as much as 10 percent of the total cost of your cruise. But tips are an important addition to most employees' often modest salaries, and you don't want to be rude when they've done so well by you. To help you figure the tipping intricacies, most cruise lines will include a tipping guide in the packet of cruise-related information you'll receive with your tickets.

Group Vacations

Perhaps you like to spend part of your vacation at Martha's Vineyard among good friends you don't see often enough. Or you've learned to ski, and you're asked to share a house at Aspen for a week during the Black Ski Summit. Or you and your bid whist partners are considering traveling to Jamaica together and wonder about sharing a villa in Mo'Bay.

Sharing vacation space can be a wonderful experience, in that it often brings you closer to the real life of the town, city, or island you're visiting than staying in a hotel will. And you have more space than you normally would in a hotel room. You also get an extended visit with friends, or become even closer to people who had been casual acquaintances before.

If you've decided to do a group share, remember to sort out several things in advance:

- Will a deposit be needed (almost always the answer to this is yes) and how much? This can be half down upon making reservations and the balance a few weeks before you arrive, or the entire amount up front, to secure an especially coveted piece of real estate.
- Who will act as banker? (Usually the person who organizes the trip.)
- What happens if anyone has to drop out? Some groups search for a new

member to absorb the fee; others prefer to divide the extra among themselves. Or they may charge the member who couldn't make the trip.

- What kind of accommodations are you looking for? Some folks just want a house or apartment that doesn't have "hotel" written all over it. Others are looking for a luxury experience, seeking a house with a housekeeper and/or cook, a pool, and other amenities. Ask the trip organizer how this will be decided.

It is easier for everyone if, as a group, you can establish some simple "house rules" that everyone lives by. A couple we know who annually shares a beach house on Long Island Sound with several other couples had to establish a rule that forbade overnight visits by their friends who hadn't actually contracted to share the space. That made it easier to explain the unavailability of an extra bed to the scores of people who suddenly felt a pressing need to visit during the hottest weekends of the year. And it kept their other shares from feeling as if their hospitality had been abused.

Other good rules might revolve around safety (all skis, ski boots, and ice skates should be left outside on the deck so no one can trip over them), common courtesy (no loud noise before 7 A.M. and after 10 P.M.), and common sense (all phone messages should be left in one central spot). Don't forget to leave your rented space as pristine as it was when you arrived.

Car Rentals

If you rent a car while you're traveling, you'll need to have a major credit card and a valid driver's license. (If you're traveling abroad, you may need an international driver's license. Any good travel guide can tell you which countries require one and how and where to apply for one.)

If you're traveling without a credit card, some companies will demand a substantial cash retainer. Check with the company you want to use.

You'll also be asked whether you want to sign on for insurance, in case of an accident. If you can, check your own auto insurance policy before you rent to see whether it covers accidents in rental cars (many do). Some credit card companies also offer standard coverage for collisions if you use their card when you rent the car. If neither is the case for you, you'll probably want to spend the extra money to make sure you're covered.

About your age: you may be old enough to have a license, but many car companies won't rent to people under age twenty-five (and if they do, there may be a Younger Driver Surcharge). Check first to see what their rules are.

Car Services

You may have the need to hire a private car sometime, perhaps to take you from the airport to a distant place, or for a social occasion. Contact a car company (usually listed in the Yellow Pages under "Limousines" or "Car Services"), tell them your needs, and ask for an estimate of the fee. Private cars are usually hired by the trip (say, from the airport to midtown) or for part of a day.

When the driver comes for you, he will identify himself ("I'm Eric, from AfroLimo; I'll be your driver this evening") and hold the door for you. Greet him by name. If you want to, feel free to chat about neutral things with him. (Most drivers tell us they prefer not to be treated like inanimate objects.) If you'd rather ride in silence, just tell the driver you have some things to think over, but to interrupt you if he has a question he needs answered: "Would you like the Bayshore entrance or the Ocean Drive entrance?"

At the end of the trip, thank the driver by name and tip him discreetly (about 15 to 20 percent of the total bill is right). If your ride is being billed to your company, check first to see whether gratuities are included in the company's monthly bill. If this is the case, tipping directly is discouraged.

Letting Friends Know You're Coming

It shouldn't need to be said, but unless you're someone's dearest friend or long-lost relative, it's polite to call before you just pop up on her doorstep. (We're talking here about long-distance travel specifically; in many parts of the country, impromptu local visits are considered a pleasant surprise.) If you're going to be in a city where you have a good friend, or many good friends, a call ahead may allow everyone to clear his schedule to get together with you while you're there. And it's nice to introduce people in the same city who don't know each other, for whom you are the common denominator.

If you happen to be just passing through (as opposed to staying in) a place where you have friends, call and let them know: "Hi, Rebecca, this is Denise Watley; Mike and I are taking Josh down to Hampton. We stopped in Richmond for a moment to stretch our legs, and I just didn't want to leave without calling to say hello." Your friend may choose to just chat with you for a few moments if she's busy, or she may try to persuade you to come by and visit for a while. Let her schedule and availability be your guide.

Hotels, Motels, Bed-and-Breakfasts

Making a Reservation

Make your reservation with the reservations department of the hotel or the central reservations office of a chain. Via toll-free number, an operator will take your reservation, noting the time and date of your arrival, the length of your stay, and any preferences you might have (an extra-long king-sized bed; a crib for your baby). She will also give you a confirmation number that you may use when you arrive if the hotel has a hard time pulling you up on the computer. All this information is relayed by central computer to the appropriate hotel. If you book a few weeks ahead, the local hotel sends a confirmation of your reservation. Bring this with you when you check in, just in case there is any confusion.

Motels were initially designed to accommodate passengers traveling by automobile, and many motels are still built close to freeways for auto travelers' convenience. It's best to call ahead here, too, and make reservations. During the summer—peak time for touring by car—motels near popular cities may be booked close to occupancy, so call well ahead if you plan to be in the area.

Bed-and-breakfasts are small inns that are operated from houses, town houses, even farmhouses. These buildings have been converted to allow overnight guests the experience of staying in a residence, often one that is architecturally or historically significant, while retaining some of the services of a hotel. B-and-Bs, as they're often fondly called, usually accommodate a specific, limited number of guests, since they normally have anywhere from two bedrooms to a dozen. True to their names, these inns offer the traveler a bed, breakfast (which might range from juice, coffee, and sweet rolls to a full-blown feast), and the insights of the owner-managers, who usually live on the premises.

Note: Many B-and-Bs consider themselves a romantic retreat for couples, so if you're planning to bring a child, ask before you make your reservation, as many have policies that forbid children under a certain age.

Registering

No matter which overnight option you choose, you'll have to register once you arrive. Tell the clerk (or manager) your name and, if someone is sharing a room with you, his or her name, too. You'll be asked for a credit card so the clerk can make an imprint of it. You'll also be asked to sign a guest card. This allows the hotel to keep track of who is under its roof at any given time and also serves as a method of head-counting, should the building have to be evacuated in case of emergency. For this reason (among others), it is essential that you let the reservations clerk know exactly how many people will be staying in your room.

Once you've registered, if you're in a hotel, your bags will be taken up to your room by the bellman. He will show you how the key works (many hotels have computer-punched plastic keys now, and it takes a moment to get the hang of using one), where the amenities are (bathrobes, honor bar, etc.), and how the heating and cooling system works. He should be tipped one to two dollars per bag.

In a motel, you will be responsible for taking your own luggage to your room unless you have some physical reason for needing assistance. The clerk will show you how to reach your room via a map or diagram.

The owner of a bed-and-breakfast will usually offer to take your bags up to your room. Because he is the owner, it's not appropriate to tip him. If he has a staff member do this, though, follow the same formula suggested for tipping a hotel bellman.

Maid Service

One of the nicest things about staying in a hotel or motel is not having to make your own bed! A housekeeper usually appears once a day to do this. For her trouble, you should try to tip her a couple of dollars a day for each day of your stay. If you're staying in a small inn and you have the same housekeeper every day, you can total the tip and give her the money at the end of your stay. If you're in a large motel or a hotel, where staff are often rotated, try to tip on a daily basis to be sure the person who cleaned your room actually receives the money you intended her to have. If you'd like additional towels, more shampoo, another glass, just request them in a small note and attach it to your tip.

Room Service

If you order meals delivered to your room, most hotels and many motels now include a gratuity for room service that is fairly significant—15 to 18 percent is average. (Your room service menu will note this clearly at the bottom of the menu.) This is the *hotel's* tariff for room service, though. The waiter should still be given a small, additional tip (a couple of dollars) in cash.

When you've finished your meal, call room service and ask that the tray or cart be removed. Don't place it in the hall, where people could trip over it and where it detracts considerably from the ambiance.

Freebies and Not-bes

Hotels encourage you to depart with certain items if you want them, such as hotel stationery, matches, and the toiletries supplied during your stay. Several other things that sometimes disappear, however, are *not* gratis: ashtrays, hotel china or silverware, bathrobes. Depart with these and they'll show up on your bill, as hotels have decided that replacement of these items adds substantially to their costs—which, ultimately, are passed on to you.

If you'd like an ashtray as a memento of your visit, or if you especially admire a hotel's fluffy complimentary robe, ask the front desk if they're for sale. They usually are.

A Word About Safety

In any strange environment, especially if you travel alone, it's essential that you make sure your doors lock properly and your windows are secure. It's equally critical for you to familiarize yourself with the layout of the hotel in general and your room in particular: Where are the hotel's emergency exits and staircases? Where is your room in relation to them? Where is your bed in relation to the door? Can the windows in your room be used as emergency exits? What kind of instructions are listed in case of fire? (These last are usually fixed to the door of the room.) Many hotel rooms have fireproof doors, and the instructions will ask that you keep them shut during a fire, as you may be safer inside than out in the hall. Be sure to read these instructions thoroughly, so if something happens you can keep a cool head.

Chapter 21

IT'S JUST NEIGHBORLY

The bedrock of individual success in life is securing the friendship, the confidence, the respect of your next-door neighbor in your little community in which you live.

Booker T. Washington

Our sense of community probably originated on slave ships, Southern plantations, and less-than-welcoming Northern cities where looking out for and relying on our neighbor could mean the difference between life and death. Integration may mean our neighborhoods are more diverse, but the principles of neighborliness are as important today as they ever were.

Welcoming New Neighbors

Whether you've moved across the city or across the country, it's a lonely feeling to be in unfamiliar surroundings. Your new neighbor may be single or part of a large family, but either way a friendly hello will be welcome. Introduce yourself, offer to answer questions about where the closest grocery store or pharmacy is, the best dry cleaner, the least expensive videos, and the restaurants that deliver. Whatever the inquiry, let your new neighbors know that you're available to help them through those first steps of getting to know the neighborhood. If you attend church regularly, you might ask if your new neighbors would like to attend with you.

"Welcome baskets" are always appreciated. These may range from a casserole, to a magazine about the city if they've just arrived, to information about the local homeowners' association.

Looking Out for Each Other

Neighbors look out for one another. Be aware of your surroundings and share unusual happenings with others in your neighborhood. Alert neighbors to unfamiliar faces lurking near their home. A potential burglary was thwarted when an observant neighbor noticed two gentlemen knocking on the door of a home where they knew the occupants to be at work. When the neighbor inquired as to whether she could be of assistance, one of the men remarked he was there to visit his grandfather and asked the neighbor if she knew when someone might be home. The neighbor, knowing no such person lived in the home, quickly called the police and attempted to locate her neighbor at work.

Good news should travel just as fast as bad news. Sharing the news of a great sale at the local drugstore will also be remembered, as will a reminder about community meetings or other neighborhood events.

When You're the New Kid on the Block

Introduce yourself and your family to your new neighbors. Ask questions, inquire about the block club or local association, and get involved in local activities. You may want to host an open house once you're settled so you can meet many of your neighbors at the same time.

Senior Citizens

Senior citizens are treasures to be respected. Widows and widowers who don't live near their families often find themselves alone most of the time. Not ones to complain or ask for favors, you should take special care to be aware of elderly neighbors and their needs. Set up a system that will allow you to know if the neighbor has not been heard from for more than a day. Notify authorities if you don't see or hear from her. The offer to run errands or tend plants will be greatly appreciated. Perhaps you can take items to the post office, pick up stamps or medicine, tend the outdoor flowers, or give a ride to church.

Remember the Days When Everyone Knew Your Mom?

There was a time (when we were little) when children playing outside could do something against the "rules" and your mother would know about it before you could run home. At home mothers and grandmothers looked out for all the children in the neighborhood. They knew them by name and who their parents were. A mother down the street was just as quick to reprimand her neighbor's child as she was to scold her own. While those days seem to have disappeared with latchkey kids and high-rise buildings, you can still look out for our youth. Monitor children playing near your home. Be alert to screams for help, cries of pain, and the child who may be lost and afraid. While some parents may view your concern as interference, it's best to err on the side of the child's welfare if he or she appears to be in danger. There's a difference between invading someone's privacy and being a part of the "village" that's helping to raise the children.

Block Clubs and Crime Watch

Join your neighborhood block club or association; it's the modern way to stay in touch with your neighbors and neighborhood activities and concerns.

Keep your eyes and ears open. Develop a neighborhood watch program. If the watch has been established, offer to participate. Be aware of your surroundings and notify authorities of suspicious adults lurking on your streets or in abandoned cars. Work with your neighborhood association or block club to free your walls of graffiti. See "Be a Good Neighbor" in chapter 38, "Thinking Twice: Life After 9/11."

Pets

There are some simple dos and don'ts that will enable you to enjoy your pet(s):

- Obey the local leash laws.
- When neighbors have young children, notify the parents of any pets in your home or yard.
- Curb your pet and if you exercise your pet outside your yard, clean up any mess it leaves behind.
- Have your pet spayed or neutered if there is a possibility it can roam the neighborhood or receive unwanted "visitors."
- Keep shots up to date (especially for rabies) and the records of them available.
- Remove a pet from guests if they are allergic to or frightened of animals.
- *Don't* allow your pet to make excessive noise.
- *Don't* let your pet wander into neighbors' yards or flower beds.
- *Don't* allow your pet, no matter how friendly, to jump on your friends or neighbors.
- *Don't* unleash your pet in a public place, such as a sidewalk or park.

Being a Good "Apartment" Neighbor

- Obey all rules of the apartment building.
- *Don't* play loud music or have noisy parties after 10 P.M. If a number of elderly people live near you, loud music may not be acceptable at all.
- *Don't* hammer or perform household chores that make noise during evening hours.
- Be mindful of thin walls.
- *Don't* buzz in strangers.
- *Do* accept UPS and other deliveries for neighbors who are not home if the delivery requires a signature.
- Be considerate of others with your pets.
- If you know your neighbor is away and you notice people entering his or her apartment, watch their activities. If you feel uncomfortable, notify the police. It's better to be embarrassed than to have your neighbor come home to a burglarized apartment.

Alerting Neighbors to a Large Party

If you're going to host a large party, notify your neighbors if it will impact their lives. Frequently street parking becomes a premium, the noise becomes unbearable, and the party lasts longer than anyone can remember in that neighborhood in over a decade. If it's a large party where a number of people won't know anyone, you might consider inviting your neighbors on either side of you. A simple invitation could ease their anxiety and make for a pleasant evening for all.

Parking Considerations When Entertaining

If parking is limited in your neighborhood and guests will have to walk quite a distance from their cars to your party, you should consider hiring a valet parking service. Make sure the valets (or your guests) continue to follow the local rules. Do not park in, or block, anyone's driveway. Do not park illegally or on anyone's lawn.

Notifying Neighbors of Construction or Renovation

It's only considerate to let your neighbors know if you are planning major construction or renovation on your home or apartment. Neighbors are much more understanding (and less ready to call the city building inspectors or landlords) if they know the nature and likely duration of the disruption.

Times of Disaster

Nothing turns people who happen to live near each other into bona fide neighbors more quickly than a common disaster or tragedy. An earthquake, hurricane, blizzard, or civil revolt will almost surely draw people together to protect their common interests. Be a good neighbor to your neighbors when disasters—natural or man-made—wreak havoc with everyone's lives.

- Keep a household emergency kit current with enough food, water, and warm clothing for your family so that you don't strain others' resources.
- Try to put by a little extra for that person who assumes such things will never happen to him, and offer to share what you can afford to share.
- If your neighbor's house is damaged or in danger of being broken into and he's not there to protect it, keep an eye on his home until he can return to do this for himself.
- Cooperate with the police and fire departments, who have been trained to handle these emergencies; vacate the premises when they demand that you do; and assist others, such as the elderly, who may be slow to leave.
- If the authorities allow you to help others by driving groups of neighbors away from danger, or ferrying them to higher ground in your boat, do so.
- Keep a cool head, and don't be the genesis of rumors that can make a tense situation even more fraught with anxiety.

During Seasonal Disasters, Such as Heat Waves, Floods, and Ice Storms

- Check on senior citizens, who are often vulnerable to extreme heat.
- Offer to shovel walkways for people too old or physically disabled to do this themselves. Share what you can (extra shovels, salt, sand, fans, etc.) with neighbors who may be in need.
- If you're a local businessperson (or a private citizen with extras), don't take advantage of the adversity by charging outrageous amounts for common household items (batteries, bottled water, disposable diapers, etc.) that are desperately needed.

Important Events in a Neighbor's Life

Even if you're not best friends and have only a distantly pleasant nodding relationship with your neighbor, you'll doubtless be aware when a new baby is born in the household or when she or a family member is seriously ill or dies. Small tokens of celebration or condolence (balloons to herald the new arrival, or a small baby gift; flowers or a plant or a gift of food for the bereaved family) are always appropriate and greatly appreciated.

Checking on the Elders

You've grown accustomed to seeing Miss Edna sweep her walk each morning when you take your children to school, but lately you've missed exchanging waves with her. Don't just assume she's off visiting her daughter's family; take a moment to knock on her door or leave her a note asking her to call. If you don't hear from her within a reasonable amount of time (you left a note at 8 A.M. and she hasn't called by dinnertime), call the police and explain your worry; they have developed procedures for making sure seniors are all right. Although it might make you uncomfortable to presume upon a neighbor's privacy like this, think how much worse it would be if she were injured or ill and unable to go to the door or reach the telephone to summon help. Your intervention could make the difference between life and death.

In nonemergency situations, try to keep a regular check on your neighborhood elders. If you can share a plate of dinner or drop off extra staples (such as toilet tissue, soap, soft drinks) that can put a dent in fixed-income budgets, do so. Little things you or your children can do—such as bringing the paper from the walk to the front porch, putting out the trash cans, or offering to go to the pharmacy for prescriptions—mean a lot.

Chapter 22

CLUBS AND ORGANIZATIONS

Organize as a group . . . those who realized the strength of their cultural group, their political demands were considered and determined by the force of their cultural grouping.

Claude McKay

Clubs and organizations have for over a hundred years played a large part in the social and cultural development of our community. From the earliest days of residence in this country, blacks have united in solidarity against the challenges of everyday existence, and sought solace and relaxation in the comfort of being with "their own." Clubs and organizations have filled a void for those separated from family and friends, have succeeded in offering an organizing base for combatting racism, and have brought laughter in the face of adversity. Black social clubs often stemmed from African Americans' exclusion from other established groups. Once driven by necessity, black clubs and organizations today remain the core of the social and cultural life within our community.

Acceptance into clubs that once spurned us has opened up membership opportunities that we eagerly—and rightly—take advantage of. We network, we enjoy sharing similar hobbies, we raise much-needed funds for social and political programs. The definition of "club" is as varied as the types of clubs themselves. A club can be a small group of parents who trade baby-sitting services, a national women's organization dedicated to furthering educational opportunities for young people, a group of professionals who share similar career interests, or just about any assemblage of people wanting to be together. Health clubs, tennis clubs, and golf clubs often refer to the facility housing the club as well as to the membership itself. "Sorry I can't join you for dinner, I'm going to my club to work out." Private clubs, once the exclusive domain of white males, have reluctantly opened their doors to minorities, and, in some instances, women. These clubs are frequently buildings that have eating, entertaining, exercise, and housing facilities for the private use of their members and guests of the members.

Frequently we join clubs because our mothers or grandmothers have been members and it is not only an honor to be asked but a family tradition. Often we join clubs to further our knowledge in an area we find fascinating but know little about. Friends are made among those who may be on a similar quest. From quilting bees to the age-old civil rights organizations that continue to address the challenges that face all of us—there's a club for everyone. In the end, it's the coming together with people "just like us" that brings us both comfort and joy.

The qualifications for membership in each of these clubs and organizations vary greatly. For simplicity's sake, think of basically two types of organizations. One type requires that you be nominated for membership; the other, that you simply sign up and pay dues.

Why Join a Club?

There are clubs for every interest, and sometimes it's the best way to meet new friends when you've settled in a neighborhood or city different from the one where you grew up. If you choose to assume a leadership role, you will gain valuable experience. If you work on the annual benefit, you will hone your organizational skills. In clubs you can find mentors, and you can have the satisfaction of being a mentor to a younger member. Club membership is not for everyone, but if you think you'll enjoy it, don't be put off by the rules for joining and what is expected of you. The experience can prove invaluable.

Joining a Club

1. Public clubs (YMCA, Red Cross, neighborhood association, NAACP, etc.): request an application, complete the application, pay the required fee, and—you're in!
2. Private "social clubs" often require that a new member be sponsored by a current member in good standing.

- If you have a close friend who is a member of your chosen club and you feel comfortable enough to ask that she sponsor you, do so: "I love the

Uptown Tennis Club and would love to join—would you be willing to sponsor me?"

- If you don't know anyone well enough to ask her to sponsor you, but would still like to join, you might consider inviting a current member to lunch and ask if the club is accepting new members. This will give the member a chance to say, "Oh, would you like to be a member? I'd love to sponsor you when new members are considered in October." If the member does not offer to sponsor you, do not ask why. You never know the politics of an organization or what is going on in the member's life at the time—accept her silence. You *may* ask if she thinks it appropriate for you to seek membership at this time.
- Don't ask more than one person to be your sponsor. If both say yes, it could prove embarrassing.
- Some clubs frown on those who seek membership—take the hint and wait it out. Hopefully your *subtle* enthusiasm will alert a member to your wishes and you will be considered.
- Sponsors are often asked to submit a written statement offering your name for membership consideration. Club rules may also require that they solicit "support" letters to second the nomination. Be cooperative.
- Some clubs require that a proposed member's name be submitted without the person's knowledge. This lessens the possibility of hurt feelings when membership is denied.
- You may be asked to interview with the club's admissions committee.
- You will be informed of the club's decision either in person, by telephone, or by an official letter.

Proposing a New Member

If you are active in a social or fraternal organization, or a private club, you will probably be asked to sponsor a new member at some point. Some basic guidelines to follow:

- If you're asked by a friend to sponsor her for membership in your club and don't feel comfortable doing it, be kind. Give her a reason for declining the request: "Bertha, I'm sorry but I don't think I'm your best choice of a sponsor. [Pick one: 1] I'm already sponsoring another candidate; [2] I'm too new a member—I think you'd have better chances of being accepted if a long-standing member proposed you; [3] We're not taking new members at this time, but I'd be happy to let you know when membership will open up; [4] I don't want to commit to sponsoring you now because I'm not sure I'll be able to devote the time later; [5] The politics of the group are such that your chances of being accepted are almost nil if you aren't sponsored by an officer or a founder of the club."

- If you are anxious to sponsor a new member: (1) don't forget to follow your club's rule regarding submission of names for membership; (2) don't push too hard—current members may not react favorably to undue pressure; (3) don't take the potential member to your private club or club events too frequently. Current members may suspect they are being forced to accept this person.

Being Blackballed

Blackballing a potential member of a club (to which members are voted in) is the act of denying the person membership. Membership voting is often held in secret, and members need not divulge publicly how they voted. Years ago, members dropped a small ball into a locked box signifying their favor (white ball) or disfavor (black ball). Following the vote, the box was opened and one by one the balls were removed. There was a collective sigh of relief by supporters of the potential member for every white ball that appeared. All it took was one black ball to be denied membership—hence the term, blackballed. If you are blackballed by a club, do not attempt to ascertain the reason. Never try to guess which members voted against you, and never ask current members why you have been kept out. You cannot buy friendship or votes. Continue to treat all those you associate with in an appropriate and polite manner. If you still want to join the club, wait a few years before making your wishes known. Circumstances may change, and your membership may be welcome.

Taking a Leave/Resigning from a Club

If you've decided to request a leave of absence or would like to resign from an organization, it is necessary for you to submit a letter stating your desires (see chapter 11, "Write On"). If you want to resign because it's too expensive, you must do so well in advance of the next assessment. Your request for a leave or resignation may not be granted if you have unpaid dues or assessments. If you are expelled from a club, you cannot ask for reinstatement at a later date. Some clubs forbid you from ever being an active member again once you've been expelled. Exceptions to this rule require you to justify an unfair expulsion.

Dues and Fees

It's best to research club fees before you ask someone to sponsor you for membership—you don't want to embarrass yourself or others when you learn that the dues and assessments are way out of your price range. Fees for private, "by invitation only" clubs usually involve initiation fees, annual dues, and any club-approved assessments for the current year.

Annual dues for civic organizations, health organizations, and special-interest clubs are usually collected at the same time each year, and often coincide with a membership drive for new members. Membership dues may be structured at more than one price and offer you access to services and activities on a sliding scale. The "golden membership" in the local historical society may cost fifty dollars and include invitations to all tours conducted by the organization, as well as the monthly newsletter. A "bronze membership" in the same organization may cost twenty dollars and include all the rights and privileges of the "golden membership" except the monthly newsletter.

Family memberships in sports facilities or special-interest groups are often available at a special rate. Students currently attending school and senior citizens generally benefit from discount membership rates in public clubs.

Loyalty and Confidentiality

Most organizations expect loyalty from their members. This loyalty takes the form of confidentiality, participation in fund-raising activities, and the perpetuation of the group through recruiting new members. Confidentiality includes not sharing the personal business of other members, and not giving out membership mailing lists.

Leadership

Clubs and organizations offer many members an opportunity to participate in the leadership process. Large national organizations are not the only outlets for learning about leadership, for honing your leadership skills, and for participating in the politics of your organization. Small social groups, quilting clubs, political forums, and a host of community organizations also offer a training ground for learning leadership skills. You may have your sights set on a congressional seat twenty years down the line, or you may simply take pride in organizing the bake sales for your neighborhood organization—whatever the reason, enjoy participating. If you belong to a club that uses parliamentary procedure when conducting meetings, purchase a book and learn the basics. As a member of a club, you have a right—and a responsibility—to participate in the organization by voting when elections are held for new members or regarding club business. You should willingly take an active role as a member of a committee (of your choice) and you should be supportive of the current leadership of the organization. If you seek an office within the organization, remember:

- Learn the duties and responsibilities of the office prior to deciding to seek the position.
- Do not show your disapproval for a current officeholder by plotting to sabotage her efforts—rather, work for a positive outcome.
- Seek the advice and counsel of former officeholders, share your knowledge with those who will follow behind you in office, and keep accurate records.

Fund-Raising

Every organization depends on fund-raising to achieve its goals. These efforts to raise money may require you to purchase or sell tickets, to entertain in your home, or to sell advertisements. In some groups, no outside fund-raising is allowed, and the members assess themselves to bankroll their activities. Ask what your financial responsibilities will be prior to accepting membership in a club or organization.

Starting Your Own Club

You may want to start a club yourself. Keep these ideas in mind:

- If you are seeking to start a local chapter of a national organization, follow the rules and regulations of the national group. Your new group may require sponsorship by an established chapter.
- What kind of club do you want to start? What do you hope to accomplish?
- Is there an established group that shares the same goals?
- Select a well-rounded, manageable group of people to be the charter group.
- Think about the number of members, frequency of meetings, and meeting location.
- Will the group be service-oriented? Or will its appeal be more social?
- Will there be open membership?

- Will there be dues?
- Will the group be coed?

Coalescing with Other Groups

As a people, we have many resources from which we can draw strength and show community solidarity. Whatever the purpose of your club, consider coalescing with other groups when you are in need of "power in numbers" or of sheer womanpower to achieve a goal.

Conventions

Many organizations hold regional or national conventions each year. As a member, you may be expected to attend these meetings from time to time. A combination of business meetings, parties, and fellowship, conventions can be the experience of a lifetime. Most organizations vary the location of their conventions each year (or as often as they are held), which enables members to experience many different communities and the social and cultural experiences that each city has to offer. When attending a convention for a social or fraternal organization, be as mindful of your manners as you would be at a professional or business convention. Some thoughts to keep in mind:

- Register on time, send the required fees, and make the needed reservations for travel and housing. Inquire through the organization if discounts will be offered through individual travel agencies, airlines, or hotels.
- Remember you are representing yourself, your organization, and your community when attending a convention. Your behavior at hotels, eating establishments in the convention city, and public events may well influence a city's desire to welcome your or a similar organization again.
- Do attend some of the business meetings of the organization, even if you are not required to do so. You will learn more about the workings of the national organization (or your local group). This information may be critical to you if you hope to serve in a leadership position within the organization.
- Take advantage of the opportunity to meet new people, visit local cultural sites, and explore a new environment.
- Keep in touch with friends and acquaintances you meet at the convention. Share knowledge, experiences, and resources.

Women's Organizations

Women's service organizations include sororities, clubs whose members' spouses are in the same profession, multigenerational groups such as Links, Inc., and Jack and Jill. There are a host of clubs that span the country but are little known outside their own communities. These organizations blend fun, sisterhood, networking, and community service.

Men's Organizations

Men's organizations vary almost as much as women's. Fraternities, Masons, professional organizations, alumni and military organizations, and special-interest or hobby groups all play a significant role in our community—just as the women's and open-membership groups do.

Sororities and Fraternities

African Americans have participated in the Greek organizational structure since the early part of the twentieth century. Traditionally, one joins a fraternity or sorority during his or her college years. In addition, many organizations offer membership to graduates and graduate students. Membership is by invitation only, and upon joining you commit yourself to a lifetime of friendship and camaraderie. Dedicated to community service and a devotion to common goals, members of Greek organizations have contributed greatly to the strength and success of the African American community. Sororities and fraternities instill in their members a sense of heritage, fierce determination, a striving for excellence in all that they undertake, unabashed pride in success, and a commitment to the organization as a means of critical problem-solving within the greater community. While many individuals and organizations across the country possess the same qualities, the sisterhood and brotherhood offered by these unique organizations have, over the years, nurtured our young as they enter adulthood, and given them an extended family from which to gain strength through their lives.

Women's sororities include Alpha Kappa Alpha, Delta Sigma Theta, Sigma Gamma Rho, and Zeta Phi Beta. Men's fraternities include Alpha Phi Alpha, Kappa Alpha Psi, Omega Psi Phi, and Phi Beta Sigma.

Some of the things you should know about life in sororities and fraternities include:

- Rites of passage into the groups are often secretive and have been known to involve hazing.

- A neophyte group being presented for membership is "the line," and upon acceptance is often presented to the general college community through public activities, including "step" shows.
- Pride in membership has resulted in widely held rivalries between groups.
- Each organization is identified by colors, emblems, and Greek names.
- Each local chapter is chartered by the organization's national body and is governed by national rules as well as local chapter rules and regulations.
- Chapters are usually connected with a local university, and in some instances housing associated with the individual organizations is available on campus.
- Alumni chapters are active in communities across the country, and continue the commitment to service locally as well as nationally. Many students have benefited from scholarships instituted by Greek organizations.
- Alumni often act as mentors to younger members who are attending school away from home, entering the workplace, or seeking to enhance their careers.
- Each organization holds local and national conclaves on a regular basis.

Initiation Process

If you are interested in joining a sorority or fraternity, either as a college undergraduate or as a graduate, contact your local chapter or a friend who is a member to get the necessary information for joining. Since membership is by invitation, it is best to learn as much as possible about the organization before letting your wishes to join be known. Secrecy within the group and about the initiation process is a hallmark of Greek organizations.

Hazing

Hazing has become almost synonymous with the pledging process. Although rarely dangerous, sorority pledges are expected to exert a great deal of time and energy in their attempt to be accepted. Be mindful of potential dangers, or of members going too far in their zeal to haze pledges.

City-Owned and Public Clubs

Residency and membership fees are usually the only requirement for joining. But even city-owned and public clubs have certain rules and regulations. After you join, make sure you, your family, and guests are familiar with and follow the guidelines.

Private Clubs

They let us in these days, but chances are you'll still be one of the few minorities in sight. Keep this in mind when selecting, and using, private clubs.

Behavior at a Club

Once you've joined a club, uphold the rules and regulations. If guests are allowed, invite friends who share similar interests, would enjoy the experience, and are compatible with the general membership. Don't take the same guest to the club all the time. Make sure your guests are aware of the club rules. It is always best to accompany each of your guests to the club, but if for some reason you are unable to, call ahead to let the appropriate club personnel know that you will have a guest arriving. Be sure all guests have the necessary passes so as to avoid confrontation.

If You're a Guest

Respect and protect the reputation of the friend who invited you. If you are unsure about the appropriate clothing (for the dining room, tennis court, golf course, or pool area), be sure to ask the member who invited you. Private clubs vary in dress codes and customs. Better to ask than to be totally mortified when they won't let you on the golf course because of your collarless T-shirt. This is not a scavenger hunt—don't peek into rooms or areas you haven't been invited into. Don't criticize the club while you're enjoying its facilities.

Health Clubs and Gyms

Physical fitness has increasingly become a more integral part of our everyday lives. Time and science have shown us that the quality of our lives can be greatly enhanced by regular physical exercise. Every time we turn around there's a new report on the latest diet or fitness craze. Many of us have found that membership in health clubs and gyms is the ultimate ticket to stress reduction and renewed energy. Take advantage of the services, but do not abuse your rights as a member or as an occasional visitor.

Some tips to remember:

- Learn and respect the club rules.
- Respect time limits on exercise equipment. If no one is waiting to use a

specific machine, you are probably welcome to use it to your heart's content. If others are waiting, keep track of your time, be courteous, and relinquish the machine within a reasonable amount of time.

- Leave the equipment clean and in the proper position for the next user. Do not leave towels lying around on equipment or on the floor.
- If you aren't familiar with how to use a piece of equipment, ask.
- When using a sauna, dress for your own comfort. Just because everyone else has decided to bare all doesn't mean you have to.
- When sharing dressing spaces and showers, leave the areas clean and neat.
- Do not stare at others.
- Secure your valuables.
- When participating in an exercise class, be mindful of others. Do not come in late and position yourself in the front row so that you can see yourself in the mirror—others arrived on time to get a good position.
- Cell phones and camera phones should be kept in your locker; don't take them onto the gym floor. No camera phones in the locker rooms! Many clubs have rules against this; violate them, and you may find your membership revoked.

Chapter 23

PLANTATION LIFE

We have been worked,
now let us learn to work.

Booker T. Washington

From the moment we dip our toes into the pool of the American workplace, most of us will spend the bulk of our waking hours at work. Work is where we'll make friends, forge alliances, master skills, and confront challenges. It's a large part of defining who we are, to the rest of the world and to us. And workplaces vary almost as much as people do. Some are very formal, with a clearly outlined hierarchy; you may never get to see your boss up close except at the annual office holiday party. Others are much more casual; the company president may walk the halls and drop in for impromptu chats, and expect everyone to address everyone else on a first-name basis.

No matter what you do or what kind of company you work in, though, some things remain basic: the employee who is cheerful, courteous, and considerate of his colleagues is always valued. If you can make criticisms that are constructive—or better yet, offer a solution to a vexing problem—so much the better. And anyone who helps to pitch in to help meet a deadline instead of turning away with "it's not my job" will stay on the company's most-wanted list. Whether you own your own business or owe your soul to the company store, reliability, trustworthiness, discretion, and timeliness are indispensable parts of your business arsenal.

Your Résumé

A résumé is a concise summary of your professional accomplishments; it also lists your levels of education, outside interests (especially as they may pertain to your career), and a way to reach you by mail and telephone. When putting your résumé together, here are a few things you should remember:

- Keep it brief. Most human-resources staff members, who will be the first people who see your résumé, warn that two pages (one double-sided page) is about maximum. Remember, *you* may be writing only one résumé, but employers receive dozens—and big companies, hundreds—each week.
- Keep it easy to read. Three pages of regular-sized type are infinitely preferable to two pages of tiny type that the personnel department will strain to read. Type your résumé on white or off-white paper—don't try to call attention to yourself with neon paper, paper with a fussy decorated border, or cutesy sayings.
- Don't exaggerate. Remember that most personnel offices do a thorough check of an applicant's credentials if the point is reached when you're considered a serious candidate for the job.
- Offer references separately, after you're asked for them. Always call people you'd like to use as references and get their approval *before* you list their names on your reference sheet. Most people will be happy to comply—but if they aren't, you need to know that ahead of time, so you don't include them on your list.

The Job Interview

Once your résumé has sparked some interest, you may be asked to come in for an interview. In that case, you should remember to:

- Review whatever information you've been able to gather on the company before you visit. Ask for an annual report. Or use the public library to look up the company in back issues of your local newspaper. You can request information from the local chamber of commerce, too.
- Dress neatly and in accordance with the company's culture. When in doubt, be more conservative. (For more information, see chapter 14, "Glad Rags.") Carry your papers and notebook in a briefcase, portfolio, or tote bag made of leather or a good fabric. If you can't afford to buy one, borrow one from a friend—and remember to return it promptly and in good condition.

- Arrive at least five minutes early. Better they know you're on time than to have them wait for you.
- Extend your hand for a firm shake when you meet your interviewer, maintain eye contact, and thank the person who is interviewing you for seeing you. Sit down *only* after he or she asks you to.

Discussing the Job

Be prepared to discuss your strengths and what advantages you could offer the company. Since you know that "Tell me a bit about yourself" will be asked of you at some point during the interview, give it some thought ahead of time. Be direct about why you'd be an asset to the company: "I have fifteen years of marketing experience, and I know what mothers are looking for when they shop for toddler shoes."

Ask questions about what the job entails, and where it stands in the company's organizational chart: To whom do you report? What things are unspoken requirements that are nonetheless expected to be part of the job? (Do you have to get coffee for your boss? Take a turn at organizing the office Christmas party?) Be frank about any areas that concern you: "I don't mind overtime, but if I can have advance notice, when possible, it would be helpful."

Be aware that questions about your age, marital status, and number of children are all illegal—but it won't stop people from asking. Assess for yourself whether such questions are a big deal or not, and answer accordingly. You may choose to be direct: "I'm forty-three." Or more indirect: "I'm about the same age as most people who graduated from college in 1974." You may not mind that your prospective employer knows you're a mother: "I have a twelve-year-old and a fourteen-year-old." Or you may decide not to share that information: "Can you clear something up for me? I'm confused as to why whether I have children is important in this job." Most employers are fully aware that asking such questions is illegal, but they also know that many times, potential employees either don't care or are too timid to protest. Letting them know—nicely—that you're aware of the law often stops that line of questioning.

Never, ever bad-mouth your current (or former) employer. Even if yours was the job from hell, you can pull together a few neutral phrases that don't make you sound like a back-stabber: "I just think I've gone as far as there's room for me to at Graves Tours." If you hated your former boss, your potential employer shouldn't be able to figure it out by your words or behavior. Most employers are justifiably wary of potential employees who speak ill of their current employers.

Follow up the interview with a note, thanking the person who interviewed you for his time, and repeating your interest in the job:

Dear Mr. Leeds,
Thanks for taking the time to meet with me yesterday; it was good to find out more about Samset and its clients. I hope if my qualifications and your needs mesh, I can look forward to becoming part of the Samset team one day. Thanks again, and please don't hesitate to call if you have additional questions.

Sincerely,

Keesha Wells

We can't emphasize enough how impressed people are when you perform this simple courtesy.

Business Cards

See chapter 11, "Write On."

Service with Some Style

If you work in a service industry, you know that to the clients on the other side of the desk or counter, your face is the company's face, so it's vitally important to be as pleasant, courteous, and helpful as possible. You'd be surprised the number of satisfied customers who actually take the time to send a company a note of praise when they have had a particularly good experience with an employee. And you'd be shocked at the increasing number of angry customers who pick up the phone to try and make heads roll when they feel they've been disrespected, abused, or slighted by "the help." Try to:

- Address the customer by name, if you know it: "Yes, Mrs. Williams. We show you in a double room for two nights at $95 a night." Or "Thanks for shopping at Bristol's, Ms. Gordon. Don't forget your card."
- Ask if you can help with anything else: "May I bring you anything else from the bar?"
- Offer to go over the bill if the client doesn't understand. Make corrections promptly, if necessary: "Mr. Blake, here's the problem. We charged you twice for liability insurance. My apologies. I'll take that off the rental total right now."
- Offer to get your supervisor if the dispute can't be resolved, or if you feel you're being abused by a customer: "Miss Perkins, that flight to

Cincinnati was canceled because of weather. I can't do anything but put you on the next available flight out. If you like, I can get my supervisor, Ms. Givens. She might be able to work something out that will make you happier."

Remember, the customer isn't *always* right, but she's usually given the benefit of the doubt, especially in businesses that rely on repeat customers.

Casual Days

Many offices now have days when, as a treat, employees are encouraged to "dress down." Sometimes this is extended to other times, too: offices that have little or no air-conditioning might allow staff to dress casually in warm-weather months. Or on the day preceding a long weekend, the "casual clause" might be invoked.

Check with your colleagues or the office manager to see what "casual" means in your particular case. Some offices are more aggressively casual than others. And some areas of the country are less formal than others. Casual in Phoenix might have a different meaning than it does in Boston, St. Louis, Atlanta, or Miami.

When Life Interrupts Work

So much of our lives is spent at work that our private and working selves eventually collide: A child or parent becomes ill. A pipe bursts in your apartment, and the superintendent asks you to come home while it's being fixed. The telephone company wants to install a phone, or the sofa you've ordered is ready to be delivered sometime between nine and five and only on weekdays, of course.

If you can arrange doctor's appointments, deliveries, and other personal matters to coincide with your days off, wonderful. If you're like most of the rest of us, you make some adjustments. If you can, try to:

- Notify the office ahead of time that you'll need to be home to receive a delivery or admit a service person.
- If there's illness in the family and you know you can't come in, call as soon as possible. If you can, let your office know how long you might be out.
- Try to keep personal calls short and infrequent. Even when it's a slow day, some offices take a dim view of employees who socialize on company time.
- A lunch hour is usually just that—an hour. In some places it's less. An

employee who arrives and departs by the clock but who takes a leisurely lunch each day (unless business luncheons are part of your normal job responsibilities) will eventually be asked to account more closely for his time.

Business Meetings During Breakfast, Lunch, and Dinner

Business meetings conducted over a meal may be as simple as pastry and coffee in a client's office or as grand as dinner at a three-star restaurant to celebrate the closure of a deal. Remember that in the United States the purpose of the meal is business, although business should be brought up after the meal is well under way.

Arrive on time, prepared to take notes, and with any other materials that might be pertinent to your meeting. (You can take quick notes in a small notebook, but your flipchart and pointer should stay in the office.) Usually, the fancier the restaurant, the fewer the items you drag out and spread on the table. It might be fine for six of you to have a full-fledged planning session in a corner of your favorite coffee shop. But lunch at El Exclusivo (unless it's in a private dining room) should be saved for general, get-to-know-you forays or business celebrations.

If you are paying for the meal, take the check swiftly and use a credit card to pay your check if you can. If your client is hosting the meal, thank him before you go.

Women in the Workplace

Not so long ago, a woman with a job was the exception rather than the rule. But since 1986, well over 50 percent of all American women work outside the home at least part-time.

Correspondingly, workplace culture has changed tremendously. Many corporations now give employees parental leave when a child is born. (Some now do this for adoption, too.) And many places are beginning to recognize that when a child or elderly parent becomes ill, the primary responsibility for that care often falls to the mother or daughter in the family.

Although adjustments in child-care arrangements and other important issues continue to evolve, there are other areas—such as interoffice dating, sexism, and sexual harassment—that still need refining. This section attempts to discuss some of those concerns.

Dating in the Workplace

With more time being spent at work, it's not surprising that office romances are flourishing. Some companies still discourage colleagues' romantic involvement, fearing that a change in a strictly professional relationship will inevitably affect work performance.

If you and a coworker decide you'd like to see each other socially, remember that the social part occurs outside the office, and try to keep your office life pretty much as it was before you started to date. By all means:

- Don't spend time in the office with each other to the exclusion of all others.
- Don't address each other in any manner but the neutrally friendly way you used before you began to date.
- Don't engage in any public displays of affection, *period.*

It's fine to attend a social function together that is hosted by your company, provided you don't hang all over each other or hold hands on the way to the buffet.

Dating Up and Down the Corporate Ladder

Veterans of the romance-in-the-workplace wars tell us that dating between two different levels of office hierarchy is less successful than dating between peers.

Dating Your Boss

Dating your boss is *very* dicey. If you and your department head are seriously fond of each other, you may want to ask for a reassignment to a different department, or project, to protect both your job and your relationship. If the romance ends badly, or simply ends, usually the company will choose to keep the employee with higher status—especially if he's male. It's not fair, but that's the way the real world usually works.

Dating Your Subordinate

This, too, is risky business. The number of sexual harassment lawsuits rises sharply each year. If you decide to go this route, be sure the interest is mutual. If an employee indicates an interest in seeing you outside the office, *make sure you proceed cautiously at every step.* Under *no* circumstances should your subordinate feel pressured, coerced, or pushed to go out with you. If you persist, the result may or may not become as ugly as Clarence

Thomas's Supreme Court confirmation hearings—but why put yourself in that position?

Deflecting Unwanted Attention

Drawing the line between innocuous, but sexist, banter and genuine harassment is becoming increasingly difficult, especially for men. Does "great suit" mean just that? Or does it mean "Your bustline looks great in that suit?" Should a compliment to your hair or perfume be taken at face value, acknowledged, and dismissed, or could it possibly mean "I find you sexy, and I'd like to explore that further?"

Traditionally, sexual harassment has been visited upon women by men, but that's changing, too, as more women enter management positions and find themselves with several employees who report to them. Whatever your gender, forcing your attention on someone who has indicated that such attention causes discomfort, embarrassment, or uneasiness is never acceptable.

If you find yourself being paid attention you have no interest in receiving, firmly notify the person who is "complimenting" you that his attention is making you uncomfortable, and you wish he'd stop. If he persists, notify his superior and your human-resources department—in writing. If you still receive no satisfaction, contact one of the several nonprofit organizations for women (9 to 5, the Women's Legal Defense Fund, etc.). If you belong to a union or professional organization, ask for guidance from them as well.

Remember that while doing this, life probably won't be terribly pleasant at work. As unfair as it is, some offices prefer simply to look the other way when harassment occurs. But more and more companies, perhaps spurred on by the number of high-profile cases that plaintiffs have won in the past few years, are beginning to take the issue of sexual harassment seriously.

Women Traveling Alone on Business

See "Women Traveling Alone" in chapter 20, "Ease on Down the Road."

Eating Alone

There are at least two options for women business travelers. Like men, some women prefer to order dinner via room service so they can put their feet up and relax while eating. Others prefer to be around people. If you're one of the latter, remember to:

- Make reservations in the hotel dining room and be sure to tell the captain you are a guest at the hotel and will be dining alone. Most hotels are used to this and will see that you receive a pleasant table.
- Ask the concierge (see Glossary) which restaurants in town might be a good choice for a woman dining alone. Request that she make reservations for you. (Don't forget to tip her. See chapter 19, "Tips and Gratuities.")
- Don't hesitate to bring a book or some work to keep yourself occupied during the meal if you're uncomfortable not having company.
- If a man stops to introduce himself or sends a drink over, don't feel obligated to entertain him. Just point out "I'm trying to get through this pile of work" or this book and tell him, "It's nice to have met you." If he persists, signal the waiter and ask him to have the maître d' urge the man to lavish his attentions on someone else.

When a Woman Conducts Business in Her Hotel Suite

Business travelers sometimes find they must host meetings in their hotel rooms. This usually poses no problem when the group is all of one gender. When men and women are meeting together, however, the most comfortable solution is to request a hotel suite. Then you can close the bedroom door and have your business meeting in the living/dining portion of the suite. If you can't get your company to agree to the extra expense of a suite, other spots in the hotel—the coffee shop, the bar, or even the lobby area—may be acceptable substitutes.

Corporate Social Life

"Corporate party" almost sounds like a contradiction in terms, but there are times when your company decides to encourage social activity. The company holiday party and the annual picnic or outing are two good examples of this.

Some people make the mistake of thinking that, because these gatherings have a social veneer, they are purely social. They aren't. Different rules apply to business parties than to social events you'd attend with your good friends, and it's a wise person who doesn't mistake the two. Here are some guidelines you may find useful:

- Don't assume the office party is an optional social function; it's work, with a fun edge. Your failure to show up may indicate all kinds of messages you didn't intend to send (it wasn't important enough; you don't like your colleagues; the rules don't apply to you).
- Don't dress for the office party as you would for a party outside the

office. If the annual holiday dinner is held at a local restaurant, leave the plunging necklines, high heels, and dangly earrings for another time. You want to look festive *and* professional.

- Take "casual" with a grain of salt, and go less casual to the office party than you would to one a friend gives. If the invitation to the annual picnic says "shorts okay," wear a fairly modest pair. Leave the "Daisy Dukes" and other kinds of short-shorts in the drawer for another kind of party. Same for tube tops, halter tops, and the top part of any two-piece bathing suit. And when the company party is a pool party, use your common sense: if you don't want to be harassed in the office, don't encourage it with a teeny, tiny swimsuit. (Men, leave those Speedo bikinis home, too!)

Other things to remember when at an office social event:

- Drink moderately, if at all. You want people to see you relaxed, not looped.
- Don't use this occasion to unload on your boss re the unfairness of office politics. He/she won't appreciate it.
- Don't confront people you've been itching to have it out with. The office party is *not* the place for a fight of any kind.

When the Boss Invites You for the Weekend

In many companies, this is a cherished invitation, one not extended to everyone. It is often considered a mark of favor and—more nerve-wrackingly—a way to see if you have the "right stuff" to move up the corporate ladder. If you accept (and you should, unless you have an unbreakable commitment):

- Ask what the weekend will entail. If you know you're going hiking or rowing on the lake behind your hosts' house on Saturday, you'll have a better idea of what to pack.
- Ask if (or how) they dress for dinner in the evening. In many places, especially rustic weekend homes, people drop the formality of changing into dressy clothes for dinner. You need to know ahead of time whether you'll be having steaks in the yard or dinner at the local country club so you can pack appropriately.
- Ask what time your hosts would like you to arrive: "We're asking people to come for dinner on Friday and stay through Sunday brunch, if you can."
- *Don't* overstay your welcome. Leave them wanting more.

- *Do* offer to help with small household chores—especially if household staff aren't in evidence. (And of course make your bed, pick up your wet towels, etc.)
- *Do* bring a small present for your host (see chapter 18, "Gifts from Me to You"), and follow up with a thank-you note right away.

If you are married, both you and your spouse will be invited—unless the occasion is a working executive retreat, which may or may not include spouses. If you are unmarried but living with someone, it is possible that the invitation will be extended to both of you *if* your host is aware of your relationship and/or has met the person you live with, and if he has no objection to unmarried couples living together. If he doesn't mention your significant other, don't bring it up, and leave your honey at home. He (or she) should understand. If the invitation *is* extended to you as a live-in couple, follow the boss's lead: If you're placed in the same bedroom, fine. If you're placed in bedrooms across the hall from each other, grin and bear it. It's only a weekend, and in this case, your boss is like your mother—when in *his* house . . .

Mentoring

Sometimes it's done *to* you; sometimes it's done *by* you. But the process of guiding another person—usually one who is younger or less experienced—through the maze of company policy and mores is a valuable one. This is especially important in places where there are few people of color; if you can help to acclimate a young brother or sister to the corporation's culture and mores, you should. Organizations such as the Coalition of 100 Black Women and the Coalition of 100 Black Men, black professional societies, unions, and guilds are vital resources to seek out and use for support and assistance, because their members have been down your path before. Don't be selfish with your expertise; if you've been lucky enough to have someone help shape and guide your career, the highest compliment you can give is to do well and, in turn, bring someone else along. Each one, teach one.

Confidentiality

Confidential information is exactly that, and if you can't keep a confidence, ask beforehand that it not be told to you. Information about salaries, perks, impending promotions, layoffs, firings, and transfers that is shared with you on a confidential basis should go no further than your ears.

Entertaining Business Associates in Your Home

Sometimes you may want to have a business-related dinner or cocktails at home, perhaps to celebrate a colleague's promotion, a department's success, or another happy occasion.

Remember that if you invite only one or two people from your department, you must keep the invitation low-key so others' feelings aren't hurt. (It wouldn't hurt to mention that you aren't inviting everyone, so discretion would be appreciated.) Keep in mind the rules about office parties in general, especially if your boss is invited, too.

If you're married, your spouse should be your cheerful backup, offering to make people at ease, check on supplies that may be running low, taking coats. The spouse who has extended the invitation is the host in chief. He or she is responsible for the tone of the evening, and the spouse is responsible for making the trains run on time.

If you're not married, but have a date or escort for the evening, he fulfills the spouse's role, doing the physical tasks—such as taking coats, freshening drinks—a spouse would. (When people send thank-you notes for the nice time they had, though, the notes will be addressed to you alone, since you're the person who extended the invitation.)

Business Associates and Special Occasions

If you have colleagues who have become very close friends, or a boss who has been particularly supportive and helpful to you, there's no reason you shouldn't invite them to your wedding or your Christmas party if you want. As with entertaining at home, if you're only inviting the colleagues you're closest to and not your whole department, try to be discreet when you extend the invitation so other coworkers don't feel left out.

Gifts in the Workplace

In some offices, it's traditional to exchange gifts during the holiday season. Or colleagues who are especially friendly may take each other to lunch on their birthdays or exchange small presents. In general, try not to make these presents too extravagant (unless your best friend happens to work in your department). And if you're giving a present to your boss, make it fairly impersonal and modest in price. Anything else looks like you're buttering her up. (Okay presents: a small leather agenda; a photo frame; a box of chocolates or other candy; a current novel you know he's dying to read; flowers. A group of employees may take her to lunch or chip in for a gift certificate for a facial or manicure or massage. Stay away from jewelry, perfume, lingerie, a really expensive accessory, such as a gold cigarette lighter or a set of golf clubs.)

Group Presents

In many offices, it's fairly common for employees to chip in for one substantial gift when a colleague gets married, retires, or has a baby. When you're asked to contribute, you can ask what the average donation has been, and use that as your guideline—but don't feel obligated if that amount is more than you'd planned to give. If you're new, or don't know the person who's being given a present, just say "Thanks, but I'd rather not." You don't owe an explanation beyond that.

Looking for a Job When You Already Have One

"It's easier to get a job when you already have one." That old advice probably exists for a reason, and people who have jobs do search for better or different ones every day. But the key to success in this process is *discretion.* Try to have your potential employer call you at home, after work hours. Well before a potential employer needs to check with your present employer, notify your supervisor that you are having conversations with other companies, "just because the opportunity presented itself." If things are getting serious, be frank with your present company and let them know.

Losing a Job

Whether you've lost your job because of downsizing or a company merger or because you've been fired, losing a job (according to psychiatric studies) is one of the biggest traumas you'll face in your adult life. Even though you're devastated, try to maintain a professional demeanor: don't sulk or mope or mumble about how awful your employer is for doing this to you. Many job losses are business, not personal, decisions (and, frankly, you probably weren't even taken into consideration on an individual basis when the decision to cut staff was made).

Keep coming to work on time and tie up any loose ends before you go. Familiarize yourself with what your benefits, postjob, might be. (Can you be retrained for another job? Will they extend coverage of your health plan for a few more months? Do you have the option of paying for health-care benefits through the company for some time after that? Do you have unused vacation time coming that you'll be paid for, or can you simply stop work at an earlier date and be paid until your vacation days are used up?)

Definitely take advantage of the company's outplacement services if they are offered. Many outplacement offices offer career counseling and the use of an office for job-hunting calls (usually not in the same building as the company's), a message service, and a business address to put on your résumé.

After you leave your job, keep busy by doing volunteer work for a local nonprofit organization in your chosen field; you'll keep your skills up, an organization that can use an extra hand will be happy to have you, and you won't spend time moping while you wait for the phone to ring. (As a fringe benefit, several people have told us they've actually *found* jobs this way, too, or gotten great recommendations that have led to jobs.)

Resigning

Sometimes you have to leave a job of your own volition. Perhaps you've found a better job. Or you simply feel burned out in the one you have now. Or you're sensing the handwriting on the wall and have decided it's time to move on. However it occurs, when you resign, make sure you inform your superior of your decision before you take anyone else into your confidence. Follow this up with a letter of resignation (see sample) that highlights your positive experiences with the company, as you don't want to burn any bridges unnecessarily. You may also be asked to have an "exit interview," which is like the interview you had before you were offered your job—only this time, you can tell the company how you found the experience, what things you enjoyed most, and which things could stand improvement. (This is not the time, however, for wholesale griping.)

Dear Mr. Rankin:

Please consider this my official letter of resignation from Bigsby Bros., Inc., effective the first of next month. As I said when we discussed my resignation yesterday, I've tremendously enjoyed my four years here at Bigsby. I've learned a lot from my colleagues and the clients I've had the privilege to serve, but I feel I've done as much as I can in my current position, and now is a good time for me to move on.

Thank you again for all the support you've given me during my time here. I wish only the best to you and my colleagues.

Sincerely,

Judith Smith

The Home Office

Corporate downsizing and more Americans' wish to be their own boss has led to a boom in home offices. There are even several publications devoted expressly to people who work at home. The advantages of doing this are many: Unless you're meeting clients, you don't have to get dressed as you would for work in a corporate office. Your time is a bit more flexible (you can work *and* let the sofa deliveryman in!). If you want to work far into the night, you can sleep until noon to make up for it. And you can slip into the kitchen and make yourself lunch instead of waiting in line at the company cafeteria.

Enchanting as the idea of working at home can be, though, there are distinct drawbacks, too. The biggest one may be other people's assumption that since you're not in an office, you'd just *love* to be interrupted for a long chat on the telephone, an impromptu lunch, a personal visit that wasn't scheduled. Or that since "you're home anyway," it "won't be much trouble" for you to feed the cat while they're away on a business trip, or let their child in after he's lost his key, or sign for their delivery packages while they're at work. To avoid this, try to establish a few ground rules:

- If you can, install a second, business line for your office calls. Use an office answering machine: "You've reached 555-1212, Ross Associates. Your message is important, so please leave your name and number at the sound of the tone."
- Keep regular office hours, so people know when they can try to reach you.
- Let people know that when you're working, you can't stop to visit or take personal calls, except for true (as in medical) emergencies.
- Have your office sound as businesslike as possible: a caller shouldn't hear any barking dogs, fussy children, or the *whump-whump* of the washing machine in the background.

Business Meetings When You Work at Home

If you have a pleasant room that is in a "public" area of the house (so you don't, for instance, have to trek through your bedroom to get there), feel free to ask people to meet with you at home. If you live in a small space, or feel home meetings are too great a burden on your privacy, schedule your meeting at a restaurant where you know you can work undisturbed for a couple of hours. (Remember that if you offer to do this, you should pick up the bill.) Or offer to come and meet your client in his office, which may be the easiest solution of all.

Race in the Workplace

"One may challenge the so-called scientific divisions of the human race," wrote Harlem Renaissance poet Claude McKay, "but we cannot abolish the instinct and the reality of race."

The poet was—and is—right. Like it or not, race permeates every part of American life. It influences where many of us live and work, it guides our choices of social associations, and it affects how we see each other. Urged on (and sometimes forced) by the sacrifices of good people of all races, this country has made tremendous strides in the past half-century in what Swedish sociologist Gunnar Myrdal once labeled "an American dilemma."

Today it is more likely than ever that if you are bright and industrious, you may well end up in a position where you are the first black person ever to have blazed a trail there. In the old days, people who found themselves in such a position would have been urged by their communities to "be a credit to the race." Some people scoff that this is old-fashioned thinking; they feel it's onerous to those among us who want to be seen as individuals. But the reality is, in America, the individual, if he is different, is often forced to be emblematic of the group he belongs to—whether he wants it that way or not. So we'd urge you to be a credit to *yourself*, and in so doing, you cannot help but make the rest of us who claim you as a racial kinsperson proud.

The Affirmative-Action Question

When you look at it objectively, *most* people hold their jobs because of some kind of preference, whether it's an unstated one (mostly white males in the U.S. Senate), a more clearly expressed one (sons and daughters of university alumni or relatives of current union members or company employees being given special consideration), or one that is an attempt to level the workplace playing field by seeking to include people who have traditionally been excluded from it.

If your competence is questioned because the questioner suspects you got your job through affirmative action, simply point out that if you hadn't been qualified, you wouldn't have been hired. And if you didn't continue to produce, you wouldn't keep your job. Emphasize that "black" and "qualified" are not mutually exclusive terms. And remember that, fair or not, you will inevitably be judged by a different, higher standard because of your race.

Offensive Racial Humor

Many companies now have zero-tolerance policies when it comes to giving racial offense. Earl Butz, the former Secretary of Agriculture, once told a vulgar joke about black men that, when it became public, cost him his job. The consequences of public indulgence in racist humor will not always be so immediate (or, for that matter, gratifying), but unless you are comfortable with ignoring it, you should always point out that racist humor is unacceptable. And it goes without saying you should never engage in it yourself. (For more information on this, see chapter 8, "Strictly Speaking.")

Racial Harassment at Work

Occasionally, especially in a profession or craft that has never had the benefit of racial diversity, some employees handle their own feelings of being threatened by engaging in a series of racially inspired harassment that can run from the low-level to the truly hair-raising.

If you find yourself the recipient of repeated racial slurs or racially inspired humor, notify your department head or supervisor, both verbally and in writing. Request that he ask his employees to stop this odious practice.

If the harassment continues, send a memo to the Human Resources department; enclose your prior written notification to your supervisor. Request that this be handled immediately.

If nothing is done, contact your union, guild, or professional association; file a suit with the local branch of the Equal Employment Opportunity Commission. Notify your local NAACP.

The Culturally Clueless

If you are an FN^2 (shorthand for what a friend wryly calls the "First Negro to . . .") working with people who've never had a black colleague, the chances are very good that they have no black neighbors or close friends, either. You'll find yourself answering questions based on assumptions about black life or physiognomy that have little fact as their foundation.

How you answer questions like these depends a lot on who's asking them and the spirit behind the question. People who've never been exposed to black folks or our culture may have no inkling that we come in all colors, have all hair textures, and that these differences can exist within one nuclear family, making us our very own mini-Rainbow Coalition. Our preference is to do the culturally uninitiated a favor by straightening them out—gently—and relieving them of their stereotypical baggage at the same time, if we can:

"No, we *aren't* all on welfare. Statistically speaking, more white people are." "Yes, you *can* be black and have blue eyes." "I was hired because I'm bilingual; being black was just icing on the cake."

If the questions have an edge of malice to them, don't hesitate to answer more pointedly: "If you're asking if Chief Jacobs got the job because he's black, I'd have to say probably not. Remember, the newspaper did say he had the highest test score and was the only candidate with a doctoral degree." Or "When I need some help, I'll be sure and ask for it. Until then, I'd appreciate it if you wouldn't follow me around your store. I have no intention of not paying for whatever I choose."

There will probably always be questions from people who are genuinely curious about our culture, but as our culture becomes more visible in America (which it is, with every day that passes), the questions will become less clueless. And that in itself can be considered progress.

Part IV

DATING, MATING, AND BEGETTING

From "Oh Baby" to Babies

The ins and outs of the dating game

marriage, living together, gay partnerships

in-laws and out-laws

babies, children, and teens

blended families

dating after divorce

Chapter 24

IT'S A DATE, NOT A MATE

Relax and have fun;
it's just a date, not a mate.

Anonymous

Reduced to its essentials, dating used to be considered a way of surveying the field in preparation for settling down with a lifemate. At least that's how sociologists might have described the traditional purpose of this particular ritual. Dating was the bridge between living with your parents and the beginning of your independent adult life. Earlier in this century, people married much younger, often straight out of high school or college, and began their families right away. Dating was done for a shorter, more intense period of time and was seen as a screening process in the search for an appropriate mate. To that end, your date was almost inevitably someone who might, eventually, become a mate.

Today people marry much later. Many go to college, some go on to graduate school, and most spend at least a few years working or building a career before they seriously consider settling down. Young women who, even a few decades earlier, were expected to remain at home until marriage may now live for several years on their own before they marry.

Because of this, the purpose of dating has changed significantly. Rather than screening a potential mate, sometimes, to paraphrase Sigmund Freud, a date is just a date. And when the pressure of considering every date a potential spouse is removed, the field widens, the process relaxes, and people begin to date members of the opposite sex they have no intention of marrying. Your dating career could be lengthy indeed: instead of a few intense years between, say, sixteen and twenty, people might date today from their early teens until their early thirties and beyond.

Dating 101

While the rigidity surrounding dating has relaxed considerably (some people would say too much!), many of the basics still apply:

- Unless a woman is being met elsewhere (say, at a restaurant after work), a man should always call for her at her home. If she lives with her parents or a roommate, she should introduce him to them: "Jerry, I'd like you to meet my parents, Alma and James Mack. Mom, I told you about Jerry; we met at that tae kwon do class I've been taking."
- A man should always go to the door for his date. He should never honk the horn or yell from the car or street. *Period.*
- At the end of the evening, a man should always escort his date to her door (or lobby) and wait until she's safely in; these days, this is a matter of safety as well as good manners.
- Even if he's had a less-than-fabulous time, he should always thank her for going out with him. If he had a great time, he should tell her. Even if it was the evening from hell and they never see each other again, he should be polite: "Thanks for coming to check out that new Spike Lee movie. I really enjoyed it." (Note he enjoyed the *movie*, not the date.)
- She, in turn, should thank him for asking her out. And even if she had a horrible time, there must be *something* nice to say about some part of the evening: "Dinner was great." Or "I'd never been to an outdoor concert at night; that was fun."
- Men should not say "I'll call you" if they have no intention of doing so.
- Women should remember not to encourage a second date if one isn't wanted. And if he asks anyway, a simple, polite refusal is kinder than a string of unreturned phone calls. If you think he won't take no graciously, a noncommittal answer at the door ("The next three weeks are going to be crazy at work; let's play it by ear, okay?"), followed by a gentle no over the phone, might be better.

Who Pays for What—and How

One of the stickier aspects of modern dating, especially now that women's pay is more closely approximate (but still not always equal) to men's, is the issue of who pays when you're out on a date. In the old days, most women had very little discretionary income, so the burden of financially covering an evening out fell to men. (The rationale here was that the pleasure of a nice woman's company should be ample recompense for whatever expense was incurred.) That's not always the case now, although many men and women remain comfortable with this traditional arrangement.

Our simple rule of thumb: *whoever asks pays.* This does vary with, for example, age (many older women, especially those who came of age before the feminist movement, still feel paying is the masculine prerogative) and geography (women in the South and Midwest, where values tend to be more traditional and gender roles more sharply defined, may feel more strongly about this than their sisters in the North and West). Too, the protocol for who pays in business situations differs from how this would be handled in a purely social instance. A businesswoman could take a male client to lunch and both could be comfortable when she picks up the check. One wise woman we know handles social situations this way: "I always assume that if he asks, *he's* paying—but I bring enough money or have a credit card ready just in case. And if *I* ask *him,* I always assume *I'm* paying, but I let him do it if he insists. And if he insists, of course I say thank you."

When He Asks Her

If a man asks a woman to dinner, especially if it's a first date, he should offer to pay when the check comes. He should encourage his date to order from the menu as she pleases, although a considerate date will keep in mind that a dinner is supposed to be a relaxed way to get to know someone, using the meal as a social lubricant. It should *not* be used as a probe into a man's financial stability: "If he doesn't flinch when I order the lobster, he's a keeper."

Although the practice has all but disappeared, in a very few, very formal, very traditional restaurants, the menus given to women will have no prices on them. If you find yourself in one of these restaurants (and we admit, the probability is slim), the safest practice is to order what looks to be neither the cheapest nor the most expensive item, which spares your companion the embarrassment of being thought too pinched to entertain a date properly—or so well off anything goes. This Goldilocks approach (not too much, not to little . . . just right) is commonly referred to as "ordering from the middle of the menu." (See ordering at a restaurant, in chapter 17, "Eating Out.")

When the bill arrives, it should be quickly but carefully scrutinized. Cash or, preferably, a credit card should be quietly left beneath the bill (or tucked into the small folder the bill sometimes comes in) and placed at the edge of the table so the waiter can whisk it away. Credit card tips are added directly onto the statement, and a total, including the tip, is penned onto the bottom line. When he pays with cash, a tip is left in the bill folder after the initial bill has been paid. (For more information, see chapter 19, "Tips and Gratuities," and chapter 17, "Eating Out.")

If coats are checked or if the valet takes the car, he should be responsible for paying for their retrieval, whether you arrived together or separately.

When She Asks Him

The same rules, generally, apply—with one exception. Many women feel it's easier for a man to accept their hospitality if the bill is paid with a credit card. "It's more discreet," one woman told us. "You just sign the bill and that's that. Some men squirm when you actually put down cash." You can even excuse yourself, on the pretense of going to the ladies' room, and give the waiter your card, so the bill will appear written up and ready to sign at the end of dinner. You can do this if you pay with cash, too: just pass the waiter's station on your way to the ladies' room and ask him to total the bill so you can pay him on your way back to the table.

Men, too, considerately order something they'd like to have, but not the priciest thing on the menu. If she's having a Caesar salad with grilled chicken, for instance, she probably doesn't expect her date to survive just on salad greens, but it would be nice if he didn't try to break the bank by ordering the biggest T-bone available, either. The exception is when she urges him to go for broke: "Sam, I brought you here because I know you love crab cakes; the ones here are great, so I hope you'll try them if you want to."

Reciprocity

If a woman would like to reciprocate for having been wined and dined by a man, but feels he may be reluctant to let her pay for the meal—even though she's invited him—there are other alternatives. Many traditional-minded women like to offer a meal prepared at home. With a nicely set table, flowers, and wine, such an offer is often a welcome change from dining out.

How does she extend the invitation? Simply: "Robert, would you like to come to dinner on Friday? I'm told I make a mean jambalaya." It's quite possible that Robert will be delighted to accept. Don't forget to ask about food allergies: before you go to a lot of trouble and expense to fix a gorgeous lobster dinner, make sure your guest of honor isn't deathly allergic to shellfish. You don't want your evening to be memorable because you spent it with him in the local emergency room.

Hidden Agendas

Reciprocity means extending an invitation as a way of saying thank you for the nice time you've been shown. It does *not* mean quid pro quo for his investment in your dinner. A man who expects to receive anything but a heartfelt thanks at the end of a pleasant dinner deserves to be disappointed. And a woman who equates "putting out" with payment for her evening out should stay in more often.

When a Single Parent Dates

Dating isn't just for teens and young folks. If you're a single parent who's getting back in the social mainstream, there are a few things to remember:

- Explain to your children that you are entitled to have a social life, but assure them it won't interfere with the time you devote to them. It's important for them to know that they come first.
- If your date comes to the house to pick you up, introduce him to your children so they have some idea whom you're seeing.
- If you're sexually involved with your date, do not allow him or her to spend the night until it becomes clear that this person has become a serious (steady, monogamous) partner. Children get attached to people they take a liking to, and yours will be devastated when they no longer have access to someone they've become fond of.
- Don't allow your date to physically discipline your children. If *you* believe in spanking, that is the sole prerogative of the custodial parent. Verbal discipline should be sparing, too; the date—even a serious one—should always defer to the parent's wishes in this department, and not undermine her with alternative suggestions.

  Do: "Max, I can't help you out, buddy. Your Mom says five minutes in the time-out corner."

  Don't: "Oh, don't send him to time-out; he won't do it again, will you, Max?"

When to Include/Exclude a Date in Family Functions

Beyond standard introductions, many people don't immediately expose their dates to their families until they have some idea of how fond they're becoming of their date and where the relationship is going. "It saves a lot of questions later," wryly notes a friend, "since in my family, if you bring a man around once, they ask about him forever after."

There *are* occasions when even a casual date can be "brought around." These would include large, festive, informal times: a family picnic or reunion, a favorite niece's birthday party, the neighborhood block club party.

Other occasions that may warrant bringing a truly special date are a special celebration for a parent or grandparent; a christening or graduation celebration for a young relative; Thanksgiving dinner, especially if the meal traditionally includes a large crowd.

And there are times when it's appropriate to include the adult equivalent of a steady date: weddings; Christmas dinner; the special birthday celebration of the family matriarch; your parents' silver anniversary party.

Finally, there are times when, no matter how close you are, your date should be left at home: a memorial service for a family member that is family-only; the reading of a will; a hospital visit—unless the patient has specifically requested she be introduced to your friend. Anytime that there is the potential that things might become contentious or volatile, it's best not to insert a new person.

When He Takes You Home to Meet His Folks

Your date asks you to his parents' home for dinner. You're delighted; you'd love to meet the people who brought up such a wonderful man. You, of course, remember to:

- Be ready on time, so the two of you aren't late.
- Wear something appropriate to the occasion (a sundress to a barbecue, something more pulled together for a Sunday afternoon dinner with his parents and their friends).
- Take a small gift for his mother (perhaps a book on her favorite hobby, if you know it, or an interesting photo frame or flowers or chocolates).
- While there, you're on your best behavior—charming, funny, relaxed. You offer to help bring dishes from the kitchen or clear the table. If the "boys" go off to chat for a moment, you take the time to get to know his mother a little better.
- When you leave, you compliment his mother on the meal (or his dad, if that's who cooked), assure them how much you enjoyed the evening, and tell them what a nice person they've raised. You send a thank-you note within the next couple of days.

When a Date Becomes a Steady

When two people are lucky enough to find they have a lot in common, delight in each other's company, and, eventually, begin to see each other seriously, that's cause for celebration. It's not, however, cause for excessive public displays of affection, using pet nicknames that make others uncomfortable, and ignoring the rest of the world to concentrate totally on each other. That behavior is perfectly acceptable between the enamored couple and behind closed doors—which is exactly where it belongs.

- *Do* feel free to hold hands or stroll arm in arm down the street. People will smile and envy you your good fortune.
- *Don't* engage in serious necking in plain public view. People will wonder why you can't control yourselves any better.
- *Do* feel free to indicate your affection using common words of endearment (honey, sweetheart, etc.).
- *Don't* use your private nicknames for each other—especially if they have sexual connotations, vague or explicit. "Sweetie" is one thing; "sweet cheeks" should be saved for later.

"Let's Get It On . . ."

It should go without saying, but in the area of sex it's always better to be safe than sorry. When a couple decides they want to add a sexual dimension to their relationship, things become a bit more complex. Given the current crop of grim sexually transmitted diseases, which have consequences ranging from impaired fertility to death, it's good manners for you and your partner to have a frank discussion about sex before you actually sleep together. It's good sense, too: your life could depend upon it.

Before either of you gets swept away on a tide of passion, some important questions have to be asked:

- Will this relationship be sexually monogamous? For your health, you should insist on it.
- Has either of you ever been tested for HIV/AIDS, or for another sexually transmitted disease? What were the results?
- Who will be responsible for birth control, and what kind will you use?
- In the event of a technological failure, how do both parties feel about abortion? About pregnancy and parenthood?

It's absolutely true that a discussion like this can take a little of the luster off a potentially enchanted evening, but these days, not asking these questions can literally make the difference between life and death. *Ask.* Better to find out now than later, when it may be too late.

And Brother, Remember

DON'T YOU DARE:

- Assume that because you paid for dinner, anything other than a thank-you is owed you.
- Be late for a date. If it's unavoidable, call as soon as you realize you'll be late and offer an explanation.
- Invite someone out and feign poverty when the bill arrives.
- Do anything that would put another in harm's way.
- Think that because you've invited a woman to your house, it's automatically her job to clean up the place for you.
- Try to convince anyone that "just this once" nothing will happen and she won't have to worry about AIDS or other sexually transmitted diseases.
- Become so sure of yourself that you feel you no longer need to say "please" and "thank you."

POSSLQs

The Census Bureau calls them Persons of Opposite Sex Sharing Living Quarters—POSSLQs. Which is an ungainly way of saying you're living with your steady boyfriend. While living together before marriage was not widely accepted in the United States before the late 1960s, it is now practiced virtually everywhere; the trend crosses all racial, geographic, and economic borders.

Just as you had to make some hard decisions before you decided to have sex, if you and your steady date make the decision to share living quarters, you both have to decide, before you share the same space, some important things:

- Will you move in with him, him with you, or will you search for a new apartment for both of you?
- Will you each keep your own places, just in case things don't work out?
- How will you divide financial responsibilities?
- Will you have one telephone or two? And if you have separate numbers, are you allowed to answer each other's telephone?
- Which finances should remain separate, which joint?
- Why are you doing this?

The latter may seem a strange question, but it's an important one. If one of you is looking at living together as a sort of trial marriage while the other considers it simply a pleasant way to spend a year or two, that's a problem. Before you break your leases, move cross-country (or even across the city), or make any otherwise hard-to-undo decisions, have a frank talk about what you both hope will come from this arrangement.

What's in a Name?

Let's assume you're both in agreement that you'd like to see if you can live together comfortably before going any further. What do you call your live-in partner? POSSLQ is ridiculous. "Lover" is a bit too in-your-face for some people. You're more than "friends." "Boyfriend" is a little coy. Maybe the best way, if you can manage it, is to simply introduce your live-in lover as "This is John."

Going Home When Home Is Out of Town

It's Christmas. Your parents are eagerly looking forward to having you home. They're also fond of your, um, roommate and would love for him to come, too. They know you're living together, which is something they're not wild about, but they're trying to deal with it. You hit the door. Hugs and handshakes all around. Your mother shows you up to your old room, while your dad escorts him a few doors down the hall to the room that used to be your baby brother's. What do you do?

Remember that old adage "When in Rome, do what the Romans do"? Modify it a little: *When at home, do what your parents want you to do* (see chapter 13 "My House, My Rules"). If they realize you're living together but they're not comfortable with unmarried people in the same bed under their roof, then sleep separately. It won't kill you, and it will keep your relationship with your folks on an even keel.

This, by the way, works with things other than sex. If your honey's parents don't smoke and there are no ashtrays in the house, step out into the yard to smoke if you must. If they don't drink but don't mind if you do, BYOB if you want wine with dinner. If they don't drink and *do* mind if you do, have water or iced tea or whatever they offer with dinner and don't complain. You're there to spend some quality time with them, and that's more important than getting to do all the things you normally do. You'll be going home soon enough.

Your honey can make the visit even more pleasant by offering to help out when he sees or thinks help is needed. If the trash cans are magically hauled to the curb so your dad doesn't have to do it; if things are returned to high shelves so your mother doesn't have to drag the step stool over to put them up; if he cheerfully attends Sunday services, even though he usually likes to sleep in when he's home, he will be fondly remembered.

Old-Fashioned Love, New Technology

Not everyone meets dates the old-fashioned way, through personal introductions. Some folks decide to cast a wider net using dating services and personal ads (these are often referred to simply as "personals"). There are pros and cons to both:

Personals reach a broad number of people, but you don't know exactly whom you're reaching. *Dating services* narrow the scope a bit, in that people have to apply and be matched, but they can be expensive. *On-line,* or *computer, dating* is a recent trend and, as more people become computer-literate, can be expected to increase.

PERSONALS

Personal ads work by placing a description of you and what you're looking for in a newspaper or magazine. Ads usually describe the gender, race, and age of the applicant, and give a general description of the kind of person he/she is seeking:

> *Single, African American female, 28, fond of tennis, Chinese food, and old movies, seeking single African American male, 27–35, for pleasant company doing same.*

This is usually followed by a number or alphanumeric code that the applicant can reply to, according to the specifications of the particular publication in which the ad appears. (Some magazines have a voice mail option, others direct respondents to a post office box.)

DATING SERVICES

Dating services are commercial enterprises designed to act as matchmakers for like-minded people. Usually you visit the service, describe what you're seeking, ask if the service has people generally like those you seek in its clientele. (Note: If you're black and looking for a black mate, many white dating services may advise you that they have little to offer, unless you would consider dating across racial lines.) If you're satisfied with the service, you fill out a detailed form listing your background and interests. You may be asked to do this via interview, on videotape, so a potential applicant can get a better feel for who you are.

After paying a fee, which can range anywhere from a couple hundred to several thousand dollars, your information is included in the service's client base, and you are contacted when a potential date wants to reach you.

ELECTRONIC PERSONALS, DATING ON-LINE

On-line introductions can be made through computer users' forums that many on-line services (such as America Online and CompuServe) have, or via other Internet connections. People often meet in "chat rooms," where they participate in (and yes, flirt) using typed dialogue, and, if they hit it off, perhaps decide to investigate each other further off-line, via the telephone or a real, face-to-face date. The same safety rules that apply to other kinds of personal ads are relevant here, too.

Meeting a Person You've Met via the Personals

Remember to describe yourself and your interests honestly. There's always a huge temptation to gloss over our real-life selves in favor of the selves we'd like to present to the outside world. But our ability to do that evaporates when we agree to actually come out in public. Your date won't be expecting someone who's a dead ringer for Janet Jackson (unless of course you are) if you don't lead him to believe that's possible in the first place. Knowing these are the blindest of blind dates, some commonsense rules apply:

- Always meet the personals date someplace public: a restaurant, hotel lobby, bookstore.
- Make sure your first date is in a similarly public place.
- Wait until a few dates later, when you know your date better, to allow him to accompany you to your door.

Close Encounters of the Tense Kind

When there are dates, there are, every now and then, ex-dates. And occasionally, they run into each other at the most inopportune times. When you make unexpected sightings of old dates you'd rather forget, smile pleasantly, speak briefly (if you're close enough that you need to speak), and keep moving. Most rooms are big enough to contain the two of you without risking the roof getting blown off.

Giving Out Your Number

You're at a reception and a man asks for your number. You think you might like to get to know him a little better, but you're not sure. What do you do?

Some women, ever safety-conscious, give their office numbers. After a brief chat, they may decide to meet the man who's interested in them for lunch or for drinks after work. Other women would rather keep the option of calling themselves: "Why don't you give me your number, and when things calm down at my office, I'll give you a call." A man can assume if she does call, she's genuinely interested in getting to know him better.

A Word About Fatal Attractions

Sometimes the date you originally thought was heaven-sent turns out to be the date from hell. There's very little way to know whether a stranger—or even someone you've gotten to know well—will turn out to be enchanting or just plain evil. Let's say you've broken it off and your former date refuses to accept reality. He calls at work and at home. He stops by unannounced and refuses to budge from your doorstep. He follows you from place to place or threatens violence.

There are several things you can do that are not only good home training—they are essential to your safety, too. If there is talk of violence—overt or implied—*run*, don't walk, to your local police precinct and carefully describe the pattern of harassment. Tell the officer who takes your information that you are worried for your physical safety and ask for advice. The police are faced with this problem frequently, and they'll have valuable suggestions for you.

If a judge orders that a temporary restraining order (TRO) be written out to keep him away from you, follow it to the letter. Don't accept a TRO and then let him in to talk things over; besides sending mixed signals, it could be very dangerous. And make sure you notify the police if he ignores or otherwise breaches it; this will make him subject to arrest. ("Judges get pretty miffed when their orders are ignored," a detective told us. "If he violates the restraining order, he *will* go to jail.")

Also, let friends know you are worried for your safety and ask them to check on you regularly. Let your stalker know that your friends and family are actively monitoring his movements and that you have complained to police.

Finally, if all else fails, change your residence for a while. Ask a friend in a safe building if you can stay with her for a few weeks while you assess your situation, if you don't think staying with her will put her in danger. Check your Yellow Pages for women's shelters and other organizations that can give commonsense, practical advice on how to keep yourself as safe as possible.

Fundamental Things

The rules for dating may have changed some over the years, but, as Sam pointed out in *Casablanca*, the fundamental things *do* apply as time goes by. And some things will always be true:

- It's still best to meet a new person with an introduction from a friend, colleague, or relative.
- Men with good home training still hold chairs for ladies, stand when being introduced, hold coats and doors, and walk on the outside of the sidewalk. Women with good home training let them.

Chapter 25

I DO, I DON'T

Marriage and Other Living Arrangements

. . . Do I love you?
'course I does!
Jump back, honey
Jump back!

Paul Laurence Dunbar,
"A Negro Love Song"

To paraphrase a children's poet, marriage can often best be described like the little girl with the curl in the middle of her forehead: when it is good, it is very, very good, and when it is bad, it is horrid. Keeping the horrid moments few and far between is probably one of the secrets of a lasting marriage. And observing some basic courtesies toward your spouse, just as you would people you know (and love) less well, is a key ingredient.

Consulting Each Other's Calendar

Few things can rub a partner the wrong way so quickly as the assumption that your time is more valuable than his. Unless you have an understanding that one of you is responsible for keeping your social calendar (and some couples do have this agreement), always try to consult with your partner before accepting a social engagement for both of you. That way, if you discover he has a violent aversion to attending a classical concert, you don't have to sheepishly call back and retract your acceptance—or nag him into going because you said you both would go. And if you aren't dying to see the latest blow-'em-up, stab-'em-up macho film, you can suggest he take his best friend—before he locks you into a foursome with his best friend and his best friend's wife.

If there are things that are annual "musts"—his great-aunt's Fourth of July barbecue, your social club's winter dinner/fund-raiser—sit down and figure out how you can both get part of what you want. Perhaps you go to his great-aunt's every *other* year, and he agrees to go solo in the years you don't go together. Or you shorten your evening to include only the dinner, not the predinner cocktail party and the coffee at somebody's house at dawn. Being willing to make the compromise counts almost as much as the compromise itself. And after time, you may actually find yourself offering to go on the years you don't have to, simply because you don't have to.

Respecting Your Partner's Family's Wishes

- Your fiancé's mother is a strict Pentecostal and shudders at the idea of being in the same room where alcohol is served, let alone having to serve it herself. Your fiancé does not share her religious beliefs, but he wants you to nix the wine when you plan the menu for a special dinner you're preparing for his parents.
- Your partner's family is fully aware you are both lesbians and openly so. They live in a different city and have always been extremely hospitable to you when you visit with your lover. But your lover's parents insist on introducing you as "Ginny's friend Frances." You'd rather they make a more public acknowledgment of your couplehood.

The rule in these situations is to try to keep the peace *if possible* and if keeping the peace does not betray your own values. If your fiancé's mother is visibly uncomfortable at the notion of being served alcohol, then leave the wine for another time. There are plenty of elegant alternatives that might suit your meal (serve sparkling cider in your champagne flutes, or iced tea in pretty stemmed goblets), and you can always share a glass after his parents depart and the dishes are washed and put away.

If your partner's parents generally treat you well, allow them the discretion of not announcing their daughter's status to people they may not want to share this information with. Smile, be gracious, and try not to rub it in by using body language that would fill in her parents' friends as to exactly *how* friendly you two are. It may well be that the parents are trying in subtle ways to acknowledge that you are permanent parts of each other's life. (Maybe they send you joint presents or display a photo of the two of you taken during your most recent vacation.) Try to meet them halfway if you can.

There are times when family requests can be unreasonable: A family is violently against interracial dating, as well as same-sex unions, or hates the idea of a May-December romance. Or is devoutly Baptist and is horrified that you're considering marrying a Muslim and are converting to Islam yourself. In these cases, you have to follow your conscience and *gently* explain to them why you can't accede to their wishes:

"Dad, I know how you feel about interracial relationships. I know what a hard time white people have given you since you were young. But Peter is the person I've fallen in love with, and I hope you'll accept that. Even though you were discriminated against, you and Mom always brought me up to look beyond color to the person beneath. That's exactly what I did. I hope, in time, you'll get to know and grow fond of Peter, too. I know he's anxious to know you better."

"Mama, I know you're not happy with the fact that I'm gay, but you don't have to be happy with it to accept that's what I am. Please stop fixing me up with your friends' daughters—it's not fair to them, or me. And Shelby is *not* my 'roommate,' he's my partner for life. You don't have to shout it from the rooftops, but I do wish you'd treat us as the couple we are."

"Aunt Ruby, our family has been Baptist for generations, that's true. But Soroya is Muslim, and that does not make her a 'godless heathen.' I hope you'll reconsider your position, because I'd sure miss my favorite aunt if I couldn't see her anymore. It's really important to me that we *both* be welcome in your home."

Sometimes they come around, sometimes they don't. But time, and your willingness to keep communications open, will help make the difference, if it can be made.

Endearing Yourself to Your Spouse's Family

One of the pleasantest things to overhear is your mother-in-law bubbling over with praise for her son's wife. Or to have his little sister enthuse to a friend how easy it is to talk with you or what fun she had when she spent the weekend at your house.

Treating your spouse well is a direct route to his family's heart. But they also like knowing that you appreciate them as individuals, and not just because they're related to someone you love. Spend time with his parents or call to check on them when he's away. Call "just to chat" sometime. When you visit, offer to help around the house; don't sit back and wait to be served like a guest.

One of the first things some new wives discover is that, along with the ring and changed status, they have also inherited—much to their husbands' relief—the chores of sending birthday cards and of shopping for the entire family! ("It ain't fair," one wife said wryly, "but it's true.") If this is your situation, find out a bit about their tastes and interests and clue your husband in on what his dad would *really* like for Father's Day, or do a little sleuthing so you can make suggestions for a birthday present his mother will actually *wear.*

Holidays and Family Traditions

You both live in a city different from the ones in which you were raised. Your respective parents miss you and exert pressure—from the charmingly subtle to the overt hammer-on-the-head—for you to spend your holidays with them. What do you do?

Millions of couples face this dilemma each year, and the savvy ones' advice: alternate! If you spend Thanksgiving with her family, agree to spend Christmas with your folks. Perhaps some years you can host both families at *your* house. What's important here is that each family gets to spend time with you.

If your family lives in the same town you do but his are far away, make a special effort to visit with them for an important holiday or urge them to come and stay with you, if that's practical. The parents who live most distant no doubt feel a little envy that your nearby in-laws can see you much more frequently—a feeling that only intensifies when grandchildren are involved. Figure out a way to include the distant parents by sending videotapes or photos of holiday gatherings and calling frequently. They won't substitute for your actual presence, but those things are, as an old phone company ad used to note, the next best thing to being there.

Ladies' (and Gents') Night Out

Just because you're married doesn't mean either of you should forget the friends you made when you were single. In fact, it's especially important to nurture these relationships after you become part of a couple, because your single friends will worry that you no longer have time for them.

If a monthly dinner with the girls was a cherished part of your life before you found Mr. Right, by all means continue. And let your husband know that he should not deep-six that quarterly bid whist game with his pals just because he has a ring on his finger. Letting each other know that it's fine to have friends in common and friends you enjoy separately is an important component of acknowledging that you have individual as well as joint needs and interests. Couples who do every little thing together are either extraordinarily lucky or, as more often the case, in danger of falling into a rut.

When Only One of You Is Invited

If people are aware that you're a couple, most of your social invitations will read "Mr. and Mrs. So-and-So." Or if you're not married, but engaged, or have dated each other exclusively for a significant amount of time, both your name and your friend's will be included: "Ms. Jennifer Staples and Mr. Christopher Parsons."

There are times, however, when you'll be invited to places alone, and not necessarily because people are trying to snub your spouse or date. Significant others may or may not be invited, for instance, to corporate dinners or retreats. Some women feel strongly that engagement parties or baby showers are single-sex celebrations, although coed parties for these celebrations have become increasingly common.

If you receive a solo invitation to an event, you have two options: to accept or decline. Don't call the host in a huff and complain that you wouldn't think of showing up without your date or mate. She may have a legitimate reason for inviting only one of you. For instance, an invitation for a fancy wedding followed by a sit-down dinner may not say "and guest" because space may be at a premium or dinner may be expensive, and this may be the only way for the bride to include friends without going hopelessly overbudget. (Some would argue that it might be more generous for the bride to have a less elaborate wedding so she could include more people, but weddings reflect highly individual preferences.)

It's unusual, however, for only one spouse to be invited to a social function. If you're having a dinner party and want your married friend to come, you must invite her husband, too. If she declines because he's not available, she may be invited to come alone. And if she wants to, she should go.

The Ex-Factor

Researchers note that nearly half of all American marriages end in divorce (although happily that figure is stabilizing) and that we, ever hopeful, often remarry. Many couples are getting married for the second, even third time. And some bring children from a previous marriage to the union.

Where does your ex—or his—fit in? If no children resulted from the marriage, he probably doesn't. You may encounter each other on an occasional basis, and you should try to remain cordial. If the breakup was particularly nasty or public, this may be difficult, but comfort yourself with the knowledge that the time you spend together will be brief, and everyone can act like an adult for the sake of maintaining a pleasant evening for the other guests.

If the breakup was amicable and you have remained friends, there's no reason not to continue the friendship—as long as you don't get together *too* much and your respective spouses are included in the gatherings. Even then, it's not appropriate to display your ex's photo (unless you share children, in which case the photo should remain in their room).

His Name, My Name, Our Name

When your mother was married, it was automatically assumed that she would change her last name to your father's. Today some women choose to do this and others don't. If a woman has become well known in her field, she may choose to keep her maiden name at work and be Mrs. So-and-So socially. Or she may go all the way and simply keep her maiden name.

If you decide to do this, remember to let people know, when introducing them to your husband, that his name is different: "Margaret, I want you to meet my husband, Sidney Hogan." Margaret will, since she knows you, be aware that your name is different from your husband's.

If you're introducing yourself to strangers who know neither of you, state both your names so your husband doesn't end up being called by your surname: "Hi, I'm Linda Massey, and this is my husband, Sidney Hogan."

If you choose to share stationery as a couple, both your names will be listed:

Linda Y. Massey
Sidney A. Hogan
3200 Wildwood Terrace
South Orange, New Jersey 07079

If you choose to be listed in the telephone book, you have two options: you can be listed separately in your respective parts of the alphabet:

Hogan, Sidney A., 3200 Wildwood Terr . . . . . . (201) 555-6256
Massey, L.Y., 3200 Wildwood Terr . . . . (201) 555-6256

or you can ask that one of you be listed followed by the other:

Hogan, Sidney A.
and Linda Y. Massey . . . . (201) 555-6256

Couples with different last names usually give the father's name to any children they may have; sometimes the wife's last name is used as the child's first or middle name, if that is practical:

Linda Massey
and
Sidney Hogan
joyously announce
the arrival
of
Michael Massey Hogan
born
23 November 1994

Chapter 26

PRIDE AND JOY

Grown don't mean nothing to a mother.
A child is a child.
They get bigger, older, but grown.
In my heart, it don't mean a thing.

Toni Morrison, *Beloved*

It's been confirmed; you're going to be a mother! For many women, especially those who have planned or longed for their pregnancies, this is joyous news. Some are anxious to share their news with close friends and family members immediately. Others prefer to wait for a few months to get used to the idea themselves—and because the first trimester of pregnancy has traditionally been the time when miscarriages are most likely to happen: "I don't want to tell everyone and get them excited about my pregnancy before I know the baby's going to be okay. I'd just rather wait a few more weeks, to be sure."

Announcing Your Pregnancy

When you do decide you want to share the news, call your family and close friends. Or wait until you're face-to-face, and when they ask, "So what's new?" you can tell them in person and watch their surprised faces. If you're a letter writer, a note would be a great way to let a distant friend or relative know you're expecting:

> *Hi, Aunt Grace,*
> *Robert and I thought you'd like to know you'll have a new nephew or niece sometime in February—I'm pregnant! When we*

see you at the family reunion, in August, someone will be waiting to claim a piece of lap. Hope you're well. We're looking forward to seeing you this summer. Bob sends his love, too.

All my love,
Carrie

Genetic Screening

Depending on your age and medical history, you may be asked to take certain tests in your first trimester that will screen for genetic illnesses, such as sickle-cell anemia or its trait. One of the fringe benefits of these tests is the revelation of the developing baby's gender. The doctor will ask if you want to know the sex of your child. Some parents prefer to be surprised; others want to know because they can't stand the suspense—and because they'll know what color to paint the nursery. Whether or not you choose to know your child's gender is up to you. And whether or not you choose to share that knowledge with anyone else is also your decision as a couple.

A Single Parent by Choice

Although births to single mothers were treated with hushed embarrassment a few decades ago, today they are so commonplace they have become, if not accepted, at least widely tolerated. As more and more women decline postponing the joys of parenthood simply because Mr. Right hasn't appeared, more babies are being born to single mothers who have planned to have them.

Whether a mother adopts or has her child "the old-fashioned way" or via a newer technology, such as donor insemination or in vitro fertilization, the baby should be welcomed with all the fanfare every new baby deserves. The mother should not be asked, "Did you plan this?" or "Who's the father?" or "Why didn't you get married before you did this?" since presumably some thought went into the enterprise. If she hasn't chosen to fill you in on the exact circumstances surrounding her pregnancy, she obviously prefers to keep this information to herself.

If you're the expectant mother and you're faced with these questions, give simple, straightforward answers that don't violate your privacy: "Yes, I'm quite excited about becoming a mother." "The father's identity is a private issue." "I don't feel marriage and motherhood are inseparable." People with good home training won't press beyond that.

Adoptive Parents

Many parents—single people of both sexes and married couples—have, in recent years, begun to adopt in large numbers. Adopted babies should be given all the same privileges other children receive: birth announcements, a baby shower or party, and so forth. Questions to adoptive parents about their decision to adopt ("Couldn't you have any of your own?" "Won't your other children be jealous of him?") are strictly off-limits.

Baby Showers

These have two purposes: they allow a bit of a fuss over the new parents (who, let's face it, will fade into the background almost as soon as Wonder Child makes her appearance), and they provide the new baby with some basic necessities for starting out in life.

For decades, the traditional baby shower was a women-only party, with dainty food and plenty of female bonding to ease the prospective mother into her new status. In recent years, though, more and more fathers have been taking an active part in their children's births, from attending parenthood and birthing classes to actually helping out in the delivery room, so coed showers are becoming more common.

If you'd like to give a shower for a friend, ask her preference as to whether she'd like only her girlfriends to be invited, or whether she'd rather include her male friends, too—and her partner's. Pick a date not too far in advance of the baby's estimated arrival time (usually a month is safe) and time your invitations accordingly. If your friend has a list of specific things she'd like to have (a baby quilt, a baby bag, a half dozen bottles, etc.), you can ask her to register for these things at a baby store, or let people know when they call to accept the invitation that she would love to have certain things. A group of friends might like to split the cost of a large item, such as a stroller, a car seat, or a high chair.

If the baby arrives early, or if it's the mother's preference to have a shower after the baby is born, be sure to let people know when the baby arrived, so they can plan their gifts accordingly. If the shower is a month after his birth, newborn clothes probably won't fit for very long, if at all.

For first babies, showers are traditionally given by a friend or relative, on the premise that an up-until-then childless household will need to be completely outfitted for a baby. There's no reason not to celebrate the births of subsequent children, but instead of a shower, it's fine for the baby's family to choose a brunch or weekend dinner to introduce the new arrival to friends and relatives. If people want to bring presents, fine. But they shouldn't feel obligated (no wish lists this time around), as many will have given gifts when the first baby was born.

If you do take the baby a present, it's nice to take a token for the older children, too, since they may be feeling a little conflicted about the new baby. Puzzles, games, books, videos, and other "big kid" toys would cheer up a former only child who's now turned into a big brother or sister.

Announcing the New Arrival

However your baby gets here, once he's arrived, friends and relatives will want to know. A flurry of calls are usually made soon after the birth or when the adoption papers are signed. But there are other people beyond your immediate family who will also want to hear your good news, and a birth announcement is a good way to let them know.

Birth announcements are usually mailed out within a month or so after the baby comes. His full name and his parents' names are always included. Sometimes the names of his brothers and sisters, if he has siblings, are mentioned, too. The birth date is always part of the announcement. And some parents like to include the weight of the baby as well.

Traditional announcements may have a small card with the baby's name attached to the main announcement via a pink or blue ribbon. More modern announcements are limited only by the parents' imagination and budget. Some sample announcements follow:

For a New Baby Girl

James and Frances Weston
are delighted to announce
the birth of
Francesca Wilkens Weston
5 April 1993

For an Adopted Baby Boy

Brandon, Nikki, and Chad Gordon
proudly announce
the arrival of
Jonathan Monroe Gordon
born 9/14/94 arrived home 11/23/94
Melanie and John Gordon

Baby Born to Single Mother

Nadine Adams
joyfully announces
the birth of
Taylor Nadine Adams
June 12, 1995
7 lbs. 5 ozs.

Baby Whose Parents Have Different Last Names

Marie Highland
and
Chris Bender
are delighted to welcome their daughter
Jasmine Marie Bender
born October 18, 1996

Caregivers

Whether you're looking for someone to stay with your baby for a few hours a week so you can do errands or you need a full-time sitter to look after your child while you work, finding and getting caregivers has got to be one of the hardest—and most important—tasks a new parent faces.

You might begin your search by asking friends with day-care arrangements how they found their baby-sitters and whether they have any advice for you as you hunt. Sometimes it's a happy coincidence that a friend's child is going off to preschool just when yours arrives, and you find a great baby-sitter who's about to look for a new child to care for. If you have a good friend with a child approximately the age of yours, you may be able to share a sitter, who would care for the children in your home or hers. Some new mothers have struck gold by putting inquiries on their church bulletin boards or by scanning the community bulletin board at local places like the grocery store. People who have been through the process feel it pays to ask around.

If you are looking for day care outside your home, you need to make several visits before you make a final decision. Ask yourself:

- Do the children seem happy and engaged, or are they constantly clustered around the television?
- What is the ratio of caregiver to child?
- Does the caregiver know CPR?

Remember, it is essential that any day-care center you choose be licensed for child care by a state board and inspected according to board regulations. Ask for the license number so you can check.

If you're investigating a large facility that is institutional, not home-based, such as a preschool, you'll want to know:

- What kinds of activities do the children do all day?
- How large are the classes?
- Does the preschool have a philosophy about how children should learn or interact?
- What is the procedure if your child becomes sick during the day?
- How are medical emergencies handled, and where would your child be sent in case of a serious accident?

As with a home-based day-care arrangement, it's vital that you be able to check on who is running the place where your child will stay for most of the day, as well as be able to investigate whether any complaints have been lodged against it. There are specific procedures for this that vary state by state. Contact your Child Welfare Bureau for more information.

And no matter what your arrangement, parents should always have an information sheet posted in a prominent area (next to a telephone is best) that includes the following critical information:

- Work phone numbers of parent(s)
- The number of your baby's doctor, in case of medical emergency

- The name of a neighbor or friend she can call, if necessary
- Numbers for the police and fire departments
- The toll-free number for the Poison Control Center

Sharing a Baby-Sitter for the Evening

It's probably hard for new parents to believe, since they've seen no evidence of it, but parents *do* occasionally manage to get out for an evening with other adults. If the other adults have children who are approximately the age of yours, you might want to consider sharing a baby-sitter's services. If this is done, the sitter's fee should be split down the middle, and you should agree ahead of time how to handle the chore of picking her up and taking her home, if she doesn't have her own transportation.

Of course you'll always remember to leave the above-mentioned information sheet where she can find it in case of emergency. Also include a general indication of where you'll be and an approximate time you'll return home: "Gina: We'll be at the Fraziers' home—555-6212—back around 10. Gerry Peters." Or "We'll be at the Cineplex on Sunset Blvd; 555-8500. They have a paging system if there's an emergency."

Birthday Parties

If you give simple parties and your child is invited to elaborate ones, don't feel you have to have your own elaborate party as payback. It's enough to invite the child who has been a host. And be prepared, when you count heads, to include at least one parent per small child, since no parent can be asked, or expected, to look after a dozen little birthday guests on her own.

If your child is old enough to help participate in choosing a birthday gift for his friend, let him. It's valuable to allow him to shop for someone else and a good spiritual exercise to give, not get, something he would like to have himself.

At the end of the party, have the birthday boy stand at the door and thank his guests for coming. Or, if he's a guest, be sure he thanks the birthday child for inviting him and tells the child's mother what a nice time he had.

Learning to Write Letters and Notes

It's never too early to teach your little one to say thanks for the kindnesses shown to him. If he's old enough to talk, a simple "thank you" and a hug are greatly appreciated. If he's too young to write a thank-you note himself for a birthday or Christmas present, pen a few lines for him and send them on: "Nancy: Stephen loved that stuffed elephant! He can't go to bed now unless Blinky is next to him. Thanks and love, Stephanie."

If your child can sign his name or form a few letters of the alphabet, check your local stationer's for children's notepaper. Some thank-yous are partially prewritten, leaving a broad space for the little recipient to scribble (maybe with Mama's help) a word or two here and there:

> *Dear ___________, Thanks for the ___________! I love it!*
> *Love,*
>
> ___________

Older children should write brief notes specifying the gift they received and expressing some interest in the well-being of the gift giver:

> *Dear Grandpa: Thanks again for that model sailboat. Dad helped me put it together, and we went to the pond at Edgewood Park to try it out. It worked great! How are you and Grandma? Mom says you might come for Christmas. I hope so. We really miss you.*
>
> *Lots of love,*
> *Max*
>
> *P.S. Morgan says to please hug Spike for her.*

The notes may not be perfectly spelled or written in a beautiful hand, but they become treasured keepsakes. And they're a good habit for your child to get into. (One smart mother we know refuses to let her ten-year-old play with any of his newly received gifts until he has written a thank-you for each. Needless to say, his notes are completed in record time.)

CHILD'S THANK-YOU NOTE

Children Visiting Adults

If your child accompanies you to an adult friend's home for a visit, keep him in sight (unless there are children his age he can play with or an older child who volunteers to watch him) and encourage him to play quietly, perhaps with a small toy or coloring book you've brought along for him, while you and your friend chat.

If he's offered a drink or snack, he should accept or decline with a "Yes, please" or "No, thank you."

If there are pets about and he is afraid of or unfamiliar with them, encourage him to stay close to your side. If you're worried about the pet's temperament (and your friend doesn't sense this and put the pet away), try to end your visit without seeming too abrupt.

Children Visiting Other Children

When children visit their friends, make sure they offer to help clean up after the afternoon of play, and insist that they follow the house rules. If, for instance, the rules dictate that nobody but adults operate the VCR, your child should defer to them—even though he may know how to work one and does, in fact, do so when he's at home. He should refrain from informing his hosts "That's stupid" if it's a rule he doesn't agree with.

In general, impress upon him that his role as guest is to be pleasant, play well, do as he's told by the adult who is responsible for him while he's visiting, and to clean up any mess he's made before he leaves. He should always thank his host for a nice time and encourage a reciprocal visit, which you should emphasize by calling to arrange to host his friend within the next few weeks.

When Someone Else's Child Visits Your Home

The same rules as above apply: you're the boss. If you don't allow jumping on the furniture but little Malcolm's mother is more tolerant, stop him from jumping and inform him that furniture-jumping is not done in your house. It should be enough for him to know that these things are unacceptable in your home. If he protests or outright disobeys, tell him that unless he can play by the house rules, you'll have to take him home, where the rules are more to his liking.

Growing Up Too Fast

There is some wisdom to the thought that children should be allowed to be children for as long as possible, especially since they seem, with each passing generation, to become older more quickly. If you feel your child is too young to wear certain things (stockings for girls under twelve, eye makeup before she's well into her teens) or to take on certain responsibilities (going crosstown to school alone; going to the movies with a group of children his age, or seeing a movie that's more mature/violent/explicit than you're ready to have him see), you should not feel uncomfortable with your decision to wait on these things. For your efforts, you'll be bombarded with the pint-sized classic "But everybody else's mom is letting them do it!" And of course you'll have the same comeback your mother gave you: "I'm not everybody else's mother. I'm *your* mother, and I'm looking out for your best interests." Classics become classics for a good reason.

If your child is invited to participate in something that you think is too sophisticated for him or her (perhaps a group outing to see a movie that's too provocative), just let the inviting parent know "we're not at that point yet, but thanks for asking."

Age-Appropriate Clothing

Just as it shocks some people to see little girls in dresses that are far too mature for them, it mortifies some children to be dressed in clothes that they feel are "too babyish." By the time preschoolers can move about easily and dress themselves, they're usually perceptive enough to scorn those sweet clothes with nursery motifs their parents and grandparents are so fond of giving them. If you can give him a little leeway, let your child participate in choosing his wardrobe. Even young children express a preference for this color or that pattern, and it's easier to get them into clothes they've had a hand in choosing for themselves. Let them know what the ground rules are ("No superhero T-shirts for school, but they're okay to wear on weekends." "No designer sneakers; we agreed not to spend eighty dollars on gym shoes, remember?" "Sorry, your ballerina dress is for dance class. What else can you pick out?") and try to work with them from there. Some parents are surprised at their children's sensible choices and good taste!

Children at the Dinner Table

Most parents feel it's an advantage to have even small children with them at the dinner table. This is a perfect way to painlessly point out how to eat properly and mete out positive reinforcement at the same time: "Callie, you're doing so well with that fork! Look at Mommy's big girl eat her chicken!" Family news is exchanged, and for a few minutes, everyone is actually face-to-face in the same room at the same time. (This probably doesn't happen in most households every night, but with a little juggling, it's not impossible to achieve a true family dinner once or twice a week.)

Very small children will probably get antsy after they have finished their meal—even if you're still in the middle of yours. If it's truly hard for them to sit still (toddlers sometimes don't mind and can entertain themselves while you finish, while preschoolers get ferocious attacks of the squirmies and ache to be off doing something else), allow them to leave the table, after they've asked to be excused: "Okay, Stevie, you can go color in the living room while Daddy and Mommy finish. If you want some cake, you're going to have to come back here and eat it with us."

Children Addressing Adults

Call us old-fashioned, but we think children should refer to adults in their lives by some title or honorific ("Dr. Bass," "Mr. Houston"), unless the adult in question specifically requests otherwise. So your best friend might be referred to as "Aunt Helena," unless Helena wants it otherwise. And strangers certainly should be addressed as "Mrs. Moore" or "Mr. Dixon"—and they should be introduced by you as such: "Mr. Dixon, I'd like you to meet my youngest son, David. David, Mr. Dixon plays the piano at our new church." (David would then shake Mr. Dixon's extended hand and tell him, "Hi, Mr. Dixon. It's nice to meet you.")

Children at Adult Functions

If the invitation specifies "Mr. and Mrs.," it's safe to assume that Junior is not invited. Some hosts, especially people in childless households, prefer all-adult gatherings. Others don't mind including children and usually indicate this in some way. Sometimes this is done on the invitation ("children welcome"); other times the host may scribble a brief line at the bottom of the invitation ("Sara, please bring David if you can; we'd all love to see him"). And certainly if the invitation is addressed to "The Pryor Family," it's safe to assume that the invitation includes all family members.

Even when children are invited, some commonsense rules should apply: if the event is past a child's bedtime, don't keep him up to attend, unless he's had a nap earlier. If the child is ill or fretful or anxious around strangers, he'd probably be more comfortable at home. And very new babies who haven't built up their immunities should be left behind, for their own sakes.

Recitals, Graduations, Parents' Night

Part of being a parent or member of an extended family is the chance to watch your young one—or a dear friend's—shine in public. If you receive an invitation to a recital, play, or other event, try to attend if you can. Young actors are delighted when an adult makes room in his busy schedule to see *Peter Pan*. Aspiring tap artists and ballerinas always remember that first bouquet from Uncle Pete or Grandma. Be enthusiastic about the performance (even if it isn't stellar) and remember to commemorate it with a snapshot.

Parents' Night has different meanings at different schools. Sometimes this is the night reserved for parental visits to teachers, to check on your children's progress. At other times Parents' Night may be the catchall phrase for student show-and-tell: the school orchestra performs, the third-grade chorus sings, the fifth-grade poet laureate holds forth. It's vitally important to children that their parents (or whoever has custodial care) attend these functions. Move mountains. Change schedules. Put off doing something that needs doing in favor of these sweet, fleeting moments. They're gone before you know it, and they won't come again.

Blended Families and the Space Question

Many modern families are the result of a trend now referred to as "blending": children from previous marriages become stepsiblings; grandparents are inherited from a new marriage or union. Add to that the extension that many African American families normally make anyway, to include close family friends, longtime neighbors, and such, and our personal communities grow even larger.

This is mostly a blessing, but there is one time when the circle of family and friends can be a problem: when tickets to a coveted event are scarce, some way has to be devised to determine who gets to go see little Adrienne be a Sugar Plum Fairy.

In small families with no grandparents nearby, it's a no-brainer: the entire immediate family gets to go see Baby Girl perform. But what happens when there are only four tickets available, and Mommy and Daddy are divorced and remarried? Do stepparents take precedence over biological ones? Should the child, if he is old enough, have some say in who comes to see him graduate?

Some parents tell us they've settled this dilemma by rotating who gets to do what. If his maternal grandma travels from Atlanta to Seattle to see Marcus graduate from sixth grade, his paternal grandparents get front-row seats for Awards Night. Or Marcus may, if he's old enough, request that his grandfathers accompany him, with his parents. There are as many ways to figure this out as there are family configurations. The important thing is to try to include everyone at one time or another. And if you can extend the celebration by having a small gathering at home after the big event, then everyone can be part of the party. Perhaps only parents and grandparents get to use the six graduation tickets, but the family barbecue the next afternoon allows uncles, aunts, neighbors, and godparents to fete the graduate, too.

As for noncelebratory occasions, it's important that the parents with whom the child lives be present to hear why, for example, his math teacher is worried about his progress. If your child from your first marriage lives with you and your second husband, you should attend the conference. If your first husband is available, he should come, too. Or be included in a postmeeting discussion, via telephone. It's important that the parent who isn't living under the same roof with your child also be kept abreast of what's happening—good and bad—in his day-to-day life. Parents who live far away are especially appreciative when this effort is made on their behalf.

And it goes without saying that it's best if the adults can agree on what's in the child's best interest and present a united front when explaining any decisions you might make together: "Stan, your Mom, Step-Dad, and I have talked with Mrs. Snipes, and we've all agreed that you'll probably do better in math if you have someone to work with you a couple of times a week. So we're looking for a tutor so you can get a better grip on algebra."

Using Children as Detectives

In short, don't use children as detectives. Whom your ex-husband is dating, whether your ex-wife is going on vacation with a girlfriend or a new boyfriend, how much anyone spent on dinner or a haircut, are questions that children should not be placed in the position of having to answer.

If they blurt out information inadvertently ("Michelle says . . ." "*Who's Michelle?*" "Daddy's new girlfriend"), try to let it slide with a bland aside (*"Daddy has a new friend? That's nice."*). The only time to become actively involved is if you suspect your child is being exposed to inappropriate things ("Kwesi took us to see *Die Hard 3*—it was cool when that guy's head got blown off and we saw his guts and stuff!") or is being abused ("Michelle spanked me hard because I knocked milk over and it went on the floor").

If these things happen, immediately inform your ex that you need to come to some agreement about (for example) age-appropriate entertainment or the question of who, if anyone, besides the parents is allowed to physically discipline the children, when, and for what purpose. (Stepparents might be allowed to do this as part of a parental unit, whereas dates, even long-standing ones, would not be given the same leeway.) It's better to do this *before* the crises erupt, but if the crisis comes first, wait until you're calm enough to discuss it rationally. ("You'd better not let that woman touch my children ever again!" is not, probably, going to get the agreement you want on who gets to spank whom.)

The Teen Years

Just as you've managed to get your children through toilet training, the perils of learning to ride a bicycle without training wheels, and the trauma of a mouthful of braces, they enter adolescence and you're knocked flat.

Adolescence is a boiling stew of contradictory things: His legs may be long enough to reach the gas pedals, but his temper might be volatile enough that he's not yet ready to take the wheel. She may fill out the top of a bathing suit so well it's scary, but have no idea the power that her new bustline brings her in certain situations—or the consequences that can ensue if she's unaware of her effect on others. Because physically they often more closely resemble adults than children, teens may often insist on acting "too grown" for their parents' comfort.

Any parent who has wandered through the minefield of adolescence can tell you horror stories of the screaming matches they've undergone while trying to protect their increasingly independent children, but they'll also tell you that with plenty of honest communication and tolerance, there's light at the end of the tunnel. And after the turmoil of their teenage years, many of them turned out to be good friends with their parents, and nice people in their own right.

With growing up becoming more complicated each year, there's no formula for how to move through the teens. Perils like AIDS and several new sexually transmitted diseases that didn't exist even twenty years ago are now very real threats to young people, who sometimes think their youth makes them invincible. (Sadly, at this writing, young people are one of the fastest-growing segments of the AIDS population.)

The "But Everybody's Doing It!" Dilemma

You know the drill: "everybody's" mother is allowing him to come in past 2 A.M.; or wear makeup in the seventh grade; or buy outrageously expensive athletic shoes. Maybe it's true—and maybe it isn't. If you have strong feelings about the request in question (a party in a house where the parents aren't going to be home, for instance), don't be afraid to point out "everybody" doesn't live under your roof, and the house rules say no unsupervised parties.

Stylin' at School

Years ago, the dress codes for junior high and high schools were pretty clear-cut; now it looks as if anything goes. (In fact, the lines are drawn at various points, but it's often hard to tell where.) Now, in many parts of the country, we not only have to take into consideration our children's fashion druthers, we have to worry that the wrong fashion can send a message that might be disastrous. In cities plagued with gang problems, wearing the wrong-color shirt or cap might provoke an attack from a rival gang. Or it might encourage the local police to conduct a routine shakedown because your child looks like a gang member.

Find out what gang activity, if any, is in your neighborhood. Talk with your local police about the clues they use to recognize gang members (hats, bandannas, jackets with certain sports teams or insignia are sometimes give-aways). Try to encourage your child to wear neutral clothes that avoid gang inferences.

Really expensive items—a watch that was a present, a costly pair of basketball shoes, a leather backpack that's one of a kind—are better kept at home.

"You Can Tell Me Everything—I'm Your Mother!"

Your five-year-old might have been eager to share every detail of her day, but your fifteen-year-old might feel that she's entitled to a little privacy. To recognize her on-the-way-to-adult status, try to give her a little space of her own. Knock before you enter her room. Don't pick up an extension phone "by mistake" to check on who's at the other end. When she has visitors and they invite you to hang out with them and watch a TV movie, do. But when it's clear that the girls want some time to themselves, discreetly leave them alone.

If you suspect she's having difficulties, try to find out in a forthright way: "Gigi, I've been worried about you for the past two weeks. Is something happening at school you want to talk about? Maybe we can figure it out together." You want to protect her from making potential mistakes—but you don't want to shatter her trust as you do it, either.

The Birds and the Bees

Although you may have had several incrementally more detailed "where do babies come from?" discussions with your child since he was young enough to ask, even preadolescents are ready for a more advanced version of that birds-and-bees talk—especially if they're receiving little or no sex education at school. And especially because children mature physically more rapidly than you may have at your child's age.

Encourage your child to come to you with questions if he has any (even if the questions make you squirm internally) and try to answer as frankly as possible. Remember that if he doesn't get straight answers from you, he'll try to seek them elsewhere, and "elsewhere" could be anywhere—including his peers, who may be as fuzzy on the subject as he is.

Now is a good time for your children to begin to ponder the issue of forced sex, too. Daughters should know that they don't "owe" a date anything for a movie and a burger and that they should be firm, even forceful, in saying no if they're pressed to have sex. Sons should be warned that "no" means "no" (not maybe) and told that forced attention is unacceptable—and prosecutable by law, if the complainant presses charges.

If you'd prefer that your children abstain from sex totally until they're older, tell them, and tell them why. (Sex involves more than just genitals, and the psychological aftereffects of too-early sex can be significant, too.) Be frank with your children about the diseases they may come into contact with if they have unprotected sex. Explain the importance of condoms, as a protection against both pregnancy and STDs—or have your doctor do this, or a family planning clinic, if you're squeamish about getting too graphic. And if you suspect he or she is having sex, ask what they're doing to protect themselves and what they'll do if things don't go as planned: "What will you do if your girlfriend gets pregnant? Have you talked about this?" Since teen years are peak fertility years, this isn't so far-fetched a question; anyone who considers himself mature enough to have sex should be mature enough to consider a game plan if the sex results in a pregnancy.

Running with the Wrong Crowd

If you have a child who has never used curse words and all of a sudden his speech is sprinkled with them, if she's always been diligent about homework and her grades are suddenly dipping, if he's not hanging out with his usual group of friends but is mentioning kids you've never heard of before, that's a warning. Young folks' peers are almost as important to them as their families; in fact, they become surrogate families in many ways. That's wonderful if the "siblings" are children you've known and met and are pretty sure are being raised in much the same way you are raising yours.

But what do you do with kids who have different values, different house rules, and who have your child enthralled? Forbid him any access to them and they just become that much more glamorous. Give him license to run the streets with them and serious trouble could result. Probably the best compromise is to encourage your child to bring his buddies home so you can try to keep an eye on them all, and hope he'll become disenchanted with them soon. Whatever inconvenience you may realize because home has turned into hangout central will be offset by your peace of mind in knowing where your child is and who his current crop of friends are.

Different values are one thing (they stay out later than your children; they watch lots of TV and yours can't; they don't have to clean their rooms and yours do); dangerous values are another. If you suspect your teen is running with a pack of shoplifters, substance abusers, or young people otherwise involved in dangerous or illegal activity, you must have a talk with him immediately. And if you're not getting through to him, ask someone he likes, trusts, and respects (a grandparent, coach, uncle, neighbor) to add some words of wisdom.

Praise Where Praise Is Due

Bad behavior certainly gets attention, and too often, good behavior is taken for granted. We never outgrow our need for praise, and teens are no exception. Do praise them when they've done extraordinary things, and also be sure to notice when they've made personal sacrifices that allow life at home to move forward more smoothly: "DeAndre, I really appreciate your letting Sammy watch that whale movie right now; I know you wanted to see the ball game." Or "Lisa, Mrs. Hooks told me she tried to pay you for those errands, and you wouldn't take a penny. She thinks you're pretty special—and so do I." Even a little encouragement is enough impetus for future acts of selflessness.

Part V

FUNCTION AT THE JUNCTION

Party All the Time

Essentials for being a good hostess

invitations for all occasions

parties for all occasions

entertaining away from home: in a restaurant,

at a hotel, in a rented facility

what you'll need to throw that party

the basics of being a good guest

Chapter 27

THE HONOR OF YOUR PRESENCE

Surprise that special someone with a different kind of invitation: a single rose in a vase with a note attached, or a handwritten message on scented stationery secretly slipped into a pocket, a briefcase, or a purse.

Barbara Smith,
B. Smith's Entertaining and Cooking for Friends

Invitations Set the Tone

Your invitations set the tone for your party. Whether written or verbal, how you extend an invitation says much about you and the kind of party you'll be giving. Think about the last time you received an invitation in the mail. Just opening the invitation gave you your first clues about the upcoming event. You immediately knew whether the party was casual or formal, who was giving the soiree, when and where the event would take place, if it was to be for women alone or for couples. With any luck, the invitations you receive will also allow you to be instantly aware of what you should wear, if a gift is required, and maybe even the occasion and the color scheme. We're not suggesting you spend a lot of money on invitations for every party—we are suggesting that you think twice about sending out a messy, photocopied flyer with no envelope as an invitation.

By Invitation Only

Don't even think about bringing, or asking to bring, anyone whose name does not appear on the invitation. The exception to this rule is when an invitation is extended to you and a guest. "Ms. Brenda Smith and guest" does not mean "Brenda and four friends." When you respond, note whether you are required to present the invitation for admission to the event. This is not likely to happen at a house party, although security concerns do require the presentation of an invitation or a master list to verify that you are actually expected. More often than not, you are asked to present your invitation at large affairs where another, smaller reception is taking place for selected guests. An example of this would be a VIP reception prior to the NAACP Image Awards.

Are Your Children Automatically Invited When You Are?

If the invitation does not mention your children by name, is not addressed to "Keisha Waters and Family," or does not specifically state "children welcome," leave your children at home.

Timing and Sending of Invitations

With the exception of wedding invitations (see chapter 34, "To Love, Honor, and Cherish"), general invitations should be sent in ample time to be received by your guests no less than two weeks prior to your party. Clubs and organizations giving large parties and requiring a response or the purchase of tickets should usually plan for their invitations to arrive four to six weeks before the event. During the holidays send invitations earlier than usual, or telephone and alert guests to the upcoming event by asking them to "save the date," then follow up with the actual invitation.

Telephone Invitations

When inviting friends to join you for an informal dinner (or anything else), be direct. Do not say, "What are you doing Wednesday night?" Instead say, "I'm having a few friends in Wednesday to meet my brother Leroy who's visiting from Atlanta—would you like to join us for dinner?" The guest is then free to accept or regret. The guest should answer immediately and not say, "I'll let you know," which sounds like she's waiting for a better offer. It's perfectly acceptable to explain that you must check with your mate to verify he hasn't made other plans for the same night. In that case, the guest should offer to call the host the next day or as soon as possible.

When It's Too Late

It's never too late to extend an informal invitation. You may run into a friend and say, "I'm having some of our old friends over for chili tomorrow night, it would be great if you can join us." It *is* inappropriate to send formal invitations to a dinner party and then telephone someone you've forgotten. Use your judgment. When a dinner party guest cancels at the last minute, and your table is now short a valuable "talker," it's quite all right to call your sister and ask if she'd like to join you. If you do end up inviting someone at the last minute, long after the other guests have been invited, be up front. It's better to know you were asked at the last minute than to feel slighted when everyone at the party is talking about how fabulous the printed invitations were.

If you need a head count to plan food, be sure to take into consideration the snail rate of the U.S. Postal Service during holidays. Give your guests enough time to respond without making yourself crazy.

Distribution

Written invitations may be delivered by mail, fax, special delivery, or personally handed out.

Mail: On social invitations always use regular postage stamps (preferably pretty ones), not metered postage. Metered may be easier, but it shows a lack of thought for your guests.

Fax: Sending invitations by fax is an iffy proposition. You take the chance of the recipient never receiving the fax and of everyone else in that office knowing the details of a party they're not invited to. Also, you may not want strangers knowing your address and directions to your home, which may very well be on the faxed invitation. Faxes are acceptable for a small last-minute party when you've been having trouble reaching the guests by telephone.

Handouts: If you aren't sure of home addresses (it's an informal party) and you're inviting coworkers or members of your class, it's fine to hand out the invitations. You may be having an open house and don't know the full name of each neighbor you'd like to invite, so by all means, hand-deliver the invitations to them.

Special delivery: Sometimes the occasion deserves a little something special. Your invitations may be an unusual size or shape that won't easily fit into an envelope or box—or that you fear will be crushed—and you opt to have them delivered by a service. From FedEx or other overnight courier services to clowns or other characters who are available to dress for the occasion and hand-deliver your invitations, the possibilities are endless. One Christmas a company hired college students to dress in tuxedos and hand-deliver invitations stuffed into individual wicker sleighs full of cookies. Use your imagination.

Responses

Guests invited to any event should respond promptly. It is the decision of the host to make a request for response and how it will be written on the invitation.

"R.s.v.p." on an invitation is written with an uppercase "R." and lowercase "s.v.p." (translated from the French—"*Répondez s'il vous plaît*"—it means "Please respond"). Often an invitation will say R.s.v.p. and give a name and telephone number for you to call and confirm whether or not you will be attending. While not the most proper way, today it is acceptable to write your request for a response as "RSVP" in all capital letters, with or without periods. An alternative is asking for "Regrets only." When you see this on an invitation you have received, the request is for you to call only if you will be unable to attend. The problem with this type of response is that the hostess may be unprepared for who will, and will not, be attending her party. Considerate guests will telephone their regrets immediately. Those who may never have received the invitation or who thoughtlessly have forgotten to call will automatically be counted as attending. Formal invitations that state "Please respond" on the invitation itself (rather than on a separate response card) require a written note responding to the invitation.

A guest should respond in the manner indicated on the invitation. If no response is required, it is still nice to telephone or drop a short note to the hostess. Good home training suggests you do the most considerate thing.

Asking for an Invitation

A serious "don't you dare!": it is *never* appropriate to ask for an invitation for yourself or anyone else. If you know the event is a large buffet or cocktail party, and you have an out-of-town guest, it's okay to call and make the hostess aware of your situation. Never just show up with an extra person—and always abide by your hostess's wishes. In particular, do not try to get yourself invited to an affair because you're attempting to network and promote yourself and you know that important people will be there.

What to Include on Invitations

Who	is giving the party
When	the date and time of the party
Where	the location
What	type of party (dinner, luncheon, swim party, etc.)
Why (optional)	reason for the party (fiftieth anniversary, to meet my niece, etc.)
Response	R.s.v.p., "Please respond," or "Regrets only"
Date to respond (optional)	Respond by (date)

Using Fill-In Invitations

Fill-in-the-blank invitations can be used for both formal and informal occasions. Which you use when depends on the quality of paper, color of ink, and font or type used. If you entertain a lot, you might choose to have your own all-occasion invitations printed, with blanks strategically placed for the guest's name, the occasion, and the date. Or you can purchase attractive invitations that serve the same function.

Sample All-Occasion Fill-in-the-Blank Invitation

Dr. and Mrs. Joe Smo

request the pleasure of

Mr. and Mrs. Dysen

company at

Dinner

on

Saturday, 18 March

25 Carlsbrook Drive

Uptown, New Jersey 08540

R.s.v.p.

If you'd like to indicate that your party has a guest of honor, you can handwrite his or her name at the top of the invitation (before your own name) or before the address line. The wording would be "To meet Ms. Charlene Drew-Jarvis."

Sample Informal Fill-in-the-Blank Invitation

PHILIP AND KIM
ARE HAVING

AND HOPE

WILL JOIN THEM.

123 Beale Street
Memphis
Regrets only (801) 555-1230

These invitations are so versatile they are often kept on hand for impromptu gatherings.

Sample Formal Invitation (Handwritten)

Mr. Kim Hunter
requests the pleasure
of Miss Odessa Taylor's Company
at dinner
on Friday, the 14th of September
at eight o'clock
No. 34 Sutton Square, NW

R.s.v.p.
No. 34 Sutton Square, NW
Washington, DC

This type of invitation is not often used.

Maps and Directions

If your home or event location is difficult to find, or unfamiliar to some guests, draw a small map and/or enclose written directions from various points. For example:

> *If you're coming from the south, take the 405 freeway north exiting on Hobo Road. Turn left as you exit and proceed four miles on Hobbs to Ghost Lane. Right on Ghost, just past the high school, to the third house on the left.*

If you entertain with some regularity and your home is difficult to find, consider typing up directions from each major route of travel and have them printed on paper or a small card that would fit in almost any invitation-size envelope.

What to Do When Someone Has Not Responded

If you've planned a small party, you'll have to call the guests who have not responded and check on them. Don't start with "So why haven't I heard from you"? A better script might read, "Hi. Everyone is so busy these days, I didn't know if you'd tried to reach me regarding the luncheon. Will you be able to come?" Chances are it slipped her mind and she's glad (although quite mortified) you followed up. In some cases, the invitation may not have been received.

If the Party Is Canceled After the Invitations Have Been Sent

When invitations must be recalled, it may be done in writing or by telephone. If it was to be a large party, the most expedient way to notify guests is to have a card printed—put it in an envelope and send. If a last-minute emergency or other time constraints don't allow you to make individual telephone calls yourself, ask a close friend (or your secretary) to take over the task. This is a perfect example of the importance of keeping a complete guest list including addresses and telephone numbers. Originally, it could have been used to mark off respondees; in an emergency, it allows a third party to notify your guests.

Sample Recall Card (Formal)

Owing to the illness of
their mother
Jenckyn and Dara Goosby
are obliged to recall
their invitations for
Saturday, the 18th of May

Sample Recall Card (Informal)

Sorry, Mom isn't doing too well
and the party is off!
Hopefully we can reschedule
sometime soon.
Jenckyn and Dara

By telephone: State the reason for canceling the party and apologize. You're probably under stress anyway, so make it short and sweet.

Considering the Invitation

There are a number of things to consider when selecting or designing your invitations. Here's a checklist:

- ❑ Paper (color, quality, store-bought fill-in card, computer-designed)
- ❑ Ink and font or type style (color of ink, fancy or simple lettering)
- ❑ Addressing (hand-addressed or labels; print from computer, calligraphy)
- ❑ Wording (who, what, when, where, why, response)
- ❑ Envelopes (color, size, return address)
- ❑ Stamps (flowers, flags, black legacy series)

Sample Invitations and Responses

Informal Invitations (store-bought for you to fill in)

You Are Invited For

On

At

By

R.s.v.p.

Invitation from More Than One Host

Dr. and Mrs. Leonard Johnson
Mr. and Mrs. C. Albert Johnson
Mr. and Mrs. Randall P. Johnson
request the pleasure of your company
at brunch
Sunday, the 26th of June
at half past noon
The Elsinore Shore Club

R.s.v.p.
Mrs. C. Albert Johnson
626 Layfette Road
Los Angeles, CA 92516

Surprise Party

John
invites you to join him
in surprising
Kim
as she turns 40!
Friday, November 8th
6:30 p.m.
888 W. Slab Boulevard
San Antonio, Texas
Surprise at 7:15 p.m. Dinner at 8 p.m.

Child's Birthday Party

PHILIP
is turning 8 and
wants to celebrate!
Please come for pizza, games and cake
May 25th, 4pm
4242 Dinosaur Street
Wild Man, Missouri
Can't come? Please call Mrs. Smith (314) 555-4986

Invitations from a Club or Organization

The Los Angeles Chapter

of

Jack and Jill, Incorporated

requests the pleasure of your company

at a reception

on Thursday, the eighteenth of March

at five o'clock

at

The Wilfandel Clubhouse

1225 West Adams Boulevard

Los Angeles

Response Card

*M*____________________________

will __________ *attend*

will not __________ *attend*

March 18th

Sample Written Responses

Acceptance

Mr. and Mrs. Paul R. Williams
accept with pleasure
Dr. and Mrs. Goosby's
kind invitation for dinner
on Wednesday, the seventh of October
at eight o'clock

Regret

Mr. and Mrs. Paul R. Williams
regret that they are unable to accept
Dr. and Mrs. Goosby's
kind invitation for dinner
on Wednesday, the seventh of October

Combination Acceptance and Regret

Mrs. Paul R. Williams
accepts with pleasure
Dr. and Mrs. Goosby's
kind invitation for
Wednesday, the seventh of October
at eight o'clock
but regrets that
Mr. Williams
will be unable to attend

Various Christmas Invitations (Informal)

Organization

The San Francisco Smart Set
invites you to join them for . . .
Sunday Morning Jazz Brunch
as they celebrate Christmas
Sunday, December 20th
eleven o'clock
at
The Ritz Carlton
600 Stockton Street at California
San Francisco
in the Restaurant

Note: No response is required because the guests were invited, and responded, by telephone before the invitations were mailed.

Couple for At-Home Brunch

Printed on square card bordered with trains and reindeer.

Santa's Choo-Choo is chugging
along to the Mitchells for
Christmas Brunch . . .
(and Birthday too!)
So hop aboard and join us
Friday, December 25th
11:00 am
Marilyn and Al's
2235 E. 69th St #405
Chicago
regrets only by December 18th
Marilyn (312) 555-1111

Impromptu Open House

Printed on 8½ by 11 paper with Christmas design around border.

Rumor has it Christmas is in a few days . . .
and I *know* I need a reality check!

Please join me for a (last-minute)

"Come As You Are &
Escape the Madness"
Open House

Wednesday, December 21st
4–7 p.m.
Very casual . . . Drop by for Chili, etc.

Hope to See You,
Karen Williams
123 S. Main Street
Tampa, Florida
(kids welcome)

Chapter 28

HOSTESS WITH THE MOSTEST

I love it when everything shined and our warm, pleasant house was at its loveliest.

Barbara Smith,
B. Smith's Entertaining and Cooking for Friends

The host or hostess of an event sets the tone for the party. The hostess who is thoughtful and takes into consideration attention to detail—from start to finish—plans an enjoyable party. If you plan a party that you yourself would want to attend, you're probably on the right track.

Inviting People Who Would Enjoy Each Other

Don't invite people just because you owe them. Invite people you think would enjoy meeting and talking with each other. Sometimes it's just old friends (Christmas Eve dinner, fiftieth-birthday party); sometimes you will entertain an out-of-town guest or business associate. Choose wisely—give it some thought!

Setting the Tone

From the moment your guests open their invitation, the party has begun. Consider the mood as your guests arrive. Carefully plan the music, flowers, seating arrangements, the "flow" of the party, and the guest list itself.

Be on Time

Don't keep your guests waiting, and certainly don't hold them hostage by serving so late that they feel like they'll never get to go home. At the beginning of the party, make sure your guests feel comfortable and have something to do when they arrive. If you're not prepared with drinks or appetizers, your guests will just be standing around.

Where to Put People's Coats

Lucky you if your home has a guest closet. In the event you don't, select a room where the coats can be placed. If the party is large, you may need to rent a coatrack. If you must put the coats in private space (like your bedroom) and don't feel particularly comfortable with people traipsing all through your home, ask a close friend to handle taking guests' coats and retrieving them at the end of the evening.

When a Guest Asks If She Can Bring Something

Usually, say thanks, and no. If it's a close friend, however, and there's something you need, be specific with your request. "I'm running late. It would be great if you could pick up a bag of ice." For a potluck, be specific (but not *too* specific) about what you'd like a guest to bring. Indicate a category or type of food. Don't say, "Bring macaroni and cheese"; ask if she can bring a hot side dish.

If a Guest Brings Wine or Dessert That Doesn't Go with the Meal

Thank the guest and ask whether he'd mind if you saved it for the family. You can genuinely appreciate the gesture without making it part of your event.

How Long After Guests Arrive Should Dinner Be Served?

If your guests are invited for 7 P.M., and drinks will be served ahead of time, dinner should be served at 8 P.M., or one hour after the invited time. If no drinks are served prior to dinner, the meal should begin to be served twenty to thirty minutes after the invited time.

How Long Should You Wait for Late Dinner Guests?

Do not delay serving dinner for more than fifteen or twenty minutes. Waiting any longer than that would be rude to your guests who were considerate enough to arrive on time. When the folks finally arrive, don't be angry, just mention that you already started because you knew they wouldn't have wanted you to wait for them.

When Friends Are Chronically Late

We've wanted to ask some chronically late friends if they'd checked with Amos and Andy lately and "simonized" their watches—but no matter how much they plead that this is the last time they'll be late, you know they will be again. Have you ever wondered whether you should tell such friends that dinner will be served at 6 P.M. when really it's scheduled for 8? There's another tack you can take. Mention to your friends that you're giving them one more time to be on time, and if they are late again, you'll consider not extending another dinner invitation. Or only invite them to open houses or cocktail parties where time is not so important.

Is a Tardy Guest Served Missed Courses?

The tardy guest is seated and starts on whatever course is currently being served. If you've already completed dinner and dessert is being served, the guest should be offered the entrée first. No other courses need be offered.

Uninvited Children

If children were not specifically invited, they should have been left at home. If a guest simply shows up with children in tow, welcome them, provide refreshments they might enjoy (a peanut butter and jelly sandwich rather than the spicy jambalaya you're serving everyone else), and cope.

Allergies and Pets, Yours and Theirs

When entertaining in your home, it's safer for all not to have your pets underfoot. You won't fret about the guest who is terrified of your dog, or have to frantically search for antihistamines when the cat has six guests about to sneeze all over the buffet table. As a guest, don't even think of bringing your pet to an affair to which you've been invited.

Seating Couples

Make the table interesting. Don't seat couples together. A meal shared with others is an opportunity to talk to people they normally don't get to interact with.

Oops, That Unexpected Guest

If some of your guests arrive uninvited, welcome them and adjust your seating arrangement as best you can to accommodate them. If an invited guest calls at the last minute to ask if he may bring an out-of-town houseguest, warmly extend an invitation to the additional person if it's convenient (or not *too* much trouble). If it's an intimate dinner party and due to space limitations and your arrangements with the caterer you are unable to accommodate the extra person, just say so. The original guest will then have to decide whether he can still come or is obligated to his houseguest. (We're hoping he had the good sense to have thought this out before he called.)

What May I Get for You?

If you are having more than eight or ten guests, and your husband or significant other doesn't offer to take on the added responsibility of serving drinks, hire a bartender for the evening. If you're serving only one or two beverages (like champagne and sparkling water), the beverage can be poured into glasses and served from a tray as the server passes through the crowd. *Never* serve drinks or appetizers without napkins.

Appetizers and Stray Toothpicks

Make sure to provide a receptacle for used toothpicks and small plates and napkins. Don't expect your guests to eat appetizers from a buffet table without having a small plate. Otherwise, the guests will end up spending their time holding down the fort at the table, because they can only hold, and eat, one thing at a time. If you will be passing appetizers, always serve with a napkin. A plate is optional in these instances unless dipping sauces are involved.

Dietary Restrictions

When serving dishes containing such items as shellfish, nuts, or dairy products that guests are commonly allergic to, be prepared with a backup entrée. Grilled chicken or a plain pasta marinara is usually a safe choice. When your guests have chosen a lifestyle and eating habits that are restrictive, you are more likely to have some prior knowledge about what they don't eat. Many people do not eat red meat, pork, or fried foods, or are strict vegetarians. Plan accordingly, or again, have a backup. Make sure your backup entrée is something that can be eaten by the family in the next day or two, or can be frozen, in case it's not used.

Uncomfortable Situations

Try to handle uncomfortable situations as quietly and unobtrusively as possible. Potential problems or situations:

- The caterer doesn't show.
- The guest of honor at a surprise party arrives early.
- Dinner is burned.
- An extra person shows up with another guest and there aren't enough seats.
- Kitchen catches fire or the stove goes out.
- It rains on your outdoor luncheon.
- A guest becomes abusive.

Anticipate what you might do in these situations so that if and when they may happen you won't be left paralyzed.

When Someone Spills or Breaks Something

Act as if it doesn't matter at all. Be gracious and kind, and put the person at ease. It's okay to whip out the club soda to soak what will soon be a stubborn stain, but don't have a fit about it. Giving a guest grief about an accident that has already mortified him will only make your other guests uncomfortable.

Toilet Paper and Guest Towels

Don't be so busy cleaning the obvious party rooms that you forget the "designated bathroom." Be it a guest powder room or the family bathroom, make sure it's inviting to guests. Always check to make sure an extra roll of toilet paper is available and that there is a sufficient supply of pretty paper hand towels or cloth hand towels. To be safe, keep a supply of paper guest towels in case they're needed.

Just Say No!

Times will arise when you have to assert your house rules to protect the other guests and make the party continue to be enjoyable. Some of these to be prepared for:

- Vulgar or racist jokes are being told. Curtail the conversation, quietly, and let the offenders know you do not approve and it is embarrassing to you.
- Some of the guests are smokers. If you don't smoke, and don't allow others to smoke in your home, you have one of two options. Ask that no one smoke, or provide an outdoor space (with chairs) for the smokers.
- Guest has had too much to drink. If the person has become sick, get whomever he came with to help. He needs to go home. If a man has come alone, ask another man to assist you. As hostess, you will help women guests, along with the assistance of another woman. Don't let the drinker drive; call a taxi if necessary. Remember that in many states, you are legally liable for any accidents caused by someone who obtained drinks at your house. (For more details, see chapter 8, "Strictly Speaking," and chapter 13, "My House, My Rules.") Finally, smooth over any indiscretions with the victims.

Asking an Offensive Guest to Leave

If a guest is unbearably offensive to you, or to another guest, take him aside and ask him to leave. Do not embarrass the offender, if at all possible. If the guest refuses to leave, ask a gentleman to escort him out. If at a "ladies' lunch" or "girls' night out," gently ask the offender to leave. If necessary, ask another friend to help you. Never physically attempt to remove a guest (or a gate-crasher for that matter). If the guest becomes violent, or is a threat to you, your family, or the other guests, call 911 immediately.

Are Soufflés Supposed to Rise? (Trying Out a New Recipe)

Never try a new recipe on anyone other than your closest friends—and even then you should 'fess up early on that you're trying something new. While some recipes appear foolproof, they can never fully take into consideration the temperature of your oven, the misread label, or the sticky "nonstick" pan. If you're trying to be fancy or try out that recipe that looked so great in last month's magazine, try it out at least a week in advance of your party. This will allow you time for adjustments in cooking time, seasoning, and portion sizes (when the recipe says "serves six" and it has never stretched to serve any six people you know).

Having Enough Food

Black folks often cook as though every family on the block might drop by. While we don't suggest overdoing it (unless you're planning to freeze the leftovers), we do recommend ensuring that you have *enough* food. People are eating lighter meals, but that doesn't mean they'll watch their portions with a pot of gumbo on the table. The smell of bread pudding, peach cobbler, or sweet-potato pie has made many a dieter fall off the wagon. Be prepared for drop-in guests—some of our friends can "smell" a good meal from miles away.

And Brother, Remember

You, Too, Can Entertain with Flair

Entertaining is not the exclusive domain of women. As a single man, a considerate husband, or a thoughtful roommate, you can add your unique flair to the festivities. For hundreds of years men have excelled as chefs, and have showcased their creative talents through their work and their hobbies. You may be a designer of compact disc (CD) covers, or a hairdresser who wields a mean pair of scissors; you may take pleasure in painting or expressing yourself through your words. Whatever you do, the same skills can make you "the host with the most."

You might start by perfecting a favorite dish and surprise your friends with your masterpiece. It doesn't have to be fancy, it just has to taste good and be something you enjoy. You may decide on chili, barbecue, fried chicken, gumbo, homemade ice cream, or a to-die-for sweet potato pie. You'll stumble at first, and feel like a mad scientist, but you'll rise to the occasion next time the call goes out for a potluck, or you just want to have some people over.

Take care in the presentation, don't leave a mess for someone else to clean up, and make it fun!

Food may be a key ingredient to entertaining, but there are other ways you can join in. You may become bartender extraordinaire, or the man with the eye for centerpieces and decorations, or the guy who doesn't mind cleaning up. Whatever it is, do what you enjoy.

Centerpieces

Set a table that is pleasing to the eye with floral arrangements or centerpieces that are not so tall your guests cannot see over them to talk. Consider what type of meal you are serving. Will it be buffet, family style, or served to seated guests?

Favors

Special parties aren't the only time you may want your guests to leave with a small gift from you. Favors are placed at each setting or handed out as your guests leave as a delightful reminder of an enjoyable event. So often we think of taking the hostess a gift, but when the mood strikes, it's lovely for the hostess to show her appreciation for her guests. Suggested favors: individually boxed truffles or hand-dipped strawberries; instant photo of the guest taken during the party; for women, individual packets of bubble bath or shower gel.

The End of the Evening

Don't spend your time in the kitchen cleaning up while your guests are still enjoying the party. The dishes will still be there—the moments of sharing with friends should not be missed.

Party's Over . . . When the Guests Won't Go Home

The party is going strong and you're on your last leg. If the guests are close friends, be up front and let them know it's time for them to go home because you have an early meeting the following day. If you don't know all of your guests well, locate a close friend and ask her or him to get the coats and suggest to the group that it's time to go "before we wear out our welcome." Try to be lighthearted about it—don't act like a dorm mother and start flicking the lights.

Hostess Record Book

If you entertain frequently, it's a good idea to keep a record of all parties you host. Things you'll want to remember and refer to later:

- Day, date, and time
- Number of guests invited, attended, and any special guests
- Occasion or theme
- Menu
- Caterer
- Any servers or other help (bartenders, waiters, cleanup crew, etc.)
- Rentals, if any
- Special music, centerpieces, and decorations
- What you'd do again
- What went wrong

Host the Kind of Party You'd Like Going To

We know you've been to the kind of party where, at the end of the evening, everyone raved about what a fabulous time they had: the guests were interesting people, the food and drinks were memorable, and time just flew. This didn't just happen with a wave of a wand, it took considerable planning on the hosts' part. If you think back on it, you might have guessed the party was going to be wonderful when their imaginative invitation arrived. When you got to the party, you were welcomed, your coat was taken. You were introduced to a few people, offered drinks. Perhaps music was playing in the background, and you don't remember anyone rushing across the room to change the tape or CD.

It's not all magic; party-giving skills can be learned by anyone who is willing to take the time. By all means, don't host parties that make you crazy because you're spending the entire time fretting over every little detail, petrified that everything will go wrong. Do consider who/what/when/where/why as you make your party plans:

Who should be invited? It's not required that your guests become each other's friends, only that they enjoy each other's conversations and company.

What kind of party will work for you? Consider your space, finances, and other constraints.

When is an appropriate time for your party? If you plan to have a spring dinner in your backyard, remember that nights in some parts of the country can be cool.

Where will you have your party? Indoors? Outdoors? Your home or somewhere else? How much room you have dictates how many people you can comfortably accommodate. For instance, a champagne sip for 150 will be tough in a studio apartment.

Why are you giving the party? You may have a special celebration or other happy occasion in mind, but if you don't, we don't think you ever have to have a reason to host a party!

Chapter 29

LET THE PARTY BEGIN

They had a great big party
Down at Tom's the other night . . .

Paul Laurence Dunbar, "The Party"

Whether it's a little get-together for close friends and families or a full-fledged blowout, you still have to figure out what you're serving, how much you'll need, and when you're going to get all the preparty work done. Some people agonize over parties before they give them, and their meticulous planning makes sure that everyone has a wonderful time (except maybe the host!) and plenty to eat and drink. Other people seem to have the gift of just making great parties happen with hardly any prior planning—even if all that's at their disposal is a pantry full of odds and ends. You may fall in either camp or somewhere in between; wherever you are on the party-giving scale, this chapter should give you some useful guidance.

Stocking the Bar

If you keep the basics on hand well before you think of inviting people over, you'll find you have less to purchase before the party. One way to do this painlessly is to make a list of what you'd like in your household bar, then purchase a bottle or two every time you shop for groceries. In a short period of time, you will have assembled the basic bar, and you can then replenish items when necessary, as they're used up. We've found that this way, we mostly end up buying only mixers (club soda, other kinds of soft drinks, juices, etc.) before the party.

And remember that although stocking the bar basically involves liquor, you'll want an assortment of nonalcoholic beverages on hand for guests who cannot or choose not to drink alcohol.

Glasses and Tools

To set up your home bar, you should have the following tools:

- ❑ Corkscrew
- ❑ Jigger
- ❑ Strainer
- ❑ Paring knife
- ❑ Bottle opener
- ❑ Citrus reamer
- ❑ Stirrer
- ❑ Pitcher
- ❑ Ice bucket and tongs
- ❑ Cutting board

In addition, you'll want a set of glasses that can be used for the basics:

- ❑ All-purpose wineglasses (for use with red or white wines)
- ❑ Champagne flutes (not the saucer kind, which will kill the bubbles)
- ❑ Highballs (12-oz or over, for water, soft drinks, and drinks that are mixed with soft drinks, such as gin and tonic)
- ❑ Old-fashioned glasses (for whiskey served on the rocks)

Later on, you might consider adding:

- ❑ Cordial or sherry glasses (small, stemmed glasses that can be used to serve liqueurs or fortified wines, such as port, claret, and madeira)
- ❑ Brandy snifters (for brandy, single-malt liquors taken without ice, eaux-de-vie [see Glossary], and other aromatic spirits)
- ❑ Martini glasses. (Die-hard martini drinkers swear the drinks taste better in these. Also use them for daiquiris and drinks using shaved or crushed ice. Large martini glasses can be pressed into service as parfait glasses.)

Most of these tools and glasses can be purchased in the housewares section of a large department store; specialty stores such as Crate & Barrel and the Pottery Barn always keep them in stock at a reasonable price.

GLASSWARE, STEMMED

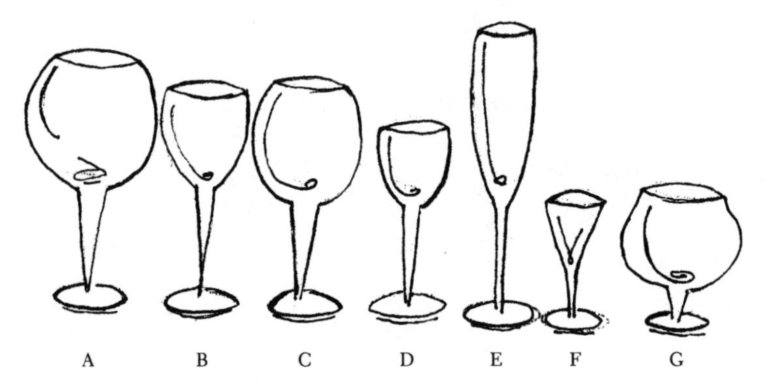

From left to right: A, water; B, white; C, red; D, all purpose; E, champagne; F, sherry; G, cognac.

OTHER GLASSWARE

Basic Liquor Requirements

Your bar should contain the basics for commonly requested drinks, and after that you can expand to include personal and family favorites (like that blackberry cordial you keep for Great-Aunt Essie).

- ❑ Brandy or cognac
- ❑ Vodka
- ❑ Rum, light and dark
- ❑ Scotch, blended and single-malt

- ❏ Gin
- ❏ Vermouth, sweet and dry
- ❏ Sherry
- ❏ Champagne
- ❏ Red wine
- ❏ White wine
- ❏ Beer

Don't forget the mixers:

- ❏ Ginger ale
- ❏ Club soda
- ❏ Cola
- ❏ Sugar-free cola
- ❏ Tonic water
- ❏ Mineral water (with and without bubbles)

After you've established your basic bar, you might want to add a few extras:

- ❏ Aperitifs (see Glossary)
- ❏ Bourbon
- ❏ Port
- ❏ Eau-de-vie (see Glossary)
- ❏ Cordials (Grand Marnier, Drambuie, Kahlúa, crème de cacao, crème de menthe, etc.)

And Brother, Remember

Giving a Toast

At times of celebration you may be called upon to make a toast. Make your remarks short—this is not meant to be a dissertation. Your sentiments may be humorous or may include an interesting anecdote. Carefully think about what you're going to say if you know ahead of time that you will be called on. Don't make your remarks either so serious or so silly that those who are joining you in the toast think that you've already had too much to drink. The main thing is to be sincere.

How to Open a Champagne Bottle

Even if you don't drink, you may occasionally be called upon to open a champagne bottle. If you remember these simple steps, you should be prepared:

1. Remove the foil from the top of the bottle.
2. Untwist the wire over the cork and remove the metal disk over the cork.
3. Wrap a towel around the base of the bottle in case it bubbles over and spills.
4. Hold the bottom of the bottle against you, with the mouth (top) pointing away from anyone who may get hurt (including you).
5. Put your hand over the top of the cork.
6. Gently remove cork by slowly rotating the bottle with one hand while holding the cork in place with the other. The bottom line—turn the bottle, not the cork.
7. Slowly ease the cork out. If you are too quick, the champagne will foam up and bubble over.
8. Before pouring, let the carbon dioxide escape. Tilt the glass just a little so the champagne won't fizz too much as it's poured.

Wine and Food: What Goes with What?

The old rule specified white wine with fish and poultry and red wine with meat and game. But that's changing, as Americans become more interested in and sophisticated about wine. Leaf through any food magazine and you'll see recipes for fish cooked or served with red wine: San Francisco's famous fisherman's stew, cioppino, has red wine in it, and roast or barbecued salmon is often served with a young red wine. The same for poultry.

If you've planned your menu but are in the dark about what kind of wine goes best with it, visit a liquor store with knowledgeable staff and ask for advice. Be sure to tell the salesperson what kind of dish you're having ("pasta" isn't very helpful—he needs to know whether the sauce you're tossing the pasta in contains cream or tomatoes, seafood or meat, whether it's spicy or bland, etc.) and what price range you want to stay within. A good salesperson will offer you a choice that will enhance your meal at a price you can afford. If you develop a relationship with a wine-savvy salesperson, you receive free private tutoring every time you visit; after a while, you unconsciously absorb the things you're being taught and can make your own selections with confidence.

Seating Your Guests

If you don't want people to pull up chairs wherever they want to, you'll have to assign them seats or indicate their places with small cards, known as place cards.

Traditionally, seated dinners followed the boy-girl-boy-girl pattern, with the guest of honor, if there is one, seated to the host's right, at the head of the table. Married couples were usually not seated next to each other, the assumption being they saw each other enough at home and would like to visit with other people.

Like everything else, those rules have become more flexible. Many hosts invite couples and singles and may well have more of one sex than another at the table. Sometimes married couples sit across from each other; often they're at opposite ends of the table—or, if there is more than one table, at separate tables altogether.

If you want, develop a seating plan that places next to each other those guests with similar interests or who might enjoy getting to know each other better. On a plain piece of paper, draw the shape of your table(s). Place yourself at the head, and working your way clockwise around the table, list the guests in the order you'd like them to sit ("Me, Marcus, Natalie, Jay, Earlene, William"). Use place cards (you can make them from stiff paper—anything about the weight of an index card will work—or buy them, ready-made in any stationery store) with your guests' first names handwritten on them to indicate where you'd like people to sit.

When two of your guests have the same first name, you can eliminate any confusion by adding a last initial. If you're having separate tables, you'll want to number each table and provide a chart that lists each table and who will be seated there, so guests can consult the chart before they go in to dinner: "Table 6: Mrs. Trinidad, Mr. Hamilton, Ms. Jones . . .")

If you're a guest and find yourself scheduled to sit next to someone you'd rather not—grin and bear it. Most hosts who use place cards have gone through a great deal of trouble to figure out who should sit where, and it is rude, rude, rude, for anyone to switch cards for any reason.

Serving and Clearing Dishes

The old rule still does apply here: lower from the left, raise from the right. Basically, this means you should always serve from the left, lowering dishes from the diner's left side, and pick up dishes from the diner's right. You'll know each person is finished with his main plate because he has thoughtfully remembered to place his fork and knife together, with handles at the "four o'clock" position, on the plate.

Scraping Plates and Stacking Dishes

Although it's more trouble to remove each plate individually to the kitchen to scrape and stack them there, please don't think about doing this any other way. It would be a shame to ruin the mood of the gorgeous meal you've gone to all the trouble to prepare by shoveling garbage from one diner's plate onto the plate of the person next to him. Take the time to take plates away two by two (one in each hand) and return until the table's empty. If someone volunteers to help and you'd like help, the work will go that much more quickly.

Cloth vs. Paper Napkins

The formality—and messiness—of the meal dictates when each is used. Save your best white damask napkins for your most formal dinners. Those bright cotton prints work well for everyday meals. And if you're serving a mess of steamed crabs, barbecued ribs, fried chicken—especially if you're eating outdoors—paper napkins are just the ticket. Most grocery stores have a good selection of pretty, sturdy napkins in several designs and sizes.

Entertaining on a Work Night

Many people choose not to entertain on a weeknight, figuring their free time during the week is so limited, there is no point in cutting into it even further by entertaining. But sometimes opportunities arise—a mutual friend is in town only for the evening; you're asked to give a fund-raiser for a good cause—that make weeknight entertaining a necessity.

We'd urge you to simplify, simplify. If you like to cook and know ahead of time you're going to have people over, make your main course beforehand and freeze it. One-dish meals (lasagna, paella, stews, etc.) are perfect for this. On the day of the dinner, you put your meal in the oven or microwave, prepare some salad and bread, open a bottle of wine, and you're done.

Also consider takeout: a Chinese feast, a Caribbean meal of jerk chicken and rice and peas, or fried chicken with all the trimmings can be picked up on the way home, as can dessert from the bakery.

Consider letting guests bring part of the meal if they ask to. A nice loaf of bread or a box of good cookies is one less thing for you to worry about.

Finally, dinner at a restaurant is a time-honored way for hosts to entertain weeknight guests. Plan the menu with the maître d' a few days ahead. If you can, give the restaurant your credit card number in advance so you can quietly sign for the bill when it is presented.

Payback Parties

If you've been entertained by many friends and have neglected to issue some invitations of your own in return, throwing everyone you need to pay back in one room at one time is not the way to reciprocate. This is the entertainment equivalent of giving a dinner party because you need to clean the odds and ends out of your refrigerator, and we're sorry, but it's tacky. Your Ladies Church Circle and the Partygirl Network may not necessarily want to know each other any better. It makes more sense to have a series of small parties with like-minded people: a champagne brunch and romantic videos for the Partygirls and tea and cookies for the Ladies Circle might be more manageable and more fun for each.

If This Is Noon, It Must Be Lunch . . . or Maybe Brunch

Having people over for a midday meal is, in some parts of the country, starting to give the traditional Saturday-night dinner party a run for the money. "It's easier to do in the middle of the day," one hostess who's switched to brunches explains. "People can come with their children, and they don't have to worry about baby-sitters." Or if they leave their children with baby-sitters, they have an easier time getting a sitter, since Saturday evenings are still prime date slots for teenage girls. "The meals are more casual, I like that. And you have the rest of the day to recover from it, instead of a couple of hours before it's time to get up for church or work."

This line of reasoning is catching on, and many hosts choose to make brunch the main meal of the day. After guests have eaten and visited with each other for part of the day, "we might have any leftovers for dinner," says another host, "or maybe just a simple meal of soup and sandwiches, because we ate so much earlier."

Selecting a Menu

As we mentioned earlier, unless you have a specific reason for doing it, you probably wouldn't want to have a meal that revolves around one thing (garlic or potatoes or lemons from start to finish). Traditionally, a meal is comprised of courses, although in modern life this has been slimmed down considerably, often to three courses: a starter, a main course, and something sweet to finish. (In the old days, a formal meal was actually seven courses long!)

You'll want to offer your guests different tastes and textures from course to course, so their taste buds don't go to sleep. If you have a spicy seafood and vegetable soup to start, you might want to segue into a calmer main course, such as grilled chicken that's been marinated in lemon juice, olive oil, and a few herbs, with rice or potatoes and a vegetable. Dessert might be something creamy and crunchy: homemade vanilla ice cream with chocolate lace cookies.

"To Your Health . . ."

Over the course of a pleasant evening, it's not unusual for a guest to offer a toast on his host's behalf—especially if the evening marks an occasion, such as a birthday, anniversary, engagement, or promotion. If you're seated at a small gathering, it's not necessary to grab everyone's attention by using your half-filled glass as a chime—although you might have to resort to this in a large room.

The person toasting simply stands and says a few words—"I've known Leah since she first came to our company, and I'm not at all surprised she's been chosen to run it . . ."—then raises his glass toward the person being toasted and takes a small drink. Other guests raise their glasses, too, and follow suit. After their first sip, it's fine for you, the guest of honor, to take a drink.

If you're the person being toasted, you may want to offer a brief response: "Thanks, Larry. And I probably wouldn't be in this job today if you hadn't taken me by the hand and shown me how everything around here—including the coffee machine!—works . . ." The tone for both the toast and the response should be taken from the gravity of the occasion. A toast before the Board of Deacons would probably vary considerably from one given among good friends who are celebrating a landmark birthday.

Guest Register

Even if you don't have a grand house or entertain often, you may want to keep a guest register as a way to enable you to look back and remember who visited with you and where they were living at the time. A visitor usually signs her name, address, and the date of the visit and may add a spontaneous comment or two if space allows: "Annie and Maceo Spinks, 173 LaFayette Drive, Atlanta GA 30303. Best shrimp curry we've ever eaten—come see us soon!" Some families use guest registers as a way of keeping their Christmas card lists and address books current. Others maintain them as family historical documents, to show children and grandchildren who visited with their family on occasions such as an anniversary celebration or reunion, or for events both sad (funerals) and joyous (weddings).

Guest registers are usually permanently bound and can be as small as 5 by

7 inches or as large as a desktop diary. You can buy them in many stationery stores, department stores, gift shops, and office supply stores. They are usually left on some flat surface (a table in a hallway, or a small table or stand moved near the door during a party) that will allow guests easy access to the book and encourage them to take a moment to sign. Don't forget to leave a pen nearby (some hosts like to attach one with a ribbon so it doesn't "wander").

Plan B

As Mr. Murphy (whoever he was) once noted, "If something can go wrong, it probably will." Murphy's Law applies to parties, too: Plan a brunch on your sunny patio, and of course it will rain. Decide upon seafood gumbo you can throw together the morning of the party, and of course when you visit the market at ten they're all out of the seafood you plan to use. Hire people to help you serve and clean up, and their car breaks down with no phone nearby.

It always helps to have a plan B ready, just in case your initial game plan goes haywire at the last minute. If the weather clouds over an hour before everyone's supposed to show up, clear your tables inside and prepare to place everything in the dining room, and encourage guests to find a seat where they can. Caterer forget to put you on his schedule? Zip out to the nearest grilled or fried chicken joint, run through the grocery store for salads that have been prewashed and sealed in bags, store-bought dessert, and cheese and crackers. (This works when you end up with half again as many guests as you'd planned on having, too. Good fast food and salad are great "stretchers.") The basic aim is to make do with what you have, don't worry about what you don't, and enjoy your guests.

Chapter 30

PARTIES AND CELEBRATIONS

A small party; a big affair.

Zaire proverb

While we favor parties for any and every occasion, some are more special than others. In this chapter we discuss ways to entertain for various occasions and events.

Birthday Parties

Birthday parties are not the sole domain of children. They can be enjoyed by teenagers and adults alike. While family celebrations are always a winner at any age, we suggest parties for each age group.

CHILDREN

Children's birthday parties need not be elaborate to be fun. An essential part of growing up and learning to socialize when you're a child, a party is not to be expected each and every year. Family dinners shared with just Mom, Dad, Grandma, and your little sister can be the most memorable, because they establish traditions. The child's favorite meal and special cake often show up year after year to sheer delight—and begin to be known as "Johnny's Dinner." When special parties are planned, we suggest:

- Rent a puppet theater for a private performance.
- Trip to local amusement park. (Take one extra adult for every three small children.)
- Treasure hunt (in your backyard or a neighbor's)
- Make-your-own-ice-cream-sundae party
- Decorate hats or T-shirts. (Buy cardboard or felt hats and glitter, paint or markers, magazines that pictures can be cut out of, buttons, etc.; and plain white oversized T-shirts and fabric paint and markers for decorating.)
- Sleep-overs (indoors or out!)
- Ethnic theme party (Mexican with piñatas and tacos, Italian with spaghetti, etc.)
- Tea party for the girls (chocolate milk in teacups, sparkling cider in miniglasses, cookies in cute shapes, everyone dressed up in their Sunday best
- Costume party. (Come as your favorite cartoon character.)
- Zoo adventure
- Disneyland or Walt Disney World

Don't forget:

- Children like to receive "goodie bags" or favors (balloons; anything they help make; coloring books/crayons; anything with their name on it).
- All birthdays don't require big parties or expensive gifts.
- Ask your child to make a wish list (you can see what he or she thinks is really special).
- Consider having one guest for each year the child is old (if you're five, you get five guests; if you're eight, you get eight guests).
- Decide whether the birthday boy or girl should open gifts at the party or later. It may be awkward either way—think about it.
- If parents of small children are invited, be sure to have refreshments they will enjoy (or at least not gag at the sight of, like "bubblegum" ice cream).

Teenagers

They're no longer children, and if you blink for a moment, they already seem "grown."

Make the party by invitation only; this is not an open house free-for-all. We're positive your teenager will let you know whether or not he or she wants a party, and what kind. Try to abide by his wishes, as long as they are reasonable. Just because Wesley had a coed sleep-over does not mean *your* teenager will be having one—make the house rules clear. While the gender requests change over the years—from coed toddlers parties, through the all-girl or all-boy parties at that "he hit me and he doesn't like me" stage, to all-out hormone-raging "I'll just die if no boys are here"—teenage years prove to be a challenge on just about every level. Don't make yourself crazy, but do make your teenager feel that his friends are welcome and you and the family think he's special. Suggested parties:

- House party with pizza and dancing
- Sleep-over (single sex)
- Take a few friends to a long-awaited concert.
- Dinner at a special restaurant
- Swim party
- Mall day (with gift certificates as prizes)
- Rent a terrific video, or take a number of friends to the movies (food included).

If the party is large, and you live in an urban area, you need to set some basic ground rules, make sure they are clearly understood by your teenager, and possibly consider security if the neighborhood is known for uninvited guests crashing parties. Just be firm, and don't do or allow anything in your home that would jeopardize the well-being of your family or any of the guests.

Adults

Despite their mature exterior, when it comes to birthdays, adults are nothing but big kids, and they like birthday parties as much as anyone. There are many things you can do to celebrate with your friends. Consider if you would like a couples party or "girls' night out" before you select an activity. Suggested celebrations:

- Dinner at home or at a restaurant. (You pay unless agreed upon *in advance!*)
- Theater party
- Hire a fortune-teller and dance the night away.
- Luncheon
- Special tour of museum or art gallery
- "Let's be decadent day"
- Spa day
- Sunday brunch and televised sports event
- Backyard barbecue

- "This Is Your Life"
- Cocktails and dancing
- Picnic
- Nighttime pool party

The bottom line for adult parties: have good food (and plenty of it), good music, friends who enjoy each other, and simply relax! It's really not necessary to have a birthday celebration every year—unless that's what you're known for. If you do have frequent parties (rather than just the *big* ones), don't expect guests to bring gifts. *Don't even think about having a party every year just to get gifts!*

Anniversaries

Anniversaries follow weddings, and luckily, until you get to the twenty-fifth or fiftieth anniversary, they are not nearly so elaborate. Anniversary parties are usually given by the couple themselves, or by their children when you get up to those big numbers. Types of anniversary parties include open house, backyard barbecue, Sunday brunch, and small dinner parties.

It is not necessary to take a gift to an anniversary party, because the couple is hosting it themselves and would just like your company in celebrating their continued happiness. Gifts may be individually given, or given as part of a group gift, when you reach those twenty-five-plus years.

Graduations

Graduation parties celebrate the accomplishments of a student (child or adult) who has achieved a goal and graduated from a learning institution. (We dare say you *could* consider a graduation party when your dog completes obedience school, but we prefer cake to dog biscuits and friends of the two-legged variety.) Many activities surround graduations from high school and college, and you may choose to entertain for one or for many of them. Graduation parties need not be held on the same day as the graduation, especially if the graduation was held out of town and you would like to celebrate in your home community.

Postprom breakfast: When your son or daughter (or you) has just spent a perfect evening at his or her senior prom and isn't ready for the evening to end, you might plan a postprom breakfast. If the prom and festivities end around 6 A.M. (the big stay-out-all-night adventure), they can extend their fun with a breakfast starting around 6:30. One thing about hosting this party at home: you'll know where your kids are and can rest easy!

Brunch or luncheon: For family and close friends following a morning or early afternoon ceremony, this may be held at your home, in a restaurant, or in a hotel restaurant or private room. The best part about hosting it away from home is you will be available to enjoy the entire ceremony, arrive with the other guests, and go home to a clean house.

Afternoon reception: An open house is perfect following a late afternoon ceremony. Friends of the graduate and their families can easily drop by after their own family celebrations.

Showers

Showers have traditionally been called such because they originated as a time to "shower" a bride-to-be with gifts. Most often given for first-time brides or mothers-to-be, there are a number of kinds of showers that can be given.

Bridal Showers

Bridal showers are most often given by a close family friend of either the bride or the groom, an aunt, cousin, or godmother. Mothers and sisters of the bride and groom are not to host showers because it gives the impression that the couple and their families are asking for gifts. If no one else is planning a shower, a member of the bridal party should offer to host the shower.

The most common themes for bridal showers:

- Lingerie
- Around the Clock: each guest is assigned an hour of the day to select a gift for.
- Kitchen
- Gardening
- China
- Crystal or glassware
- Book (any book that would benefit her married life)
- Linen

Bridal showers are traditionally for the bride and her friends, but recently coed showers have begun to appear. For a first-time bride we prefer "ladies only" showers because this is one of the last times the bride and her friends can let loose as "the girls" and talk about the impending marriage and the groom-to-be. That's not to say grooms are not entitled to some fun—but everything doesn't have to be shared with everyone.

Showers for the Second or Third Wedding

Until recently, showers were given only for the first-time bride. Given all of the divorce and remarriage in our country, there is something to say for celebrating any type of happiness and wishing the couple well. Women may choose to give a lingerie or "pamper yourself" shower for a close friend, and coed showers are perfectly acceptable for the second-time bride.

Coed Showers

Some suggested themes for coed showers:

- Honeymoon (things to use on the honeymoon)
- Barbecue or backyard (things to use entertaining outside)
- Romance (use your imagination!)
- Gourmet (gourmet items they wouldn't normally get themselves—but would love)
- Hobby or sport (anything related to an activity they've learned to enjoy together)
- Entertainment (tickets to movies/theater; CDs; electronic items for entertainment center)

Family Showers

Family showers can be given for the bride and groom or for the bride alone. The groom's family may choose to host a similar shower for their family. (This may not be the time for the families to meet for the first time!) For the bride in particular, it's a time for her family to reinforce their belief in her, and that she will always be a part of their family, no matter what her name is. Some suggested themes:

- **Family wisdom.** Each member of the family imparts family wisdom, which is recorded or given to the bride in a family album with a picture of the family member who shared this wisdom.
- **Heirloom.** The family shares heirloom treasures with the bride, along with, we're sure, a serious admonition not to give the heirloom away or leave it behind if she leaves her husband.
- **Family tree.** The family puts together a written family tree, with pictures and anecdotes if possible.
- **Quilt.** The family presents the bride with a family quilt either made by members of the family or inspired by them—telling the family history.
- **"This Is Your Life"** (and don't you forget it!)
  A scrapbook filled with pictures of the bride at various stages of her

life and stories from family members who remember those times

A videotape where each family member tells a "remembrance"

An evening at home with family—telling stories about the bride—that is audio- and/or videotaped

Home Office Shower

If the bride-to-be is quitting her "day job" and will begin working from a home office, a home office shower is the perfect thing. Often given by soon-to-be-former coworkers, this shower can also be given for a nonbride who has decided to leave her job and start out on her own as an entrepreneur. Below is a sample invitation (for coworkers):

To: ______________________________

Re: ______________________________

It's Party Time!

For: ______________________________

of ______________________________ *Department*

at ______________________________

Date: ______________ *Time:* ______________

Kind of Shower: ______________________________

Regrets Only Contact: ____________ *Ext.:* ____________

Games at Showers

Games can be fun or the most boring things in life—it's your call as to whether you would like them played at a shower hosted by you. It's more important to host a party where you can keep things moving than just to play games to keep people occupied.

Gifts

Gifts are either selected from the bride's wedding registry or randomly selected to fit the theme. Shower gifts are always opened at the shower and displayed for guests to admire. That's half the fun!

If you are the hostess, your gift to the bride-to-be is the party itself. It is not necessary to present another gift. Some hostesses, however, give the bride a shower gift just because they want to.

When You're Having More Than One Shower

You should never have more than three showers (unless one is out of town) no matter how many friends offer to host one. Decide on the types of showers you would like to have and come to a decision with your hostesses.

Each hostess (given there are three showers) should be invited to at least one of the other showers, but should not be expected to bring a gift.

Unwedding or Divorce Shower

At first, you might think, "Why would I possibly want to give, or be the honoree at, a party to celebrate the demise of a marriage?" We don't suggest celebrating the divorce, but rather celebrating your friendship and reminding the honoree that her friends are there for her. The gifts may be gag gifts, kitchen items given because her ex ran off with everything, or simply things to "pamper" her.

New Job or Promotion

Celebrate all the good things in life—and a new job or promotion certainly falls under that category. If you're staying in the same office and have made an upward leap, your coworkers may want to have a special potluck lunch or treat you to your favorite restaurant near the office. It can be balloons and candy to the lucky person, or cocktails at home hosted by the spouse of the new-title holder to celebrate his or her accomplishment and announce the new position. Whatever, at least open a bottle of champagne or sparkling cider and toast the special day.

Retirement

Those twenty-five years have flown by and now you, or a friend, are retiring. Retirement parties are usually hosted by a friend or organization, not the retiree. They may take the form of a luncheon, dinner, or large reception. If it is organized by a group and they are asking that guests pay for admission to the event, the fee usually includes the meal as well as a contribution to a group gift for the honoree. If you are not familiar with the coworkers and employment experience of a friend you've known for years, you may decide to have your own "retirement shower" for a woman who is about to become "a lady of leisure." Ask guests to bring something for the days when the honoree will have "nothing to do." This would also be great for a man who will finally have a chance to work in his garden or read those books that have been piling up for decades.

Farewell Party

Everyone knows a friend or neighbor who chooses (or may have had the decision made for him or her) to move away from the area they've called home. Suggestions? Of course:

- The soon departed (still alive, just moving!) may give an open house as a way to see many friends at one time.
- A neighbor may host an open house for the neighborhood to say good-bye. This is especially appropriate for the student going away to school or the young girl leaving to go live with her grandparents.
- A friend may host a brunch, luncheon, or dinner for a group of close friends.
- If it's a woman moving to be with her future spouse, a "pamper yourself" party may be in order (we obviously like these!).
- If it's a man moving to a new city to be with his future spouse, perhaps a "guys' night out" would be appreciated.
- "Remember When": ask each guest to bring a photo and story to place in an album for the honoree, and have a videographer at the party to record "farewell wishes."
- A surprise potluck, after the movers have packed everything up, might be a welcome boost to a rough day. Check with a close friend to see if it's an imposition, then ask invitees to bring a dish in a disposable container, disposable dishes, glasses, utensils, and even though everything in the house is packed up, you can have fun—throw everything away—and let the honoree know how much she or he will be missed. (Be sure to bring garbage bags to haul the mess away.)

Open House

An open house is a delightful way to entertain more people than would normally fit in your home for dinner, and it doesn't require a set "come and go" time. Some reasons to host an open house:

- Holiday season (any party will do—but we must have parties!)
- Neighborhood party to introduce new neighbor
- Tradition of the family (eve before New Year's Eve, etc.)
- "Meet our new son" (or daughter) when you've adopted a child
- Elderly person's birthday. (It's Grandpa's one-hundredth birthday, please come for cake between 3 and 5 P.M.—then have guests sign one big card for him.)

Card Parties

Who cares if it's poker, bid whist, or bridge, card parties are an inexpensive way to entertain and enjoy the camaraderie of friends. Things to remember:

- Invite the correct number of people for the game you'd like to play.
- Set up appropriate number of tables and chairs.
- Have cold cuts or some type of nonmessy snack that your guests can help themselves to when they're not playing cards.

Tea Parties

Give us tea in the afternoon and we are happy campers, indeed. Tea parties may be given for any reason, or better yet, for no reason. Tea parties conjure thoughts of people dressing up, women wearing hats and gloves, light conversations, and a stress-free environment. One thinks of finger sandwiches, tea cakes, scones, minidesserts, sherry, and of course tea. Not as noisy as cocktail parties, you can actually hear yourself think at a tea party, and you can enjoy a peaceful conversation with other guests. It's "being a lady" or a "gentleman," it's an image of manners to the hilt. It's a spa for your soul. Tea parties can become a staple of your entertaining traditions if you remember a few things:

- Tea parties are usually not catered unless they are very large. It's a cinch to make (or purchase) ahead of time the food you'll be serving.
- Custom dictates that certain foods are served at tea, including finger sandwiches, biscuits or scones, and, of course, tea. After that (and maybe before that if you hate scones), it's whatever you choose to serve, as long as it's finger size and you set a pretty table. If your friends would rather have hot wings than watercress sandwiches, by all means serve them. Just remember to put them on a lovely serving dish and be prepared for them to be a bit more messy than cucumber sandwiches. The key is to set a lovely table.
- The tea table is usually set on the dining room table or another large table. A cloth is placed on the table unless it is glass. A large tray at either end holds coffee service (one end) and tea service (the other end). Arrange food trays and silver (if possible) serving pieces so that they are easily reached. Stack small plates and napkins (which should match tablecloth) so they, too, are easily reached. Supply forks if cake will be served. There's no need to pass food on trays, so most likely servers will not be required. Just make sure the table is inviting. Place cups and saucers within easy reach of women who will be pouring coffee and tea.
- Tea service:
  Pot of boiling water and pot of tea
  Cream pitcher, sugar bowl, sugar substitute
  Thin slices of lemon on small plate

Tea bags (if you must!)
- Coffee service:
  Coffee urn (with flame beneath it)
  Cream pitcher, sugar bowl, sugar substitute

COFFEE SERVICE

Time of Party

Tea parties are usually held starting at two o'clock in the afternoon and ending not later than five or six o'clock. Most often invitations will read "3–5 P.M." or "tea at four o'clock."

More Things to Remember

- Guests should not pile their plates with food; they may return to the tea table for more.
- Hostess should introduce guest of honor to other guests as they arrive.
- Since it's an informal affair, even if you don't know anyone, just introduce yourself and start conversations.
- When you're ready to leave, thank the hostess and say good-bye to the guest of honor.
- Although the term "high tea" often appears on invitations, what we do in America is actually "afternoon tea." High tea is a heartier meal (like supper) and always includes meat dishes.
- Pots and urns with flames should not be lit until the serving piece is in place on the table.
- Use "real" plates and cups/saucers. If you must use paper goods, make them the prettiest ones you can find—and match the tablecloth and napkins. Even if you use paper plates, you should still use "real" forks and spoons.

- If your guests will be seated at tables, rather than eating off their laps, assign one friend to each table to keep the conversation moving along.
- The women who pour the tea or coffee are honored friends of the hostess.
- Even though you prepared the food yourself, you may want to hire someone to serve and clean up, so you and your friends can all enjoy the party.
- Tea and coffee are not the only drinks appropriate to serve. Sherry is a standard, as is champagne. Feel free to serve sparkling water or fresh juice in warm weather if you think your guests will enjoy it.
- Tea for two can be a party in itself on a cozy afternoon.

TEA SERVICE

Cocktail Parties

Cocktail parties can be large or small, formal or informal. All food is served as finger food and it's a safe bet that if you provide small plates for your guests to sample from the buffet, they won't be standing at the buffet all night trying to finish the appetizer in their hand before they can manage another. If drinks or appetizers are passed, the server must offer the guest a napkin each time the guest has something new.

Telephone your invitations for a small party, send written invitations for a large gathering. If there is no buffet being served, it is appropriate to state, "Cocktails 5–7 P.M.." If buffet is served, state "Cocktails at 5 P.M." or whatever time you expect to serve. Be sure to have nonalcoholic drinks in addition to whatever alcohol you will be serving. And, if it's a large party, plan on two glasses for each guest. (They put them down and get another.)

Surprise Parties

Think twice before planning a surprise party. Some people *hate* surprises, and some are overjoyed. Know your guest of honor and your guests. One big mouth can ruin the whole surprise. Even if your children will be included, don't tell them about the party ahead of time—they will be hard-pressed to keep the secret, and it's not fair to put them in that position.

Sweet 16 Parties

Sweet 16 parties can range from a slumber party to a coed dinner dance. Whatever your daughter has her heart set on, try to accommodate her. We don't mean splurging on an activity the family can't afford, we mean allowing her to have a luncheon for a few friends, or a day in another city with a single friend if she'd prefer that to a large dance party. She may be the only one in her class without a date to her own Sweet 16—let her make as many decisions as possible. Again, let her know there are limits. Better yet, devise a list of possibilities and let her select a type of party from the list.

Sporting Event Parties

Parties for sports events, especially the Super Bowl, have become a tradition in many cities. It rarely matters whether your team is playing, it's simply a chance to fellowship with friends and forget your cares. The ingredients for a good sports-themed party? Good food (as usual), adequate selection of drinks, enough television sets so the die-hard fans don't have to sit in the same room with the people whose main interest is when the chili will be served and how innovative the halftime program is.

Chapter 31

MOVEABLE FEASTS

A feast is made for laughter, and wine maketh merry.

Ecclesiastes 10:19

Are you often at a loss as to where to entertain? Is your apartment too small, but restaurants are too expensive? Here are some of the factors to consider when deciding where to entertain, and if you will host alone or with others.

At Home

You know you'll have a pleasing menu and good food, an attractive atmosphere, and congenial company. What you aren't sure about is the music, centerpieces, lighting, layout of home and the "flow" of the party, who's going to cook, serve, and clean up.

In a Restaurant

- Select a restaurant with food your guests would enjoy (don't take a group of vegetarians to your favorite steak place).
- If you're entertaining for business, make sure the room will be quiet enough to conduct business.
- Would your guests rather go to a "famous" restaurant or a neighborhood place with great food?

- If you're inviting out-of-town guests, will they have appropriate clothes for the restaurant you select? (It's very dressy and they've just come from camping.)
- Invitations should name the restaurant so guests know what to expect and what to wear.
- If it's to be very casual, say so—so guests won't overdress.
- If it's going to be outside, let guests know so they can dress accordingly.
- If you invited your friends, you pay, period. It's not the same as a group of you deciding to have lunch together and going dutch treat.
- If you are a stranger in town and would like to entertain, you might ask the person you're taking out if she would like to suggest a restaurant and you make the reservations. You can always ask the concierge (see Glossary) of your hotel or consult a local guidebook.

Once you've decided on the restaurant and the day has arrived:

- Get there early to confirm plans, make sure the table(s) has been secured, and be ready to greet guests. If some of the guests are late, feel free to order a drink while you wait with the others.
- You can pre-order the meals or let your guests select from the regular menu or from a few choices you've narrowed down for them. If ordering individually, the waiter will take each order separately.
- Help guests with suggestions if they've never been to the restaurant.
- Even if they're your closest friends, let them know by suggesting lobster or some other expensive dish that the sky's the limit, that you're prepared for whatever they order.
- Also let guests know if they should order courses or just an entrée. You may have pre-ordered the courses, and they are to select their entrée.
- If you notice a guest is not eating her food, inquire if everything is all right. The hostess should take care of the error right away. It is not the guest's place to complain or give orders to the waiter or management.
- Your job is to make guests comfortable. If you have not pre-ordered dessert, urge guests to have dessert—even if you have to order one for yourself first.
- Don't forget to order wine or other beverages. Ordering by the bottle ahead of time is much more economical than ordering individual glasses. Plus, you'll have better choices by the bottle. Even bottled water is less expensive if ordered for the table by the bottle.

In a Hotel

Hotel restaurants vary slightly from other restaurants in that often they have private rooms, and a variety of foods can be ordered from quite a large menu. Work with the manager or maître d' to discuss details of the party. These include: selection of room or area; linen; flowers; place cards; menu cards; gratuities; menu; and beverages. Ask how early you may get in on the day of the party to arrange seating, bring favors to place on the table, have birthday cake delivered, etc. Some guidelines:

- If no gratuity is included in the arranged price, give 20 percent of the total food bill to be split among the waiters who served the party.
- When selecting wine by consensus at the table, the host or hostess will order and the wine will be brought to him or her for inspection.
- After initial pouring by the waiter, the host may pour wine for others if the waiter has not returned.
- The hostess should be the only one to summon the waiter to meet the needs of her guests.
- All other rules of restaurant dining apply to hotels also.

In Another's Home

When entertaining jointly, or borrowing a friend's home to throw a party, treat the home as if it were your own. Anticipate every need, plan ahead, and set up for the event at a time convenient for the residents. Be sure to clean up or arrange for cleanup before you leave. Check with the residents of the home following the party to ascertain there is nothing missing, broken, or damaged. Reasons you might entertain in another's home:

- Your home is too small for the type of party you've planned.
- Your home is geographically undesirable to your guests.
- Parking is inadequate for you to entertain in your home.
- You're out of town, celebrating your daughter's graduation from the local college, and would like to entertain family and friends in the warmth of a home rather than a restaurant or hotel.
- You're giving a surprise party in the guest of honor's home (but only with the permission of the spouse, roommate, or parents).

Never take for granted that even the closest friends will grant you the use of their home. Do *not* abuse the privilege. And do remember to thank the homeowner(s) with a gift as well as a note.

Rented Facilities

If you're hosting a party at a rented facility (community hall, clubhouse, church, sorority/fraternity house, university club, etc.), do your homework and investigate the following:

- Days and hours available
- What can be served? Can you bring in your own food and liquor or must their caterer provide them?
- Capacity of room—for sit-down eating vs. reception or dance
- Security
- Parking
- Cleanup
- Hidden costs (microphone, speakers for music, air-conditioning, maintenance man on premises during event)
- Are tables, chairs, dishes, flatware, glasses, tablecloths on hand and available—what must be rented?
- When can rental deliveries be made? Picked up following event?
- Is live music permitted?
- Is an outside disc jockey allowed?
- General rules and contract including deposit and charges for canceling

Business Entertaining at Home

Business entertaining is very similar to regular entertaining, the biggest difference being that many of your guests may not be known to you. Whether you're entertaining your own business associates or hosting an evening for your spouse's colleagues, plan efficiently for a hassle-free evening. Have someone else oversee kitchen duty and serving, including cleanup. This frees you to be a charming host or hostess whose biggest duty is to greet guests, make introductions, keep the conversation and drinks flowing, and intercept any potential crisis. If at all possible, familiarize yourself with the names of your guests—the ones you don't know—prior to the party.

Groups and Hostessing Together

Once you've decided that your club or a group of friends will cohost a party, put your cards on the table. Discuss, early on, the following and (hopefully) avert any misunderstanding:

- Type of party, day, date, and time
- Number of guests and how the guest list will be decided
- Menu, and whether each (or all) of you will cook, purchase food and wine, or hire a caterer
- Additional costs that may be incurred: valet, servers, rentals, liquor and soft drinks, ice, security, invitations, stamps, music

Outdoor Dos and Don'ts

- *Do* plan as carefully as you do for indoor parties.
- *Do* let guests know the party will be outside so they can dress accordingly.
- *Don't* plan outdoor events during times of the year when there's little *chance* of sun.
- *Do* consider the setting and comfort of your guests: Where will the sun be when party is in full force? Will you need umbrellas or tents for potential extreme weather (hot or cold) or outdoor heaters?
- *Don't* use breakable glasses for drinks to be served on concrete or poolside decks.
- *Do* select buffet foods that will not wilt or become rancid in hot weather.
- *Do* have sweaters available for guests in the event the weather changes, or be prepared to move the party inside.
- *Don't* plan centerpieces that could blow over or candles that could ignite a fire if it becomes windy.
- *Do* situate barbecue grills away from crowds.

Miscellaneous Things to Consider When Entertaining

- Rentals
- Seating
- Caterer
- Setup
- Servers
- Cleanup
- Do you want to spend all of your time in the kitchen?
- Should you engage a party or event planner?
- Is this going to be the kind of party you'd like to be invited to?

RENTALS

Rental tables, chairs (folding ones for informal parties, gilded ones for more formal affairs), and linens are a help when you're having a lot of guests. You can also rent china, flatware, glasses, and serving dishes, usually for a fairly reasonable cost. Remember to keep track of how many of each item you've requested, as the rental company will count all items when they return to pick them up. You'll be charged for any missing or broken items.

Chapter 32

BE A GOOD GUEST

Do not leave your host's house
throwing mud in his well.

Zulu proverb

Just as there is an art to being a good host, there is a corresponding art to being a good guest. Ask someone who entertains a lot some of the characteristics of their favorite guests, and you'll get a hint: "If they offer to help and I say, 'Thanks, but I just want you to relax and enjoy yourself,' they take me at my word." "She helps to keep conversation going and encourages the shy guest to speak up, too." "He talks to my children without talking down to them." "They don't expect room service when they visit; they just fit themselves into the family routine." In other words, a good guest acts appreciative to be in his host's home, whether it's for a few hours or a few days, and tries to contribute something to make the visit a success.

Responding to Invitations

Invitations to informal parties and dinners are often conveyed over the telephone, especially if an event is put together on short notice. If this is the case, respond as quickly as possible to help your host with his head count. It's fine to respond in the same way the invitation was extended: "Stella, this is Ebony. Scott and I just got your message and we'd love to come on Saturday night to meet Debbie and her husband. Wasn't it nice they got a last-minute trip out this way? We'll see you at six-thirty, and please let us know if we can bring anything."

In that one short call, you've just confirmed that you received the message, repeated the time stated in the invitation, and offered to bring something your host might need.

Changing Your Response from "Yes" to "No," and Vice Versa

If you need to change from "yes" to "no" when you've given your response to an invitation, let your hostess know immediately. If it's an open house, your call will be more of a courtesy than a practical matter of having enough chairs or giving the caterer the correct number. Telephone your regrets because it gives you a chance to give your hostess an explanation.

If your change is from "no" to "yes," you probably declined originally for a legitimate reason. Perhaps you were going to be out of town on business and the trip was later canceled. If the invitation was for a seated dinner party, you are probably now out of luck, since your hostess has more than likely filled your seat. If it is to be a large party or reception, call the hostess and explain. Ask if it will be possible for you to attend. If you're close to the hostess of the small dinner party, still call and let her know you'll be in town, even though you don't expect her to rearrange things to accommodate you. If she didn't expect you to attend, please don't let her hear from someone else that you were actually in town; it would be dreadful if she got the wrong impression and believed that you made up that story just to slight her.

Not Showing After You Said You Would

If it's absolutely impossible to reach your host to let him know that an unexpected emergency or illness will cause you to miss the event, call the first thing the next day. (Don't call so early you wake him up after a big night!) Apologize and explain. Do ask how it went. Let your host know you're genuinely sorry you had to miss the festivities. If illness or another emergency keeps you from calling the host yourself, have someone make your regrets for you. As soon as you are able, call the host yourself.

When You Have Out-of-Town Guests

Let your hostess know. Unless space is very limited, most hostesses will accommodate your situation and extend an invitation to your guest, too. If you suspect an additional person will be an inconvenience, check with your houseguest and see if she has other plans that will occupy her during that time. If she doesn't, you may have to decline the invitation in order to keep your houseguest company.

Offering to Bring Part of the Meal

If you ask your host if you can bring anything and she says "sure," find out what she'd like and how much. If you offer to bring dessert, for instance, you need to know how many people are coming to dinner: "I thought I'd make lemon meringue pie if that's okay with you. Do you think two will be enough for ten people?" Other things a host might find helpful are bread, salad, and wine or soft drinks. If you offer to bring part of the meal and your host says, "Thanks, but I've got everything taken care of," take that as your signal that she has a specific menu in mind, and don't press by insisting.

Presents for the Host

Being told by the hostess that she doesn't need anything doesn't mean that you should arrive on her doorstep empty-handed. Your gift to your hostess doesn't have to be fancy or expensive: it's really just a token to let her know you're grateful for her hospitality. If you're coming for dinner, you might bring a bottle of wine, a box of cookies, or a jar of fancy preserves. Flowers are almost always welcome.

If you know your hosts are serious barbecuers or avid experimenters with hot sauce, for example, you could always come with an exotic barbecue marinade or a hard-to-find bottle of hot sauce. Chocoholics always appreciate anything chocolate. And if there are children in the house, it's nice to remember them, too, with a small puzzle, game, or set of crayons.

Bringing Uninvited Children

Don't bring your children if they haven't been invited. If your baby-sitter comes down with a cold, and your child-care arrangements fall through, notify your hostess that you have a crisis and let her know you can't come because of it: "Cheryl, I'm sorry to do this to you at the last minute but Rita, our baby-sitter, has come down with the flu, and we can't find anyone on short notice. I'm afraid it means we're going to have to miss your party." It's up to your hostess to decide whether she wants to invite all of you, or wait for another time for a family visit. If she doesn't immediately say, "Oh, bring Teddy with you; he'll bc fine," it means she was planning for an adult party and that children would not be appropriate.

Love Me, Love My Dog

Some people are pet lovers, some aren't. Many, if given the "love me, love my dog" ultimatum, might make a choice that would hurt your feelings. To spare your animal the trauma of being around lots of strangers (which often causes pets to act unpredictably—much to the dismay of the guest and host), leave him home.

If your hostess has pets and you are afraid of or allergic to them, let her know when you hit the door. A considerate hostess will always offer to put the dog in the yard, or secure the cat in the bedroom, to spare her guests an evening of sniffles and watery eyes, or edgy surveillance whenever Rex—even if he loves having company—strolls through the room.

Being Fashionably on Time

Because many people have gotten so haphazard about arriving anywhere near the stated time on the invitation, there are hundreds of anecdotes about aghast hosts opening the door at seven with their shirttails untucked, dinner still cooking away, and the table unset. If your invitation says 7 P.M., arriving by 7:15 gives the host a little more leeway for last-minute tinkering (although the major things should have been done by now). A half hour after the requested time is the absolute limit to arrive and still be polite.

If you know you're going to be delayed for some reason, call ahead and let your hosts know. There's nothing worse than a roomful of starving guests who are being denied their dinner because the anxious host is waiting for the last two people to come. Always urge your host to start without you, and when you do arrive (full of apologies, of course, even if the delay isn't your fault), just try to catch up with everybody else at whatever stage the evening's in. If you arrive at 9 P.M. because you got stuck on the freeway and dinner was at 7:30, don't ask for a plate unless the hostess offers you one—which she almost certainly will.

When the Invitation Says . . .

Drinks at 6:30, dinner at 7 P.M.: This means the host plans to serve drinks for a half hour and move people into dinner promptly after that. If you plan to skip drinks, arrive by seven sharp so you don't hold things up.

5 to 7 P.M.: This means the party is looser than a sit-down meal, and perhaps only drinks and hors d'oeuvres will be served. You can come for part, or all, of the designated two hours. If you come at 6:00 and leave at 7:00, that's fine. Don't come at 6:45 and expect to stay until 8:00, however, unless the host is urging everyone else to stay on, too.

Children Welcome: You're free to make it a family event, provided you take the responsibility for keeping an eye on your young children if they accompany you. This is not the responsibility of your hosts or the other guests.

Children over 12 Welcome: This means exactly what it says. Sometimes for liability reasons (the host has a swimming pool with no safety gate, or a deck perched over a steep slope with widely spaced railings little ones could slip through, or a collection of crystal or African sculpture that inquiring little hands could devastate) or just personal preference, a host asks that small children be left at home. This is nothing personal; it's just a way of forestalling potential disaster. (Do you want to even *think* about trying to replace a family heirloom your toddler inspected—and dropped?)

Being an Honored Guest

You're in town for the weekend visiting your college friend and her husband, and they give a small dinner in your honor. Your duty as guest is to be friendly and charming to your hosts' friends, to act pleased that your hosts have gone to the trouble of bringing people together to meet you, and, generally, to be gracious. You might, even though you're the honored guest, ask to give a toast to your hosts, thanking them for their hospitality: "I'd like to take a moment to thank Ken and Nina, who, no matter where they've lived, have always really meant it when they said, 'Our house is your house.' From the time I met them when they were in graduate school, when they put folk up on the living room sofa, till now, when we're given a beautiful guest room, they have been warm, gracious, and generous. It's so good to be back here, in my second home."

Compliments

If it's a great party or delicious dinner, tell the hostess, who would appreciate hearing that her guests are having a good time. If you know she's spent considerable time and labor remodeling her kitchen, tell her how much you admire the job. If you see some artwork by one of her children and think it's charming, make an effort to let the child know.

Clearing the Table

Of course you should offer to clear the table, then follow your host's response. If she says, "Sure, just put the plates on the kitchen counter," put the plates on the kitchen counter. If she feels she can better decide what goes where in the postdinner confusion and she prefers that you sit and visit with the others at the table, do as she asks. Don't insist, over her objections, that "two sets of hands are better than one" and proceed to bully your way into cleaning up. Some hosts are very particular about how they do this, and your overbearing manner will be thought more irritating than anything else.

If you do receive permission to clear, ask your hostess where things go before you put them up; it could save her a lot of aggravation when she's searching for them later: "Do you have bowls for leftovers you want to use? Just point me in the right direction." "Which drawer does the plastic wrap go in?" If she's out of the kitchen and you're working, place everything you cannot figure out places for in one central spot and let her know when she returns: "Edna, I didn't know where you keep the soup ladle, this bread basket, and the plate the corn bread was on, so they're on this counter here."

If You Break or Spill Something

Own up to an accident right away. Finding red wine spilled down the back of a white sofa twenty-four hours *after* it's been spilled is enough to make even the most generous host livid. If you break an ashtray, pick up the pieces and go off to ask your host for a broom or hand vacuum, whatever he usually uses, so you can finish the job. If a drink splashes on the floor, grab a handful of napkins to wipe up the bulk of the mess, and ask your host if he uses anything special on the floors, or if a damp cloth is okay. Dark stains on light fabrics should be attended to immediately, before they soak in, so notify the host as soon as the damage is done and clean up according to his instructions. (The host may prefer to do this delicate job himself; if he does, let him.)

Always offer to replace the broken object if it is replaceable. A family heirloom is not, since the sentimental value attached to it is often at least as great as the monetary one. You should apologize profusely.

Nonheirlooms that are one of a kind cannot be replaced exactly, but they can be approximated. If your elbow has knocked over a favorite flea-market pitcher your host loved to serve lemonade in, you might take some time to visit local flea markets and swap meets for a similar vessel and send it on, with a note of apology.

If the item can be repaired, you should offer to do so immediately, and ask your host if he has a preference where such repairs should be made. If he insists on repairing the damage himself, ask around and find out the estimated value of such a job and send your host a check for the repair.

Disposing of Cocktail Odds and Ends

You're at a cocktail party, and your host is passing trays of crab claws, shelled shrimp, or sausage skewered on little toothpicks; what do you do with the inedible remains? Look around: often there are a few plates or baskets with liners that are intended as communal receptacles for the little odds and ends you cannot eat. If not, quietly place the shell, toothpick, or whatever in a paper napkin and toss the napkin in a nearby wastebasket.

When You Can't Eat What They're Serving

Maybe you arrive at an open house to discover the two main dishes contain things you're allergic to or have to pass up because of a medical condition or religious reasons. If you can, try to fill your plate with things you *can* eat—salad, bread, side dishes—and refrain from making a big deal of it. If your hostess notices, she may offer something else to supplement your meal. If she doesn't, don't ask for it.

If your hostess asks whether there are foods you cannot eat, let her know when you accept the invitation. "Paula, I'd love to come, but I should tell you I'm allergic to dairy products" allows Paula the chance to switch from her planned main course of four-cheese lasagna to a pasta dish that doesn't contain cheese. And it enables you to eat the same thing as everyone else. Most people will willingly accommodate your dietary restrictions if they aren't too numerous, and if you give them enough advance notice.

Becoming Ill When You're Out

It happens: Dinner was delicious, but it gave you an upset stomach. Or you feel your temperature beginning to rocket upward. Your back goes out when you bend down to pick up a napkin you've dropped.

If you become ill or hurt when you're out, quietly notify your host and, if you can get home on your own steam, do. If you're too ill to drive yourself, ask your host to call a taxi or enlist another guest to drive you home—or to the emergency room, if the situation is urgent. The objective here is to get the help you need without, if possible, bringing the party to a halt.

When Only One of You Can Attend

If the invitation is addressed to you and your spouse, but your spouse is traveling or has a previous engagement, let the situation dictate whether you accept or decline. An invitation to an event that is all couples (maybe seats at a concert or a sit-down dinner) means you should send your regrets. And you should let your hostess know why you can't come: "Sylvia, we would have loved to join you to see the Dance Theater of Harlem on Thursday night, but Marcus is away on business. I'm really sorry." This leaves your hostess with the option of offering the tickets to another couple or perhaps pairing you with another friend or colleague: "That's all right; my friend Denise wanted to go and we couldn't get another ticket, so why don't you come anyway? We can just seat you together."

You could accept an invitation to an open house or informal dinner served family style and come alone if you tell your host that your partner will not be able to attend. In looser social events such as the ones mentioned above, it's desirable to have more than just couples anyway, and there will probably be other unpaired people there, too.

Running on Empty

It only takes one time to be stuck in the bathroom at a large party and discover—too late—that the host is out of toilet paper or hand towels. If none is in evidence, take a quick look in the places it might usually be kept—under a counter, beneath that tank-top ballerina's wide, crocheted skirt—and hope for the best. If there is facial tissue on the counter, it can be pressed into service. Otherwise, you might have to crack the door and beg a passerby to come to your rescue.

If you notice that bathroom supplies are running low, tell the host, ask if he'd like for you to replenish the items, and, if he says yes, ask where you can find them. Do this quickly, so no one else ends up in the same predicament.

Being an Overnight Guest

If you're invited to spend a weekend with friends, whether at their main home or a vacation house, you'll want to be remembered as a good guest. Here are some things you can do to get that coveted "good guest" gold star—which of course means you'll be asked back often.

When you accept the invitation, find out when your host would like you to come. If he's planning for weekend guests, he might not want anyone to show up before noon on Friday. And he certainly won't expect to entertain you until 9 P.M. Sunday. Ask when he'd like for people to arrive and leave. You'll usually be given a general window of time: "We'd like it if people could get here on Friday sometime between late afternoon and dinnertime so we can have drinks and introduce everyone; plan to stay through brunch on Sunday, if you can."

Also inquire about means of transportation: "I've never been to the Outer

Banks. Can I just drive down the Carolina coast to get to Nags Head? Will I need to book passage on a ferry to reach your part of the island?" Your host family will have all that information for you and can probably share copies of schedules and maps with you if you need them. If you're visiting their weekend house, ask for the address and telephone number, so someone back home knows how to reach you in an emergency.

Arrive on time, with goodies for your host. A household with children always appreciates games and puzzles that can be played if the weather turns nasty. Cards, tapes, and compact discs of popular music are other nice choices. A jar of popcorn (or better yet: popcorn and an inexpensive electric popper) is usually welcome. And things that can be consumed over the weekend—breakfast pastries, jam or preserves, fresh fruit, wine and fruit juice—are always good.

Stow your things where the host indicates. If you have your own room, make up your bed and pick up your things as soon as you're up for the day. If you're sleeping on the futon or sofa bed in the living room or den, strip the bed, fold the sheets and blankets, and return the bed to its upright position. Ask your host where you should store your bed linens when they're not in use. If you don't have a separate bathroom, keep your toiletries in their case so your things aren't strewn around a room that several people may end up using.

A *good guest always fits himself to his host family's rhythm:* If you're a night owl and normally sleep in but your host family is up with the birds, make the adjustment and get up when they do. (The exception here is if your hosts urge you to sleep as long as you like; if you do this, though, don't expect anyone to serve you a separate breakfast.) If the family usually eats breakfast together, you, too, should appear at the table, even if you only choose to have coffee and juice.

On any weekend visit there is always some downtime when guests are encouraged to explore the city they're visiting or simply laze around the house, if that's their preference. Bring along a few things to amuse yourself: a book you've wanted to read but couldn't find the time to; some letters you've wanted to catch up on; needlework or some other portable hobby you'd enjoy doing. If there's a nearby health club, you can call to inquire about day rates if you want to work out. If you're visiting near a beach or ski trail, find out how to get there (or hitch a ride if the family makes a couple of daily trips back and forth). In general, remember that it's not your host's duty to keep you occupied every moment of the day.

Be as helpful as possible: help to clean up; offer to take a turn feeding the dog; ask if you can fix dinner one evening or take them out to eat. Leave your room and surroundings as you found them when you go. Guests who do these things are cherished by their hosts and are always welcome for return visits.

General Guest Etiquette

- When you're invited to something, don't ask "Who else is coming?" before you accept or decline.
- Wait for your host to offer seconds before you take them, especially if there are unexpected, last-minute additions who may have stretched his capacity to serve everyone.
- If a condiment you usually use is not on the table, don't ask for it, as this is an insult to the chef. It implies he hasn't seasoned things properly. Don't salt and pepper your food before you taste it, for the same reason.
- Never reach across another guest to retrieve the salt, bread, butter; ask that they be passed to you. If you're asked to pass the salt, automatically include the pepper, too.
- If you have a drink that's sweating but no coasters are available, use several napkins to blot the moisture if you must place a glass down. If you can, just hold onto it and use the napkins to absorb the moisture. *Never* place a wet glass or hot cup on top of a fine piece of furniture; you could damage the wood forever. (It is, however, all right to place one on a glass or stone tabletop if you have to.)
- When you've finished dinner, don't push back from the table or rub your stomach or (gulp!) burp with satisfaction. Those gestures might be appreciated in some cultures, but unless your host is *of* that culture and you're positive you have the cultural shorthand right, just compliment the cook on a fine meal.

If You Want to Be Asked Again

Arrive with a small token for your host. Follow the host's instructions: if he doesn't want company in the kitchen, stay out of his work space. Don't venture a less-than-complimentary opinion about someone who might turn out to be your host's best friend. Do spend a little time with the host's children, if they're part of the evening, and compliment the host on the terrific kids he's raising. Stay away from volatile subjects, such as politics, abortion, religion. Come close to on time, don't overstay your welcome, and always, always call or write the next day to thank your hosts for the nice time you had.

Don't Even Think It!

Never neglect to R.s.v.p. and then show up anyway. Never accept an invitation and not show up without calling to explain you cannot come. Don't make yourself at home by taking off your shoes—unless your host urges you to. Don't walk through the doorway and ask for a tour; if you compliment the hostess on her home, she may well offer to take you around and show you the rest of it. Don't walk away with the centerpiece from a dinner party, or other decorations, unless they're offered to you.

Part VI

MILESTONES

Important Stops on the Road of Life

Christenings, coming-out, coming-of-age ceremonies

weddings a to z

divorce, illness, and death

helping someone "pass over"

Chapter 33

RITUALS

Out under the moon and the stars, alone with his son that eighth night, Omoro completed the naming ritual . . . Carrying little Kunta in his strong arms, he walked to the edge of the village, lifted his baby up with his face to the heavens, and said softly "behold—the only thing greater than yourself."

Alex Haley, *Roots*

Rituals are ceremonies or actions imbued with a special significance that is often spiritual or religious. Often we use rituals to mark the watersheds in our lives, to commemorate such things as birth, coming of age, marriage, and death. The ceremony can be as simple as holy water sprinkled on the head of a sleeping baby or as elaborate as the union of two people witnessed by the "village" that helped to educate, nurture, and guide them. Whether humble or grand, rituals are special times.

Christenings

A christening is the way many Christian families choose to commit a baby's spiritual life to the family's religious community. Although many religions christen (or baptize) children quite soon after they are born, others wait until they are old enough to be conscious of the decision they are agreeing to undertake.

Some churches christen children at specific times of the month, and, if there are several children whose families want their children christened, the minister christens them all at once. Other churches arrange for a private, postservice ceremony where the baby's family gathers with the godparents around the baptismal font.

If you are asking a close friend or relative to be godparent to your baby, first check with your church to see if there are any barriers before you make your request. The Roman Catholic church, for instance, requires that both prospective godparents be Catholics in good standing. Other denominations have other requirements (some request that godparents take a short course of religious instruction before they assume their duties), and a few have none, other than the request that the prospective godparents be good human beings who will provide proper moral guidance to their young charge, as necessary.

Remember that many people consider godparents as guardians who, in case of family emergency or tragedy, can step in and raise a child when his parents cannot. If you are asked to become a godparent, which is a great honor, be sure the parents clearly outline what they would consider your responsibilities to be.

Christening Clothes

For children who are christened as infants, a simple white gown and cap are traditional. These can be bought or borrowed, or handed down from generation to generation. (Some of the latter are quite beautiful and intricate.) The cap or bonnet is removed before the minister pours a thin stream of holy water over the baby's head as he is baptized.

Toddlers and preschoolers who are baptized often wear white, too. Little girls might come to the altar in frilly white dresses and white shoes, while boys might wear white shorts, shirt, and tie (perhaps with a vest or jacket) or a suit (with short or long pants) in white, gray, or navy.

Older children would wear any kind of church-appropriate clothes (a nice dress for girls, jacket and tie for boys).

After the Ceremony

Although usually only the immediate family and the godparents attend a christening or baptism, it's very common for the christened child's family to invite more people to their home after the ceremony to celebrate with them. Often invitations are extended by a short note or telephone call. The party, often a brunch or lunch, is held sometime shortly after the church service. In addition to the luncheon menu, a christening cake is often served as dessert. Some families have a toast with champagne or champagne punch.

At the luncheon, godparents often give their godchildren a present that has some religious significance. Others give traditional presents, things that will last and be handed down as a future heirloom: a sterling spoon, cup, or bowl, for instance. Girls are sometimes given a tiny string of pearls or a small gold bracelet or earrings.

REMEMBERING THE CHURCH AND MINISTER
Some churches have set fees for christening ceremonies; others don't, but would be happy to receive a donation from the christened baby's family. This should be handed, in an envelope, to the minister who performed the ceremony. If there is a postchristening celebration, you should be sure to invite the minister and his or her spouse to attend. (Many ministers, because of their multiple duties, won't be able to, but they always appreciate being asked.)

First Communion

In many Christian faiths, very young children don't take communion because they're deemed too young to absorb religious instruction that would allow them to understand the significance of the ritual. The Catholic church feels that children around age seven are ready to take this step, so first communions are usually held around the time of the first or second grade. Catholic girls don white dresses; they also wear headbands to which small veils have been attached. Boys wear white or dark suits.

First communions are held during mass, but the new communicants are asked to approach the altar first. The rest of the church comes after.

Although the ritual surrounding first communion is usually associated with the Roman Catholic church, several Protestant denominations that prominently feature communion in their services also make some acknowledgment of the time a child takes his first communion. As with christenings, first communions are often followed with a family luncheon that honors this new milestone in the child's life. Godparents may offer presents with some religious significance at this time: a child's personal Bible, a religious medal, a crucifix or rosary beads (for Catholics), or a small cross made of precious metal.

Joining a Church

Most children are baptized at a very young age, well before they are able to agree to the spiritual commitment that has been made for them. For that reason, a number of denominations also have a ceremony that acknowledges a young person's decision to become a part of his congregation; this is considered a milestone that publicly notes the confirmant's acceptance of his religion and his willful entry into the religious community.

Most religions require that people joining a denomination take a course of religious instruction first, so that the history of the church, its basic beliefs, and its current practices are understood before the actual ceremony. In some denominations, the ceremony will be much the same as a christening but without the godparents. The minister may simply anoint the new member's head with holy water as he is blessed, or there may be a full-immersion baptism, a ritual many religions follow in the belief that this is how John the Baptist baptized Jesus.

Full-Immersion Baptism

Full-immersion baptism is a very moving ceremony. It is one that has an honored place in the African American community, as for centuries many of our ancestors underwent this ritual. The ceremony may take place inside a church, if the church is equipped with a baptismal pool. Or in rural areas, baptisms often take place at the edge of a local river or lake, and are frequently followed by a big, family-style luncheon or dinner, a sort of church-wide celebration of the new spiritual souls who have been welcomed into the midst of other true believers.

During a full-immersion baptism, the person about to be initiated into the church will be helped into a baptismal pool or other body of water. He will probably wear a robe or simple clothing; many women wear robes and some choose turbans to protect their hair. The minister asks if they are ready to accept Christ into their hearts, and after affirming this and taking a deep breath, the prospective member is quickly dunked underwater for a few seconds as the minister pronounces the baptism. When the newly baptized member breaks the surface of the water, he is presented to the church, blessed again by the minister, and helped from the baptismal pool, where several other church members wait to dry him off and escort him to a room where he can change into dry clothes.

If the church you plan to join uses full-immersion baptisms and you are anxious about being held underwater—a common worry—talk with your minister. Most churches have, over the years, figured out ways to "dip" quickly, so that even the most water-wary congregants can enjoy the ceremony without fear.

As with the christening of a baby, the baptism of an adolescent or adult is often followed by some sort of quiet celebration, a way of acknowledging the start of a new spiritual commitment for the baptized person, and a way to emphasize his ties to his congregation. Adults who are confirmed via this ritual often sponsor their own celebrations, such as a luncheon or dinner following church, to which family and friends are invited. The parents of an older child usually host a celebration on his behalf.

Coming-of-Age Ceremonies

Cotillions

Perhaps the best-known modern coming-of-age ritual is the cotillion, a dance that traditionally marks the transition that girls have made on the road to becoming women. Originally, the cotillion was a European device used to indicate that young ladies of marriageable age were now "out" in society, eligible to be courted, with the ultimate intention of choosing a husband from the field of suitors. Young women made their debuts in society around age eighteen, via a very formal dance held at home or in a grand hotel, or a less formal ritual, such as an afternoon tea, at the home of their parents or a relative.

Cotillions used to be thought of as exclusive to the socially prominent WASP parts of American society. But the last hundred years have seen this expand to include groups of all ethnicities. Black families have participated in cotillions for more than a half-century. While initially the process of producing a debutante was roughly akin to the way white society did, the original exclusivity of the black cotillion (where only the daughters of well-to-do or prominent families were featured) has, in many segments of the black community, given way to a broader celebration, one that recognizes young black women who are accomplished in their own right, while raising funds for important philanthropic causes. Another critical difference between black and white debutantes is age: black debutantes usually come out a year earlier than their white peers. Since most young women now marry a great deal later than when cotillions were originally invented, black families whose daughters come out do it for a different reason: "The purpose of the debut is not to announce their availability for marriage," explains one woman who has overseen cotillions for years, "but to celebrate their transition to another phase of their lives, in this case, the fact that they're leaving home and beginning life as young adults at college."

Today's black debutantes may come from all walks of life and are chosen as much for what they have accomplished in their short lives as for who they (or their families) are. Our cotillions are usually sponsored by social, civic, or fraternal organizations (the Links, the Girl Friends, Alpha Kappa Alpha, etc.). Young women frequently are invited to participate as much as a year ahead of their intended debut; they spend the next year in community service, being schooled on their next transition (choosing and applying to colleges, finding out what to expect once you've been accepted) or a socially significant project. They may also, in the last few months, be requested to learn the basics of the cotillion drill: how to waltz, promenade with an escort, and curtsy gracefully.

Debutantes are usually presented as a group, at a formal dance. The girls wear white gowns and long gloves and carry a floral bouquet. Each girl is presented to the assembled guests by her father (or father figure, such as her stepfather, a favorite uncle, or godfather). How she is presented varies from place to place. A deb may simply step into a spotlight, curtsy deeply to the assembled audience, and then be escorted from the floor by her father or escort. Other cotillions are more intricate; in some places, the debutante circles the room as her accomplishments are announced, stopping at strategic places on the perimeter to curtsy to the assembled guests.

Tradition dictates that each girl have an escort. They may be cousins or close family friends, even brothers. (Interestingly, boyfriends are often discouraged as a choice of escort because, as one mother noted, "boyfriends come and go; cousins are forever.") Their function is usually to take turns dancing with the debutante and other young women at the party. At formal presentations, both fathers and escorts wear white tie and tails. Over the years, many cotillions have stopped insisting on white tie, feeling it an expensive anachronism. Instead, men involved in cotillions will be asked to wear a black tuxedo.

While cotillions seem to be making a resurgence in popularity, it's important to note that this is a ritual that is better suited to some families than others. A debut, even a group one, can be costly (there are cotillion fees, the price of the gown and flowers, and many parents give a separate party before or after the cotillion in addition to the big ball). It's highly social and involves a lot of patience, and it may not appeal to all girls and their families. Many women who have participated in cotillions have enjoyed the process and have made friendships they've maintained for life. Others have chosen not to participate in the ritual, feeling their time and money can be better spent in other ways.

Beautillions

A more recent phenomenon in some parts of the country is the beautillion, a reverse twist on the traditional cotillion. In a beautillion, the focus is on the young man. Dressed in a tuxedo, he is introduced, via a formal dance that is often a fund-raiser, to assembled guests. He may walk alone to his place in the spotlight and bow to the guests. Or he may be escorted by a female friend (called a belle), who is dressed in a formal gown.

Initiations into Manhood—and Womanhood

Gaining in popularity are ceremonies that publicly acknowledge a young person's first steps away from adolescence and into adult life. In many African societies, this is a hallowed tradition, a personal watershed for the young man or woman being presented to his or her community. It may be marked by feast days, a retreat for personal meditation, or a physical challenge (killing a wild animal, performing an intricate dance, receiving ritual scarification marks, taking a communal purification bath), which culminates in a village-wide celebration of the young person's passage into adulthood.

Believing, as our ancestors did, that "it takes a village to raise a child," many black Americans are now choosing to participate in coming-of-age ceremonies for their children. These may be a relatively simple process, such as a church-sponsored service for young teens where they swear before congregants to forgo the temptations of drugs and premarital sex in order to be good role models to younger children and productive members of society. Or they may take the form of a series of classes, sponsored by a fraternal or civic organization, culminating in a communal dinner, where each young person is given a mentor, someone who will help guide him over the sometimes rocky path of adolescence into mature adulthood. And the young initiate, in turn, promises before those assembled to behave in a righteous and responsible manner that is worthy of imitation by the young people who will, one day soon, look up to him.

Many of these ceremonies have been given an Afrocentric flavor, with parts of traditional African ceremonies adjusted to New World practicalities. A coming-of-age ceremony for girls, for instance, might involve the initiates spending the night together before they are presented to the community as emerging young women. Over the course of the evening, they exchange information about growing up, their eventual responsibility as wives and mothers and independent citizens, while overseen by a responsible adult. The following day, they tell assembled onlookers the pledges they've made to themselves: "I promise always to behave in such a manner that I am a credit to my community, to choose the uplifting course, not the negative, to stay true to myself and my parents' teachings, no matter what others my age are doing or urging me to do." The event might be capped with a celebratory dinner full of songs, hugs, and congratulations. In many of these ceremonies, participants choose to dress in traditional African garb, to emphasize their ties with the motherland.

Some of these ceremonies began as long as twenty years ago and have now become traditions in their communities. Others are free-flowing, tailored to the needs and interests of the participants and their families. If you are interested in starting, or taking part in, a coming-of-age ceremony for your child, local chapters of organizations such as Jack and Jill of America, Concerned Black Men, Inc., and African American Women On Tour can send you guidelines for the ceremonies they have devised.

REMEMBRANCE DAY
Honoring the ancestors has always been an important part of our culture, and Remembrance Day is a way to pay homage to those who have gone before us. Although this ceremony may be called different things in different parts of the country, the essentials are the same: a family or church congregation or community gathers at a specific time each year where their family (or church) members are buried and, together, beautifies and tidies up the burial grounds. Children ask about relatives who died way before they were born ("How is Aunt Mamie related to me?") and get to share family anecdotes. Relatives who haven't seen each other for some time can visit and reminisce with each other. The day often culminates with a group luncheon under the trees or in a park nearby.

Kwanzaa

Since 1966, when it was first introduced by Maluana Karanga as an African-inspired celebration of the first harvest, Kwanzaa (sometimes spelled Kwanza or Quanzaa) has grown in popularity in our community. Many families celebrate both, which is easy enough to do, since Kwanzaa begins on December 26 and ends on January 1.

KWANZAA TABLE

If you're interested in having a Kwanzaa celebration, you'll need to set up a Kwanzaa table. This can be the centerpiece of the room, or placed on the side, but certain elements—a tablecloth, usually of African or African-inspired fabric, a gobletlike communal cup, fresh fruits or vegetables, and Kwanzaa candles in red, black, and green, among other things—are a must. There are several good guides to this holiday now on the market; many are available in hardcover and paperback. (Two favorites are Jessica Harris's *The Kwanzaa Table* and Eric Copage's *Kwanzaa: An African American Celebration of Culture and Cooking.*)

Family Reunions

For black Americans through the ages, family has been an important source of strength, guidance, and support; family has gotten us through hard times when nothing else could. And the family reunion is a way of acknowledging the importance of this institution.

Some families gather annually, others come together every few years or so. Whatever the time cycle, this regular assembly of relatives from far and near allows us to revel in the strength and love of our families and renew our connections to one another. Old folks can recite the family history to young ones, who will one day be expected to do the same for their young ones. Young cousins separated by distance become friends. Children who have been born since the last reunion make their debuts. And the family can, together, note the passing of members who have died since the last time they were together.

Many families have developed specific parts of their reunions that have become cherished traditions. Some have a church service incorporated into the reunion time. Others choose to make their reunions a minivacation and come together for a trip. Many print directories with each relative's address and telephone number. And quite a few have chosen to offer souvenirs—T-shirts, key rings, bumper stickers, etc.—that advertise their family pride and the site and date of their reunion: "Givens Family Reunion, Mound Bayou, Miss., July 4–6, 1993."

Gatherings like this take a considerable amount of planning and hard work, but all involved agree this labor of love is definitely worth the trouble. Because of the increasing popularity of family reunions in our community, several books have been written full of valuable how-to information and checklists for those who are interested in having reunions. Consult your local black bookstores to see what's available. Back issues of magazines such as *Essence* and *Emerge* can be great resources; and check the *Reader's Guide to Periodical Literature* at your local library.

Chapter 34

TO LOVE, HONOR, AND CHERISH

There is no secret to a long marriage—it's hard work. . . . It's serious business, and certainly not for cowards.

Ossie Davis

Before You Read Another Word

Be Sweet

Has your mother ever admonished you to "be sweet" when she foresaw troubled times brewing? If this warning came as you entered into the challenging times of planning your wedding, all we can say is . . . *your mother was right!* From the moment you agree to marry the love of your life to the moment you leave on your honeymoon (which won't be a minute too soon), you will be scrutinized. You've dreamed of your perfect wedding since you were seven years old, and now reality strikes. You are beginning a journey where you will (hopefully) meld two families. At times you will try to please everyone, and end up pleasing everyone but yourself. Be considerate of the wishes of others, but not to the extent that you lose yourself and begin to question who you are. As you plan, remember this is a day you'll remember forever—so don't try to be too trendy or cutesy. It *will* haunt you.

For the Record

Although we try to offer you the basics of wedding planning and hope to steer you away from some of the pitfalls, this chapter does not begin to cover everything you will need to plan your wedding. In deference to the importance it is to your life, and out of space considerations, we suggest you consult the hundreds of books on weddings that line the shelves of every library and bookstore. We won't leave you without answers; you just may not get them all here.

The Engagement

Announcing the Engagement

Once you've decided to marry, tell your parents before you share the news with anyone else. Tell both sets of parents on the same day so no one's feelings are hurt. If your parents are divorced, call one, then the other. Now that you've told your families, you're free to tell the world. It is inappropriate to send out printed cards announcing your engagement (see below). It *is* perfectly wonderful if you, or your family, host a small party to make the announcement to all of your close friends and extended families at one time. If you choose to send the information regarding your announcement to your local newspaper, ideally the announcement would appear in the paper the day after your announcement party, if there is one. Call your local newspaper for a checklist of what information they require, what their deadlines are, whom to send the announcement to, whether they are willing to run a photograph, and what the costs involved are.

Sample Engagement Announcement

> Mr. and Mrs. Vincent X. Bender of Roanoke, Va., have announced the engagement of their daughter, Jasmine Marie Bender, to James LeRoy Carter, son of Mr. and Mrs. LeRoy Eugene Carter of Philadelphia, Pa. A September wedding is planned.
>
> Ms. Bender is a magna cum laude alumna of Howard University, and is a curator of 18th-Century African Art at the Smithsonian Institution's Museum of African Art, in Washington, D.C. Her father is a retired public information officer for the Roanoke Transport Authority. Her mother is a homemaker.
>
> Mr. Carter, who is known as Jamie, is a summa cum laude alumnus of Howard University, and holds a master's degree in journalism from American University. He covers local politics for the *Washington Post.* His father is a director of customer relations for the West Philadelphia region of the United States Postal Service. His mother is a high school chemistry teacher.

Terms of Endearment

A groom-to-be is usually referred to as "fiancé," while a bride-to-be is referred to as "fiancée." Other terms include the "betrothed," the "intended," or in reference to the future bride, the "bride-elect."

Length of Engagement

The rules are no longer hard-and-fast. Once you've decided to spend your life together, carefully select a date for your wedding. Some of the factors that may influence your decision:

- You may want to wait until you've finished school or an internship.
- You may have just started a new job and feel the planning might interfere with stabilizing your employment.
- A loved one may be very ill and you choose to push the date up—or back—to accommodate the situation.
- Family and close friends who live far away may need time to plan to attend.
- Your "dream wedding" may require some extra time to save enough money to allow for those little extras.
- The church or reception hall where you'd like to have the service is booked solid for the next year and you have to find either a new location or a new date.
- You may know you want to get married, but want to spend some time considering when that should happen.

Rings

While your knight in shining armor may be a genius when it comes to computer programs, chances are he doesn't have a clue about engagement rings and what you would like to have. Best deal: groom-to-be selects a number of rings he likes (in his price range), then takes his fiancée to the shop so she can choose from his selections. Engagement rings are not essential, and some brides elect to have a special wedding band rather than an engagement ring and a band. Think about the ring you'll wear for years to come. Instead of a traditional diamond, would you rather have another stone? Or custom-made matching bands that reflect your cultural roots? Some gentlemen may offer their loves heirloom rings that have been handed down in their family. Accept graciously—you'll have anniversaries to get the ring you want. It's a man's choice as to whether he'll choose to wear a wedding band.

And Brother, Remember

You now have a responsibility to live by the promises you have made. Things looked pretty terrific the night you proposed, but the closer it gets to the wedding, you're sure you're marrying a crazy woman. Your future bride may become so wrapped up in the details of planning the wedding that you may sometimes feel slighted. Have no fear, this, too, shall pass. (If it doesn't, you weren't meant to be together in the first place!) Traditionally, wedding plans, as well as the cost, have been left up to the bride and her family. While these decisions are now usually made jointly by the two of you, many brides' families still absorb the bulk of the financial burden. You have responsibilities as the groom (don't think you're getting off that easily), and you have a right to voice your opinion (gently) if there are things about the ceremony that make you crazy. Remember, choose your battles and be willing to compromise.

Prenuptial Agreement

Some people frown on prenuptial agreements because they think of them as self-fulfilling prophecies—because you *know* something will go wrong, and you better protect yourself. Prenuptial agreements are simply written statements that spell out the financial arrangements each of you has agreed upon should the marriage fail. In most cases, it protects the assets accumulated by each partner prior to the union, and sometimes addresses assets that will be earned or acquired during the course of the marriage. Either partner may choose to include stipulations that protect financial rights of children from previous unions. It's your call. If it's an issue for either partner, discuss it between you and then seek separate legal counsel to represent each of you.

The Master Plan

Where Do We Begin?

Before you begin calling your favorite hotel to reserve the ballroom for your reception, there are a number of things you, the bride, should think about. At this point, think this out alone without outside input. Get a notebook, and write down, "In my perfect world . . ."

I'd get married in the month of ______________________________
The day of the week would be ______________________________
The wedding would begin at ________________________ (A.M. or P.M.?)
The reception would begin at ______________________________
I'd like a religious ______ or civil ______ ceremony.

I want a big _____ or small _____ wedding.
I'd have the ceremony at ______________________________
____________ would perform, or officiate at, the wedding ceremony.
The reception would be at ______________________________
I would follow tradition on these points . . .
I want to do "my own thing" when it comes to ______________
These family traditions are important to me . . .
I can convince my fiancé to tell me how he really feels about being included in the wedding planning and preparation.
The wedding will be given by ____________________________
I'd have ________ guests. (Don't forget to count two people per invitation.)
Children will _____ or will not _____ be welcome at the wedding and/or the reception.
The wedding will be formal _____ or informal _____.
I want my invitations to be formal _____ informal _____ or casual _____.
My bridal/wedding color would be ______________________
The entire wedding budget would be ____________________
My wedding gown would look like _______________________
I'd like ________ bridesmaids.
The one thing I *must* have in my wedding is _______________

Ready, Set, Go

Now that you've thought about what you'd like in your dream world, it's time to get down to basics. At this point share your desires with your mother. While you certainly want to consider your fiancé's wishes, and hopefully he's thought about them, there's no reason to discuss *everything* with him. Do discuss the "bones" of the wedding, and the size and general "feel"—no need to discuss the details of your dream wedding gown. Ascertain early on how much input your fiancé would like to have in the overall planning. He may tell you he just wants to be told where to show up on the given day—but, in reality, the music and what you'll serve at the reception really do matter to him. (My husband-to-be has expressed these things as important to him: joint officiants with his minister participating also; his sister being asked to be in the wedding; wearing traditional tuxedos with kente cloth ties and cummerbunds; we write our own vows; his buddy Johnathan will sing a solo; the honeymoon will be a surprise and I'm not to ask about it.) Take his wishes into consideration.

Traditional or Not?

Decide whether the wedding will follow traditional guidelines or will more closely reflect the two of you. You may decide to have a traditional wedding but would like to incorporate Afrocentric touches such as "jumping the broom" following your vows. You may choose to have a traditional wedding and a very nontraditional reception. Or you may choose to skip the ceremonial madness and have a small wedding at home.

Many traditional rules governing weddings no longer apply, or at least not as strictly. Variations may occur regarding:

- Invitations
- Ceremony and vows
- Music
- Location of ceremony
- Reception
- Parents' participation. (Both parents give bride away; both parents walk down the aisle with the bride; mother gives bride away; bride stops after ceremony to remove flowers from bouquet and gives one each to mother and groom's mother—groom kisses the mothers and shakes hands with the fathers.)
- Favors—for the guests to take home—can be almost anything.
- Table settings to display new china, crystal/glassware, and flatware (especially when the reception is held at bride's parents' home)
- Cakes can be carrot, chocolate, or a little of everything.
- Groom's cake—regional, cultural (frats, hobbies, etc.)
- Receiving lines are often abandoned, and it becomes responsibility of couple and bride's parents to circulate through the party and try to speak to each guest.

Don't plan an extravaganza that's so long and involved that the players will need scripts as they fall over the "set" and the props.

Types of Weddings

Church or other spiritual service: Once you have spoken to the minister, priest, or spiritual leader and asked him (or her!) to officiate at your service, and a date has been agreed upon, ask for the church's (or other house of worship's) rules governing weddings and if there is a wedding liaison or coordinator you should confer with. Ask whether you are obligated to use the in-house wedding coordinator. Inquire early on as to costs involved in using the facility. These may include facility rental, security, lighting coordinator, air-conditioning, or baby-sitting services. If you are asking the officiant to perform the service outside of his religious facility, ask if there are any special requirements you must heed.

Civil wedding: You may be married by a judge, justice of the peace, or other legally authorized individual. The ceremony may be just as elaborate, or as simple, as a church wedding. If marrying outside of your home state, call for legal requirements well in advance of your intended wedding date.

Private ceremony: Small weddings, often just for family. A reception may be held later the same day or at a later date.

Evening wedding: Evening weddings, which are most commonly held at eight o'clock, can be elegant affairs. While the details in planning parallel daytime weddings, the time of day dictates the bridal party's attire, the attire of the guests, whether the ceremony will be held indoors or outdoors, food served, and the attendance of children and the elderly.

Officiants

You may choose to be united by a minister or other legally accepted religious leader, a judge, or the justice of the peace. Once you have decided if you will have a religious or a civil ceremony, confer with your fiancé and your family regarding who will perform the ceremony. If the service will be held at your home church, and your fiancé feels especially close to the minister at his own church, you may decide to ask them to co-officiate. It is important that this decision is made in the early stages of your planning, and that you ask the potential officiant(s) as soon as possible. Remember, the officiating person will have input as to the wording of the vows, restrictions within his or her church, and special classes you may be asked to attend as a condition of marriage. The same holds true for civil servants. They alone can tell you what is required. Another reason for finalizing your selection is to ensure they will be available on the date you have selected. Once you know whom you're going to ask, simply call the person(s) and ask if he or she will do the two of you the honor of performing your marriage ceremony. The call should be made by the person (bride or groom) who is closer to the officiant.

Who Gives the Wedding?

Traditionally, the bride's parents give the wedding, and for the most part that is still true. With today's economy, and the fact that many brides are older when they choose to marry, they may want to give the wedding themselves, or contribute to the wedding. The groom's family may also offer to contribute, but it is the bride's family that either accepts or rejects that proposition. Don't assume anything. If the wedding expenses are split fifty-fifty by the bride's and the groom's families, then the groom's parents are entitled to have their names shown on the invitation as hosts also. The more money you contribute, the more say you have in decisions. Sad, but true.

Who Pays for What?

By tradition, the entire wedding is paid for by the bride's parents, with just a few items being delegated to the groom's family. The groom's family gets off easy by simply being responsible for the rehearsal dinner. The groom himself is expected to pay for the bride's engagement and wedding rings, the marriage license, the bride's bouquet and corsages for the mothers, the boutonnieres, the officiant's fee, and the honeymoon.

In today's real world, often the costs are split among the bride's parents, the groom and his family, and the couple themselves. While not automatically even splits, the bride's family most often still contributes the greatest amount if the bride and groom are not giving the wedding.

Frequently, the bride and groom are older and do not feel comfortable allowing the bride's family to foot the entire bill—even if it's their wish to do so. The bride and groom may elect to pay for certain "extras" and major items such as flowers, music, the cake, or the engagement party.

Establishing a Wedding Budget

A number of items must be considered when planning your wedding budget. The number of guests you invite is directly related to your budget, as is the formality of the ceremony and the reception. Ten thousand dollars to host a wedding with three hundred guests is a very different proposition than spending the same amount of money on one hundred guests. Disregarding the groom's responsibility for financing the bride's rings and the honeymoon, a typical wedding budget consists of:

- Reception
- Bridal apparel
- Photography and videography
- Flowers (wedding, reception, bouquet, etc.)
- Music
- Invitations
- Cake
- Bridal luncheon
- Bridal consultant (optional)
- Miscellaneous: engagement party; attendant gifts; transportation; bride's stationery; ceremony fees; rental of ceremony and/or reception site; favors; mother-of-the-bride apparel; parties for out-of-town guests; programs; special lighting; security; postage; valet; newspaper announcements—the list goes on and on!

Start with a ballpark figure that those giving the wedding expect to pay. Whatever amount you start with, the hidden costs will astound you and must be anticipated. Take the total figure and estimate the percentage, or the amount, you wish to allocate to each category. After you pick yourself up from the floor and regroup, try again. Eventually, you will come to a realistic budget.

A simple way to evaluate your wedding budget is to obtain cost estimates for your desired reception based on your estimated number of guests. If shrimp and an open bar mean fewer guests, you must decide what's more important to you—more guests or a formal sit-down dinner.

If at all possible, don't save for a big wedding for a longer time period than the marriage will last. This is your big day, but it is not the *only* day.

The Parents' Role

You may find today's parents taking a larger role in the wedding preparations, or no role at all. Parents should be supportive, take an interest in the plans of the bridal couple, offer financial assistance and expertise when able and desired by the bride and groom. Traditionally, the mother of the bride assumes the role of hostess at a wedding given by the bride's parents. Today the father of the bride may join his wife, and even the groom's parents, in assuming some of the usual duties.

Choosing a Site for the Ceremony and Reception

Once you've decided if you'll be married in a religious ceremony or a civil ceremony, you can begin to explore your options. Consider the following:

- If you'd like to marry in a church or other house of worship, does your home church meet your needs (size, decor, availability, air-conditioning or heat)?
- Will your chosen officiant agree to perform the ceremony anywhere?
- Outdoors or indoors?
- Weather and time of year
- Seating capacity
- Does the ceremony site have adequate reception facilities?
- Will the reception site allow you to bring in your own caterer and drinks, or must you use theirs?
- Does the reception site have adequate seating, dishes, silverware—or must you provide rentals?
- Do you and your intended love the ocean, the mountains, or the desert?
- Is the site geographically desirable for your guests?
- Is the reception site within a reasonable distance from the site of the ceremony?
- Does the site have handicapped access (if needed)?

Unusual Sites to Say "I Do"

Once you've exhausted the old standbys—house of worship, hotel, clubhouse, or home—be creative. Art galleries, museums, the chapel of your alma mater, in the park at sunrise, on a cliff overlooking the ocean at sunset—the possibilities are endless. If you volunteer at the local YMCA and want your after-school program students to attend, you might request the facility's gym. Gardens are always a lovely choice, and large cities usually have a listing of potential wedding sites for you to explore. Couples have begun their lives together in hot-air balloons, underwater, at the zoo, or at their favorite bookstore where they met. Use your imagination, it doesn't hurt to ask!

The Guest List

What seems like a simple task—compiling a guest list—is often what gives you your first ulcer. Start your guest list as soon as possible after deciding to marry. Use a starting figure, determine how many guests, or what percentage of guests, will be allocated to each family and their friends. Since the bride's family most often is giving the wedding, the majority of invitations are designated for the bride's side. Ask your fiancé how many guests he thinks he would like to invite, and work backward. In addition to the names, list the mailing address (including zip code), how the invitation should be addressed ("Dr. and Mrs. Benjamin Hill" rather than "Benny and Carole Hill"), and a telephone number if it's readily available. Telephone numbers come in handy for last-minute verifications (when a guest *thinks* she's bringing an extra five guests just because your wedding will be the biggest of the year). As you merge your fiancé's list, your parents' list, his parents' list, and yours, an updated telephone book begins to emerge. Having a complete list (in the computer, or printed on individual index cards alphabetized by last name) will eliminate duplications, and come in handy for putting together shower guest lists, addressing thank-you notes, and remembering your friends when sending out your first joint holiday cards.

Who's Going to Give You Away?

Whoever you feel deserves the job and will make you happy. Father, stepfather, uncle; either parent, grandfather, mother, brother—it's your call. Don't intentionally hurt anyone's feelings, but you may feel that the grandfather who raised you has more of a right to give you away than the father who just emerged for the first time since you were three years old.

The Wedding Team

No matter how large or how small, no one person puts on a wedding without help. From the very beginning you assemble a team of experts to advise, counsel, and (hopefully) make your life easier.

Wedding Consultant

A wedding consultant can coordinate your entire wedding. Wedding consultant's services range from securing a caterer and having favors made to organizing every detail after consultation with you. Although these experts have a great deal of experience in planning weddings, take their suggestions as just that—suggestions. *Never* allow anyone to manipulate you into believing that a major change in plans was your idea, when actually you were so exhausted you simply took the path of least resistance. Discuss with your family and/or your fiancé just how much you'd like to do yourselves, and what would be better left to the experts. Interview wedding consultants prior to agreeing to use their services. Do your homework. Sometimes you think you don't know what you're talking about—when in reality you're just uncomfortable because this is unknown territory. Wedding consultants may be recommended by the facility where your wedding will take place, they may be part of the wedding package at your house of worship, or they may be affiliated with the bridal salon where you're shopping for a gown. Many freelance consultants have unspoken agreements with other wedding services, such as caterers, party rental businesses, or stationery shops. Be sure to ask if you will be able to select your own services, or if you will be expected to use companies of their choice. Many a lovely wedding (even huge ones!) has been executed without a wedding consultant. Be realistic. You or a member of your family may be the most creative party giver that ever graced a ballroom—but time constraints and circumstances may indicate the need for someone to do your "follow-up" and allow you to take care of the rest of your life.

Locating and Hiring Services

Start by asking friends who've recently entertained for a suggestion of a caterer. Think of the weddings you've been to that you most enjoyed and ask the former bride if she'd mind sharing some of her resources. Begin to keep a list of potential service companies and individuals. Often bridal magazines and special editions of women's magazines offer suggestions for bridal services. Ask for suggestions as you begin to visit bridal shops. Remember that the earlier you order various items, the greater chance you will have a product you are pleased with and the price will be right. Last-minute requests don't allow for changes when mistakes have been made, often incur "rush" charges, and will certainly add to your increasing frustration as the big day nears. Good cake makers and caterers will offer you samples of their products free of charge. Hotels and restaurants will offer you complimentary meals that you propose to serve, or at least will reduce the price. Taste, look, sample, compare prices, and think some more before making decisions. Secure a written contract for all services you engage. Be sure the agreement includes services to be provided, total cost or cost per person, deposit and final payment schedule, conditions of partial or full refunds, whether a prior approval is required by you prior to delivery (for instance, a proof to be checked for invitations), and the conditions of and day and time of delivery.

Services for Consideration

While you may have a pool of talented people in your circle of family and friends and will not need to hire anyone, the following services should give you guidelines for planning:

Caterer: You may be looking for the best person to cater your favorite meal or you may be looking for a caterer that can offer you suggested menus within your budget. Remember it's not just how good the food tastes, it's also the presentation and how pretty the buffet tables or individual plates will look. Check for references if you are unfamiliar with the caterer. A wonderful cook may be notoriously late and your guests will be kept waiting for hours! When purchasing food on a "per person" basis, try to ascertain just how much food that will be. You certainly don't want your guests to come to a full sit-down dinner and go away still hungry. (We've all been to one of *those* events.)

Florist: When determining your floral needs, think about how many venues will need flowers. You may require flowers, decorated pews, and bridal party bouquets for the church, and table centerpieces, hostess corsages, and decorations for the dance floor area at the reception. You may need flowers for your parents' home if out-of-town visitors and gift deliverers will be stopping by unexpectedly during the wedding week. Again, ask friends who were pleased with their florists. Ask to look at photographs of previous weddings and large events they've provided floral decorations for. Compare prices and whether or not one florist is equipped to meet all of your needs. Consider one florist for the ceremony site, and another for the reception if it will be held somewhere else. This allows the florist to focus on one venue, and there's a greater chance each will be set up on time. If you do choose separate florists, be sure to coordinate the "looks" if that is what you'd like.

Photographer and videographer: You may want a professional photographer to record your formal photographs of the ceremony, the bridal party, your families, and the setting. Specify if you would like color photographs, black-and-white, or a combination of both. Videographers are becoming more and more popular as a method of recording your precious moments with movement and audio. Videos provide a "living" record for grandparents and others whose health may not have allowed them to attend. You probably *think* you'll remember every minute of the "big event," but chances are far greater that you won't remember a thing! If candid shots are your pleasure, even if you have a professional photographer, enlist a friend or two to take candid shots at the reception. Close friends can capture those special to you and unspoken moments that will bring you joy when you see them. One way of ensuring that all guests at a sit-down reception will be photographed is to provide a disposable camera for each table, and ask that they photograph the guests at their table, then return the used camera to a designated hostess. It's also a way to get the guests to be active participants in an informal reception. The bottom line: never hire a photographer whose wedding pictures you have not seen.

Wedding cake baker: With your fiancé, decide what flavor cake and filling you would like to consider, and make the rounds testing the goods. Bakeries will offer suggestions for types of cakes, size based on the expected number of guests, and decoration of the cake. Let the baker know your color scheme, the formality or informality of the reception, and how the cake is to be served. An eight-tired extravaganza might be pleasing to the eye, but quite difficult to maneuver if the correct serving utensils and help are not on hand to cut and serve. A baker that will not provide you with taste samples should be avoided, if possible. Our people love pretty cakes (look at pictures of other wedding cakes they've done)—but not nearly as much as they like *good* cakes.

Musician(s) and disc jockeys: Decide whether you will have live music, recorded music, or a combination of the two. Much like the floral arrangements, you may require different musical enhancements for the ceremony and the reception. If you would like to have a soloist or duo sing at your wedding, try to remember the last event where you heard that person or persons perform and contact the hostess for a referral. If you're interested in chamber music or jazz quartets, investigate the possibilities with the music department of your local university or music school. Music agents exist that allow you to select live performers from videos designated by type of music. Rather than listening to a cassette recording of the group or individual, the video allows you to evaluate their look and their performance style as well as their musical ability. If you will be using live music at the reception, you may choose to record taped selections that can be played during breaks. If you require a master of ceremonies or someone who can make announcements, ask the music leader if he is willing to provide this service. Disc jockeys can be referred by friends or even the teenage children of your friends. Review their musical selections and your special requests prior to entering into an agreement. If you would like your musicians to dress in a certain attire, it is only fair to discuss this with them, or their agent, prior to signing a contract. Organists and soloists can often be provided by, or referrals offered by, the facility hosting the ceremony.

Transportation and valets: List your transportation needs and decide if you will require valet parking for the ceremony and/or reception before you begin to interview potential companies. Your best references will continue to come from friends and relatives. Do not assume that limousines are the only mode of travel—perhaps a summer wedding party will arrive in convertible vintage cars. For both hired cars and valets, check their insurance coverage before finalizing any agreements.

Stationer or printer for invitations: If your dream is to create your own invitations, consult with a printer for recommendations as to the most effective way to proceed. Whether you use a commercial printer or select your invitations from a catalog, list all printed pieces that you will need prior to making a decision. Some standard catalog invitations do not carry all the items you may wish to have (invitations; response cards; at-home cards; announcements; pew cards; thank-you notes; printed ribbon; programs; printed boxes for favors; etc.).

Dressmaker for bride's gown and/or bridal attendants: Ready-made dresses may not offer you the range in style, size, and color that suits your fancy, or you would like a custom dress. If you have not used the designer or dressmaker you're considering, ask for referrals, and actually look at finished pieces. Custom dresses for the bridal party are more difficult to manage when a number of the attendants reside out of town and would not be available for regular fittings.

Rental attire for groom and groomsmen/ushers: Consider the size and build of the groom as well as the attendants. Will you be attempting to add Afrocentric touches through kente ties, vests, or cummerbunds? If so, shop with your eyes open for tuxedo shops that are able to provide you with these accessories. While most rental shops are full service, all do not offer a size range that suits our men's particular needs when it comes to that perfect fit.

Miscellaneous needs: favors, runner for bridal procession, pillow for ring, printed napkins, special lighting, heaters or tents for outdoor events, equipment rentals (tables, chairs, dishes, flatware, glasses, stoves, generators, umbrellas, tablecloths, napkins, cake stands, etc.), gifts for attendants, calligrapher for addressing invitations, and everything else that comes up at the last minute.

Keeping a Wedding Planner

The only way to stay on top of all that you will have to organize and remember is to keep a wedding planner. Commercial (store-bought) planners include timetables for completing wedding tasks, as well as suggestions. A loose-leaf notebook or blank diary will serve just as well. Even if you *think* you'll remember every suggestion you received for a caterer, and will *always* know where that stray piece of paper or business card is with her telephone number, record *everything* in your wedding book. When it becomes a bit overwhelming, at least you will know that all information is recorded in a single place. Make yourself a list of things to be done and assign completion dates to them. Keep a small calendar in the beginning of the book for scheduling.

Bride's Checklist

The bride's checklist is actually her individual things to be done, the overall wedding things to be done, and a copy of her fiancé's things to be done.

As we mentioned earlier, we don't expect to answer all of your wedding questions. We do offer a general checklist for getting yourself organized. Don't put off until tomorrow what you can do today. And above all, don't become so caught up in the planning that the "wedding" becomes more important to you than the marriage.

- ❑ Announce your engagement (remember, family first!).
- ❑ Select time of day and day of the week—then date.
- ❑ Choose the kind of wedding you'd like to have.
- ❑ Decide, along with family and fiancé, on officiant(s) and invite participation.
- ❑ Select the location and reserve the date.
- ❑ Check with officiant to determine if premarital counseling is required.
- ❑ Agree on who will pay for what (bride's parents, the couple, groom's family).
- ❑ Settle on a realistic budget.
- ❑ Choose a color scheme.
- ❑ Decide on the number of guests (and who will make the final decisions when the list is too long!).
- ❑ Decide if you would like to use the services of a bridal or wedding consultant.
- ❑ What attendants would you like in the bridal party? Number? (Matron of honor? Ring bearer? Train bearer? Candle lighters?)
- ❑ Invite your maid and/or matron of honor and bridesmaids to be in the wedding.
- ❑ Invite other members of bridal party to be in the wedding.
- ❑ Keep working on that guest list.

- ❑ Select your gown and headpiece (needless to say, you'll need shoes, too).
- ❑ Begin to look for bridal party attire (store-bought or custom-made?).
- ❑ Investigate gift registry possibilities.
- ❑ Select a caterer (make sure she/he saves the date!).
- ❑ Select florist (might consider one for church, another for reception).
- ❑ Begin to think about musical selections you'd like to have played (ceremony and reception; live music or recorded; disc jockey; etc.)
- ❑ Think about whether you want still or video photos, and color and/or black-and-white.
- ❑ Select a photographer (look at his wedding work before you hire him—and get referrals from friends who were pleased with their wedding photographs—and actually received them the same decade they were married!). Videographer too, if desired.
- ❑ Start tasting wedding cakes—select one as soon as you're satisfied.
- ❑ Reserve the reception locale if different from wedding (same time as wedding, to coordinate availability).
- ❑ Order invitations and thank-you notes.
- ❑ Help fiancé make selection of groomsmen attire.
- ❑ Finalize selections for bridal party attire and schedule fittings.
- ❑ Remind fiancé about the need to obtain a marriage license.
- ❑ Make a doctor's appointment for checkup and required tests.
- ❑ Change your name on your driver's license and Social Security card (if you choose).
- ❑ Get marriage license (don't wait until the last minute—bureaucracy is rough!).
- ❑ Stick to budget.
- ❑ Keep working on that never-ending guest list.
- ❑ Consider fiancé's wishes.
- ❑ Plan bridal luncheon.
- ❑ Ask others for referrals of people to hire for various services.
- ❑ Get everything in writing (arrangements; date gown to arrive; when bridesmaids alterations will be complete; church expenses; etc.).
- ❑ Keep a notebook with all arrangements and agreements.
- ❑ Ask your maid of honor to remind you of important items you're afraid you'll forget.
- ❑ Remember, you're only Queen for a Day (on your wedding day), *not* for the entire year leading up to the big day!
- ❑ Be sweet . . .

Groom's Checklist

- ❑ Announce engagement.
- ❑ Consider inviting both sets of parents to lunch or dinner so everyone can begin to get to know each other—and get started on a good foot. It will show them that family matters to you both.
- ❑ Select wedding rings.
- ❑ Submit guest list to bride.
- ❑ Ask friends to be your attendants (ask the best man first—consider your father or brother).
- ❑ Get a calendar to schedule appointments, follow-ups, rehearsal, parties, etc.).
- ❑ Plan honeymoon.
- ❑ Arrange for passport, visas, and shots (if needed).
- ❑ If not leaving on honeymoon until the day following the wedding, book a hotel room in town for your wedding night.
- ❑ If you're surprising the bride with the honeymoon plans, at least be sure she has the appropriate passport and knows what kind of clothes she should pack.
- ❑ *Calmly* let bride know if you have special requests regarding the ceremony and/or the reception (music, scripture, participants, favorite food, type of cake, etc.).
- ❑ Shop for bride's gift.
- ❑ Plan/arrange for rehearsal dinner with your family.
- ❑ Arrange for accommodations for out-of-town guests.
- ❑ Arrange for transportation for bridal party.
- ❑ Purchase gift for your attendants.
- ❑ Select attendants' (and your) attire.
- ❑ Discuss seating and special arrangements with ushers.
- ❑ Pick up rings and check the fit.

Last week:

- ❑ Pick up wedding attire and make sure it fits.
- ❑ Have dinner (just you) with your family.
- ❑ Arrange for someone to drive the "getaway" car.
- ❑ Review schedule of events.
- ❑ Confirm honeymoon plans, pick up tickets.
- ❑ Confirm accommodations for out-of-town guests.
- ❑ Pack for honeymoon.

- ❑ Attend rehearsal (and be on your good behavior).
- ❑ Prepare checks for officiant and any other services that must be paid for on wedding day (give to best man to deliver).
- ❑ Make "to do" and "to take" lists for wedding day.
- ❑ Attend bachelor party (not the night before!).

Wedding day:

- ❑ Give ring to best man.
- ❑ Be where you're supposed to be, when you're supposed to be—and don't upset anyone.
- ❑ Call your parents (and siblings) that morning just to say "good morning."
- ❑ Relax and enjoy yourself.
- ❑ Don't drink too much, and remember to eat.

Reality Check

Your wedding can be dramatic, but this is *not* theater! Get a grip. Make a pact, in the early stages of planning, with your family or closest friend to alert you as the need for a "reality check" becomes apparent. Retain your humor, perhaps with a code word that needs no explanation. If you hear them say the word "aardvark," you know you're about to go over the edge. If your mother is helping you plan the wedding, you'll probably need a code word that you issue to her!

Coordinating the Bridal Party

Asking Friends to Participate

Once you've decided how many attendants you would like to have, and the friends you'd like to share your big day with, call them as soon as possible. Many costs are involved in being a member of a bridal party, so don't expect even your closest friends to respond immediately. As much as they may love you, many factors will come into play. For the out-of-town attendant, or if you're planning your wedding far away, talk frankly about the costs involved. If you are financially able, you may offer to pay the travel or wedding-attire costs for your bridesmaids. If at all possible, ask each attendant at about the same time—so no one thinks they're an afterthought.

Bride's Attendants

Maid and/or matron of honor: Consults and assists the bride; takes responsibilities and stress off the bride; signs registry as "witness" for the bride; if there is a receiving line, stands to the left of the groom; sits at groom's left at bridal table; holds bride's flowers and assists in adjusting veil as needed; pays for her own attire; collects for and purchases gift if bridesmaids decide to give a joint gift to bride. While often your sister or best friend, you may choose your mother to be your matron of honor. If both maid and matron, maid takes precedence over matron.

Bridesmaids: Pay for own attire and make sure it fits properly; act as deputy hostesses at reception; may stand in receiving line; attend rehearsal and dinner.

Jr. bridesmaids: Girls usually between the ages of eight and fourteen (too big to be flower girls and too young to be bridesmaids). Their family pays for attire, and the girls attend the rehearsal and the rehearsal dinner—not necessarily any other festivities.

Flower girls: Usually young relatives of the bride or groom; they scatter flowers before the bride; are about three to seven years old; attend rehearsal; their family pays for attire; if they attend showers or other parties, it is for only a short time (depending on their age and parents' wishes).

Ring bearer: Between the ages of three and seven; carries ring on cushion (fake; real rings with best man and maid of honor); his family pays for attire; attends rehearsal.

Other small attendants: Train bearers hold the bride's train, and are very little boys; pages are small boys who walk in the procession but do little else.

Children in general: Don't have too many children in the bridal party, no matter how cute they are. In addition to how many things can go wrong, they may steal the show!

Groom's Attendants

Best man: No matter how small the wedding, a groom always has a best man (just as bride has maid of honor). You can ask brother, relative, close friend, or your father. Duty to relieve groom of stressful responsibilities; makes sure the groom is properly dressed and "at the church on time"; holds the wedding ring; in Christian ceremonies, enters church with the groom; signs wedding registry as groom's witness; attends rehearsal and keeps other attendants "on the job"; delivers payment to officiants and others on wedding day (groom will have given him envelopes with checks in each); helps groom prepare "getaway" transportation.

Ushers: Direct guests to their seats, to the reception, and dance with bridesmaids. Some of the ushers will serve as groomsmen in the ceremony, others will simply assist with the guests. You should plan on approximately one usher for each fifty guests. Assign a family friend to be head usher. Head usher escorts the mother of the bride and the mother of the groom to their seats. Ushers may be assigned to place the white carpet, or runner, down the aisle for the procession. If ribbons have cordoned off special pews, two ushers remove the ribbons after the section has been filled. Ushers pay for their own rental of wedding attire. Ushers also distribute programs.

Jr. ushers: Between the ages of eight and fourteen. They dress like the other ushers, but walk behind them. Sometimes if there are two junior ushers, they take responsibility for the pew ribbons.

Dressing the Wedding Party

It's probably fair to say that, next to the proposal, the most important question the potential bride will face is "What are we going to wear?" Depending on the time of day and type of wedding, the choices vary hugely. The important thing to remember is context: it's entirely appropriate to get married in a simple, romantic dress and flat sandals if your ceremony is in a field and the guests are casually dressed. A long, beaded dress with a train would look out of place in the same setting—unless the "field" is a formal garden in a parklike setting at a country club or an estate.

The same rules apply for the time of day. Strictly speaking, a wedding after six o'clock in the evening is considered formal, and the bridal party should be dressed appropriately. Although tradition usually dictates that in a formal wedding the groom and his party would be dressed in white tie and tail coats, many modern formal weddings choose a broader interpretation and opt for the less-daunting (but still elegant) tuxedo instead.

We've included both the traditional and what we call the real world corollaries for the wedding party's clothes.

The Bride

At an Informal Wedding During the Day

Traditional: A short dress or suit (sometimes a very, very simple long dress—but no train), in white or off-white, with a small headpiece or hat and short veil (the veil optional).
Real world: Same.

At a Formal Wedding During the Day

Traditional: Long white or off-white gown. May or may not have a modest "sweep" (as the name indicates, it's only slightly longer than the dress and barely sweeps the floor) or "chapel-length" train (which extends four feet from the waist of the dress). Veil is optional.
Real world: Same, although brides often wear more elaborate gowns, traditionally seen at evening weddings, in the late afternoon.

At a Formal Evening Wedding

Traditional: Long white or off-white gown, may be quite elaborate and very sophisticated. Train, if any, usually parallels the gown in mood: a simple gown would have a sweep or chapel-length train; more elaborate ones will need a more substantive train. And the fanciest, most regal dress could command a cathedral-length train, which usually extends two and a half yards from the waist). Unless you're marrying royalty (or *are* royalty), forget about the twenty-five-foot train.
Real world: Same.

Bridal Accessories

"Something borrowed, something blue, something old, something new," of course. Jewelry should be in harmony with the dress: If you have a simple gown, a lustrous strand (or a choker) of pearls would be beautiful. Or small pearl earrings, or diamond studs. We'd suggest that the fancier the gown, the more beading, seed pearls, crystal, and so forth, the simpler the jewelry.

And keep it to the minimum: what you most want your guests and groom to remember is not how beautiful the dress was, but how beautiful you looked *in* it.

Don't choose anything that would distract from your happy face.

The Bridal Attendants

These dresses should match the bride's in mood and harmonize with her type. (If she's chosen a *Gone with the Wind* hoopskirt kind of dress, her attendants will probably be matched in something akin to it—even though they'd much rather the streamlined, one-shoulder sheath they spied on the sample rack). If there is a maid or matron of honor, her dress may be a slightly different hue of the same color family (i.e., attendants in pale pink and the maid of honor in dusky rose).

At an Informal Wedding During the Day

Traditional: Short, dressy dresses that harmonize (or contrast happily) with the bride's. Satin shoes, often dyed to match. Headpieces and veils optional.
Real world: Same.

At a Formal Wedding During the Day

Traditional: Long gowns that correspond to the bride's, in pastel or bright colors. (Contemporary brides sometimes choose to have their attendants in white, too, perhaps with colored accents, such as jackets or sashes or trim.)
Real world: Short, dressy dresses or long gowns.

At a Formal Evening Wedding

Traditional: Long gowns that correspond to the bride's, in pastel or bright colors. A new trend shows many bridesmaids in deep colors for evening weddings (navy, chocolate, etc.), even black.
Real world: Same.

THE FLOWER GIRL
Traditional: A long or ankle-length gown, in white, off-white (may have a colored sash), or a pastel reflection of the bridesmaids' gowns.
Real world: Same.

THE GROOM

For an Informal Wedding During the Day

Traditional: Dark business suit, dark shoes and socks.
Real world: Dark business suit or jacket; dark jacket and contrasting trousers (i.e., navy linen jacket and white linen trousers for a summer wedding). Vest, shirt, and trousers (for a *very* informal wedding).

For a Formal Wedding During the Day

Traditional: Black or oxford-gray cutaway, gray vest, black-and-gray-striped trousers. Black shoes and socks.
Real world: Dark business suit. Tuxedo (black only).

For a Formal Evening Wedding

Traditional: Black tailcoat, black trousers with satin trim, white pique shirt with wing collar, white pique bow tie. White pique waistcoat. Black patent-leather pumps or oxfords, or black kid oxfords.
Real world: Black tuxedo (white dinner jackets in warm weather, but never a white tuxedo); black patent-leather oxfords or simple black kid oxfords.

AND REMEMBER . . .
It's the attention to details, as with any party, that will make your day successful. Your bridal party is an integral part of the wedding, so make sure you have thought out your wishes. We offer you a list you may not have thought of.

- Do you want attendants to wear certain color nail polish or lipstick?
- Do you prefer that they wear their hair up or down?
- Do you really want attendants to wear big watches or earrings?
- How do you feel about ushers wearing earrings?

- If attendants dress together, where will they keep their handbags, keys to car and house, and other valuables?
- Check the dresses in a full-length mirror. Can you see through them in the light?
- Designate a friend to have a first-aid/emergency kit at the wedding. It should include safety pins, tape for mending uncooperative hems, needle and thread, any medication that may be required by the bride and/or her attendants, extra stockings, a mirror, etc.
- Don't forget to reapply lipstick after ceremony and eating—the pictures will be much better.

The Groom's Attendants

In each situation, same attire as the groom.

Ring Bearer

His dress should be a miniature version of the groom's attendants'.

Mother of the Bride

Traditional: For an informal wedding during the day: a very dressy short dress or suit. For a formal, daytime wedding: a long dress in a color of the bride's choice. Evening: a long gown, again in a color chosen by the bride.
Real world: Informal: short, dressy dress or suit or simple long dress. Formal day: dressy short or cocktail-type dress, or simple gown. Formal: long gown.

Mother of the Groom

Follows the guidelines for mother of the bride. She will not, unless by mutual agreement, wear the same color as the mother of the bride, but may choose a color that harmonizes (or at least doesn't clash) with the bride's mother's dress.

Father of the Bride

Wears the same thing as the groom and his attendants, in the same circumstance.

Father of the Groom

If he has no participation in the wedding, can opt for a dark business suit, black shoes, and dark socks. Or he may choose to wear what the groom and his attendants are wearing.

MOST FORMAL—SEMIFORMAL—MOST FORMAL—SEMIFORMAL
EVENING GARDEN DAYTIME

GROOM'S ATTIRE

AND REMEMBER . . .

Everyone in the wedding party should wear the same kind of clothes: a formally dressed bride and groom should have formally dressed attendants. No mixing and matching. (Remember your wedding pictures!)

The smaller the wedding, the fewer the attendants. (If seventy-five people come to see you get married, twenty of them shouldn't be standing at the altar with you!)

When we say "tuxedo," we mean *black* tuxedo—black tuxedo with plain white shirt. (In warm weather, a white dinner jacket can be substituted.) We do *not* mean tuxedos in rainbow hues with ruffled shirts in matching, pastel colors. Nor do we mean white tuxedos—those belong on the little man who stands on the top of the wedding cake.

Invitations

Visit your local stationery or specialty shop to get an idea of the invitations that are offered in their catalogs, or that can be handmade in the store. The selection may be overwhelming. Don't make a hasty decision. Invitations may be formal, or handwritten by whoever is hosting the event.

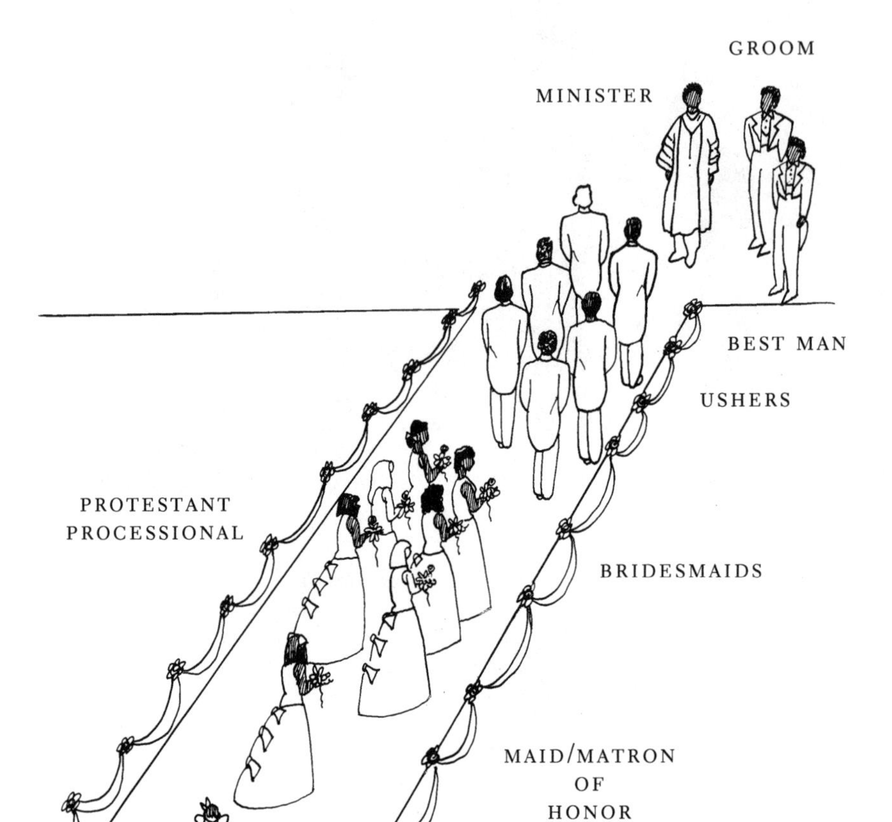

Selecting and Ordering

The formality of your wedding will dictate the formality of your invitations. Consider the paper, the size of the invitation, the style of lettering, the color, the ink color, and if the invitations will be printed or engraved.

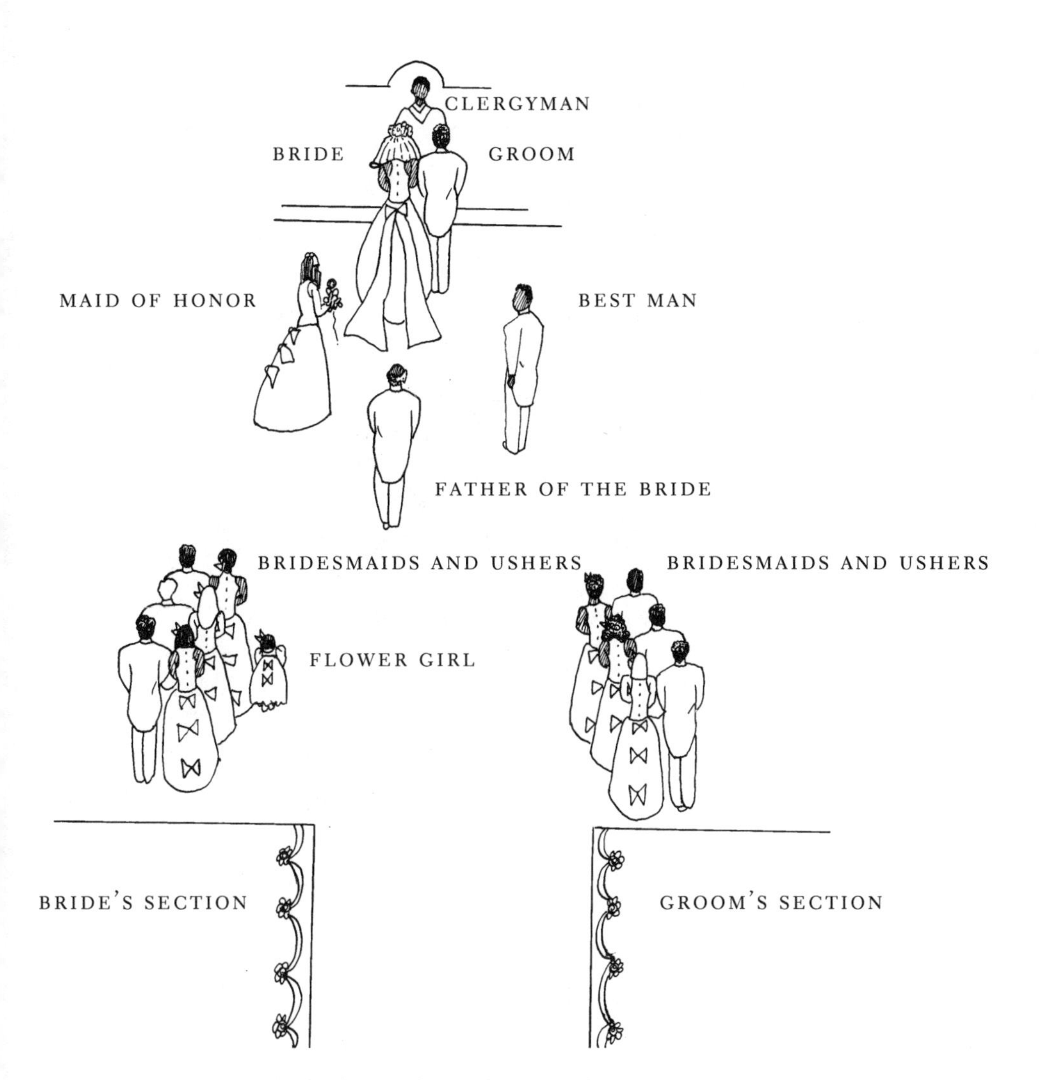

GROUPING AT THE ALTAR

Your Personal Touch

Invitations set the tone of your wedding, just as they set the tone for all parties. Alternatives to the traditional formal invitation are as endless as your imagination. Creative suggestions:

- Select a color paper, or ink, that matches your wedding colors.
- Include a short poem or inspirational passage that reflects your thoughts.
- Include a photograph of the bride and groom.

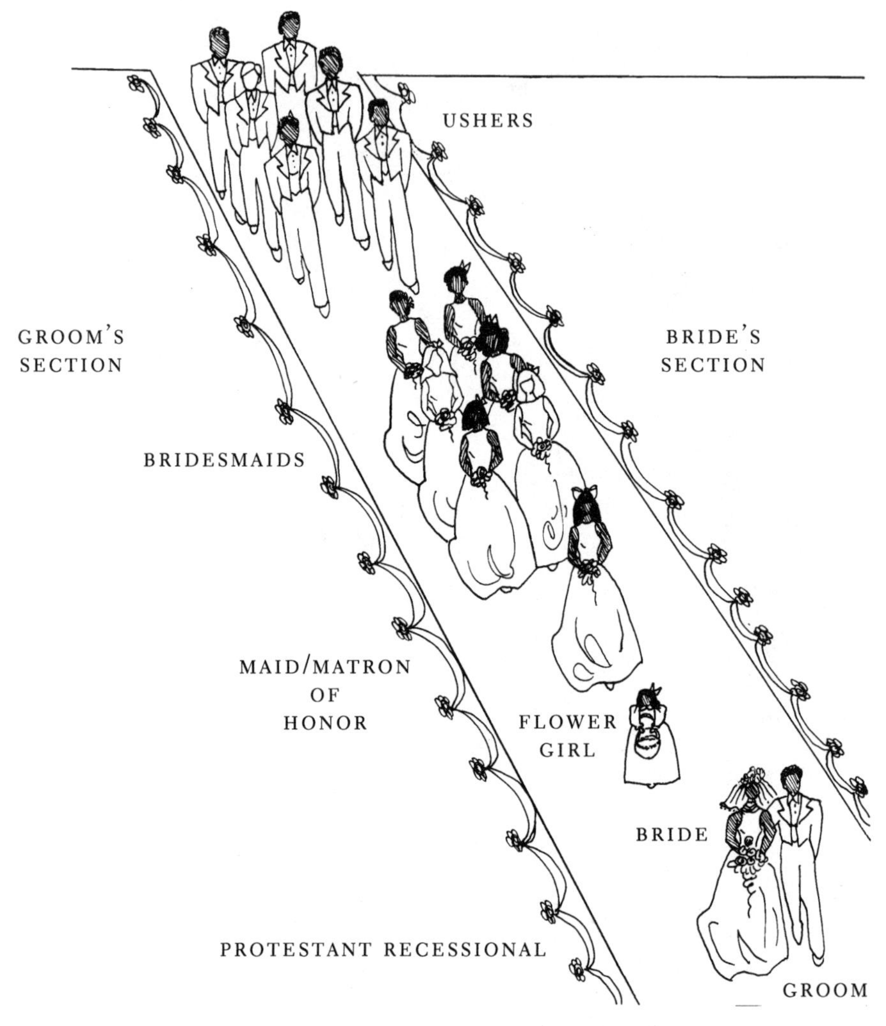

RECESSIONAL WITH BRIDESMAIDS AND USHERS GROUPED SEPARATELY (AN ALTERNATIVE TO EXITING IN COUPLES)

- Select invitations from a traditional source (catalog or stationery store) and personalize them with silk flowers, seed pearl arrangements, or ribbon or cloth that reflects your culture or heritage. Simple invitations can be "jazzed up" by hand-painting a flower with watercolors.

TIMETABLE

Select your invitations as soon as possible.

Three to six months before your wedding: Order invitations, announcements, personal stationery, and thank-you notes. Send "save the date" cards to out-of-town relatives and friends so they can plan vacations and travel arrangements.

Three months before your wedding: Finalize the guest list, who will address the invitations, and how they will be addressed (handwritten in black ink by a freelance calligrapher, your aunt, or you and your fiancé).

Two months before your wedding: Address and stuff invitations.

Four to six weeks before your wedding: Mail invitations (invitations to small weddings may be sent up to ten days prior to the wedding).

One month before your wedding: Address and prepare announcements—if you're sending them—for mailing the day *after* your wedding.

Parts of the Invitation

- Invitation
- Pew cards (for reserved seating at the front of the church)
- Admission cards (for weddings that attract the public—cards that allow you to enter the wedding site)
- Response cards
- Maps or directions
- At-home cards (to let friends know your new address)
- Inner envelope
- Outer envelope

Wording Your Invitation

Formal invitations follow timeless guidelines, while informal invitations may showcase any wording of your choosing. The essentials to the wording of your invitation are:

- Who is giving the wedding and/or reception
- Names of the bride and groom
- Day, date, and time of event
- Location of event
- Response required

Wording of Parents' Names on Formal Invitations

If . . .

- *Both parents are medical doctors:* Doctor and Mrs. James Ellis Johnson, *or* The Doctors Johnson, *or* Doctor Belinda Jackson Johnson and Doctor James Ellis Johnson.
- *Mother is a medical doctor, father is not:* Mr. and Mrs. Edward Grant Roper, *or* Doctor Brenda Bass Roper and Mr. Edward Grant Roper.

- *Mother kept maiden name:* Dara Jenckyn Goosby and Eric Paul Young.
- *Father is a judge:* Judge and Mrs. Sherman Wendell Smith III.
- *Mother is a judge, father is not:* Mr. and Mrs. Steven Wesley Washington, *or* Judge Sarah Baker Washington and Mr. Steven Wesley Washington.

Note: The use of "and" indicates that the people giving the wedding are married to each other.

The Formal Invitation, Line by Line

Traditional wedding invitations are known for their simplicity. Each invitation follows a time-honored order and includes the following:

- Invitational line
- Request lines
- Bride's name
- Joining word
- Groom's name
- Date line
- Year line
- Time line
- Location
- Street address
- City and State
- Reception line (if to be held in the same location as the ceremony)

Addressing Invitations

Wedding invitations are to be hand addressed in black ink. *Never* even think about addressing envelopes for your wedding with computer-generated labels.

- Proper titles for addressing envelopes of invited guests (see chapter 11, "Write On")
- Married couple: The outer envelope is addressed with the full name of the couple.

  Mr. and Mrs. (full name) ______________________________

  Inner envelope (if used) is then addressed:

  Mr. and Mrs. ______________________________
- Married couple using different names: the woman's name is first, with "and" joining the two names to indicate a married couple.

  Ms. ______________________________
  and Mr. ______________________________

Inner envelope:

Ms. ______________________

and Mr. ______________________

- Married couple, when the woman is a doctor (only medical doctors' titles are recognized on social invitations, unless the person is always referred to as "Doctor.")

  Doctor Brenda Bass
  and Mr. Edward G. Roper

  Inner envelope

  Doctor Bass
  and Mr. Roper

- Unmarried couple living together: the woman's name comes first, followed by the gentleman's name. You may address the woman as Ms. or Miss.

  Miss ______________________
  Mr. ______________________

  Inner envelope

  Miss ______________________
  Mr. ______________________

- Married couple with children under eighteen living at home

  Mr. and Mrs. ______________________

  Inner envelope

  Mr. and Mrs. ______________________
  Alexis and Philip

- Daughters over eighteen living at home

  The Misses Delaney or *Miss Bessie Delaney*
  Miss ________ *Delaney*

  Inner envelope

  The Misses Delaney

- Son and daughter over eighteen living at home

  Ms. Brittany Scottish
  Mr. Ozzie Scottish

  Inner envelope

  Ms. Scottish
  Mr. Scottish

- Single woman and date

  Ms. (or Miss) Karen R. Jones

  Inner envelope

  Ms. (or Miss) Jones and guest, or Ms. Jones and escort

Assembling Invitations

Wedding invitations are assembled for mailing in order of size.

- Invitation first
- Enclosure cards are stacked on top of invitation (not inside, if a folded invitation):

  Reception card is on top of invitation.
  Reply envelope is placed face down on reception card.
  Reply card is slipped, face up, beneath the flap of reply envelope.
  Any other enclosures (directions, pew cards, etc.) are added face up in order of size.

Placement in the Envelope:

Single-fold invitations: invitation and enclosures are placed inside the envelope, with the fold of the invitation at the bottom of the envelope and the engraving (or printing) facing the back of the envelope. You can tell if you have stuffed the envelope correctly by removing the invitation with your right hand. If you can read the invitation without turning it around, you have assembled and stuffed it correctly.

Double-fold invitations: Enclosures are placed on top of the lower half of the invitation, in the same order as in single-fold invitations. The invitation is then folded top-to-bottom over the enclosures. Place invitation in envelope with fold toward the bottom of the inside envelope. Again, the invitation has been correctly stuffed when it can be read, without being turned, after removing from the envelope with your right hand.

Once stuffed, the inside envelopes are inserted into the outside envelopes. The front of the inside envelope should be facing the back of the outside envelope.

Tips for Composing and Sending Invitations

- Weddings held in a house of worship read "the honour of your presence."
- Weddings held in other locations read "request the pleasure of your company."
- "Honor" and "honour" are both accepted spellings.
- Wedding receptions that do not take place on the day of the wedding are not properly referred to as "wedding receptions." Instead, they are simply parties or receptions held in honor of the recently married couple.

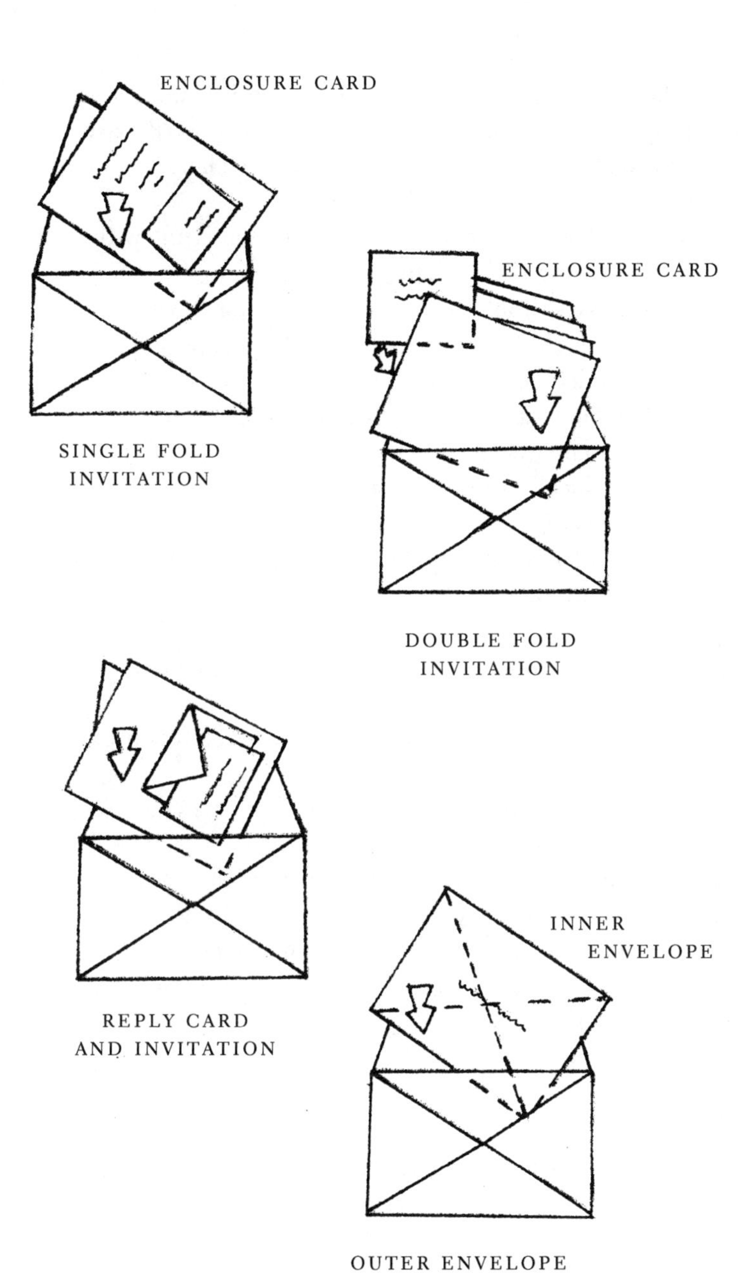

ASSEMBLING INVITATIONS

- Consider sending "save the date" cards to out-of-town guests who need prior notice in order to plan vacation time and travel.
- The term "black tie" should never be printed on an invitation. If you feel compelled to let your guests know the event is black tie, print it on the reception card in the lower right-hand corner.

- If the families and invited guests of the bride and groom speak two distinctly different languages, consider using a booklet-style invitation, and printing the information in duplicate (one language on each side of the fold).
- Weddings announcements are to be mailed anytime within one day to one year following the wedding.
- Return addresses should be on the back flap of the invitation envelope.
- Tissues, once included with invitations to ensure proper drying of ink, may be included or not (we say not!). If you must use them, place tissues over the text of the invitation and enclosures.
- If you have many pieces in your wedding invitation, consider mailing them at your local post office and asking the postal employee to hand-cancel the envelopes.
- Postage should *never* be applied with metered stamps. Select pretty stamps (love, flowers, black heritage) and individually stamp the envelopes.
- Be sure to have a complete sample invitation weighed, to ensure correct postage.
- Return envelopes for responses should be prestamped prior to enclosing.
- "No children" should never be printed on your invitations. If you don't want children to attend your ceremony or reception, simply don't invite them. If children's names do not appear on the invitation envelope—they're not invited!
- Don't use any abbreviations on your invitations.
- Although not formally correct, you *may* use initials for ministers who are known by them (Rev. J.B. ________).

Sample Invitations

♦ Formal invitation and response card:

Mr. and Mrs. William Johnson
request the honour of your presence
at the marriage of their daughter
Ellen Valentine
to
Mr. Michael James Joseph
Saturday, the twenty-seventh of June
one thousand, nine hundred and ninety-seven
at six o'clock
West Angeles Church
1234 Spiritual Way
New York, New York

The favour of a reply is requested
before the tenth of June
M ________________________
_______ *accepts* _______ *regrets*

♦ Informal invitation and response card:

Our joy will be
more complete
if you will join us as we
"Jump the Broom"
Saturday, June 27, 1997
11 a.m.
at the home of
Philip and Alexis Smith
1234 Starlight Lane
Memphis

Belinda White and Terrence Small

M ________________________
will attend _______
will be unable to attend _______
Belinda and Terrence's wedding

♦ Handwritten wedding invitation:

Will and I are getting married Wednesday, the seventh of October at 8 p.m. at Founder's Church of Religious Science. We'd love for you to join us for the ceremony and for dinner afterwards at The Four Seasons.

Love,
Karen

Gifts

Bridal Registry

Bridal registries are a boon, both to the couple and to the guests who are searching for gifts that would please them. Investigate registries at various stores before you make your final choices. Some of the things to consider prior to selecting items from a particular store:

♦ If your spouse is interested in helping to select your china, crystal, or flatware patterns, in addition to the miscellaneous household needs, by all means consider his feelings. It might be easier if you, the bride, make "possible" selections on an initial venture out into the department and specialty stores, and then return another time with the groom, so that you may consult together on your already narrowed down selection.

♦ Investigate the price range of gifts at your chosen store—and find out if they accept credit cards. This will give your invited guests more freedom in their selection, and also allow them to shop by telephone.

♦ Decide on how many stores you will register with. You might include a full-service department store, a specialty housewares store, and a nationwide chain store in the event many of your friends and relatives live in other cities.

♦ Always ask about the store's return policy so that you don't find yourselves with twenty-three ice cream makers. Even though you have registered, often the items are not deleted from your list when a purchase is made, and you end up with duplicates.

♦ More and more stores nationwide are offering brides the opportunity to be "card brides" rather than "gift brides." In this case, when a guest purchases something from your registry, you are sent a card announcing the gift and the giver, rather than the gift itself. In the case of your stemware patterns, this allows you to receive fifteen water goblets, eight champagne flutes, ten white-wine goblets, and four highball glasses—and simply shuffle the cards and notify the store you would rather have a complete set of ten of each piece, instead of uneven numbers. This is also a nice service when you are having a reception in a city you do not currently reside in, and would rather not open, repack, and ship each gift. Once you've notified the store, they can ship the items directly to your home. This also comes in handy when you've been too busy to open gifts; many may be brought to the reception only to remain unopened until you return from your honeymoon. This is a safe way to guard against theft while you are away. The store will be happy to work with you when you've settled down from the hectic pace of the wedding.

♦ Also consider stores that service many of your friends and families, and where it is expected you will be registered. "Oh, I know Gayle must be registered at Geary's, that's where everyone goes." This allows the guest to call the known store and inquire about your registry without having to contact your family to find out where you're registered.

♦ Don't register at too many stores. One large store, and one or two specialty stores, should serve your registry needs.

Wedding Presents

Wedding gifts are truly your expression of joy and happiness for the wedding couple. Bridal registries have made making your gift selection much easier—they're the path of least resistance, with full confidence that you're purchasing an item the couple would actually enjoy having. Marriage is a milestone in the couple's lives, and the closer you are to them, the more thought you should give the gift. Rather than simply select something from the registry, you may choose an heirloom from your family that you'd like to share. For those acquaintances you're not close to, but would like to honor with a gift, you should consider something that fits their lifestyle, and would be fun and relaxing. Anything from a case of wine to tickets to the theater will be welcomed. If they love to roller skate or Rollerblade, consider matching T-shirts or caps with their names embroidered on them.

Gifts are to be sent or delivered prior to the wedding, if at all possible. Be sure and enclose your gift card, either in the box or attached with tape, so the frantic bride will not spend countless hours trying to determine who gave them a particular gift.

Choosing a Wedding Gift

Wedding gifts will be welcomed, whatever they are. If you'd like to contribute to the couple's china pattern or crystal and do not know the name of the chosen pattern, call the bride's mother or a member of the bridal party. Gifts may be informal or quite elegant. Some appropriate choices include:

- Anything for the home
- Items for the dining table (glasses, flatware, placemats, tablecloth, etc.)
- Crystal candlesticks or a crystal vase
- Small kitchen appliances
- Serving trays (pottery, glass, silver)
- Picture frames
- Original artwork
- Anything from the bride's registry
- Check or gift certificate

Monograms and Engraving

You may use your married initial or his last initial on your linen and flatware. Traditionally, the bride had silverware monogrammed with her initial, but that is not commonly done anymore.

Linens are monogrammed as follows:

- Towels: in the center of one end so when folded lengthwise in thirds it shows when hung on a rack
- Tablecloths: center of each long side midway between table edge and center of cloth
- Dinner napkins: diagonally on one corner or centered on rectangular fold
- Sheets: monogrammed so when top sheet is folded down, letters can be read by person standing at the end of the bed
- Pillowcases: two inches above the hem

Engraving: for tips on engraving, see chapter 18, "Gifts from Me to You."

Taking Gifts to the Wedding or Reception

In certain regions and cultures it is perfectly acceptable, and expected, to take your gift with you to the wedding and reception. While this may seem appropriate, when you think of it from the bride and groom's point of view, it's not. When the reception is held away from the couple's new home, someone must be responsible for packing up the gifts, taking them to the couple's home, and ensuring security for the unopened presents. And no one wants to see you the morning of the wedding—best to wait until after the honeymoon to deliver the gift. In short, the thoughtful guest either sends or delivers the wedding gift prior to the wedding, or in the weeks following the ceremony.

Receiving and Recording Gifts

Open all gifts promptly in order to return any damaged or broken items. In either a notebook, or on 3″×5″ cards, record all gifts received (engagement, shower, and wedding). Your gift record book should include:

- Date received
- Item, including quantity and brief description ("8 fluted champagne glasses—crystal pattern" or "4 hunter-green placemats")
- Who the gift is from (list all names)

Be sure to keep track of cards sent from stores notifying you of guests' selections from your registry. Most often the card will let you know the approximate time the gift should be received. If it is to be sent to you within four to six weeks, record this on a calendar so you can follow up if the gift does not arrive. Don't forget to list all "out of stock" cards in your gift book.

Acknowledging Gifts Promptly

Shower gifts should be acknowledged, and a thank-you note written, prior to the wedding. Shower thank-yous should go out within two weeks of the shower. Wedding gifts, like shower gifts, must *all* be acknowledged with a written thank-you note. Thank-yous can be written as soon as a gift is received—try to send as many as possible prior to the wedding (for gifts received in the weeks preceding the wedding). All thank-you notes should be completed and mailed within three months of the wedding. Given today's hectic times, the bride who has to go back to work, set up a new household, and adjust to married life might need a little more time. Six months is the absolute deadline. Each person who was kind enough to give you a gift should be acknowledged sincerely, and with a handwritten note. Printed thank-you cards will not do. Traditionally, the bride sent the thank-yous, but there's no reason why the groom cannot help out, especially with his family and friends. Each note should mention the gift, how it will be used, and if the giver was unable to attend the service, that he or she was missed.

Exchanging and Returning Gifts

Not a problem! Wedding gifts are frequently exchanged or returned as a result of duplications, the desire to balance out your table settings, or simple dislike of a gift that you know you will never use. In such cases, return the gift to the appropriate store promptly. Thank the giver for the gift he or she gave—there's no need to explain you already received fourteen popcorn makers, or that it was hideous—simply return it and enjoy the new item. Most guests truly want you to have what will make you happy.

Bride and Groom Gifts

The bride and groom may decide to exchange gifts in celebration of the beginning of their new lives together. While they are free to select any type of gift, these items are usually timeless and meant to be keepsakes. For the groom, it may be a watch; for the bride a pearl necklace or special earrings.

Gifts for the Bridal Attendants

Bridal attendants' gifts range from a piece of jewelry to wear on the wedding day (earrings, pendants, bracelet) to a frame that can be used for a picture from the big day. Select whatever you think your attendants would like—but keep in mind that it should be a keepsake gift, rather than a disposable one.

Favors

Favors, or small gifts of cake, candies, or remembrances of the day, are traditional at weddings. Be creative; select whatever you would like to give your guests. It may be a lace-wrapped praline, a tiny box of chocolates, or a small tin of jellybeans with the bride and groom's names and the date painted on the can. It may be a small card or scroll thanking the guests for their attendance and expressing the couple's sentiments of the day. Favors can be anything you want them to be!

Displaying Wedding Presents

If your reception is to be held at your family's home, you may choose to display a number of the gifts you received *prior* to the wedding. In some regions, a dining room table is set to display the bride and groom's china, crystal, and flatware selections. Usually this display table will remain in place for a few days following the wedding, for close friends to drop by to see. Be sure to provide security or someone to stay at the home during the actual wedding ceremony, and for anytime gifts will be visible from the outside.

Giving to a Couple that Elopes

If the family approves of the marriage, often announcements will be sent by the bride's parents. The bride and groom may even decide to send their own announcements. It is then your choice to send a gift or not.

Celebrations

There's no better time to enjoy yourself than during the months leading up to the wedding—so celebrate!

Engagement Party

If you and your intended would like to have an engagement party, it should be given by the parents of the bride, the parents of the groom, or the bride's godparents or grandparents. Guests should include immediate family of the bride and groom and their closest friends. This is not a big party, just an intimate affair to announce your engagement to those you hold dear. (When everyone finds out at the same time, hurt feelings are avoided.)

Showers

See chapter 30, "Parties and Celebrations."

Bridal Luncheon

A luncheon is usually given by the bride for her bridesmaids. This gives the bridal party a chance to get to know each other, and for the bride's closest friends to have a special celebration. Although the domain of the bridal attendants, the bride is welcome to invite whomever she chooses. Often the bride's mother, grandmother, cousins, siblings not included in the wedding party, and the groom's mother and sisters are asked to join the fun. This is the time the bride gives her gifts to the bridesmaids in appreciation of their participation and as a keepsake of the special day. While luncheons or teas are traditional, you may choose to have a Sunday brunch or dinner due to attendants' busy schedules. This party is typically given during the final week or two prior to the wedding; if at all possible, wait until all out-of-town attendants have arrived.

Bachelor Party

Have fun—don't put anyone in danger by allowing them to drink and drive. Include the groom's dad and siblings (maybe the bride's father, too), and don't do anything that will bring on a divorce before the happy couple is married! Do not have the party the night before the wedding (we don't care who is arriving from out of town). Anywhere from a week or two to three days before the wedding is acceptable.

Bachelorette Party

Enjoy the friendship and camaraderie of your best buddies. No need to invite the mothers of the bride and groom. Don't allow anyone to drive drunk—and have the party at least three days prior to the wedding, preferably a week ahead. Even if the hostess doesn't know the bridesmaids well, all are to be invited.

Rehearsal Dinner

The groom's family traditionally gives the rehearsal dinner and sends out the invitations for it. The bride is consulted in order to coordinate the dinner with her chosen rehearsal date.

The wedding party and the immediate families of the bride and groom are always invited. You may invite the spouses (or dates) of the wedding party, out-of-town guests, extended family, and the officiant(s) and spouses. The invitations may be formal or informal. Small dinners can use fill-in invitations or handwritten notes.

The Rehearsal

Always schedule a rehearsal for the entire wedding party. This is the one chance all of you will have to practice together. Determine the rehearsal date after consulting with the officiant, your families, and the facility where the ceremony will be held. With the exception of the bride, all participants should practice walking just as they will on the big day. *It's bad luck* for the bride to walk down the center aisle during rehearsal—so usually the maid of honor or another attendant will stand in for the bride.

The Big Day

It's a Reflection of You

Your wedding ceremony and reception are a reflection of you, your values, and your taste. Make sure that as you plan, you don't allow the event to become "someone else's" wedding. If you have a particular cultural tradition that you'd like to include, by all means do so. African and West Indian customs are often innertwined with American wedding traditions. And we haven't been to a Creole wedding yet that didn't have a "second line" dance before the reception was over. If necessary, consult with your wedding officiant on combining ceremonial parts from your chosen cultures. Wedding coordinators can also supply ideas of how to incorporate your wishes into your special day.

Please Be Seated—Who Sits Where?

The bride's guests are seated on the left, and the groom's guests are seated on the right. Ushers escort female guests by offering their right arm; they walk on the left side of male guests. With couples, they offer their right arm to the woman, and the gentleman walks a step or two behind them. If a group arrives to be seated at the same time, the eldest woman is seated first.

The Processional

The bride and her father (or whoever is giving her away) are always the last to enter. The bride's mother is the last guest to be seated, and the processional begins immediately after an usher seats her. The bridesmaids and ushers are the first to enter, with the groom and the best man already situated at the altar. Next are the flower girl(s), ring bearer, maid of honor, and finally the bride on her father's right arm.

The Recessional

The recessional is the processional in reverse. The newly married bride and groom begin the exit, with the bridal party following in the same order in which they entered. The bride and groom's families then exit, followed by the other guests. The bridal party may leave the altar as couples, or with bridesmaids and ushers separate.

The Reception

Hostesses at the Reception

You may need to ask good friends, or friends of your mother's, to act as hostesses during the reception. If they agree to serve, you may ask them to wear a color complementary to your bridal colors, but it is not necessary. It is nice if they are identified with a corsage. Hostesses act in the place of the hosts in greeting guests and answering questions. Make sure all hostesses know where each available rest room is, where a public telephone is, and what to do in case of a medical emergency. There are a number of stations where hostesses can serve. Don't ask them to hostess the entire reception—break it up into shifts. They should be able to enjoy themselves, too. Stations include:

- Greeting
- Guest book
- Cake
- Gift table and money box
- In the area where the couple's new "dining table" is on display

Guest Book

Do have one, and in an area of the reception where guests will surely see and sign it. No way will you remember who was at your big event—it will be great to look back on later. Do not hold up guests' entrance to the reception as they wait in a long line to sign the guest book.

Photographer

After you've selected your photographer, make clear your wishes:

- List the shots you'd like taken (ceremony and reception).
- Take a black-and-white photo of the couple and their parents for use in newspaper (if that's part of the plan).
- List special guests you'd like photographed.
- Assign a hostess to work with photographer identifying family members and close friends.
- If you have a videographer, clear his presence with the church, and establish where he can, and can't, stand, during the ceremony. Pretty much give him free reign at the reception.

Be a Good Guest

- For wedding attire for guests, see chapter 14, "Glad Rags."
- How long do you have to stay at the reception? Theoretically, at least through the cutting of the cake.

Toast to the Bride and Groom

At a sit-down bridal table, champagne is served as soon as the party is seated. The bride is served first, then groom, maid of honor, and around the table. Best man proposes a toast, and all stand but the bride and groom. Then the groom stands and thanks best man and proposes a toast to his new wife. At a large wedding, only those at the bridal table offer toasts. At a smaller wedding, anyone can offer a toast after the best man.

Dancing the Night Away

Dancing at an evening reception does not start until dinner has been served and eaten. Protocol requires that the bride and groom dance the first dance together—often to a song they have selected for the occasion. The remaining dance sequence is:

- Groom's father dances with the bride.
- Bride's father cuts in and dances with his daughter.
- Groom dances with the mother of the bride.
- Groom dances with his mother.
- Bride's father dances with the groom's mother.
- Groom's father dances with the bride's mother.
- Groom dances with the maid of honor.
- Best man dances with bride.

- Ushers dance with bridesmaids.
- All guests are invited to join in the dancing.

Dancing at afternoon weddings is acceptable before and after the meal is served.

CUTTING THE CAKE

Together, the bride and groom cut the first slice of cake from the bottom tier. Traditionally, the couple feeds each other a piece of cake (pushing the cake into your new spouse's face *really* isn't necessary), and the caterer or a designated person takes over the job of serving the cake. The bridal couple and the attendants are served first, followed by the parents and immediate family of the bride and groom. On a multitiered cake, the top layer is saved for the bride and groom. At a sit-down meal the cake is cut just prior to dessert being served, so that the cake can be served to the guests at their tables. At a buffet reception, the cake is cut later, following the meal.

Spreadin' the News

It used to be that no marriage was complete without a newspaper announcement. Mainstream newspapers—especially ones in large cities, where competition for space was (and is) fierce—often ran brief announcements following the wedding, unless the bride, her groom, or their parents were very prominent. Hometown papers and the Negro press tended to include more information, such as where each member of the bridal party was from, what the bride and her attendants wore, who sang the solos and played the piano.

Many people no longer do this, and many newspapers now charge substantial fees to place an announcement. If you decide you want to do this, check with the social editor of your local paper (or your hometown paper, if you want an announcement placed there); ask what kind of information is required, whether or not they'll accept a picture (even so, there's no guarantee it will be published with your announcement), and what the fees and deadlines are for delivery of copy. The paper will also give you guidance for special situations, such as how to word the announcement if your parents are divorced or one is deceased. Some examples are listed below:

Sample Wedding Announcement

> On Sunday, June 30, Camille Renée Thornton, daughter of Mr. and Mrs. Neville P. Thornton, became the bride of Harris Anthony Richmond at Main Street Presbyterian Church in Birmingham, Alabama. A reception followed the evening ceremony in the garden of the bride's parents' home. They were married by the Rever-

end Louis Hall, who married the brides' parents and, later, christened the bride.

Patricia Jean Thornton-Smith, the bride's sister, served as matron of honor, and Melanie Anne Richmond, the bride's sister, served as maid of honor. Shelley P. Reed and Imani Johnson were bridesmaids, and Alana Johnson was a flower girl. The groom's best man was his brother, Theodore G. Richmond. Sylvester Monroe and Gregory W. Thornton were ushers. The bride's nephew, Henry Lee Smith, was the ring-bearer.

The bride is a graduate of Spelman College in Atlanta. She holds a master's degree from the London School of Economics, and is Director of Development for the City University of New York. Her father is the principal of the Lehigh School for Boys in Birmingham; her mother is president of the board of Foster Care for All Children, a Birmingham-based nonprofit organization.

The groom holds a bachelor's degree from the University of the West Indies in Kingston, Jamaica, and master's and doctorate degrees from Stanford University. He is an overseas investment analyst for Lazard Frères, in Manhattan. His late father, the Honorable Hamish T. R. Richmond, served as chief magistrate of the Jamaican Supreme Court for two decades. His mother is an artist.

Sample Wedding Announcement

At eight o'clock on Saturday evening on June 29, Jasmine Marie Bender became the bride of James LeRoy Carter. The candlelight ceremony was performed in Rankin Chapel at Howard University. The Reverend T. Arthur Willoughby officiated.

Sara Louise Carter, sister of the groom, was the maid of honor. Jason C. Brandon served as best man.

The bride, daughter of Mr. and Mrs. Vincent Bender of Roanoke, Va., is a magna cum laude graduate of Howard University. She is a curator of 18th-Century African Art at the Smithsonian Institution's Museum of African Art in Washington, D.C. Her father, now retired, was the public information officer for the Roanoke Transport Authority. Her mother is a homemaker.

The groom, son of Mr. and Mrs. LeRoy Eugene Carter, is a summa cum laude graduate of Howard University, and holds a master's degree in journalism from American University. He is a reporter for the *Washington Post*. His father is a director of customer relations for the United States Postal Service. His mother is a chemistry teacher at St. Brendan's School in Mount Airy, Pa.

Following a honeymoon trip, the couple will live in Washington, D.C.

It's Your Thing

You've Done This Before (Second and Third Marriages)

Many of today's brides and grooms have "walked the walk" before, and now are looking down that aisle again. When planning your second or third marriage, use the same care in planning that (hopefully) you did the first time. While it may be a large affair, rarely is it formal.

The "Golden Oldies" Couple

Be happy for the fortunate couple that they're not alone in a senior citizens' home. Once in a while a loving son or daughter objects to his or her mother or father remarrying at such an advanced age—go figure. They deserve a life, too—and last time we checked, it's their life, not their children's. Some things to remember:

- A son may give his mother away, but usually there are no attendants.
- If a son is not giving his mother away, the bride may either walk down the aisle alone or enter from the side door with the officiant.
- If the party is large, make sure there are enough ushers to seat the guests.
- Older couples are entitled to flaunt tradition and have whatever kind of ceremony and reception that pleases them. They can serve the food they know their friends enjoy, and wear the clothes they want (within reason)—offer gentle suggestions if needed, but don't rain on their parade.

Double Weddings

Double weddings are most often with sisters as the two brides. Although the brides do not have an obligation to dress alike, they often choose similar dresses. Each set of bridesmaids wears their own dresses, but the dresses are complimentary to the other bridal party. Ushers and groomsmen from both parties are expected to dress alike.

The Pregnant Bride

Remember, this is an occasion to be celebrated. It helps if the families are supportive and everyone (at least almost everyone) is happy. Think about your situation when planning your wedding. If you've already got your hands full, you might want to keep the wedding small and simple. The wedding should be dignified—don't flaunt your situation, and don't be embarrassed that you have, or are going to have, a beautiful child. It's done now. We're just glad you'll be a family and a once fatherless child will have a daddy.

When People with Children Get Married

The children, depending on their ages, may or may not be part of the ceremony. If they are very young, certainly bring them to the ceremony, but be prepared for whoever is caring for the infant to escort the child out if he becomes cranky or unruly, disturbing the bride and groom.

When the Couple Has Been Living Together

Couples who have been living together even for a number of years, can still have a traditional wedding. Couples who have been together for a long time might prefer a small ceremony with a reception (of any size) to follow. Another alternative is a small ceremony with announcements sent out afterward.

A Rose by Any Other Name

Think about it. Don't base the decision to keep or change your last name solely on the current trend or what your friends are doing. If you decide to keep your maiden name, take into consideration what name your children will go by so it's not an issue down the road.

Interracial Marriages

Interracial marriages continue to pose a problem in some families and their communities. The old adage, "Date 'em, just don't bring one home for keeps," still rings loud and clear in many households. The reality is, if you choose to marry outside your race, or are biracial and have been raised in a culture that is different from your intended spouse, be realistic. Openly discuss the pros and cons with each other. As a couple you must feel confident that you *really* want to get married, and must understand the uncomfortable situations you may find yourselves in at various stages of your married life. This is still America—you know the rest. Consider how important, to each of you, your family's feelings are, and the challenges facing biracial children and the community in which you live. If you've truly explored the ups and downs and decide to marry, by all means do so. If you are marrying against your families' wishes, once you have made up your mind to begin life as a couple, be respectful of those who are hurt by your decision. There's no need to think your parents are *obligated* to give you a big wedding, and there's no reason for them to disown you or refuse to celebrate your happiness. Being together is more important than the entrapments; invite those people who you know are happy for you, but always extend an invitation to immediate family members.

Interfaith Marriages

Many of the same challenges faced by interracial couples confront those choosing to marry outside of their religions. While Christians of the Protestant faith are more likely to have little, if any, opposition from their individual denomination, those crossing the boundaries of Christianity and Judaism may be headed for many lectures. The same is true for devout followers of any faith. Again, discuss the situation openly with each other and your families. Consider how deep your religious commitment is, in what faith you would like to see your children raised, and if you will be ostracized in any way from your family or current house of worship. Again, it's your decision. Remember that, just as you have a right to do as you choose, others who genuinely care about your welfare are entitled to have an opinion.

Same-Sex Unions

While same-sex marriages have only recently begun to be recognized by state governments and in the workplace as they relate to spousal benefits—they do, in fact, exist spiritually, although rarely legally. Perhaps even more overwhelmingly than couples choosing to marry outside their race or religion, those entering into same-sex unions with the same expectations as other married couples must be prepared to face resistance. If you choose to marry, and would like to have a wedding celebration, do it however you feel comfortable. Just as in traditional weddings, the possibilities range from small, intimate gatherings of close friends to elaborate events.

Reaffirmation of Marriage Vows

If it feels good, by all means do it. Do not register for, or expect, gifts. Friends may choose to bring gifts to celebrate your continued joy—that's up to them.

Don't Get Caught Off Guard

In-laws, Outlaws, and Other Delicate Situations

What Shall You Call Your Fiancé's Parents?

Whatever they want you to call them! Prior to the engagement you may have called them Mr. and Mrs. Johnson, and at this point they may ask you to call them by their first names—or Mom and Dad. Abide by their wishes.

When You Know Your Parents and His Don't Get Along

Don't force the issue. Try to include them in activities where other friends (of each of them) will be present. Don't apologize for your family or his. Time will tell. If it's a racial problem—and they're dead set against you or anything about you—don't even try at this point. Concentrate on your new husband and your life together. You'll have enough challenges to deal with. Perhaps in time, actions rather than words (and grandchildren, hopefully) will at least bring them to the point of being civil to you both.

When Your Mom Hates Your Dad's Girlfriend

If your father and his girlfriend have been together for quite a while—and your mom won't really go into cardiac arrest—invite her if your dad wants her there. Just keep them on opposite sides of the room. Consult your dad, and be considerate of your mom. They *might* surprise you.

When an Attendant Must Bow Out at the Last Minute

If a bridal attendant must bow out at the last minute due to illness, family emergency, or an unexpected pregnancy (and that dress will *never* fit), be calm. The attendant is still responsible for any expenses she incurred, and should offer to pay for her dress even if a stand-in is asked to replace her. If the dress can be worn by someone else, and there's time to have it altered, perhaps the two can split the cost. If you are unable to replace the attendant, simply reposition one of the groomsmen so that he continues to be part of the bridal party, but without an escort.

If a groomsman must bow out, it's a little easier. Hopefully he has not rented his bridal clothing yet, and another gentleman can be asked to take his place, presuming he has time to be fitted for his tuxedo (or suit).

Never, when asking a friend to replace someone else, make them feel as though they were an afterthought, or your last resort. If there's no way to do this tactfully, leave it alone.

When the Wedding Must be Postponed

Weddings are occasionally postponed due to unexpected illness or death in the family. When time permits, each guest is mailed a formal announcement of the postponement. The announcements are printed on the same paper, and in the same style, as the original invitations. Guests may be notified by telephone if there is not enough time to notify them by mail.

When You Don't Yet Know When the Wedding Will Take Place

Mr. and Mrs. ___________________________
regret that the illness of their daughter
____
obliges them to recall their invitations
to her marriage to
Mr. ___________________________
on Friday, the thirteenth of September

Then, when the new date has been set:

Mr. and Mrs. ___________________________
announce that the wedding of their daughter
____
to
____
which was postponed, will now take place
on Saturday, the third of November
at six o'clock
Church of the Advent
Los Angeles, California

When a New Wedding Date Has Already Been Set

Mr. and Mrs. Thurgood Marshall
announce that the marriage of their daughter
____
to
Mr. ___________________________
has been postponed to
Saturday, the third of September
at six o'clock
Church of the Advent
Los Angeles, California

When the Wedding is Canceled After Invitations Have Been Sent

Mr. and Mrs. ___________________________

are obliged to recall their invitation
to the marriage of their daughter

____

to

Mr. ___________________________

as the marriage will not take place

Returning Gifts When the Wedding Has Been Postponed or Canceled

If the wedding has been postponed due to an emergency, and you're sure the ceremony will still take place in the immediate future, there's no need to return the gifts. If the wedding is canceled, all gifts (unless engraved or otherwise personalized) should be returned with a short note showing your appreciation, and stating the necessity to return the gift. Shower gifts should be returned as well. If friends insist you keep the gifts, do so. If you keep either a shower or wedding gift from a friend who insisted that you do—and you become engaged again—inform your friend that you are inviting them to your wedding (or shower), but that you do not expect them to give another gift.

When Not Everyone Is Invited to Both the Wedding and the Reception

In years gone by, weddings were often quite large, as it was the custom in many black churches to welcome all members of the congregation to a wedding held at the church. Receptions, on the other hand, were only for invited guests, resulting in fewer attendees. In contrast, today's couples sometimes prefer to have small, private ceremonies—for a select group of family and friends—and larger receptions for all of their guests.

In such a case, reception invitations are sent to all invited guests, and invitations to the actual wedding ceremony are extended by telephone, handwritten note, or a separate enclosure card.

When You'd Prefer to Have Donations Made to Charity, Rather Than Gifts

Sometimes couples getting married for the second or third time realize that they have already established households, and would really like their invited guests to contribute to the couple's favorite charity rather than purchase a gift. *Do not* note such a request on the wedding invitation. It's essentially the same as asking for a gift or money. Spread the word the same way you let people know about the bridal registry. If people call and ask, feel free to share the information. *Never* make a guest feel obligated to contribute.

Don't Even Think It!

- Spangles and glitter before evening? NOT! Evening clothes to a simple wedding that's held in the morning or afternoon? NOT!
- Bare shoulders, plunging necklines, and backless backs that almost show your, um, *assets* should be covered (with a jacket, coat, or shawl) for church weddings. Undrape at the reception if you must. But remember, this is the *bride's* time to shine, and it's bad home training to try to upstage her with your skimpy little piece of a dress.
- Toasting the bride and groom? Never, ever bring up either's past indiscretions! ("Jay, you finally pulled it off. I remember when you had four dates in one night and ended up breaking up with Sheila because of it. Congratulations on settling down, buddy.")
- Don't sit and stage-whisper about how you "liked her other boyfriend better." Even if the groom can't hear you, his family or friends may be nearby. And even if no one's nearby—it's tacky!
- If you're in the wedding party but hate your bridesmaid's dress (which certainly wouldn't make you unique in the history of bridesmaids), suffer: you've got to wear it for the entire reception. Even if chartreuse isn't your color and you hate that bustle in the back. Wedding photos should show the entire wedding party dressed in wedding clothes. For the duration of the wedding reception, just consider it a uniform, okay? (If there's an after-party, you can change then, and the ushers can feel free to unknot their ties, remove their jackets, etc.).
- Weddings are celebrations and usually entail something of a festival atmosphere. Don't let *festival* slip over the edge into *carnival:* chug-a-lug contests, competitions to see who can dance most suggestively with the groom (wasn't there enough of that at the bachelor party?), and other things that shouldn't be done by people who are dressed in their best clothes are verboten.
- If one or both of the couple has been married before, don't bring the former spouse into it. ("Well, I gotta tell you folks: I've liked all my daughter's husbands, and Mike, you're no exception. Welcome to the club, son.")
- We all know what wearing a white wedding dress *used* to symbolize, but that strict interpretation of virginity has given way to equating white with joy and new beginnings. Even if the bride has been living with the

groom for three years, don't loudly announce, "Girl, I don't know why you're wearing *that* color!" even in jest. She will *not* be amused. Neither, probably, will her mother.

- A congratulatory kiss to the bride or groom by someone of the opposite sex is supposed to be warm and friendly and administered on the *cheek*. With a *closed* mouth, thank you.
- Never, ever sidle up to the new bride (or groom) and whisper: "Call me if it doesn't work out." If it doesn't work out, you'll know soon enough, if you're meant to.

Chapter 35

AND THIS, TOO, SHALL PASS

Sometimes I feel like a motherless child
Sometimes I feel like a motherless child
Sometimes I feel like a motherless child
A long way from home
A long way from home.

Spiritual

If we're stumped at how to proceed during joyous times, it's even more frustrating to try to figure out what to do when we're mired in the midst of an unhappy event. This section is intended to give you guidance for those times when your hands are full just dealing with what fate has dropped in your lap. And remember what the old folks told us: no matter how gloomy the immediate present is, this, too, shall pass.

Announcing a Separation or Divorce

When a marriage comes undone, it not only affects the married couple who are dissolving their bonds, the circles ripple outward through friends, relatives, and community. Everyone is concerned (sometimes even depressed or threatened) by your news.

It may help to tell your closest friends what's about to happen. This can be done via a phone call or a note, depending on what you feel you're up to handling. If you choose a note, it can be brief:

> *Sandy:*
> *I wanted to let you know that Craig and I have decided to separate and will probably be divorced sometime early next year. We're*

> *sad that things ended this way, but we both hope our friends will keep in touch with each of us. I'll write in a few weeks, when I've found a new place, and will look forward to seeing you when I get to Boston in May.*
>
> *All the best,*
> *Erica*

You may each have people whom one of you is closer to than the other (his best friend from childhood, your college roommate), and it would probably be best for the person closest to that friend to break the news.

People will ask, "How? Why? Can't you try to fix it?"—it's a natural reaction. It's enough for you simply to say, "We were both very unhappy," and leave it at that.

Party of the First Part

It's always better for everyone involved in a divorce to be as charitable as possible toward the almost ex-partner, but it's not always practical, especially if there have been contributing factors to the breakup. A public midlife crisis, a scandal, or an extramarital affair makes it harder for the wronged partner to remain neutral and aloof.

You'll have to decide how much you want to share about the reasons for your divorce. If the contributing factor has been very public (a widely known embezzlement; an affair), it may be harder to give just a simple explanation—but there may not be a need to. It's enough to say, "After what's happened, I thought it best that we separate. And I really don't feel like discussing it further." That should tell inquisitors—well-meaning and otherwise—that additional questions are unwelcome and inappropriate.

Telling Your Children About Death, Divorce, and Other Traumas

Children, even really young ones, are very quick to pick up on the changes around them. They may not be able to fully articulate what's going on, but little ones are extremely sensitive to the nuances of adult anxieties and emotional changes. So don't insult their intelligence by telling them everything's all right when it clearly isn't. Give them brief explanations of what's happened, and be honest with them about your feelings:

"Tommy, I have something sad to tell you. You know Grandpa has been sick for a while, and last night he died."

"Aisha, you know Daddy and I haven't been getting along very well for some time. We've decided we don't want to live together anymore, so we're getting a divorce. But we're divorcing *each other*, not you. We both love you a lot, and we'll always be your parents. But we won't be living in the same place, the way we are right now."

"Lisa, Daddy's company is closing its office in our city, and in order for Daddy to keep his job, we're going to have to move away so he can work in another branch of the company. That means we're going to have to move away from this house, to a new neighborhood. And you'll meet new friends, because you're going to be in a new school."

If, in giving the bad news, you can pass along some reassurance ("Yes, we have to move, but you'll make new friends at your new school"), so much the better.

Children often worry that family catastrophes may be their fault, and it's important to tell them, emphatically, that this is not the case:

"No, honey, Grandpa didn't die because he gave you too many piggybacks; he had a sick heart and he was very old. It wasn't anybody's fault Grandpa died."

"We're not fighting about you, sweetie; we're fighting because we're angry and unhappy with each other. And we think we'll stop fighting and like each other better if we live apart."

Explaining a Child's Death to a Child

To a child, the idea of a peer's death is not only sad—it's terrifying. "Why did Andy die? Will the same thing happen to me? Did it hurt?" are all normal questions your child can be expected to ask. If his friend's death is the result of an illness, let your child know that pediatric sickness usually isn't fatal and that such things are unusual for children to experience: "Andy had a very rare blood disease; very few children have it, and many recover from it. But Andy's body couldn't get better, and so he died. Most children don't usually get sick enough to die; it's not very common."

If the death is the result of an accident, you might explain how the death occurred and emphasize that this, too, is unusual: "A car hit Andy because the car's brakes failed and the driver couldn't stop in time. It was an accident, and the man who was driving feels very, very bad. He has a little boy, too."

If a child dies as a result of foul play (something that, sadly, is becoming more and more common), it may be best to give the briefest outline and stress instead the need to pay attention to the family safety rules: "A bad man invited Paul to get into his car and took him away. You remember, don't you, that Mommy and Daddy never want you to get into a car with a stranger—even if he says he knows us?" Do point out that such behavior by adults is more the tragic exception than the rule: "I don't know why anyone would want to hurt a little child like that. Maybe he's a bad man. Maybe he's sick and doesn't know what he's doing. Most adults look out for children and try to protect them—but it's important to remember our rule: *only go with adults you know.*"

Comforting a Family When a Child Dies

In addition to assuaging a child's fears, the family of a dead child is going through anguish that is comprehensible only to someone who has had the same misfortune. The best thing you can do for a bereaved family is be there to listen and console, or to reminisce about happy memories, if the parents want to: "Remember the time they all decided to make mud pies—in the kitchen?" Or to take telephone messages, keep track of flowers and food that people leave for the family, and to do the work involved in setting up a memorial fund.

If you have an especially good photograph or memento of the child that his family might cherish, it would be nice to share it, with a note:

> *Dear Leah and Bob:*
>
> *We found this in our photo album and thought you might like to have it. It's the way we'll always remember Andy—laughing and up to something. (This was taken on the day the boys decided to "dye" the dog with grape juice!) Although we know your loss is so much greater than ours, we wanted you to know how much we loved and will miss your very special little boy. Please let us know if there's anything we can do to help you get through this.*
>
> *With all our love,*
> *Jocelyn and Ed*

Encourage your children to write to their friend's parents and let them know how the child's friends love and will miss him. One of the biggest condolences to a bereaved family is the assurance that their child's life touched others, and that his memory will live on.

Abortion, Stillbirth, and Miscarriage

When a pregnancy ends in miscarriage or stillbirth, the mother needs your comfort and sympathy, since this is one of the hardest things a woman (or for that matter, a man) may face. Do offer sympathy and understanding. Don't try to cheer her up by telling her, "You'll have other children," or "Well, the baby was here too short a time for you to become attached to him," or "Maybe it was a blessing, since he would have been born with a serious birth defect." No parent will be comforted by such words.

Terminating a pregnancy is not a decision most women make lightly. Whether she ends the pregnancy because of health complications (her own or the developing child's) or because she feels circumstances in her life do not permit her to carry a child to term at the time she makes the decision, most women go through a fair amount of anguish before they arrive at this decision. If you have had or are considering an abortion, you may want to confide only to a close friend or family member. If a friend confides in you, reserve judgment, however you feel about the issue yourself, and be the friend to her you would want her to be to you if the situation were reversed.

Illness

During a temporary illness, the potential patient may need help in the hospital or at home. A person who is hospitalized for the removal of an appendix or for a fractured leg knows she'll be fine in the long term, but in the short term may have some specific problems she can use help with. Whether you've promised to water her houseplants, feed her fish, or collect her mail and drop it off at the hospital, don't forget to do what you've offered to do, because you're being counted on.

People who are confined and not feeling too bad often welcome visits and relish news of the outside world. Keep your visit short, cheerful, and full of the kind of chat you'd like to be caught up on if you were the person who was bedridden.

People with chronic illnesses that do not require hospitalization may decide to keep their illnesses to themselves and tell close friends or associates if and when the need arises. Don't pry, if you haven't been told the specific nature of the illness, but do try to go with the flow, according to how your friend feels on a given day. If your plans fall through because she's just not up to going out, reassure her that there will be other times: "Hey, Joy, if you're whipped, we can go to the movies another night; I'm sure this one will be around for a few weeks."

Hospital Visits

If you've ever been "incarcerated" in a hospital, you know the feeling of watching time draagggg by, and remember how things quickened when you had things or people to engage or amuse you. If you have a friend or colleague who is hospitalized and he encourages you to visit, go. Call just before you plan to leave, to make sure that your patient is still up to the visit. Stay for a short period of time. And bring a little gift (see chapter 18, "Gifts from Me to You").

COMMON COURTESIES AND HOSPITAL ETIQUETTE

- Stay a short while (ten to fifteen minutes max, unless you're urged to stay longer).
- Don't bring a party to the room; be considerate if the room is being shared. (And do offer your friend's roommate a goody or two, too.)
- Stay at home if you're ill—don't "gift" someone with your cold or flu.
- Leave if the patient begins to look ill or tired—even if you've only been there for a moment.
- Step out when the doctor visits, when a bath is given, dressings are changed, etc. (unless you're asked to help).
- Don't volunteer to read charts or other medical information even if you are an MD.
- Don't ask about the prognosis for serious diseases if one isn't volunteered. Remain upbeat.

Patients in Nursing Homes or Senior Citizens' Residences

These patients may be well enough to leave the hospital but are in need of rehabilitation or close supervision. Because patients who are residents of long-term facilities are away from their home environments, it's particularly nice to bring them things that can help to establish a comfortable, welcoming home away from home. Framed photos of family and friends are a wonderful addition, as is a cozy quilt or afghan, which provides color and warmth to rooms that often feel clinical. A few books on tape, with a Walkman, might please a patient who loves to read but is having a hard time, physically, doing this. Warm socks, slippers, or a handsome bathrobe are good choices.

Home Visits

Once a patient is home from the hospital, there are a number of small things you can do to make his life easier:

- Offer to bring lunch to share.
- Bring dinner, all ready to be warmed.
- Take the kids to a movie or for the afternoon.
- Vacuum or dust.
- Do the grocery shopping—especially if he or she isn't allowed to drive yet.

- Offer to write letters, mail bills, or type notes your friend might need to send out.

Long-Term Illness

- If you know the nature of the illness, do some research to understand what the patient might—and might not—be up to. If you know, for instance, that people who suffer from sickle-cell anemia sometimes go through crises where they are bedridden and in pain, you'll know the sorts of assistance your friend can use when this situation arises.
- Offer to contribute an hour or two to your friend each week: grocery shopping, physical therapy exercises, reading and answering mail.
- If your friend has no nearby family to lend support, organize and coordinate a care group of friends who can pitch in on a regular basis to help your friend out.

Sudden Tragedies: Accidents, Critical Diagnoses

Sometimes bad luck seems to drop on us out of the blue: a car runs a red light and you find yourself in a body cast. Or the nagging cough you've been trying to ignore indicates a far more serious problem than you'd ever imagined. Beyond the psychological shock that accompanies the accident or diagnosis, there may also be physical disabilities that prevent the patient from carrying on his normal activities, which still have to be attended to.

- *Ask what you can do, and do it.* If your friend has taken a bad fall and you know she has a small dog or other pet, get the key, and feed and walk the animal. Or, if you can, bring it home until your friend can care for it.
- *Help the patient to research or assemble information on his injury or disease:* How long does it take for a broken pelvis to heal? What have the advances been in chemotherapy? What are some of the new treatments for AIDS that might keep a patient comfortable and healthy? Where can the patient find a physician for a second opinion?
- *Offer to be a chauffeur.* Some medical procedures leave patients too medicated or wiped out to drive themselves home afterward. If you can offer to drive your friend to and from physical therapy or an arduous set of tests or some in-and-out surgery, you'd be considered a lifesaver.

Surgery

Forget the friendly family doctor who made house calls in the middle of the night. He's been replaced by a behemoth medical establishment bristling with release forms, disclaimers, and a battery of claims analysts whose job it is to decide if you *really* need the services you're asking for. Because the administration of medicine has become so complicated, a trip to the hospital for surgery is probably even more anxiety-producing than it used to be. Keeping that in mind, there are some things you should know before you walk through the hospital doors:

- Before you undergo surgery, make sure you get a second opinion—something most insurance plans require before paying for any major surgery anyway.
- Be sure to have surgical consent forms brought to you well before you're taken down to surgery (ideally a day or two ahead of time, if possible), when you can read them at your leisure and receive explanations if you need them. Don't let anyone rush you into signing anything, especially in a nonemergency situation.
- Don't be afraid to ask questions: it's your body, and you need to be fully informed as to what's going to happen to it.
- It's critical that you have an advocate, a friend or relative, who can hassle the hospital and your doctors on your behalf if you're too groggy or too distracted to do it yourself. If you are the advocate, you will need to lobby on your friend's behalf: Ask for extra blankets if she's cold. Remind her nurses that her pain medication hasn't yet arrived. Ask them to take her temperature and draw blood when she's awake, if she's having a hard time getting her rest. Keep visitors down to a manageable number, and ask them to leave if they're wearing her out (especially if she's too embarrassed to tell them she's not up to the visit).

Acknowledging the Nursing Staff

Nurses are the backbone of any hospital system and are often the way the patient measures the success of his stay. Good nurses are, to paraphrase the Bible, more precious than gold. If you're fortunate enough to have a nurse or nurses you think are fabulous, don't keep that information to yourself:

- Send a letter to the head of the hospital, commending the unit, staff, or individual nurses you feel were instrumental to your (or your loved one's) recovery.

- Don't send flowers: nurses get the overflow from patients all the time.
- Do send food that can be shared: sweets, snacks, gourmet coffee, or a gift certificate to the local deli or pizza joint will be greatly appreciated. As will fresh fruit.
- Ask around to see what the nurse's station needs. If you are able, you could make a donation toward a fund for an especially coveted piece of equipment that the hospital budget can't or won't cover.

Helping in a Crisis: Illness and Death

Not only the patient but her family can use nurturing and support during a crisis. Make dinner for them and drop it off. Or have them over to dinner—they may need to get out of the house. Bring a care package of videos, microwave popcorn, and soft drinks so a tired, anxious family can unwind a bit at home. Look after (or temporarily adopt) a beloved pet. Call friends of the terminally ill and ask that they write or call your friend if he's taken a turn for the worse. People want to know they'll be remembered and that they have meant something to others. Some ways to show you care:

- *Be there.* Sometimes it's just enough to have you nearby.
- *Listen.* People who do this well are treasured friends.
- *If you see something that needs doing, do it.* If the refrigerator's bare, if the laundry's undone, if the dust is drifting over the surfaces of furniture, don't wait to ask if you can tackle it. Just do it.

Violent, Unexpected Death

The sad reality of modern life is that while we've made tremendous progress in some areas, we've slid back on the developmental scale in others. The rise of violent crime and fatal accidents that are the result of carelessness continues to worry most of us.

If you have friends or relatives who have suffered a loss from a murder, a collision with a drunk driver, or other sudden tragedy, undoubtedly they are reeling from the shock. One of the kindest things you can do is refrain from indulging in the agony of "what-iffing" (What if she hadn't used the ATM that night? What if the underground garage had been patrolled better? What if they'd taken the next plane?), since it doesn't help things and may only make the pain worse.

If you can act as an advocate on behalf of the family to speak with police or rescue workers, this might be useful. If you can stand it, you might spare a grieving relative the pain of identifying the body or collecting the personal effects of the deceased.

When a Contemporary Dies

This is one of the hardest things to face—our natural human reaction is, "That could have been me!" Everyone who has died before a ripe old age dies too young. Reach out to the support network that kept your group of friends together in life, and offer your help to her family in planning and/or participating in her funeral or memorial service. And honor her life and what she meant to you by participating in something that was meaningful to her, which allows her memory to carry on, and which helps a cause that was important to her.

It's unpleasant, even frightening, to think of any of these things occurring, especially to us or someone we love. Tragedy in any form is hard to deal with, but it's doubly traumatic when we're unprepared for how to handle it and how to do the mechanical steps that are necessary in its aftermath. You will find in situations like these that knowledge will help to strengthen you. And remember what our elders told us about walking in the Valley: even though it feels interminable when we are at our lowest point of despair, this, too, shall pass.

Chapter 36

SWING LOW, SWEET CHARIOT

Black people have always clung to a genuine love for each other. That's why a funeral said so much. You can't let this person die as though it was nothing happening. A great loss had been suffered. I learned to cry at funerals.

Vernon Jarrett,
syndicated columnist, *Chicago Sun-Times,* 1979

Funerals are, and always have been, taken very seriously in our community. Virtually every African civilization has a ceremony or ritual honoring those who have died before the living who are now honoring them. In the New World, African descendants even while enslaved found ways to stop and acknowledge when one of us "passed over" into the Promised Land.

Some of today's largest black insurance companies had their humble beginnings as burial assurance businesses. Each week, these organizations would collect a pre-agreed-upon amount, sometimes as little as a dime, sometimes as much as a dollar, to ensure that, when the time arose, the policyholder would enjoy a proper funeral. From those humble beginnings have sprung corporate giants such as Atlanta Life, North Carolina Mutual (Winston-Salem), and Golden State Mutual (Los Angeles).

There are even cinematic references to our fondness for a well-produced send-off. Remember *Imitation of Life?* That was the 1934 film in which Louise Beavers costarred (with Claudette Colbert), as the indomitable Delilah. The movie's denouement comes when Delilah dies, and, per her instructions (and lifelong savings), she has "the biggest funeral Harlem ever did see." Throngs turn out to witness her stately procession: Her coffin rides in a glass-windowed cortege drawn by white horses wearing plumes. A brass band walks behind playing mournful dirges, and white flowers are thrown in her path.

Most modern funerals are hardly so elaborate, but our traditional wish for a way to gather together and mourn the loss of a family member or friend remains undiminished. And while most of our funerals (unlike Delilah's) no longer take an entire day to conduct, great care goes into comforting the bereaved and making sure everyone involved is looked after.

In the Beginning

There are several ways to notify people when someone dies. Quite often a relative of the person who has passed will take it upon himself or herself to notify the immediate family, who often go on to call their own close friends. Or a dear family friend may volunteer to relay the sad news to people the family wishes to be notified immediately. Many people find having someone else do this an immense relief; they're in enough shock at the passing of their loved one. Having to describe, over and over, the whats, whens, and whys of the death is excruciating for some. Others will welcome the task as a way to keep busy.

What Friends Can Do to Help

When someone dies, everyone wishes to chip in and assist a family to get through this tough time. If you are a close family friend, some things you might ask to be allowed to do, which the family might find helpful, are:

- Calling others to notify them of the death
- Answering the telephone at the family's home, taking condolence messages
- Keeping track of floral arrangements and gift baskets that may arrive so that thank-you notes can be sent later
- Baby-sitting, or entertaining small children for a few hours
- Helping to entertain visitors who stop by on condolence calls
- Providing food for visitors and relatives who have come to call

At a time like this, when large numbers of people are circulating through the house for several hours on end, perhaps for several days, you can bring by certain things that can be lifesavers:

- A large stack of paper goods, such as sturdy plates and napkins
- Plastic forks and glasses
- Cases of soft drinks
- A large container of ground coffee and a jar of instant decaf, a box of sugar, and cream or milk

- Snack foods—cheese, crackers, fresh fruit—that can be nibbled on between meals
- An extra cooler filled with ice

Never be afraid to pitch in and do a chore that needs doing, even if no one has specifically asked for it: no one will object if you make that sinkful of dirty platters disappear, or empty those overflowing ashtrays, or whisk away that pile of crumpled napkins that someone left on the coffee table.

Perhaps more than anyone else, black Americans and food are closely intertwined. (Have you ever been to one of our funerals when you *weren't* fed afterward?) Traditionally, the postfuneral meal was sustenance for travelers who had journeyed far to pay their respects. And in the early days, food was the only material thing many of us had to give, and it was given lovingly and without reservation. Today feeding funeral-goers is a way to bolster sagging spirits, allow people to visit with each other, and to remind mourners that even in the midst of death, life goes on.

Planning the Service

Before you plan the service, you'll want to consult with your minister, as he's done this several times and can walk you through much of the process. If you are not a regular churchgoer and don't have a minister of your own, ask friends for suggestions, or tell your mortician you will need a minister to perform the service. Mortuaries usually have a relationship with several clergy persons and will be happy to suggest a minister. (Be aware that a nominal cost is involved here.)

While many religious institutions have their own standard order that is usually followed, there is almost always room for deviation from that standard. Basically, you should let your heart and your common sense work hand in hand to design a service you're comfortable with and one that you think represents the personality or wishes of the person who has died.

The Program

If your loved one has left special instructions about the service, try to honor them. Perhaps he had a favorite hymn or passage from the Scripture. Or he has designated a special friend to read her eulogy. Or he has requested a very short service with a brief prayer and more music than anything else. These are things that can usually be accommodated by the pastor, especially if he knows that the deceased felt strongly about them.

When you have decided what you'd like included in the service, you need to prepare an order of service, which indicates who does what, when (see sample), and a brief biography for inclusion in the funeral program. (This is another task a close friend might be called upon to perform.) A good likeness of the deceased is always appreciated, especially if the person who has died struggled with a long illness first. Try to pick a photograph that would allow guests to remember him or her as a happy, vital person: one teacher's family chose to use a photograph that showed her smiling, surrounded by her laughing students. A professional photographer was depicted focusing intently through the lens of a beloved camera. And the family of a veteran who had proudly served as a Tuskegee Airman chose a photo that showed him in full dress uniform.

A Service Checklist

- ❑ Contact your minister.
- ❑ Choose a mortician.
- ❑ Decide on method of disposal (burial, cremation, donation of body to science).
- ❑ Select a casket or receptacle for ashes.
- ❑ Decide on what to include in the service, and the order in which these things will be done.
- ❑ Select a photograph for inclusion in the program.
- ❑ Choose a cemetery plot or crypt and a gravestone or marker.
- ❑ Write the eulogy, or ask someone else to.
- ❑ Ask friends to participate in the service if you'd like for people to make remarks.
- ❑ Ask friends to serve as pallbearers.
- ❑ Choose acknowledgment cards to send as thank-yous afterward.
- ❑ Notify the newspaper, if you'd like a death notice placed.

Sample Order of Service

Processional	Music played as the minister, family, pallbearers enter church
Opening Prayer	Senior minister
Song	Solo, choir, or congregation
Scripture Reading	Auxiliary minister, church elder, or good friend
Solo	
Acknowledgments	Read by close family friend. Note: These do not take the place of thank-you notes.
Resolutions	Read by a representative of a club or association of which the deceased was a member
Remarks	Remembrances by friends and colleagues

Obituary Read silently
Musical Interlude
Recessional
Interment

Planning Your Own Service

Perhaps you've been to funerals that have struck you as particularly moving or beautiful. Or maybe you've returned from one swearing, "I'll *never* let that happen at my service!" If you have definite feelings about what (and whom) you'd like included in your service, you might give some thought to writing it down and letting someone close to you know where your instructions are. (Some people, to be safe, make two copies—one for a family member and another for a close friend or the minister or the mortician, if you know whom you'll be using.)

Sometimes the planning is purely hypothetical: you're not planning to die anytime soon, but if you do, this is how you want things done. But sometimes the planning is a nod to practicality: more and more, people who are in the final stage of a terminal disease are choosing to have a say in how their services will be structured. This is especially important when there might be some controversy surrounding your death. Many AIDS patients have taken great pains to specify that their life partners be included in the ceremony, given a place of honor as a chief mourner, and generally treated as a spouse, especially when their families did not approve of the relationship. The same is true for couples who are living together but not married. If you are single and want your partner to be seated and treated in the same manner a spouse would be, there's a much better chance your wishes will be fulfilled if they're written down and easy to find: "Please seat Lorraine in the first row, next to my mother and father, and list her as a survivor in my obituary."

Donating Organs

Organ donation really is giving the gift of life to someone who might languish without your help. Record numbers of black Americans die each year of kidney failure and heart and lung disease. Thousands of us require cornea replacements for cataracts. Yet our numbers on donor registries are few. If you'd like to leave part of yourself to someone who would be grateful for your kindness, contact your local hospital or your branch of the Red Cross and ask for organ donor forms. In some states, you may do this by filling in a line on your driver's license application or renewal form; this will identify you as a potential organ donor to medical staff.

Practically speaking, however, many doctors are reluctant to honor your wishes if your family is dead set against them. If you'd like to make a gift of some or all of your organs, make sure you have the donor form properly filled out; have a written statement notarized indicating your intention to donate; and talk with your family and explain that this is your wish and, should something happen to you, you would like to donate some or all of your organs. Their ability and willingness to reinforce your wishes could prove essential.

Clothes for the Deceased

Bodies are usually dressed in less-casual clothes: dresses or suits for women, suits with ties for men. But it's fine, especially if the deceased requested it, to place someone in a favorite outfit that is not a suit or dress, too. If Uncle Victor wanted to be buried in a polo shirt, slacks, and a golf sweater, fine. Parents might choose to dress a child in her favorite party dress. A member of the armed services, even if he's retired, may ask to be placed in his uniform. If your great-grandmother loved pink and had many pink clothes, it would make sense to have her placed in her favorite pink dress.

Ask your mortician what you'll need to bring to be sure the deceased is properly dressed. Bring the outfit and everything that goes with it (a dress would require proper underwear: slip, bra, and panties) that would be worn in life.

If the departed always wore a specific-color makeup, let the mortician know. And try to have a good color likeness of the person, so the makeup artist can try to make her look as much like herself as possible.

Viewing the Body

If you choose to have a viewing of the body (sometimes called visiting hours) or a wake, your mortician will contact you when the body is ready and ask for a family member (or someone the family designates) to inspect and approve the body's appearance. This gives you some private time with the departed and also allows you to check on small details that can be corrected to allow the person who died to look the way everyone remembered: "Aunt Sara looks great—but she never wore pink lipstick. Can you change it to deep red?" Or "Daddy always wore his part on the left; we should switch that."

Some families prefer to have a viewing or wake the evening before the service. This custom allows friends and family a last look at their loved one, so for that purpose, the casket, if there is one, usually remains open. A wake is by no means mandatory but is considered traditional in some communities and religions where "visiting hours" are offered. The family may or may not be in the same room as the casket but is often somewhere nearby to receive condolences. Whether or not this is done, as well as whether one has a casket open or closed, is entirely up to the family. Do what makes you comfortable.

In many instances, at the end of the service, people who attend the funeral will be invited to go to the front of the church or funeral home for a final viewing. You don't have to view the body if you'd rather not; just remain in your seat and let others pass by when the ushers gesture for you to go forward.

Video Presentations

Just as weddings, graduations, and other milestones are often videotaped, many families are choosing to include a brief video presentation at the funeral service or wake. This is a compilation of photographs and brief comments on the deceased's life and personality captured on film for those at the service. Video biographies may include snippets from old home movies, remembrances from close friends, shots of favorite haunts (the business someone started, the favorite restaurant where a group of friends met monthly for lunch). If you choose this option, check with your pastor or funeral home before requesting that a video technician work on this project for you, as not every place is equipped for video presentations, and some places (churches especially) may not feel comfortable doing them yet.

Photographing at Funerals

Unless the person who has died is very prominent and the funeral is something of a state affair, cameras should not be used during the service. Traditionally, family members have gathered following the service to sit for a group portrait. Or candid shots are taken as people relax over the postservice luncheon.

Notifying the Newspapers

If you'd like for an obituary to be placed in the paper, you or someone who was close to the deceased will have to compose a short piece containing some basic information:

- ❑ Name of the deceased
- ❑ Date of death
- ❑ Cause of death (optional, and up to the family)
- ❑ General biographical information (where born, schooled, when married)
- ❑ Professional and social affiliations

- ❑ Survivors
- ❑ Day, date, and time of service, if open to the public
- ❑ Family's wishes re contributions or flowers

Years ago, this service was provided to anyone who wished it by the local newspapers. Today some newspapers (especially ones in large cities) choose only to run obituaries of prominent citizens, but will place a death notice for anyone. A charge is usually associated with the latter. Sometimes the mortician can arrange this for a modest fee.

SAMPLE OBITUARY

GERALD LEMOYNE

Gerald Antoine LeMoyne, founder of ABC Accounting Corporation, died on April 24 in New Paltz, New York. He was 65 years old.

Mr. LeMoyne moved to New Paltz from his native Louisiana at age 21 in 1952. A graduate of Dillard University, Mr. LeMoyne served in the Army during World War II, and received two Bronze Stars. He was a founder of the National Certified Public Accountants' Association, a member of Alpha Kappa Psi fraternity, past president of the Dillard Alumni Association and a deacon of Ward Street Presbyterian Church. In addition, Mr. LeMoyne served for several years as treasurer on the board of the NAACP Legal Defense and Educational Fund.

Besides his wife, Mary Hankins LeMoyne, Mr. LeMoyne is survived by two sons, Gerald A. LeMoyne, Jr., of Manhattan, Charles Hankins LeMoyne of Atlanta, four grandchildren and several nieces and nephews. Funeral services will be held Wednesday at 2:00 p.m. at Ward Street Presbyterian Church, with interment immediately following at Cromwell Memorial Park in New Paltz. In lieu of flowers, the family asks that any contributions be sent to the NAACP Legal Defense and Educational Fund, where a scholarship is being established in memory of Mr. LeMoyne.

Asking Friends to Participate in the Service

One of the highest compliments a friend can ask of another is to participate in a loved one's service. If you are asked to read a Scripture passage, give a verbal thank-you on behalf of the family, or read a citation or resolution, try to accept, as it will mean a great deal to the friend who has asked you to do this. If you don't feel you'll be able to get through the service without breaking down yourself, explain to your friend why you don't feel you can accept this honor. People usually understand.

If you ask someone to participate, be clear on what you need him/her to do, and when: "Natalie, we'd be so pleased if you'd read one of Mother's favorite passages from the Bible. It's from the Book of Micah, and I'll have it typed out for you. Your part would come just after the soloist sings 'Deep River.' "

If you are asked to participate, make sure you know what your friend wants of you. If you're asked to give brief remarks about the deceased, write them out beforehand, go over them a few times in your head, and use them as a guideline when you speak. Keep it brief, and remember that what you're really doing is painting a verbal portrait of the person who has died, so any anecdotes or remembrances that are particularly typical of the person would be appropriate: "I grew up in Nan Spencer's home right along with Alice: I can still hear her calling *both* our names when we were in trouble! It didn't matter that Alice was her child and I wasn't; as far as Nan was concerned, *everybody* was her child, and that's pretty much how she lived her life."

Special Participants

If the person who dies was a member of several organizations, representatives of these often request to be included in the service. Members of Masonic temples (the Masons), for instance, usually participate in the graveside service. Daughters of the Eastern Star frequently read a resolution or take some other active part in the service. Sorority and fraternity members often attend en masse, or ask to be of service at the reception (pouring tea, serving plates, etc.). If you are approached by members of an organization your loved one belonged to and was active in, try to accommodate them if you can. Again, this is an individual preference.

Military funerals usually follow a specific protocol. If you choose a military funeral, you will be advised on the customary procedure. Contact your local Veteran's Administration for guidance.

Dressing for Funerals

Black is still considered the traditional color of mourning in the United States and Europe, although white (especially in warm weather and in certain parts of the country) is always an acceptable alternative. Neutral colors—gray, beige, navy—are often seen and are entirely proper. Any sober color and quiet pattern is appropriate. (In some places, deep purple is considered a mourning color, too.)

What's *not* appropriate: anything flashy, anything more suitable for a festive gathering (such as a cocktail party) than a sad occasion. Women should keep jewelry simple, personal exposure discreet (thigh-high slits, plunging necklines are out), and accessories low-key. Funerals are not the time to wear your spike-heeled mules, carry your gold lamé purse, or wear lace-patterned stockings. Men should wear ties that are appropriately sober and dark business suits. Sunglasses should not be worn indoors. (For more guidance, see chapter 14, "Glad Rags.")

Children at Funerals

Our preference is not to have young children at funerals, period, unless the person who has died is a grandparent, parent, or sibling. There will be time enough to attend these sad occasions in the years ahead. Little children who are bewildered—or frightened—by the proceedings just add to the stress of an already stress-laden occasion. If you feel this way, ask a close friend to sacrifice attending the service so that small children may stay at home with him or her while you attend. Adolescents should follow the same guidelines as adults.

As we said, the presence of children is a personal decision. Many people feel strongly that having small ones with them during the service brings a measure of comfort and, under those circumstances, who could deny them? If you choose to bring your child to a funeral, dress her in something you know she'll find comfortable. Bring a small stuffed animal or other toy to keep her engaged—and be prepared to step into the corridor (or ask a close friend to do this if you cannot leave) if she gets restless or upset.

Always explain to older children what is going to happen in clear and simple language. You might tell a six-year-old, for instance: "Michael, we're going to say good-bye to Grandpa this afternoon. There will be a big box at the front of the church with flowers on it; that's called Grandpa's casket. The minister will say prayers for Grandpa and we will, too. You might see some people crying, and that's okay. They're sad because Grandpa died, and they loved him and they're going to miss him, just like we are. I know you're sad, too, and it's okay for you to cry if you want to." It's important to warn a child old enough to understand the proceedings that the adults around him may be weeping; often the sight of a parent in distress is more upsetting than the death itself.

For a child, viewing the inert body of someone he has known and loved may be traumatic. Never insist that a child view the body, or "give Grandpa one last kiss and tell him you love him." If he chooses to go to the casket, stay close so he can be reassured: "Didn't they make Grandpa look nice? It doesn't look like he was as sick as he was, does it?" Don't force him to get any closer or stay any longer than he can bear.

A Word About Pallbearers

Most caskets now slide on gliders and, to a large degree, pallbearers now perform a purely ceremonial function. Occasionally, if the service is performed in, for example, a church with steps, pallbearers may be needed to convey the casket down the steps, or steady it as it is slid into the back of the hearse. For that reason, active pallbearers are usually chosen from the ranks of the young and/or fit. There are six or eight, depending on the size of the casket and the preference of the family. Pallbearers are usually close family friends or even relatives of the deceased. Because a casket is heavy, pallbearers traditionally have been men, but occasionally a woman serves in this capacity, too.

Honorary pallbearers are people who are not actually enlisted to carry the casket, but whose honorary status indicated they are special friends of the deceased and his family. Honorary pallbearers can be any age or gender, and can be larger in number than active pallbearers. Sometimes members of the deceased's sorority or social organization or union are listed as honorary pallbearers. They may or may not enter the church or funeral home together, and exit, walking two abreast, before the casket.

Interment

Interment is simply the process of placing a body in the ground, although it is often broadly used to indicate placing a body in a mausoleum (aboveground burial, usually in a crypt or sepulchre—see "Entombment" on the following page) or placing ashes or other mortal remains in a crypt before it is sealed. Some families prefer to do this privately; in that case, the program would read: "Private interment, St. Alban's Cemetery, immediately following service." When a private interment occurs, guests who have attended the service are usually invited to the church hall or a relative's home, and some refreshment is given while they wait for the family to return.

Cremation

Cremation is the obvious alternative to burial, one that many people choose. If the body is to be cremated, a funeral can be held before cremation. The mortician then takes the body to be cremated, and the ashes are given to the family shortly thereafter. Or the body can be cremated and a service performed at the crematorium, before the ashes are placed in a crypt. Sometimes the ashes are placed elsewhere, according to the deceased's wishes:

perhaps they are spread over a favorite hiking trail or gently scattered over the sea.

Entombment

Bodies that are placed aboveground in mausoleums or crypts are entombed. The same procedure for funerals is followed, except instead of being interred, the casket is put in a family mausoleum, an aboveground crypt, or a wall crypt.

Memorial Services

Unlike a funeral, which usually has a casket in the room at the time of the service, the memorial service does not. It may be held soon after a private funeral and burial, or it could occur several weeks, even months, after death. When the deceased has family who live all over the country, or when he has many friends who will not be able to attend the funeral, a memorial service is appropriate. The memorial service is largely similar to a funeral service, although the venue may change. Memorial services have been held in churches, fellowship halls, school auditoriums, campus amphitheaters, museum courtyards, and public gardens. And while funerals are usually given by the family, memorial services may be held at the request of family, friends, or admirers of the deceased. (After writer James Baldwin died, for instance, there were several services in addition to his Harlem funeral, including one in his adopted village, St.-Paul-de-Vence, and a large one in Paris, which was attended by Parisians and expatriate Americans alike.) Where and when this is done depends on the preference of the memorial service sponsors.

Mass Cards

Having a mass said in memory of the deceased may be an appropriate and much appreciated expression of sympathy when the deceased or his family is Catholic, either in lieu of flowers or in addition to them. Masses may be arranged either through the parish office of the local church attended by the deceased, the funeral home where the wake takes place, a Catholic religious order of priests (e.g. Jesuits, Franciscans, etc.), or a Catholic church close to one's home. Depending on local custom and where you are making the arrangements, the mass (or masses) may be scheduled to take place as soon as available, a month after the date of death (sometimes referred to as a "month's mind" mass), or to coincide with the first-year anniversary of death. The person scheduling the mass for you will need to know the name of the deceased, and will accept a modest stipend ($3–$25) according to one's means. In return, mass cards and envelopes are provided, which may be left at the funeral home (if there is a wake service) or mailed to the family. Family members may wish to attend the mass if time and place are convenient.

Mass cards may be sent by non-Catholics as well as Catholics. It is appropriate for the family receiving a mass card to send a note of acknowledgment.

Where There's a Will . . .

In movies, the will is read directly following the funeral, as anxious relatives perch tensely on the edge of their chairs. This happens sometimes in real life, too (especially if relatives from far away gather for the funeral), but more often than not, disclosure of a will's contents is much less dramatic. The lawyer or the executor of the estate will contact you if you are mentioned in a will. (In some states, the executor has to be a lawyer; in others, it can be a family member or close family friend or someone the deceased or the family has designated.) If you are left something by a friend or relative who has died, by all means be grateful to have been remembered and refrain from expressing any disappointment about what you didn't/should have/wanted to get. If you feel you must, for some reason, challenge a will (perhaps your grandmother has said, several times, that she'd like her family photographs to be passed on to you, but someone else claimed them first), hire a lawyer and let her make all contact with the will's executor. Try your hardest not to get personal about the disputed items; a family split is the last thing most people envision when they draw up wills.

Delicate Situations

With any gathering of people there is the potential for tension. Add the sadness and anxiety that funerals produce, and things can get downright explosive. To that end, some things to remember when attending a funeral:

- Ex-spouses should not sit with the family (unless the family specifically requests it), but in another part of the church.
- Spouse equivalents should be seated with the family, especially if the deceased has requested that they be treated as family.
- Extramarital partners should exhibit good home training and refrain from attending the funeral, especially if it's a small one and the deceased's family will become upset or enraged.
- Children should be seated with the family, even if the deceased was divorced.
- Don't lecture the bereaved family about what you want them to do or

how you want them to act: "Nita, you should have had the casket open." "Kwasi, why didn't you view your father one last time?"

♦ Don't give an Oscar-winning performance as a mourner if you hardly knew the deceased: no throwing yourself across the casket or into the grave, no histrionics.

Let Us Break Bread Together

As we mentioned earlier, for our community, funerals and food go hand in hand. From the first hot meal that arrives in the family's kitchen as soon as the sad news is known to the last piece of cake lovingly wrapped and pressed on a departing guest, food has always been our solace and sustenance.

Postfuneral spreads do not need to be lavish or expensive. Often part of the cost and burden is borne by family friends, who among themselves decide who's bringing what and appear, like angels, to set up the kitchen or dining room while others are still in church. (To do this, they usually sacrifice attending the service, so they can admit visitors who couldn't attend the funeral but wanted to drop by and sign the guest book.) Whether it's chicken in a bucket or a catered meal, the postfuneral repast enables mourners to gather over plates of food, to linger and rediscover each other awhile, and to revel in happy memories of the newly departed that take away some of the sting of the loss everyone has just suffered.

A floor-basket floral arrangement

Acknowledging Kindnesses

It does seem pretty unfair that, after having gone through the trauma of losing a loved one, you must write thank-you notes to people who have acknowledged that loss—but you must. Those who have sent contributions, given time and personal service, taken the time to send flowers, condolences, or attend a funeral service deserve to be thanked.

Tradition dictates that these notes be handwritten, but like all aspects of etiquette, this, too, is changing. These days, a small printed card is often sent to everyone but the deceased's closest friends and family, especially if the funeral was a very large one. The sentiment on the card is fairly straightforward, and people often personalize the cards by writing a line or two at the bottom:

The family of
Sarah Jervis Jackson
thanks you for your kindness
in our time of sorrow.

Try to send handwritten notes to very close friends and family. One or two lines is enough: "*Natalie—Thanks for coming; thanks for caring. It meant a lot to have you with us. Much love, Cynthia.*"

Part VII

LOOKING FORWARD

Life in the New Millennium

Maneuvering through life after 9/11

simple talk about the new technology

taking care of the whole you: your health,
your relationships, your financial well-being

important information for raising your child right

Chapter 37

ON THE FLY

Everybody is always after us to get a phone.
We hate phones! . . . If the phone company installed a phone
for free and paid for a man to stand there and answer
it for us, seven days a week, we still wouldn't want a phone!

—Sadie Delany,
Having Our Say

If you feel as if your life used to be home-cooked and now it's being microwaved, you're not alone. Plenty of studies show we're busier and moving faster than ever. Our lives seem filled with shortcuts as we try to fit more and more into our waking hours. The "convenient life" is one we've all embraced at one time or another. From prepared meals we can pick up "on the fly" to instant messaging, from e-mailed invitations to Web sites that share every detail of upcoming nuptials, the advantages of such shortcuts are boundless. But, too often, in our haste, we forget the basic rules of etiquette. We might not be able to slow things down all the time, and we wouldn't want to, but hopefully this section contains some of the things you'll want to take a moment to think about. Ready? Set? Go . . .

Cell Phones

In the span of a few years, cell phones have become smaller and filled with more options, and are more prevalent than ever. Some people use them as their main phones, and nearly everyone who travels relies on their cell phones to bypass the sometimes-outrageous phone charges that hotels like to add to the bill. (Now hotels have caught on, and many are adding a flat communications charge whether you use your phone or theirs.)

Although cell phone transmission has improved greatly in the past decade, the downside is this: Now that people can talk anywhere, they do. In elevators. In restaurants. On commuter trains. And on airplanes. If you can do it quietly and you simply must make a call (tell someone where to pick you up or leave an important message), do. Otherwise, please refrain from sharing your business with people who don't care about it and would rather remain ignorant of it.

Cell Phone Safety

Virtually every cell phone sold comes with earphones, and a lot of people don't use them. While there are no widely available studies that show a connection between the alarming uptick in brain cancer and cell phone usage, be conservative: keep your calls short (no three-hour phoneathons!), and always, always use your earphones or a headset. Far easier to do that and laugh if the brain tumor hypothesis turns out to be wrong than to disregard the possibility and be saddened to discover it's right. Make sure your children, who will probably spend as much if not more time on their cells as you do, use their earphones, too.

Children and Cell Phones

It used to be that only overindulged children had cell phones. Now, some as young as elementary school students have them—in order that their parents can reach them in an emergency. If your child has a cell phone, make sure your various phone numbers are programmed into his speed-dial so he can reach you right away, and tell him how you want his phone used (not for hours-long conversations, not to play video games, and not to lend to all his friends to call *their* friends, etc.). Emphasize that cell phones are a privilege, not a right. Especially if you're paying the bill. Make sure he knows he has to ask your permission before he downloads ring tones to individualize his phone. And stress the need to keep it charged properly (or else you won't be able to reach him).

Cell Phonies

Have you ever seen someone totally engaged in a conversation on her cell phone while everyone around the person is apparently traumatized by chaos? Or have you ever wondered how each time you approach a desirable person with the hope of meeting him or her, that person is suddenly chatting away on his or her cell phone? These people may very well be "cell phonies," people who carry on imaginary conversations on their cell phones in order to avoid unpleasant situations. From the woman who doesn't want to be hit on to the employee who is late for a meeting and feigning an important conference call, cell phonies master the art of using cell phone conversations as an excuse to ignore others.

Camera Phones

Cell phones with cameras can be lifesavers ("Officer, this is what the side of my car looked like after he ran into me. . . ."), but they can be privacy-busters, too. Digital imagery saves time and money. Camera phones can record useful information that will make your life easier in the long run. Without having to lug around an additional piece of equipment, camera phones provide instant reminders of that unforgettable sight on your vacation, that must-have piece of furniture you've found and want to show your spouse before purchasing, or they can document a home remodeling project as it progresses. You can take photos of your children and immediately e-mail them right from your phone to their eager grandparents. However, just because you've become the star photographer of the family doesn't give you a right to abuse the technology. Never use your cell phone to take photos in restrooms, dressing rooms, locker rooms, and other places where privacy is desired. Camera phones should not be used where photographic equipment is typically banned: movie theaters, concerts, museums, and courtrooms. Camera phones should not be used to take anyone's photo without his or her knowledge and consent, and particular care should be taken when photographing children under the age of eighteen. Bottom line: respect the privacy of others as you would expect them to respect yours. Think before you click. Period.

Handheld Devices

Personal digital assistants (PDAs) are the electronic equivalent of an address book, a calendar, and a to-do list combined. Some even have built-in phones. Most, if not all, have infrared capabilities, so you can "beam" telephone numbers or "text message" short messages to someone nearby. It's certainly acceptable to send necessary information—especially if a colleague needs some help and sends a text message similar to the following:

> *Sam: Uh-oh, alarm. He's going to ask the How Much Did We Gross in 2000 question, and I'm drawing a blank. Help!*
> *Alana: 3.5 million, or somewhere in that neighborhood . . .*

It is *not* okay to carry on a protracted, private conversation with someone else in the middle of a meeting or group gathering. Save that for when you can be face to face. Ditto flirting: *You look hot in that suit* doesn't have a place in the middle of the department head's lecture on downsizing.

Remember to regularly back up your data. You should do this once a week, in case your little machine were to suffer shock or trauma and lose your data. (Live by the battery, die by the battery . . .) And you should make sure you have some kind of security mechanism to keep your personal business and information from becoming everybody else's. A flavor-of-the-month starlet had her PDA hacked into recently, and her celebrity friends' numbers were on the Internet in a flash. You can imagine how happy they were with that.

The advantage of devices such as Blackberries and Treos is that having one means people can reach you instantly, by e-mail or phone, if they need to. The disadvantage: family and colleagues assume you're available to them 24/7. The solution? Don't have a knee-jerk reaction to your Blackberry. If you have to immediately e-mail a reply as soon as you receive communication, you've become one of those people who is addicted to his "Crackberry." Be selective about when you return calls and e-mails.

The Internet

The Internet has given more mortals instant access to information around the globe within seconds. Anyone with a computer or other device (PDA, select cell phones) that has Internet access through one of the many service providers is privy to a wealth of information and services.

Surfing the Net

Surveys say the vast majority of Americans know how to use a computer, and more than two thirds of American households have one. A home computer can be a great help for research (medical, genealogical, historical, financial, etc.), errands (some states let you renew your driver's license on-line; some libraries allow you to check your book's due date and extend it), and business (information about things like the closest cab company and best kennel are a click away). You can get driving directions, check the academic performance of your child's school, do your banking, purchase postage stamps, or search for your favorite recipe or the best deal on your next car or home. While the possibilities of Internet uses are endless, some of our favorites include the following:

- Research local ordinances and fees for services (dog licenses, parking tickets, marriage licenses, etc.) on-line by typing your city's name into a search engine such as Google or Yahoo.
- Find out hours of operation for government offices (the library, the Department of Motor Vehicles, etc.).
- Download government forms, pay taxes, or request tax extensions.

- Apply for a fictitious name for your business if you're doing business under a name other than your own.
- Access information if you belong to an organization that posts its activities on-line (fraternity or sorority, family reunion, or social organization). Many groups' sites include calendars of upcoming activities, and the information is usually accessible with a protected password, so people who happen to stumble upon the site don't have access to private addresses and photos.
- Locate hard-to-find items, antiques, and art, the world over.
- Keep on top of schoolwork. Many schools now post homework on-line—so there's no excuse if your reluctant student "forgets" to write the assignment from the board. Both of you can see that Ms. So-and-So's history assignment is due . . . uh, *tomorrow*. On-line homework has rescued many an imperiled academic career.

Security on the Web

Your screen name, user name, and password are your keys to unlocking the Internet and the world. *Never share your password with anyone.* Every time you sign up on a company's Web site to obtain information designated for their select readers, you will be asked to provide a user name and a password. Passwords should be kept in a secure place—and not on a list labeled "passwords" stuck to your computer. Treat this information as you would the combination to your trusted safe.

Getting Spammed

It's not just for dinner anymore! Spam, which stands for Self Promotional Advertising Message, is not only a canned-meat subject but the name for the flood of unwanted e-mail that cascades into your on-line mailbox. Some of it is annoying, but benign. Some of it can be lethal to your computer. Protect it and you: Never, ever open an e-mail from an unknown source. It could contain a computer virus that could destroy your machine. Report it as spam to your Internet service provider (ISP), then delete.

Banking On-line

Some love it, others are leery of it. Talk to your bank representative about security measures if you would like to be able to check your bank balance, pay a bill, or move money from one account to the other via on-line banking. If you have direct deposit, you can check your account from the privacy of your home to ensure that the deposit has been credited. If you use a bank-issued automated teller machine (ATM) or debit card, you can print a record of your recent transactions to keep track of your available balance. However, unlike writing checks, which we are trained to record, using a debit or an ATM card is so easily done that it often leaves us reeling when we realize we've automatically made a frequent number of withdrawals.

Paying bills on-line: You're often credited the same day—and you don't have to use stamps! Check your monthly statements to make sure the correct amount of money has been withdrawn. Banks aren't infallible.

Shopping On-line

Shopping on the Web is easy to do and saves a lot of wear and tear on the shopper, just make sure that the site has a secure shopping mechanism, so your credit card doesn't go places you don't want it to. Look for the little padlock icon on your computer screen or an indication from your computer: "You are now entering a secure site." Consider establishing a secondary e-mail address for Internet shopping and Web sites you subscribe to.

If you've resisted the urge to shop solely for yourself and are sending a present to someone else, make sure you provide both your name and billing address *and* the gift recipient's name and address to the store's Web site. Indicate that the purchase is a present. Write the wording you'd like to have placed on the card that will accompany the gift. On-line bridal and baby registries are a godsend. Not only can you view the recipient's wish list at a number of stores without having to leave your desk, the store can wrap and send the gift, saving you the trouble.

Entertainment (movie tickets, restaurant reservations, travel/ hotel bookings, frequent-buyer discounts)

Entertainment, travel, and leisure activities are but a click away on the Internet. You can search for the best deals in airfare, hotels, tours, and package deals. While the airline and hotel chains have sites that allow you to view special discounts, other sites pride themselves on one-stop shopping for the lowest fares at all the airlines. Simply enter your departing and arriving cities, the dates you would like to travel, the number of people traveling, and if your travel dates and times are flexible. In less time than it takes to dial your neighborhood grocery store, your travel options appear before your eyes.

The days of waiting for a restaurant to answer the phone, put you on hold, and then lose your reservation are a thing of the past. Restaurants often have Web sites that allow you to view the menu as well as make reservations and cancellations on-line. Many cities are part of Open Table, an on-line service that searches for reservations at a host of restaurants, based on the type of food you would like to have, the neighborhood you'd like to eat in, and the time you'd like to dine. A few clicks, and all your options appear.

Tired of waiting in line at your local theater only to find out the movie you've been dying to see just sold out? Movie tickets are also available on-line in most cities. Simply view the "What's showing" icon and select your show time, enter your credit card information, and you're set to go. Upon arriving at the theater, pick up your tickets at one of the ticket kiosks. It doesn't get much easier than that!

The Internet offers everything from weight loss support groups to game plans for hosting the ultimate party. If you're looking for a recipe for your favorite red velvet cake, wondering what wine to serve with seafood, or looking for a resource that can ship you all the makings for a backyard luau, the Internet can be your guide.

News and Events

Miss the news? If your computer has enough memory, you can watch it as it "streams" on-line in real time. Many universities offer graduation broadcasts on the Internet, just in case you want to watch your godchild graduate but can't make the trip across country.

Web Pages

Domain names, or Web site addresses, are not just for institutions and corporations anymore. Individuals and small businesses can register domain names and host their own Web pages. If you have a personal Web page, maintain it. Send links to your friends and associates and update it regularly. Blogs, or personal web page journals, are an excellent way to communicate with family and friends.

If you have a business Web site, keeping it up to date is even more important. Make sure your Web address is on your business stationery. You might also want to advertise in the Internet Yellow Pages.

Wireless Connections

"Hot spots" are locations that allow people with laptops and other Internet connections to "plug into" their servers without wires. Such spaces have become tremendously popular in a very short time, and soon hot spots will be widespread. While it's great to take your laptop out into the world, remember that wireless capability makes you more vulnerable to hacking and other kinds of computer mischief. If the document you're working on is confidential, financially delicate, or otherwise not for public consumption, don't work on it in a hot spot.

E-mail Basics

Love it or hate it, e-mail is here to stay. E-mails are messages sent electronically via a computer network. Just like you have a mailbox at your home, if you have e-mail, you have a personal mailbox on the Web. Your e-mail address allows other people who have Internet access to send you messages instantly. And there are advantages:

- E-mails save you telephone charges and cut down on the time you spend on the phone.
- E-mail can be sent twenty-four hours a day, to any time zone worldwide—allowing you to communicate with someone on the opposite coast while he or she is sleeping.
- Via attachments, you can send documents, presentations, recipes, digital photos, drawings, etc., with no lag time. (Grandmas love this.)
- Unlike faxes, e-mail is private and can only be viewed by the addressee.
- While regular or "snail mail" may take a couple days to travel two blocks, e-mail can be sent, and responded to, within minutes.
- Often you are asked for your e-mail address by businesses that would like to keep in touch with you. Signing up for restaurant or department store e-mail offers can mean receiving discounts and special offers sent to you by e-mail.
- Airlines frequently have cheaper fares on-line.

Are there disadvantages? Of course there are:

- You may find yourself spending too much time on your computer and forget you have a job to do, errands to run, and a family to actually talk to.
- Nothing replaces handwritten personal correspondence. E-mail can feel cold and impersonal.

Here are more tips:

- Pick a user name you can remember.
- Choose a name that won't embarrass you. "Stinky105" might seem funny in the middle of the night . . . but not when a human resources person asks you to send your résumé via e-mail.
- Lots of Internet service providers (AOL, Yahoo!, etc.) allow more than one user name, so consider picking one for personal correspondence

(okay, Stinky105, if you must) and one for more public use (FX-Smith@whatever.com).

Personal vs. Business E-mail

It's a good idea to separate personal e-mail from business e-mail, when possible. We're sure your employer does not want you spending your time (and her money!) chatting with your friends by e-mail all day, and if you use e-mail for business purposes, you should have a separate business e-mail address. Even if you don't have a separate e-mail address at your workplace, most Internet service providers allow you to have more than one e-mail address for a single price. Think of your personal e-mail address as one that you give out to friends and family, and a separate home business e-mail address as one that you use for community projects, business transactions, or anytime you fear your address will end up on a master mailing list without your knowledge.

When sending e-mails at work, check the address once, twice, even three times, before sending. Your job could depend on it, especially if you were to accidentally send an e-mail that was unflattering, untrue, or confidential. Your boss, for instance, probably wouldn't react well to receiving the following:

> "My idiot boss is being made Senior VP!"

Remember: Anger is transient; e-mail is forever.

E-mail Etiquette

If you choose to share your e-mail address with others, it's the same as giving out your home address. People assume if you have an e-mail address, you actually use it. Even if you don't use it very often, check it regularly. You'd be surprised by what you might be missing.

Try to respond to e-mails within twenty-four hours. Monitoring your e-mail regularly and replying in a timely fashion prevents your in-box from filling up and lets people know you've received their e-mail. Other things to keep in mind:

- E-mail fonts need to be large enough and dark enough for people to read them.
- When sending out mass e-mails, protect your recipients' e-mail addresses. Consider using the "blind copy" feature for multiple recipients.
- If you change e-mail addresses, send an e-mail to friends, family, and business associates to let them know.

"Out of Office" Notice

If you're going out of town or will be away from your office for an extended time and will be unable to access your e-mail, check to see if your e-mail software or Internet service provider offers you an "Out of Office" or "Out of Town" message, so people who e-mail you know why they're not getting a response. Sometimes you can customize an accompanying message:

> *"Hi. I'm traveling for the next two weeks and won't have access to e-mail. I will check all messages when I return."*

Note or E-note?

A handwritten note is always appreciated, especially these days when they're scarce. Use e-mail for casual conversation if you want to check up on friends and let them know you're thinking about them *("Hey—I saw your sister when she was in NY last week—she looks great! The baby is HUGE!")* While it's better to send paper notes as thank-yous for parties and dinner gatherings *(Lynne: We really enjoyed dinner last night—I'm still amazed by what good cooks your children are! Thanks again, Brenda)*, you can get away with an e-note. You should send a paper thank-you note in response to presents, long stays, and serious favors *(Eileen: Thanks so much for writing a letter of recommendation to your alma mater for Michelle; she's crossing her fingers Spelman says yes. We'll let you know. Love, Renee)*.

A simple paper card or a note written on stationery is most appropriate when offering condolences. A personalized note is a lovely addition to a sympathy card that contains a printed sentiment.

E-mail Introductions

It's okay to introduce, via e-mail, two friends with mutual causes or interests or someone who is new to town to another friend if you've checked beforehand to see if they want to be connected:

> *Deloise: I wanted you to know that my niece, Marie Thomson, is moving to Atlanta in June. She's going to work in ad sales at the* Journal-Constitution. *If she has questions about her new town, may I tell her to contact you? She'd probably enjoy hearing a friendly voice. Let me know when you have a moment, and if it's okay, I'll pass along your e-mail addresses to each other. Fondly, Shelley.*

Whether corresponding via e-mail or handwritten note, don't blindside someone without asking first.

Mailing the Masses

Oh, okay, if you have to send an e-Christmas card, we can't stop you. Ditto solicitations made on behalf of your favorite cause, sorority, school, or social group. But if you must send such communiqués, do it in a way that protects the e-dentities of the recipients. The person who gets your missive shouldn't know who everyone else is on your mailing list and how to reach them.

You have an obligation to protect your recipients' privacy and not give spammers (or scammers) the opportunity to glom onto them.

Chain Letters

Don't, don't, don't. Especially the kind that threatens dire results if you don't respond, or don't respond in a specific period of time. *Don't.*

Jokes and Vulgar Humor

Whether it be by e-mail or any other mode of communication, it is in bad taste to send or relay jokes that are vulgar, pornographic, or racist. Period.

Who Would Have Thought . . .

- That invitations would become electronic? We can't say we love the e-vite—it doesn't make us feel very special—but it is convenient. We'd advise that you not post all the invitees, though. Too much information.
- That wedding pages would become popular? But a caution: It's a wedding, not a coronation. We'd love to see photos of your Big Day, but the chronology of how you met, the details of every aspect of the courtship, and photos of the multiple showers . . . let's don't. Just let the rest of us know where you're registered and include a link to those Web sites, and call it a (very happy) day, okay?
- Electronic baby announcements would supplement or replace traditional birth announcements? Sure, why not introduce the newest addition to your family on the Internet? If you never get around to sending birth announcements (and with a new baby in the house, a lot of people don't), at least we'll know what he looks like before he's old enough to drive himself over and let us take a look. Photos of the newborn and his family are great. Photos from the birth room and the actual birth? Um, let's pass on those.
- One could attend a virtual funeral? Though we're not sure why, we have witnessed "streaming funerals," which broadcast the event in real-time

on the Internet. Some families are now posting memorial collages of their dearly departed on a Web site, complete with an e-guest book for people who would like to have attended the funeral but couldn't. You can leave a message to the family on the site, but it's best to also send a handwritten note or card.

Chapter 38

THINKING TWICE: LIFE AFTER 9/11

What can you do to promote world peace?
Go home and love your family.

—Mother Teresa

World War II was more than a half century ago, but people who were alive long enough ago to remember back then can still tell you, in vivid detail, where they were when President Franklin D. Roosevelt announced the attack on Pearl Harbor and America's entry into the war. Others can tell you with startling clarity where they were and what was happening around them when they learned of the assassinations of John F. Kennedy and, later, Martin Luther King, Jr. One thing we often hear in the wake of such momentous events is "we knew life would never be the same after that."

The same can be said of September 11, 2001. That's when the terrorist attacks occurred in New York (and Pennsylvania and suburban Washington, D.C.), when Islamic fundamentalists slammed planes loaded with passengers and highly combustible jet fuel into the World Trade Center towers and the Pentagon. Almost three thousand people lost their lives in New York alone.

After the horror of what's almost universally referred to as 9/11, life in the United States did indeed change and will not, in many important ways, ever be the same. Everything from the simple mechanics of airline travel to expressing your opinion in public is being done differently in "life after 9/11."

At one time, natural disasters were our only cause for concern. Today the threat of terrorism is very real, and it will be a part of our society in years to come.

Potential Threats

While threats may come in a variety of forms, from suicide bombers to hijackers, it's the unknown that poses the greatest threat. We certainly aren't suggesting you live your life in constant fear, only that you prepare for potential disasters. We may no longer be surprised by the thought of airplanes being used as weapons, but most of us are much less familiar with the more lethal, and potentially widespread, threats of chemicals. Familiarize yourself with the most common threats and their possible signs. These include:

- A *biological attack* is the deliberate release of germs or other biological substances that can make you sick. Agents such as anthrax can be dangerous but do not cause contagious diseases; others, such as the smallpox virus, can result in communicable diseases. Most agents must be inhaled or eaten, or enter the skin through a cut to make you sick.
- A *chemical attack* can poison people and the environment through the deliberate release of a toxic gas, liquid, or solid.
- A *nuclear blast* is an explosion with intense light and heat, a damaging pressure wave, and widespread radioactive material that can contaminate the air, water, and ground surfaces for miles.
- A *radiation threat*, or "*dirty bomb*," is the use of common explosives to spread radioactive materials over a targeted area. Unlike a nuclear blast, which would be immediately apparent, the presence of radiation would not be clearly defined. It is important to avoid breathing radiological dust and to limit any exposure to radiation.

Be Prepared

Being prepared can reduce anxiety, fear, and the loss of loved ones. You and your family, as well as your community, should know what to do in the event of a terrorist attack. Much like a natural disaster, you should be prepared to be self-sufficient for at least three days. Usually this means providing your own shelter, food, water, first aid, and sanitation.

If 9/11 taught us anything, it's that we need to have some basic plans in place when disaster strikes. And not just the historic, man-made emergencies, but the natural ones, too. Some parts of the country have hurricanes every year or frequent earthquakes. However, once the blowing or the shaking is done, we tend to forget that the event can—and probably will—happen again. So give some thought to your personal emergency preparedness plan before a time comes to put it into action.

Consider how you and your family will get in touch with each other. If you all have cell phones and the cells work, great. If you have to get in touch in a piecemeal fashion, think about choosing someone who lives out of town (and presumably won't be affected by the same emergency you are) and use him or her as your touch point. Then you can say to every member of your family: "Here's Aunt Paula's number. If there's ever a huge emergency, call her immediately. She's going to help us keep track of each other." (You might also consider an emergency meeting place, if you're sure everyone would be able to get to it.)

Keep some cash in a safe place. After the 1989 Loma Prieta earthquake that rocked the San Francisco Bay Area, power went out in a lot of places, but not everywhere. One mother whose cupboard was bare got ready to order pizza for her rattled children and then realized she'd need to borrow a couple dollars from her neighbor. "I was going to go to the ATM after I got home . . . but none of them were working!" Uh oh. Think about how much easier it would have been for her to tap into the "emergency stash." (And remember: the power can be out for a little bit—or a long time. On the East Coast, residents in some parts of the Carolinas were left with no power for up to ten days in the wake of Hurricane Hugo. Which meant cooking charcoal, lighter fluid, and ice suddenly got very expensive in some neighborhoods.)

Keep a short list of rental-car companies in your wallet so you can order a car if you're stranded at the airport. After 9/11, some people who thought quickly were able to grab their cells and order rental cars and drive home (in some cases, across the country) while planes were still forbidden to fly. But planes get grounded for other reasons, too, and having rental companies' numbers right at your fingertips gives you an important advantage.

Keep good copies of your important personal records (wills; birth, marriage, and death certificates; passport info; immunization info) in a place outside your home, maybe in a safe-deposit box.

Do not wander off. No matter how badly you want to wander off alone for some much-needed private time, *always, always, always* tell *someone* where you've gone and when you expect to return. We'd hate for your romantic getaway to turn into an all-points bulletin when someone fears you're the victim of foul play. It's simply good manners. In this day and age, it's important that your family be able to reach you in an emergency.

For more information on emergency preparedness, visit the Federal Emergency Management Agency (FEMA) Web site at www.fema.gov/areyou ready/why_prepare.shtm and www.ready.gov.

Racial Profiling

Pre-9/11, driving while black (DWB) was a perennial problem in the black community. It's still a problem, but now black folks have company: DWM (driving while Middle Eastern or Muslim) goes onto the list, too. Early on after 9/11, newspapers were filled with reports of men, women, and children who were pulled off airplanes or detained by the side of the road because nervous observers thought they "looked suspicious." In virtually every case, the people involved were documented foreign nationals or American citizens, but because their looks closely paralleled those of people from Egypt, Pakistan, Saudi Arabia, and other countries where there are militant Islamic operatives, these people were questioned closely and aggressively—even harassed.

The terrorists who drove planes into the World Trade towers were indeed Muslim, but that should not brand all Muslims everywhere as anti-American or anti-Christian. Sadly, after 9/11, many Muslim families living in the United States reported feeling feared, isolated, and scorned by people heartsick over the 9/11 carnage. If you have friends, coworkers, or neighbors who are Muslim, it's important not to treat them guilty by association. The 9/11 terrorists weren't representative of Muslims any more than O. J. Simpson represents all black people.

Air Travel

The pre-9/11 days of buy-and-fly are history. Thanks to heightened screening practices and much more invasive screening measures, traveling by plane is much more involved than it used to be. Here are some things to remember before you fly:

- *Be prepared with a valid government-issued photo ID for domestic flights and a valid U.S. passport for flights outside the country—even to Canada and Mexico.* (You may not need them to leave the United States, but you will need to prove your citizenship to reenter the country.) Passport applications are available at any U.S. Post Office or on-line at http://travel.state.gov/passport.
- *Check ahead for what is, and isn't, allowed in your packed and carry-on luggage.* Obviously, guns, explosives, and other dangerous items are forbidden for normal passengers. (People who carry guns in the line of duty—law enforcement officers, Secret Service agents, etc.—have different rules and know what they are.) But things such as butane cigarette lighters, nail scissors, and other items may also be forbidden. Gift-wrapped packages are also a no-no. Don't try to board with that lovely, beautifully wrapped present for your mother; it will only be unwrapped in the interest of security. Most airlines have information on what you can and cannot carry aboard (or in checked luggage) on their Web sites, and many include a portion of this information in recorded phone messages. Check with your airline.

- *Resign yourself to the metal detector.* You may argue over its efficacy and whether you have to, by law, remove your shoes, but in the end, your fate is in the hands of the security personnel who are staffing the metal detector. According to the Transportation Security Agency (TSA), you don't have to remove your shoes, but they warn that if you refuse, you will greatly increase the probability that you will be pulled aside for a time-consuming random search. Don't want to remove your grandfather's stainless-steel wristwatch? Wince at the idea of your bare feet hitting the dirty terminal floor? You can protest, but what happens is that your time is taken up while a security agent watches calmly as you get more and more wound up explaining why you don't want to do what you've been asked to. Just remember: you're trying to catch a plane—they're not going anywhere. So it's in your best interest to consider ahead of time how to speed yourself through the line:
- Remove large jewelry—especially if it's not precious metal—and place it in a zipped space in your carry-on luggage.
- Remove any loose change you might have in your pockets and be ready to place it in the little containers the security staff provides.
- Secure the closures on your purse, briefcase, tote, or other carry-on bags. If security staff needs you to open them, they'll ask you.
- Inform the security agent if you have something in a bag that may catch his or her attention on the X-ray: "I have a digital camera and a cell phone in the side pocket. . . ."
- Wear shoes that can be easily stepped out of and into again. It's up to the individual agent to decide whether you get to keep them on as you go through the detector. Some people wear soft shoes with no metal in the soles or metal eyelets, assuming that they'll be able to sail through. Don't bet on it. So protect yourself: If the thought of direct contact with the terminal floor gives you a serious case of *eeewwww,* take socks you can easily slip on and then stash in the side of your bag.
- When you're through the other side of the security check, grab your things from the conveyor belt as quickly as possible so that the people behind you can move on, too.
- In some instances, you will be required to submit to a pat down, or worst case scenario, a strip search. You have a right to have the search done by a security agent of your same gender—don't be intimidated or let anyone tell you otherwise.
- *Get to the airport in plenty of time.* Post-9/11, there's very little chance you can dash to the airport at the last minute, sprint through the airport, and trot onto your flight with moments to spare. Plan to arrive at the airport at least ninety minutes ahead of time for domestic flights, three hours ahead of time for international flights.
- *Ticket holders only* means just that. You might be able to accompany a

traveler inside the terminal to a certain point. After that, security dictates that only people who are actually boarding a plane be allowed to go beyond that point. Arguing, wheedling, etc., will usually get you escorted out of the terminal.

Dropping Off/Picking Up

It's not just the airport, it's all public transportation: post-9/11, terminals are very wary of idling cars. So if you're dropping someone off, plan on enough time to remove his or her luggage and for a quick hug, and be gone. Passenger drop off is no longer the place for extended good-byes or last-minute instructions.

Train Travel

At this writing, train travel is not as tightly scrutinized as plane travel, although some of the same rules apply:

- Have your ticket in hand, with a photo ID, just in case.
- It won't always happen, but there could be a random check of your bags.
- On board, stow your things quickly and make sure you don't take more than your allotted storage or seating space.

Bus Travel

After 9/11, many Americans did something they hadn't done in a long time: they took the bus. Ground transportation seemed safer, you could buy a bus ticket at the last moment, and bus fares were (and generally are) still cheaper than flying. Again, some of the same rules apply:

- Arrive in time to purchase a ticket, if you haven't bought one ahead of time.
- Don't take up more than your share of space once you're aboard.
- Remember that bus travel can get a little colorful at times—one wag defined a long-distance bus trip as "a magnet for eccentrics." Plan accordingly: bring a big book or headphones to politely indicate that you're not up for your seatmate's life story. Don't be afraid to switch seats if one is available (*"I think I'm going to try the view over here for a little while, excuse me"*). And when the bus stops for refueling or food, make sure you're back in plenty of time, so people don't have to wait for

you—or so you won't be left behind. (The driver is keeping to a schedule, right?)

Crises While You're Traveling

If your car breaks down and you're a member of the American Automobile Association (AAA), call them and ask for assistance. If your car has an onboard assistance service (OnStar is very common), let the operator know immediately the nature of the problem and be as specific as possible. *(I blew out my right rear tire and had to drive off the road. My grandpa is in the backseat, and I think he's having a heart attack. We're being chased by some boys in a huge pickup—I don't know what they want, but we're worried about what's going to happen when they catch up with us.)* OnStar will send help, pronto. Also, most highways have emergency call boxes for your convenience.

If you're on a train, bus, or plane and you think there may be a problem, notify a member of the flight crew, a conductor, or the driver immediately *(Should the engine over the wing be making that noise? Did the train just run over something on the track? Driver, I think that lady in the back row is going into labor.)*.

If the crisis occurs when you're in another country, call the American embassy. It's part of the State Department's job to protect and assist Americans when they are abroad. Before traveling, check to see if the country you'll be visiting has an American embassy, and keep that information handy.

Things the American embassy can help its citizens do:

- Apply for a new passport, if the one you're traveling with is stolen.
- Notify your relatives at home that you're in trouble and need help.
- Suggest a local medical facility or doctor if there's a medical emergency.
- Work with the airlines to get you home if there's a family crisis.

Some credit card companies tell their holders that they will assist in an emergency abroad. American Express, for instance, can help locate a doctor when your migraine strikes at midnight or provide more traveler's checks if you lose yours or if they're stolen. Check with your credit card company to see what services it offers when you travel internationally.

Before going abroad, check with the U.S. State Department (http://travel.state.gov) to make sure your destination is okay to visit. There are travel advisories for countries that are experiencing unrest or where anti-American sentiment is strong. Tourists are discouraged from visiting those areas, and businesspeople or relief workers are urged to proceed with their work while using extreme caution and all protective measures. (This means anything from hiring a local "fixer" to smooth the way with local residents to wearing protective gear and traveling with a bodyguard.)

Be a Good Neighbor

Used to be, being a good neighbor was the friendly thing to do. Post-9/11, it's also the smart, *safe* thing to do. And because you're looking out for each other, it increases safety. (And neighborliness.)

- Tell your neighbors when you're going to be out of town and ask that they tell you when they're not going to be home overnight or for several nights.
- Leave an emergency number with one of your neighbors, in case something happens while you're gone. (A friend's pipes burst in a bitterly cold winter, and his neighbor called while he was out of town to tell him he was trying to do something about the lake that was rapidly forming in his front yard. . . . It would have been much worse without the call and the assistance.)
- Pick up newspapers and mail for your neighbor, if necessary, so that it doesn't look as if nobody is home.
- Collect packages if you know your neighbors are expecting one, or collect the post office or delivery service receipt so the package can be picked up upon their return.
- If you see people lurking around your neighbor's house, peering in the windows or otherwise casing it, let such people know that someone is next door—pull up your blinds, call for your dog (even if you don't have one), etc. Don't be afraid to call the police and tell them that you think a burglary is in process.
- Become part of or form a block club. Exchange information about what's going on in your neighborhood. Police say block clubs and neighborhood watch teams are invaluable assets in preventing crime's start or spread.

News Overload!

Back in the day, believe it or not, the national television news lasted for fifteen minutes in the early evening. There was no CNN, no entertainment tabloids, and no screamathons masquerading as news talk shows. Now, we not only get a half hour of national evening news, it's usually preceded by an hour of local news, with recaps laced throughout the evening. If you want "all news, all the time," there are cable networks for that. And someone has decided that we need news streaming on our computers and, yes, our cell phones. Oh, and did we mention talk radio?

So if you're feeling as if your head needs a vacation to a place where all electronic communication is banned, you're not alone. Consider doing the next best thing: *Put yourself on an info diet.* You know how some folks say they eat just because the food is in front of them? Well, there are people who suck up the news just because it's in front of them. Don't. Do some triage and decide what you really need to read, watch, or listen to. Here are our suggestions:

For the morning:

- One (or maybe two) good newspapers. Preferably one national and one regional, if not hometown, so you'll know what's happening far and near.
- A bit of trustworthy news radio. We'd be partial to National Public Radio (NPR) even if one of us didn't work there.

But you may have other preferences. Choose what you feel covers the news in the best and fairest way. Your local all-news radio stations are your best bet for the most up-to-date information if there's an emergency in your backyard.

And in the evening:

- Good radio *or* television news. Either will give you an overview of what happened during the day.

And always, always consider the source: some sources are more partisan than others. Check out your local black newspapers and the news offered on black television and cable stations. Note that some media pay for interviews. Good ones never do.

All bets are off when tragedy strikes. We find comfort in our insatiable quest for news. Do what feels comfortable for you and your family.

Telling Your Children About Terrorism

This is a difficult talk to have with young children, and it's a delicate balance to strike. On the one hand, you want them to take joy in exploring life and their surroundings. On the other, you're painfully aware that the world they're growing up in is vastly different from the one you enjoyed as a child. We suggest using news events as they happen as a jump-off point of conversation. *Could that happen here? We hope not, but possibly. What would happen if it did? Mommy or Daddy would come to get you, or Grandma would, or Aunt Eileen. Someone you know and trust would come to get you.* (Here's a good time to reinforce the importance of having a plan and knowing how to check in.)

I, Too, Sing America

Some of the saddest fallout from the 9/11 attacks is the tendency of some people to question the patriotism of others because they disagree about the measures that are needed to keep America safe and free. Having different visions for how that should be accomplished doesn't make one anti-American—but it can make one a target for people who feel their vision should be the only legitimate one.

- *Don't allow others to slur your patriotism.* Black Americans have fought in every war in which America has engaged, and many paid the ultimate price. Black and American are not mutually exclusive terms.
- *Don't be an uncritical American.* Are we perfect? Hardly. As a country, we've done some things very well (moving forward after the civil rights movement), and have some areas where we need to improve (racial profiling, anyone?). Don't be blindly critical or blindly supportive. Be honest.
- *Be a good representative of America to non-Americans when you meet them here or abroad.* Often, their impressions of our country will be formed by you. Not the president, not the evening newscast, but the person who was nice enough to keep the automatic door from closing on their two-year-old child. Or the person who was kind enough to help them figure out how the subway card works, and which train to take. *You* are America for a lot of people who meet you.

We're All in This Together

The world is, in fact, getting smaller and smaller. Events that happen on one side of the globe have repercussions on the other. Things that affect our neighbors affect us. Be alert, report suspicious activity to the proper authorities, when warranted, and do what you can. We *are* all in this together, which is exactly why the Golden Rule has never been more appropriate.

Chapter 39

YOUR BEST POSSIBLE YOU

[Strong black women] taught me I was entitled to have the best in life by refusing to settle for less themselves.

Susan Fales-Hill, *Always Wear Joy: My Mother Bold and Beautiful*

Susan Fales-Hill, daughter of the incomparable singer/actress Josephine Premice, says her mother often reminded her in no certain terms that no matter how hectic life got, no matter how many demands were placed upon her, she was obligated to remember her own needs as a human being and woman. Good advice then—and now. Oprah Winfrey says the same thing, but a little differently; she describes it as living your best life. We call it finding a way to be the best possible you.

Find Your Bliss

In the flower-power 1960s, we were urged to follow our bliss—but don't you have to find it first? Think back to times that made you especially happy. What were you doing? Who was with you? Therein may lie the clue to a profession or volunteer career that will allow you to look forward to going into the office (or not, if it's a non-office-related job) every day. If, as the T-shirt saying goes, "Life is too short to drink bad wine," it's far too short to shackle yourself to a job that drains you because you hate it.

Remove the Toxins in Your Life

Do you really need a "friend" who is ultracompetitive with you, or ultracritical of you? Do you need a significant other who spends more time pointing out your liabilities than he or she does your assets? Do some relatives just love to drag you into their drama—but are never there when you need support? Ask yourself this crucial question: Do you feel better being near them, or worse? If the latter, steer clear.

Attitude Is Everything

We don't mean nose-in-the-air attitude, we mean positive attitude. Although it's annoying to hear the when-life-gives-you-lemons-make-lemonade speech, there's a kernel of truth in it. Looking at life through a positive lens, rather than peering at it through a negative one, actually enables us to tackle challenges more successfully. Studies have even shown that optimists live longer than pessimists and enjoy better health. Reason enough for your glass to be half full, not half empty.

Set Goals to Achieve What You Want

Sometimes half the getting is in the planning. If you want to stop renting and become a homeowner, for instance, recognize that as a goal and list the steps you'll need to accomplish it: regular savings, less splurging. Recognize that a starter house won't be your final house, but it may be the first step to the house of your deams. If going back to school to get a degree (or finish one) is a cherished goal, outline what you need to do to get it done, and start. Want to lose weight? Maybe the first step is breaking the weight loss into sections, to make it seem more achievable; each completed stage will then bring you closer to your goal. (*"I'm trying to lose thirty pounds—I lost my first ten, which means I'm a third of the way there!"*)

Be Responsible to Yourself and Others

- Keep your word. If you say you're going to do something, follow through.
- Guard your health.
- Stay away from situations you know might lead to destructive behaviors. (Are you a shopaholic? Then it's probably better for you to leave

your charge cards at home when you're "window shopping," so you don't accidentally buy what's in the window.)

- Take the keys when you're out with a friend who's had too much to drink—and be prepared to hand over yours to a designated driver if you're the person who has overindulged.
- Take your walks or runs with a friend, in safe places, even if it means a few laps around the local mall.

You're Still Black and in America

- Don't allow people—however well meaning—to isolate you from your cultural community or assume you're the exception to the rule. "I didn't mean you; I meant most black people" is not a compliment.
- Don't allow stereotypes to remain unchallenged. ("I'm surprised to hear you say that; I've lived in a black neighborhood all my life, and I've never seen what you described.")
- Don't accept racist observations or racist humor from anyone. You can object to the offense without becoming offensive yourself. ("Jack, you're the company president. If you think my objection to having the office party at a club that excludes blacks is being 'overly sensitive,' you might want to think instead about what it says about this company that you're willing to spend stockholders' money in that fashion.")
- Don't allow others' bad behavior to be projected onto you, simply because you both have one obvious thing in common. Just because a black celebrity is behaving badly doesn't mean you condone or imitate that behavior.
- Do speak up if you don't appreciate nonblacks who speak to you in what they think is "black talk." Let them know if you'd prefer not to be addressed as "girlfriend" or "homey."

The Superwoman Syndrome

Okay, so as the song says, you can bring home the bacon, fry it up in a pan—but do you have to clean up afterward and take out the trash, too? If you're juggling a bunch of balls, toss a couple to others, especially if they ask if they can help. There's no shame in saying yes! and taking them up on it, whether it's picking up cookies for Women's Day at church, giving your child a ride home from soccer practice, or offering to send out the save-the-date notices for your club's big fundraiser. Don't lift that bale all on your own—asking for help is a sign of sanity. And don't forget to offer to help when you see someone is as overwhelmed as you sometimes are.

Your Personal Style

We all can't be Audrey Hepburn or Diahann Carroll, but we can cover the basics before we leave the house: a clean face with minimal makeup (we've learned that dark glasses and lipstick make us look far more put together than we really are) and neat clothes are a good start, even on casual days. (For instance, if you're going out in sweats, make sure they don't have dog drool on one leg or the results of an especially productive burp dribbling down the back on one shoulder. . . .)

Clothes that you wear "out in the world" should fit properly, suit your style, and be in good shape. Safety pins are wonderful things to have for emergencies, but they shouldn't be a regular part of your wardrobe.

Entertaining: Whether it's a thrown-together meal for friends who dropped by or a long-planned party, remember that the most important part of entertaining is for you to make guests feel welcomed and cared for. (For details, see chapter 28, "Hostess with the Mostest."

Living Without Regrets

If we make the right choices, we tend not to regret them. A friend says that when she is faced with the decision about whether or not to do something, she asks herself, "When I look back ten years from now, will I be sorry I didn't do this?" If the answer is yes, she takes the plunge. If it's no, she passes. Basically what she's doing is looking ahead to imagine how today's decision might affect her in the long run. You can't always make important decisions this way, but it does help to examine your reasons for why you're contemplating something before you do it. ("Which do I want more—the raise this new promotion will give me, or more time with my family and friends?" or "Am I pressuring Stephen to go to this college because it's prestigious, or do I really think this is the school where he'll be the happiest?")

By all means, don't let your failure to spend time with family and friends be something you'll look back on and wish you'd done differently.

Being Present

"Yesterday is past; tomorrow is not promised, the present is all we have." That's certainly true, and it doesn't mean we shouldn't plan for the future. (Optimism, remember? It's good to think that we're going to *have* a future!) Being present means not counting on the future to take care of things that we should be addressing in the present. Don't fail to discipline yourself to save

what you can when you can, simply because you have this vague idea that you'll come into money later on. Unless Miss Cleo has told you that Publishers Clearing House is going to knock on your door in five years and two months, it's better to keep saving. Often, we spend so much time looking forward that we are not engaged in taking care of the present and being grateful for what we have right now. That friend you keep meaning to spend the afternoon with? Pick up the phone and make a date. That child you've been promising yourself to find and mentor? Check into the local chapter of Big Brothers and/or Big Sisters of America and start to help shape a life. That family you're dying to have, but Mr. Right seems infuriatingly elusive? Maybe talking to adoption agencies is the first step to making your own ideal family.

Humanity

"Community" can be as small as the group of people who make up the floor of your apartment building or as large as your neighborhood, political district, or ethnic affiliation. However you define it, we're bound together by common interests and obligations. Remember that you're part of a community—probably several communities—and be a responsible community member. Participate in your neighborhood block association. If you're a churchgoer, remember that financial contributions and involvement are important—even monied churches don't run themselves. If you're unhappy with a situation in your community, join your neighbors to help change it. ("The only public library in a three-mile radius will be closed three months from now if we don't petition the Board of Aldermen to reconsider. Please help us get enough signatures . . .") *E pluribus unum* ("out of many, one") isn't just a phrase on the back of our currency: it indicates there really *is* strength in numbers.

Handling Fame

"In the future, everyone will be famous for fifteen minutes." Artist Andy Warhol had it almost right—with all the publications devoted to the coverage of celebrities, it feels as if just about everyone *is* famous. Problem is, someone forgot to set the alarm, because this fascination with fame has gone way past its allotted time. If fame's searing spotlight swivels your way, remember the basics:

Tell the truth. Or if you can't, or don't want to, discuss a particular aspect of your life when you face the press, just say, "No comment."

Remember that fame is fickle. The public that adores you today could abhor you tomorrow.

You're still you. Just because your circumstances change doesn't mean you have to. Keep the people who were your friends before you became "all that" close to you; they'll keep you grounded.

You've heard it before. Never forget where you came from and always remember those who helped you get where you are now.

Celebrations, Big and Little

You know that milestones (turning twenty-one or sixty, graduating, getting married, etc.) are cause for celebration. But don't neglect other important things that aren't traditionally celebrated:

- Your childhood friends are all in the same city at the same time for the first time in years.
- Your best friend successfully completed chemotherapy.
- You paid off your credit-card debt.
- Your daughter finally decided to stop seeing the man who was making her miserable.
- You've kicked your nicotine habit.
- Your grandchild is starring in the school play.

These are all occasions that allow you to celebrate, whether it's you who has achieved a coveted goal or someone you know. Recognition and congratulations are in order.

Lifelong Learning

Learning doesn't start when we enter school or stop when we leave it. Someone we can't remember at the moment urged us to "live life like you'll die tomorrow, learn like you'll live forever." And even if you don't live forever, you will enjoy life a lot more when your mind is engaged and challenged by learning. Whether the learning is academic (taking a poetry class, learning a new language, finally grasping trigonometry), "just because" (tango lessons, cooking classes), or practical (swimming lessons, CPR instruction, computer classes), *do it*! As the ads proclaim: "A Mind Is a Terrible Thing to Waste." Don't waste yours.

From Techno-Peasant to Techno-Proficient

If a computer is that thing you dust around and everyone else uses, think about making friends with it. If you growl when all the pay phones on a street are broken or vandalized but you don't carry a cell phone because "I don't know how to work one of those things," and if you still can't program your VCR or set up your answering machine, consider some technical assistance. Virtually everyone older than the age of about ten (and sometimes considerably younger) can show you the basics of how to send e-mail and how to enter important numbers into your cell phone. (It's still in the box, isn't it? And you're paying for monthly service you're not using, aren't you?) It's not hard, and once you're set up, you'll wonder how you ever lived without such modern conveniences.

The Best You, Physically

You definitely owe it to yourself to stay as healthy as possible. You can start by eating well and getting some exercise. Eating well doesn't mean restricting yourself to a punishing diet (unless your health and your doctor dictate that)—it means eating a good balance of grains, fruits, vegetables, and proteins. It means using "good fats," such as olive oil and canola oil, to prepare your food and staying away from high-cholesterol-inducing saturated fats, or using them very sparingly. It means using fast food as an occasional treat, not a way of life. You can make small changes that, over time, can contribute to a big difference, especially controlling your portions. Eat fruit instead of drinking high-caloric fruit juice; you'll be consuming delicious fruit plus important fiber. Trade that chocolate-topped doughnut for whole wheat toast with a small amount of all-fruit preserves—you'll experience great taste, fiber, and no trans fats. Use ground turkey in your chili and spaghetti sauce, and enjoy the meals with less artery-clogging fat. Switch from whole milk to 2% or 1%—your taste buds won't be able to tell, but your scale will.

The U.S. government's dietary guidelines say that eating well is part of the battle; regular exercise is another. And it's not just for vanity's sake (although if vanity is enough to get you to put on your walking shoes, fine). As more Americans—and more Americans of color—slip into a state of obesity, the danger for diabetes and heart disease increases, too. Even a loss of ten pounds on an overweight person can lower blood pressure and lessen the risk of heart disease.

Type 2 diabetes (often referred to as adult onset diabetes) is at an all-time high in our community, and more black Americans are demonstrating signs of prediabetic conditions. Obesity (technically, thirty percent or more of the suggested maximum body weight for your height, gender, and age) is an important factor for developing diabetes. Controlling your weight by a reasonable diet and regular exercise are two huge steps toward keeping diabetes at bay (for more suggestions, go to www.diabetes.org). Gradual changes in your exercise routine, like your diet, can make a difference—you don't have to commit to becoming a marathon runner to get results.

- ♦ Walk a few flights of stairs instead of using elevators.
- ♦ At malls and grocery stores, park as far away from the store as you can and walk.
- ♦ Walk around the block a couple of times at work, or around your neighborhood when you're home. Increase the walk by five minutes every day until you reach your maximum.
- ♦ Talk someone into being your exercise buddy; you can encourage each other when one of you starts to lag.

Diet Scams and Fads

That old adage about "if it sounds to good to be true, it probably is" was on the money when it comes to diets and diet aids. Anything that promises to make you "lose twenty-five pounds in two weeks, naturally and healthily" isn't telling the truth. Nobody loses twenty-five pounds in two weeks without being seriously sick. Weight-control professionals tell us that safe weight loss is between 1.5 and 2.5 pounds a week. So those ads for miracle pills that will erase hunger or let you eat all that you want without gaining weight? Save your money. As Oprah likes to say about weight loss—and she's had some experience with it—"There are no short cuts. Look, if there was an easy way to do this, don't you think I would have found it by now?" Listen to the experts.

Necessary Tests

In addition to controlling our weight and getting some exercise, we need to be faithful about scheduling medical tests that can save our lives—and following through and keeping the appointments.

Yes, you're busy. And yes, a mammogram isn't the most fun way to spend the morning, but do it. Breast cancer affects women of color—especially African American women—disproportionately. Part of the reason it does is because we wait so late to have this important annual exam. Breast cancer caught early is curable almost ninety-five percent of the time. Reason enough to keep the appointment.

- ♦ *Don't let modesty be a barrier:* Worried about who's going to be doing the imaging? Most clinics have all-female technician staff; they're not only familiar with the female body, they *have* one.
- ♦ *Don't let money be the issue:* Most communities have free clinics or free-exam days where breast screenings are held. Call your local hospital or a branch of the American Cancer Society (www.cancer.org) to find out more.

Don't let gender be a barrier: If your significant other is putting off a prostate exam for all the reasons men do (the doctor's going to put a finger *where?!*), nag him until he goes. Or have a male friend he likes and respects nag him for you. Just make sure that the adults in your family get those critical exams by any means necessary. (No, Malcolm wasn't referring to medical exams back then when he coined the phrase, but he probably would say that to be black and know the statistics on cancer in the black community and to not do anything to protect yourself is akin to genocide.)

Oh, and one more nag: Need we say that cutting out smoking cigarettes and drinking excessive alcohol will prolong your life and greatly lessen the probability of contacting some of these diseases to begin with?

Tests That Could Save Your Life

For Everyone:

- Cholesterol (HCL/LDL, lipids)
- Blood pressure
- Eye exam for glaucoma
- Occult blood test in stool
- Colonoscopy
- Blood test to screen for diabetes

Just for women:

- Mammogram (annually, after age forty)
- Pap smear (annually)
- Bone density test (every other year after age sixty or sixty-five)

Just for men:

- Prostate screening

Brushing Up . . .

And don't forget your dental checkup. Besides making sure you have the brightest smile to flash, a regular checkup can make sure your gums are healthy. And since more adults lose teeth to gum disease than tooth decay, that's something to follow up on, isn't it?

The Best You, Spiritually

If you're a regular churchgoer, don't allow a mountain of unsorted laundry or lengthy grocery list to keep you from enjoying the church and your church community. Yes, clean clothes and a well-stocked pantry do make the week easier, but being fed spiritually helps to keep you on an even keel, too, so don't "starve" yourself.

If you're not a churchgoer, the inner you still needs time alone. You might want to spend time meditating or just sitting somewhere peaceful and thinking quiet thoughts. You can do it at home by going into a room and closing the door, turning off the phone, and just settling into the silence.

Or maybe you're an outdoor type: a walk through a local park, a hike, a stroll along an uncrowded stretch of beach or lakefront (feeding the ducks can be very therapeutic!)—all can help you to unwind and face the world again.

Family is another source of spiritual replenishment. And family doesn't just mean blood relatives, but the friends we choose to make part of our extended family. They're not only relatives and companions, they're part of a critical support network for our balance and mental health. Appreciate people for that, and be supportive in turn.

Try to manage to see close friends regularly if you're physically able. If they live too far away for that, frequent calls and e-mails can keep the bond strong. Knowing someone has your back—and that you have hers—can make all the difference.

The Best You, Romantically

A favorite William Wordsworth poem begins "the world is too much with us." We don't know many couples who wouldn't agree. It might be impractical for you and your honey to steal away to an island paradise every couple months, but dinner and a movie you both want to see are a good start. Or a visit to a museum exhibition with drinks afterward. Or an evening in, perhaps with another couple, sharing laughter and a meal. We get pulled in so many different directions all of the time, any time spent as part of a twosome that reinforces the fact that you *are* a couple will help you start to feel like one again in no time. Other suggestions we've heard and liked:

- *Pajama Party for Two.* Ditch those boxers and ratty pj's (yes, they're comfortable, but they're not romantic!) for an evening and put on better night clothes (maybe the special occasion you're saving them for is now?). Bring a tray with some take-out food up to bed and snuggle while you share Thai food and a couple of romantic DVDs.
- *Early-to-Bed Night.* Instead of sprawling over the living room sofa, why not take the papers, all those magazines you've wanted to read but haven't gotten to, and a cup of tea or cocoa up to bed a couple hours before you normally hit the sack and read side by side?

- *Long Drive to Nowhere.* You don't have to have a destination in mind, just a scenic route and maybe a restaurant along the way. Better yet, pack an elegant picnic lunch. Then get in the car, admire the scenery, and stop somewhere along the way. Who knows? This could turn into a sunny day tradition.
- *You've Got Skills Date.* Always secretly wanted the two of you to in-line skate but never got up the nerve to ask? Or wanted to ride a bike trail from point A to point B? Or take a yoga class? Or learn how to refinish that old end table your grandmother let you have? Propose a try-it-out date. You can bond over picking up a new skill or laugh together when you decide this one isn't the glue that binds.
- *Dance Date.* You say the last time you learned a new dance it was the hustle? Maybe it's time to update your dancing repertoire. Sign the two of you up for a dance class. The rhythm, the music, the body contact, the ability to move together as one . . . could be the start of something very romantic.
- *Wine Appreciation Class or Cooking Class.* There's nothing like being able to drink or eat your homework. If the two of you enjoy and want to know more about it, maybe a cooking class would be fun—especially if you can get another couple to take it with you.

The Best You, Financially

Do you know if anyone has tried to use your name or identification to open credit in their own name? Do you know what your credit score is and why it matters? A good credit rating can be a tremendous asset—you're offered lower interest rates, higher lines of credit, and in the event that you need it, bigger loans if you're deemed credit-worthy. So consider doing these things to protect your credit:

- Make photocopies of your credit cards. Place your credit cards on a copy machine and photocopy the back and front (and don't leave the extra photocopies lying about!). File these copies in a safe place. If you're ripped off, you can quickly and easily provide your card numbers to credit card companies to cancel your stolen cards and request new ones. Being robbed is stressful enough—keep the stress level lower by saving yourself from having to wade through your checking account statements and bills.
- Savvy money managers suggest that you shred as much as possible to try to ensure that your identity isn't stolen. They suggest shredding credit cards, bills, bank statements, ATM receipts, credit card receipts, and preapproved credit card offers.

- With identity theft at an all-time high, it's wise to check your credit report from time to time. Make sure nobody else is using your name or Social Security number to establish accounts in their names with your numbers by requesting a credit report once a year or every six months. If you notice suspicious activity on an account (a charge card you didn't ask for or don't use that still has a bill; several charges on cards you do use but didn't make, etc.), notify the card company immediately. Most cards don't have more than a $50 liability—many don't hold the theft victim liable at all—but it's easier to nip theft in the bud than it is to retrace a thief's steps and try to correct bad-faith purchases he's made in your name but hasn't paid for.

Pay Yourself First

This is the mantra of bankers and financial advisors: when you're paid, put aside what you can, consistently, in a savings account for yourself. It can be as little as $20 a week, but if you get paid weekly, that adds up. Such savings can become an important nest egg to fall back on if there's an emergency or a situation where money is really needed. You'd be surprised how satisfying it is to watch your money grow. If you are paid via direct deposit, many banks can divert funds into a savings or money market account on a regular basis.

Don't Spend Everything You Make

Just because something is on sale doesn't mean you have to buy it. Just because everyone else has an item doesn't mean you have to have one, too—especially if you don't really care about it. Just because there is an updated version of your stereo, car, computer, cell phone, or DVD player doesn't mean you have to go out and buy it or upgrade.

When the Name on the Bag Isn't Yours

Wearing brand names on the outside of your clothes isn't announcing how sophisticated you are—it's giving the clothing manufacturer free advertising. (One Italian designer decided to strike back in his ads with this very effective motto: "When Your Own Initials Are Enough.") A monogram here or there on an eyeglass temple or watch face might be unavoidable if you like the style. *But unless you're in the entertainment industry, you really don't want to make a habit of turning yourself into a walking billboard of brand names.*

The Changing Job Market

Maybe you've been downsized in a corporate merger. Maybe your company's gone bankrupt. Maybe you took several years out of the workforce to raise your children or look after a sick parent. If there are gaps in your job history, consult a person or guide that will help you restructure your résumé to minimize inconsistencies. For instance, listing your work experience by paid and unpaid (volunteer) work can be helpful. Those years you were raising children also involved skills: fundraising for your school's PTA, running your church's after-school tutoring service, volunteering for a local politician's campaign—all of these are jobs, whether or not you received a salary for doing them.

Preparing for the Future

Your Earthly Possessions

To paraphrase the dairy industry's classic ad: Got Will? If you don't, get cracking. There are several computer programs that can help you write a will or a living will (in the event that you have special considerations, don't want extraordinary measures to keep you alive, etc.), which you can then take to a lawyer or notary public to make everything official. If you do have a will, update it periodically. If the last time you wrote a will you had two children and now you have three, keeping your wishes current will make things much easier later on when you won't be able to make those corrections yourself.

If you have young children, you need to appoint a legal guardian for them, just in case. And it's essential that the guardian know that he or she has been given that honor. Don't, under any circumstances, let that special person be surprised when the will is read. That's not fair to the potential guardian, to you, or to your children. If your children are old enough to help make the decision, let them, stressing this is *hypothetical:* "Remember that movie we saw on TV? If something like that happened to Daddy and me, who would you want to live with? I'm pretty sure that won't ever happen, but you're eleven, and I thought we should take your thoughts into consideration as we're making these just-in-case plans. . . ."

Their plans might be different from yours, but it would be good to be able to talk about the whos and whys of guardianship *("I want to make sure you're taken care of, no matter what happens. . . .")* well before it becomes a practical necessity.

Organ Donation

Organ donation really is the gift of life, and there's a desperate need for organ donors in the black community. The reasons people don't sign up for donation are varied. Sometimes it's just too disturbing to contemplate *("They're going to put my heart in someone else's body? I don't think so!")*. Some people feel their religion would frown on an organ donation or transplant. Some are superstitious *("They're going to let me die just so somebody else can have my kidney!")*. But think about it: If you're in an accident or otherwise die suddenly, and your heart, liver, or kidneys could allow someone to live to see his or her children grow up, wouldn't you want that option if the situation were reversed?

Organ donation is as easy as checking off a box on your driver's license renewal application. Or you can go to www.organdonor.gov, the U.S. Department of Health's Web site that will connect you to your state's organ donor registry. It's quick, it's simple—and a donated organ could save your life or the life of someone you love.

Saving for Retirement

If you're like most of us, your money is being pulled in fifteen different directions: health care, house note, car note, maybe school tuition, church contributions, groceries, . . . but somewhere in there, you want to remember to put a little something in the pot for your retirement. With the U.S. population rapidly aging and the economy constantly in flux, more of us than ever will be retiring soon. And unlike our parents and grandparents, who often had made provisions for an adequate—or better—retirement, today's impending retirees are going to have to be more aggressive. So when a windfall comes your way, tuck in into the retirement fund.

- Consult a financial advisor for ways you can increase your retirement savings.
- Determine what the balance should be between what you should be maintaining of stocks, bonds, and your savings account.
- If Uncle Sam sends you a tax refund consider putting some or all of it into your retirement fund. You'll thank yourself when you're finally able to retire.

Sophisticated Gents

And finally, a few reminders for the brothers, our sophisticated gents. Some things men we love have taught us over the years and that we're passing on:

- A gentleman is judged by his character, not by his wealth.
- A gentleman doesn't talk about or display his wealth.
- A gentleman never disrespects women.
- A gentleman eases the way for others, if possible, in business.
- A gentleman works hard and earns his own way; he doesn't assume he's entitled to anything but an equal opportunity to prove his worth.
- A gentleman offers his seat to an invalid, elderly person, or lady.
- A gentleman doesn't discuss his wife or her business with his boys.

- A gentleman doesn't lose control of his temper when the going gets rough.
- A gentleman doesn't drink more than he should.
- A gentleman will not let a friend drive drunk.
- A gentleman doesn't wear his hat or cap indoors.
- A gentleman still opens doors for ladies.
- A gentleman cherishes his mother, grandmothers, sisters, and aunts.
- A gentleman remembers where he came from.
- A gentleman celebrates the accomplishments of others.
- A gentleman keeps up with current affairs and can discuss them.
- A gentleman supports his community.
- A gentleman is willing to try new things without complaint.
- A gentleman remembers birthdays, anniversaries, etc.
- A gentleman keeps confidences when they're told to him.

Chapter 40

CONTINUING THE TRADITIONS

There will always be some curveballs in your life.
Teach your children to thrive in that adversity.

Jeanne Moutoussamy-Ashe

The great, barrier-breaking professional tennis player Althea Gibson liked to say she was keenly aware that she got to where she was by standing on someone's shoulders. She was paying homage to the people who had come before her, both known and unknown, whose presence and sacrifice had allowed her to become who she was. And she was acknowledging her debt to them.

We, too, are where we are because the people who came before us have lifted us up. Sometimes we know them and can thank them. Sometimes we don't, but we can still thank them and acknowledge our debt to them by carrying ourselves as if our grandmothers were looking over our shoulders. Their greatest pride was when someone complimented them on their children by saying, "That child's been raised right."

It was good practice then, and it's good practice now. No matter how much they protest, it is your responsibility to instill in your children the basic manners we all learned growing up. So to enable you to carry on the traditions begun by your family and your community, this chapter includes some advice for the next generation.

When They're Away from Home

How often has someone complimented you on your child's manners, causing you to say to yourself, "*I wish he used them at home!*" Well, if your children can't be perfect all the time, it's nice they're saving their "company manners" when *they're* the company—even if it is somewhere else and you don't get to see the end result of your good home training.

Let your children know what you expect of them when they're in someone else's home:

- Abide by the house rules.
- Be respectful to your friends' parents.
- Be respectful of others' property.
- At mealtimes, offer to help serve or clear or whatever the hostess wants.
- Check in with home. If you're supposed to be home by five o'clock and you're invited to stay for dinner, you need to get permission to stay and call home to give some idea of when you'll need to be picked up.
- Thank the host and/or hostess for having you as you're leaving.

Out and About on Their Own

Whether the situation is a group movie outing, shopping expedition, dance, or church school trip, emphasize to your child that you expect him to behave as if you were right next to him. Hollering, shoving, squealing? Those things shouldn't be happening. Nor will you abide superloud cell phone conversations or loud exclamations that are basically just showing off. ("What? You Charge *How much* for that burger?!" simply isn't the way to tell the waitress that you think the restaurant's hamburger is a little pricey.)

Family Traditions

Birthdays (Theirs)

Everyone celebrates birthdays differently, but most of us feel pleased when our birthdays are remembered. Some families mark them by allowing the birthday boy or girl (or Mom or Dad) to choose his or her favorite dinner. Others have a flat-out party every year. If there's something special your family members love to do, do it, and emphasize to younger children why the ritual is special: "*When your big brother turned three, he told us he wanted fried chicken for every single birthday, so Chicken Birthday Dinner has become what we do on his day. Now you're old enough to choose your special birthday dinner, so we're telling you ahead of time so you can have plenty of time to think about what you want.*" Everyone wants to feel they're the center of their family's attention for a day.

BIRTHDAYS (EVERYONE ELSE'S)
Try to remember everyone's special day: mark it on the family calendar or have your computer send you a reminder. Plan to add a few days' "padding" in your reminder system for out-of-town birthdays.

When you forget a birthday? Call, or send an "I blew it!" card, to let your friend or relative know you're thinking of her—you're just a little slow at the moment. . . .

If the birthday is on or near Christmas, try not to roll it into the holiday. Most Christmas babies will tell you they always felt they got less than their siblings did because their birthday fell on the one day of the year when everyone gets presents! Two special days that fall on the same day still deserve two special observances. We know one mother who celebrates her Christmas baby with a birthday party for him in July each year.

Cultural Appreciation

Plan activities as a family to explore cultural traditions. Keep abreast of museum exhibits, books, plays, and movies that reinforce your child's appreciation for his history and culture. Researching family genealogy and collecting photographs of your ancestors is an excellent way for your child to learn about his family and the contributions each member has made to the family you are today.

Team Sports

Team sports teach principles of character, cooperation, and fair competition. Boys and girls both enjoy team sports and should be encouraged to participate.

If your child is involved in team sports, stress to her the importance of:

- Attending practice regularly, as scheduled.
- Arriving on time, or even early.
- Being a good host to the visiting team. Treating them as she'd like to be treated.
- Helping out with team fundraisers.
- Not whining when a call doesn't go her way.
- Never trying to injure a teammate or opponent purposefully.

- Being a good sport when she loses.
- Remembering that, in the end, it's just a game. Real life will go on.

Public Performances

- If he's been chosen to be in a school play, is going to recite a poem, or sing a song with the rest of his class, remind him that rehearsals are important and help him to memorize his lines.
- If he's part of a group effort (a play, a choir) he should remember that his performance counts—he shouldn't slack off on the assumption that his fellow performers will make up for what he isn't doing. (What if they *all* thought that way?!)
- If he's going to be in a spelling bee or will be participating in a debate, stress the need for him to try his best, but remind him there will be other competitions throughout life; this one won't make or break him.

Clubs and Organizations

Whether it's the Boy or Girl Scouts, the French Club, or Jack and Jill Club, the basics are the same. Your child should:

- Attend meetings and show up on time.
- Help with fundraisers that are designed to benefit the group or another designated cause.
- Wear the appropriate clothing. If a uniform or a certain style of dress (dark pants and white shirt, a Cub Scout uniform, etc.) is required, be sure to wear it.
- Act in a way that reflects well on the group when you're out with them. (*"We would have those Girl Scouts back to our museum anytime. They really listened to the docent and asked great questions as they went along!"*)
- Understand the importance of paying group dues and fees *on time.*
- Abide by the group's rules.

School Days

When your child grows up and goes out into the real world, she'll find out soon enough how great she had it in school. For now, though, school *is* her work, and she needs to do it well. For beginners, your child should:

- Arrive at school on time.
- Arrive ready to work.
- Refrain from distracting other students from their work.

Homework

Encourage your child to get correct and complete homework assignments (no sense in doing all that math if you're studying the wrong page, hmmm?) and to call a classmate if he doesn't know the assignment or wasn't in school that day. Also remind your child to:

- Hand your homework in on time.
- Make it neat. A teacher with thirty-five papers to correct doesn't want to see that seventeen of them are smudged, torn, and filled with lots of cross-outs.
- Never do anyone's homework for them—or let them do yours for you.
- Complete quizzes and tests as best you can.
- Never cheat, and never help someone else cheat.
- Keep your locker organized so you can easily find what you need between classes.
- Keep your backpack organized so that your papers aren't smushed and crumpled at the bottom.

Respect for—and Occasionally Disputing—Authority

While your child is at school, the administrators, teachers, and coaches are your child's protectors and guardians. Emphasize to your child that she should be respectful to the adults at school at all times. If your child has a disagreement with a teacher, instruct her not to resolve it herself. She should come home, tell you what happened, and let you and the teacher sort it out.

Participating in School Activities

Book learning is a big part of what goes on in school, but it's not the only part. Encourage your child to become involved in school activities—clubs, organizations, and team sports. These things will put him in contact with a wide spectrum of people and allow others to see him as a different person than who he is in the classroom. Perhaps he's stumped by math but is a formidable soccer player. Maybe he can't sink a basketball to save his life, but he can cause jaws to drop when he sings the show stopping finale of the school play. Remind him we all shine in different ways, and encourage him to find his own light—and not to hide it.

Odd Boy or Girl Out

One of the biggest pressures in school is to be like everyone else—which is funny, because when we're adults, what we want to do is stand out from the crowd. But not as kids. If your child worries that she isn't like everyone else, point out to her that some of the most famous people in the world were different from their peers: Martin Luther King, Jr., Albert Einstein, Maya Angelou. All started out as "different"—and ended up magnificent. Encourage her to think for herself, to be comfortable with her differences, and to keep things in perspective: junior high and high school don't last forever. Kids who don't fit in now are often sought out *for* their individualism later.

Hazing, Bullies, and Other Bummers

If you think your child is being bullied psychologically or physically, it's vitally important that the situation be addressed. Recent years have seen an uptick in teen suicides and sometimes suicides in children as young as eight or nine: in virtually every case, bullying had made the child's life so intolerable that he or she chose to end it far too early. Help protect your child, even when you're not there.

Keep lines of communication open so he feels comfortable talking to you about what's happening in school. He may not always discuss it directly: "That mean kid, Calvin? He's been hitting Joshua at lunch every day. . . ." Joshua might not be the only kid Calvin is pounding on. Dig a little deeper, gently.

If you hear a child has been a particular problem for other children, have a word with the teacher and let school authorities know you're concerned via a letter or e-mail. It's always better to have a tangible record of these kinds of communications. Unfortunately, sometimes schools are reluctant to rock the boat if the complaint is only verbal.

If your child has been physically attacked, take photos of the abuse so you can share them with school authorities—and go see the school authorities right away. They need to see any marks or bruises while the injuries are fresh.

Inquire about your school district's policy on bullying. Stress to your child that she is never to bully another child. If you hear that she has, confront your child about it. Explain what the consequences will be if she bullies again, and have her apologize to the child she has wronged.

If the bullying is hazing—punishment as the price of admission to get into a club or organization—check to see what the school's rules are regarding such organizations, and inform the principal that hazing is going on. Follow up with a letter.

Racial slurs or incidences should be dealt with by you swiftly and directly.

Cleanliness Is Next To . . .

Impossible, if you're the parent of a young teenage boy. We don't want to stereotype, but at that age, girls are cleaner—if only because they want a clean "canvas" for their makeup! (We'll get to that in a moment.) But not their gender opposites. Apparently, being stinky is somehow connected to young men's budding masculinity. (Go figure.) So while preadolescents and adolescents are growing into themselves, tell them what the essentials are:

- Brush your teeth twice a day: once in the morning, once at night. (And maybe after that garlic jalapeño burger?)
- Floss once a day. (When we asked the dentist years ago, "Do I have to floss?", he cheerfully replied, "Only if you want to keep your teeth!" So we floss regularly. Feel free to use the specter of a toothless adulthood if it gets them to floss.)
- Bathe or shower daily. (You might opt for a daily bath in warm weather and/or quick washups daily in extremely cold weather. Many Europeans are astonished by how often Americans bathe, but we say *vive la différence!* While those hormones are zinging around, teens can be especially fragrant, and hot weather exacerbates the problem. Stress how much more pleasant they are to be around when they have a regular relationship with soap and water.)
- Deodorant does exactly what it implies: it *de-odorizes.* (Let your youngsters choose their own deodorant. They'll probably use it more often if they do—and that's what you want, isn't it?)
- Hair should be clean and neat and conform to school rules. If the rules say no dye, that green streak will have to wait until summer (or use the shampoo-out kind just for the weekend). (If your child's school allows Afros but not huge ones, he or she shouldn't show up looking like Bootsy Collins or Angela Davis in their heyday.)
- Regarding body ornamentation, pierced ears are probably acceptable (girls, anyway), if the earrings are small and not too dangly or distracting. However, hoops and studs for noses, tongue studs, and jewelry for pierced eyebrows, upper lips, and anywhere else we forgot to mention all need to stay in the jewelry box until it's party time.
- Ankle bracelets, waist chains? Uh-uh.

Also, girls can save their bare midriffs for parties—preferably beach parties—and boys can save their bare arms for wherever it is men wear tank tops (the same beach?). Neither are appropriate for school.

Dressing Your Age

Here's where, we're told, girls are more difficult than boys. Every girl wants her first pair of heels, and age-appropriate heels are a good thing. Those spiky stilettos she can barely walk in? They belong on someone who doesn't still sleep with her teddy bear.

Many girls are avidly interested in making themselves up and dressing to look much older than they actually are. If you've been to a high school prom recently, you've probably gasped at the skintight, plunging gowns and the ultrasophisticated hair.

Call us old fogies, but we say there is time enough for that later. Let's leave them something to look forward to when they're older. So we're hoping you'll encourage the young lady in your life to remember:

- What she wears telegraphs who she is to people who don't know her. If she's uncomfortable with men whistling at her in the streets, if she squirms at the looks she's getting on the bus, she may need to reconsider her wardrobe.
- There are "party clothes" and "school clothes," and while one could, we suppose, wear school clothes to a party, one cannot wear party clothes to school. The glittery tops, the micro-minis, the midriff-baring tube tops, the gold eye shadow, . . . none of that goes with a book bag. And most schools don't allow it, anyway.
- Too much makeup doesn't make her look sophisticated—it just makes her look like she's wearing too much makeup. Less is more becoming.

If her friends are allowed to dress more provocatively than you're comfortable with, simply tell her that's between them and their mothers—but as her mother, these are her dress guidelines.

Hello? Cell Phone Use

Yes, we give them cell phones so we can keep in touch and make sure they're safe, but cell phones aren't toys. Tell your child that his cell phone comes with rules:

- Cell phones are to be turned off when he is in school and at other places where cell phones are inappropriate.
- Is he text-messaging like crazy? Remind him that the cost of this service adds up, and it shouldn't be used indiscriminately—unless he is going to pay for the service.

- Text messages shouldn't be sent as a high-tech form of whispering. Just as it's rude to leave others out of the conversation, it's rude to communicate electronically while he is in the room with other people.

Helping Out at Home

Even the youngest children can do this, and should be encouraged to. Setting the table, taking recyclables to the bin, picking up the newspaper each morning, filling (and emptying) the dishwasher. All these tasks make children feel as if they're an important part of their households. In addition to being loved, they're needed.

Exposing Children to New Experiences

One of the best gifts we can give our children is the expansion of their worlds through new experiences. Visits to museums, trips to cultural events, regular outings to the library (we feel about library cards the way American Express feels about its product: Don't leave home without it), all serve to show us more of the world. Emphasize to your child that going to cultural events is not a chore, it's an adventure. And if she grows up doing these things, chances are she'll appreciate them enough that *her* children will, too.

Travel is another way to capitalize on new experiences. Whether at home or abroad, encourage your child to enjoy meeting new people, to immerse herself in a different culture, and to respect the local customs of wherever you are. She'll gain a better understanding of the world at large and also gain a better appreciation for her own country.

What Every Young Person Should Know

In case you were wondering, there are some basics that we think children should know at certain ages.

Ages Two to Five

- How to say hello clearly without turning away.
- How to say please and thank you.
- How to respond to basic questions from friends and family (*"What's your name?" "Is this your doll?" "Would you put that cup on the table for me?" "How old are you?"*).
- To begin to recognize when he has done something he shouldn't and how to respond: "I'm sorry" (for hitting my friend, pulling the dog's tail, writing in the book Daddy was reading, etc.).

- Respect for elders.
- To know his name, his parents' names, and his phone number, in case of emergency.

Ages Six to Ten

- How to shake hands firmly and look adults in the eye when being introduced.
- How to carry on a basic conversation in more than one word or syllable (*"Sammy, I hear you're in the third grade this year. How is it?" "It's HARD—but I like my teacher. She lets us draw every day."*).
- How to express preferences for things without whining (*"Mom, I hate okra! May I have the leftover broccoli instead?"*).
- How, if she's lost or scared, to tell a teacher or policeman her parents' phone number.
- How to call 911. (Practice dialing on a phone while the receiver is on the hook, and coach her through telling the dispatcher what he needs to know: *"My mom fell down and hit her head and she's bleeding. She won't wake up!"*)
- How to take a simple phone message.
- How to pick up after herself.
- How to feed her pets.
- How to write a basic thank-you note:

> *Dear Auntie Kare,*
> *Thank you for the cool game you gave me for my birthday. I already beat my dad!*
>
> *Love,*
> *Jordan*

- How to sit still for up to an hour in church, at a concert, or during a play, without squirming or acting out.
- To know her parents' names, home address, and emergency phone numbers.

Ages Eleven to Seventeen

- How to speak to his friends' parents and siblings.
- How to flatly refuse cigarettes, alcohol, and drugs.
- How not to be afraid to say no to things he knows he shouldn't be doing.

- How to sometimes put his wants behind others' ("*Grandma, you can have the last brownie. I had two yesterday—and I know you love chocolate!*").
- How to tell the truth, even if it's inconvenient or awkward. ("*No, Jacob's mother isn't going to be home; she has to take Amina to Brownies. Does that mean I can't go?*").
- How to walk away from, rather than toward trouble.
- How to speak to the police (see chapter 42, "In Case You're Wondering").
- How to help around the house, whether it's hauling recyclables, babysitting for younger siblings, doing the dishes, setting the table, walking the dog, or cleaning the hamster's cage. (*Hey, whose pets are these, anyway?*)

The Payoff

All this struggling to rear a child and where does it get you? You're helping to raise a child who will grow into an adult you'd like to know.

Part VIII

AND FURTHERMORE

More Proof Your Mother Was Right!

Odds and ends you wanted to know

but were afraid to ask and

two *very* opinionated lists

Chapter 41

APPLAUSE!

♦♦♦

A singer starts by having his instrument as a gift from God . . .
When you have been given something in a moment of grace,
it is sacrilegious to be greedy.

Marian Anderson

You've waited and waited to see the play that had all the critics raving, and it's finally come to your town. You stood in line for two hours to get prime tickets—and you had to work overtime to pay for them. But you figured it would be worth all the trouble once you entered the darkened theater and the play began . . .

. . . And it *would* have been—except for the couple in your row who arrived well into the first act, stepped on your feet getting to their seats, crackled the cellophane on their chocolate-covered raisins, and, to top it all off, chatted throughout the performance, much to everyone's annoyance!

Maybe they didn't know any better. But don't let that be *your* excuse. Here are a few guidelines that can help everyone enjoy the movie, play, or music.

Movies

- Do arrive on time so that you don't disturb others.
- Don't talk to the characters on the screen during the film ("Girl, let the man kiss you!").

- Do take your children to age-appropriate movies so that you don't disturb others explaining every scene to them.
- Don't take children to inappropriate movies (i.e., those with violence, nudity, or bad language).
- Don't rest your feet on the seat in front of you (or anywhere else!).
- Do refrain from critiquing the film aloud; we don't need to know you think you'd have been a better director than Spike.
- Don't purchase a single ticket at a multiscreen theater and sneak into other screenings.
- Do let a theater employee know (as you're leaving) that you've spilled your snacks and made a mess.
- At drive-in theaters, don't park in nondesignated areas, honk your horn, leave your lights on, play loud music during the movie, or encourage a woman to go alone to the snack counter.

Theaters

- If you're in the lobby, go into the theater when the lobby lights flash.
- Don't rest your head on your hand, sigh loudly, or otherwise appear bored.
- Don't eat snacks in the theater; do this in the lobby during intermission.
- If you have a coughing or sneezing fit, leave your seat until it passes.

Concerts

- Don't stand during a performance; you may obstruct the view of others behind you.
- Don't sing or hum along with a familiar song, let alone dance to it.
- Don't shove your way through a large crowd.
- At outdoor concerts, if a picnic is part of the event, take your trash and garbage with you when you go.

Symphony

- Do dress appropriately; some evenings (such as opening night) may require special attire. (See chapter 14, "Glad Rags").
- Don't hum along (please!).
- Don't applaud between movements.

Opera

- Do applaud when the conductor comes to the podium.
- Do applaud, if you want to, at the end of an aria or act.

All-Purpose Rules

- Don't bring your video recorder to any of these events, as most venues have rules against using them during the performance. The same is true for cameras and tape recorders.
- Do turn off your cell phone or pager. You can check during intermissions for messages and return the urgent ones.
- Do, as a rule, remove your hat. Men should always do so, women only if the hat is large and can obstruct others' view.
- Don't bathe yourself in strong cologne, perfume, or after-shave lotion—a wave of your favorite scent can be offensive to others. (See chapter 4, "Best Foot Forward.")
- Do leave your children home if they aren't capable of sitting through a performance without talking and fidgeting.
- Don't leave during a performance unless it's absolutely necessary.
- Do refrain from complaining about an awful performance until you're safely in your car or home. That way, you can be sure you haven't hurt anyone's feelings.
- Do remember that seats are sold on a per-person basis. If you bring your child to an event, you must pay for a seat for him—even if he chooses to sit on your lap instead.
- Don't kick the seat in front of you.
- Don't assume that just because there are empty seats in the front of the theater or concert hall that they have your name on them!
- Do carry cough drops (sans plastic wrappers or cellophane, please) if you are afraid that your coughing (or clearing your throat) might be a distraction to those around you.

Chapter 42

IN CASE YOU'RE WONDERING

Space didn't allow us to put every single thing we wanted to in this book, but we saved this chapter for the little odds-and-ends questions that pop up and deserve answers, too. Meanwhile, in case you were wondering:

Q: Are there things I absolutely, positively shouldn't ask someone?

A: We think there are. Although the recent trend, buttressed by a slew of talk shows, has been for people to tell all their business to people they hardly know—and conversely, to ask intimate questions of people they hardly know—we think there are things you can and should refrain from asking: Have you gained a lot of weight, or are you pregnant? How much do you make? What did you pay for your house/car/dress? You don't look too hot; are you sick? What does the doctor say about the diagnosis? Is it terminal?

Q: Is it tacky to use a personalized license plate frame?

A: Lots of people use the frame that holds their license plates to display their fraternal associations ("Omega Brother"), alumni status ("Hampton University"), challenge or accomplishment mastered ("Boston Marathon, 1984"), or religious belief ("I Love Jesus"). Best to leave alone anything sexually suggestive ("Your Place or Mine?") and anything politically controversial that could invite aggressive response from others ("I'm pro-choice"; "It's a black thang").

Q: What do I do if I'm stopped by the police?

A: Pull over as soon as it's safe to do so. Remain in the car unless the officer asks you to get out. Have your license and registration ready. If you have to reach into your purse or your glove compartment, inform the officer *before* you begin to do this ("I keep the registration in the glove compartment; I'm going to have to open it to get it out for you") so he knows exactly what you're going to do. You may ask why you've been stopped, but if you don't agree with the reason (you didn't run that red light; it was turning from yellow to red when you passed through it), don't argue with the officer. You can always choose the option of going to traffic court and defend yourself there.

If you're asked to exit the car and wait at the side of the road while the officer conducts a search of your car, do it. If you speak to the officer in a neutral tone, he'll usually respond in kind. If you disagree with the officer's interpretation of the situation, don't challenge him at that moment; veteran police officers tell us this only angers them more and puts you at a further disadvantage. Complain at a station house *after* you and the officer have parted ways. If you are unfortunate enough to be arrested or ticketed, the officer's badge number is on all the required paperwork, and you can identify him that way.

Q: May I drop by someone's house without calling? What if it's a good friend's home?

A: This varies from place to place and with individual preference. In many urban areas, where schedules are hectic and private time is precious, calling ahead—even if it's from a pay phone or your cell phone at the curb—is a common courtesy, since you don't want to be an intrusion or want your host to feel obligated. Lots of things may prevent a person from rushing to the door if she doesn't know who's on the other side; women or elderly people of either gender who live alone might hesitate. A person who's brought work home won't want to be disturbed. Neither will a couple who's planned a romantic evening alone. Even if you suspect a good friend would love to see you, try to call.

In many places, particularly the South, people enjoy impromptu visits and take pleasure in the unexpected friend who drops by to say hello. Too, during a bereavement period, it's fine to stop by and offer condolences to a family in mourning, especially if you're coming with flowers, food, etc. Emphasize that you just wanted to check on them, that you don't expect or want to be entertained, and always, always ask if there is anything you can do. (See chapter 35, "And This, Too, Shall Pass," and chapter 36, "Swing Low, Sweet Chariot," for more suggestions.)

Q: Help! I'm at a cocktail party where they're passing hors d'oeuvres, but there's no place to put those little toothpicks and plastic spear things the hors d'oeuvres came on. What do I do?

A: A good hostess will leave small plates somewhere obvious so you'll know you can discard these here. Never put them back on the serving tray or in an ashtray. If you don't see a discard plate, just roll the picks in a napkin until you find a wastebasket. If you order a sandwich and it comes with toothpicks in it, remove them before eating and place them on the edge of your plate.

Q: I drove by someone today who was obviously having car trouble; how can I help the next time this happens? I want to be a Good Samaritan, but I don't want to get carjacked or mugged trying to do the right thing.

A: If it's car trouble and not an accident, call the state Highway Patrol from a roadside phone, your cell phone, or a pay phone, and inform them there is a disabled car and stranded motorist near the such-and-such exit of your highway: "I'm on the New England Thruway, and there's a family in a stalled car just past the downtown Bridgeport exit." If you spot an accident, especially if you think someone has been hurt, call 911.

Q: What happens if I'm the stranded motorist?

A: If you have a car phone, call 911 and report your location. If others stop and ask if they can assist you, remain in the car, and ask them to call the Highway Patrol for you.

Q: Someone came to my front door and asked to use my telephone. I didn't feel comfortable letting a stranger in, so I said no. Should I have let them?

A: No! It's much better to be safe than sorry. Offer to place a call for them, if you like, but leave them outside.

Q: A neighbor of mine has obviously been ill, but he hasn't mentioned what's wrong, and I don't know if I should ask, so I can help. What should I do?

A: Accept the fact that you'll only know what's been offered to you. No matter how anxious you are over his condition, it's his right to tell you what he wants you to know. You can, of course, offer help in a very general way: "You know, Mr. Bradley, I go grocery shopping a couple of times a week; I'd be glad to pick some things up for you if you want me to. Why don't I check with you before I go?"

Q: I'm in love, big-time, but my lady doesn't like it when I hug her on the street. I've tried to tell her to loosen up, but she says she's not comfortable "being mushy in front of other people." I say she's being too uptight. Who's right?

A: Sorry, but our vote goes with the sister. Holding hands or walking arm in arm down the street is sweet. Tongue-wrestling matches, groping and pawing, and other public displays of attraction are tacky. Period.

Q: How can I get guests to go home after spending all night at my house?

A: Sometimes the best approach is the most direct: "Folks, I love ya, but I have to get some sleep! Let me help you find some coats." Even the dimmest guest will get the hint.

Q: Can you give some quick do's and don'ts for courtesy at the theater, ballet, etc.? I'm tired of having my Alvin Ailey experience ruined by people with pagers!

- Do put your pager, if you must bring one, on "vibrate" so only you will be disturbed.
- Don't wear a huge hat that obstructs the views of the paying patrons behind you.
- Do come on time so you don't have to climb over others after the event has started.
- Don't turn your cell phone on at the movies, opera, etc.
- Do enjoy the music—but don't sing along with it. People paid good money to hear the orchestra, not you.
- Do remember that not everything is appropriate for children. Don't bring them to something you'll have to explain throughout the event. (There are child-sized introductions to ballet, symphony, and operas that come to most major cities; try one of these, instead of asking a five-year-old to sit through two and a half hours of *Romeo and Juliet.*) Don't bring them to movies that are violent, use adult language, or feature overt sexuality. (And don't count on the movie rating code to do your work for you. Read reviews in newspapers and magazines carefully, as reviewers often are more candid about the age-appropriateness of a particular film.)

Q: I've never heard of it, but is there such a thing as camera etiquette?

A: Yes, indeed, and it's really simple:

- If you see a photo being taken, don't walk in the photographer's field of vision.

- If you see a group of people trying to take a picture together, you can offer to take the photo so the photographer is in the picture, too. (Make sure it's a camera you know how to use, or can be instructed to use on the spot.)
- If you're taking pictures at a wedding reception or graduation, get your shot quickly and get out of the way; others want to do the same thing.
- If you're taking a picture of people you don't know (in another country, neighborhood, etc.) and you're close enough that they're aware their photo is being taken, ask permission first.

Q: My brother and I are planning to give our parents a fiftieth-anniversary party, but our folks have been definite about not wanting people to bring presents. How can we indicate that tactfully when we invite their friends?

A: Include a small card or a line that says, "No gifts please . . . your presence is the only gift we want." Good guests will honor that request.

Q: I am tired of shopping in fancy stores and being mistaken for the help—especially when I don't dress any differently from the other customers. How do I respond when people ask, "Does this come in a size 8?"

A: Sweetly reply: "I have no idea; I don't work here. Perhaps a salesperson could give you the answer." Most people have the good sense to apologize right away.

Q: In some stores—especially if I am the only black customer—salespeople seem to feel obligated to follow me closely, which I find offensive. How do I nip this in the bud?

A: We suggest turning on your heel, looking straight into the face of the tailgating salesperson, and saying, "I know you're trying to be helpful, but I'd rather browse on my own. I'll let you know if I need assistance." If you suspect they're worried about your departing with merchandise that hasn't been paid for, tell them you find the inference objectionable—and inform them you're taking your money elsewhere, someplace you'll be treated with respect.

Q: What about when the opposite happens? I was at a cosmetics counter and the saleslady took two other customers before me—even though she saw me waiting first.

A: Speak up! "Excuse me, I was here first." If the saleslady balks, or says, "Well, just let me get this out of the way, because this lady is in a rush," let her know *your* time is valuable, too. If you still get no satisfaction, ask to see the manager or go to the store's customer service department and take the time to register a complaint. Since stores rely on customer goodwill, you can bet that your complaint will be looked into.

Q: If a group of us is being served, when can we begin to eat?

A: It's polite to wait until everyone has a plate in front of him, and then you can begin. If you're having dinner in a private home, you can begin after the hostess picks up her fork.

Q: Where's the proper place for your napkin? Can't it go anywhere your clothes need protecting?

A: Sorry, no. When you're seated at the table, the first thing you do is put your napkin in your lap. It shouldn't be tucked into your collar, or your belt, or kept on the table next to your plate—unless you've finished and want to indicate it's all right for the plate to be cleared.

Q: Can guys throw their ties over their shoulders or tuck them into their shirts when they're eating so they don't spill anything on them?

A: If guys are old enough to wear ties, guys are old enough to eat neatly and keep their ties in the proper place.

Q: I just joined a health club. Are there rules, besides the club's, I should know about?

A: Many clubs request these anyway, but here are some pointers:

- Use towels to absorb sweat when using exercise machines and equipment.
- Wipe off machines after you're finished with them, so no one sits in/slips on your sweat.
- Refrain from using equipment, such as treadmills and stairmasters, for longer than the maximum allowable time.
- Keep your belongings in a locker, and not spread them about the locker room.
- Refrain from coming into class late and going to the front of the room, where on-time members have positioned themselves.
- Return all weights, balls, stretch bands, etc., to their proper places.
- Clean off exercise mats before returning them to their proper place.
- Refrain from wearing clothes that are too skimpy, odorous (yes, you go to work out, but you shouldn't smell as if you already have before you even start!), or have offensive or provocative language written all over them.

- Don't go if you have a cold; it's the considerate thing to do for your fellow members.

Q: Can I hold someone's place in line at the bank or grocery store?
A: If she appears promptly when it's her turn, sure. You can't hold everyone up on behalf of someone who's in another part of the store, though.

Q: Is there such a thing as line etiquette?
A: Of course: you form an orderly, single line (unless instructed otherwise) at the grocery store, in the post office, bank, etc. You don't step in front of people or invite friends who arrive after you to step in with you. (You can offer to take their money and buy stamps for them, though, or add a quick transaction to yours.) You leave an appropriate amount of space between yourself and the person before and behind you. If you're driving, you don't tailgate, or change lanes without using your signals. The only exception we can think of offhand is ladies' rooms and small children: when they gotta go, they gotta go. If you're a mother with a squirmy little one, ask the person at the head of the line if you can go next. If you're the person at the head of the line and you're aware of a small child's distress, offer to let him go first.

Q: What do I do with that wet umbrella?
A: If you're visiting someone, your hostess may have a specific place she wants you to leave it: an umbrella stand, a powder room bathtub, or someplace else. You can also always leave it, closed, in a corner of the front porch.

Q: Who says the blessing at the dinner table, and how?
A: If a minister is present, it's traditional to ask him to do it. The head of the household or the eldest person at the gathering is often asked. If a child has been taught to say the blessing and isn't shy, it's nice to have him do it. If you know your guest has done this before and doesn't mind doing it, you may ask if he'd like to give the blessing. Try not to put anyone on the spot, in case he/she doesn't know what to say.

If you're seated, you may simply bow your head and fold your hands in your lap while the blessing is said. If you're standing, you might all hold hands. Either way, you may feel free to repeat "amen" when the blessing is concluded.

If you don't normally say a blessing and you're in the household of someone who does, do what everyone else does: bow your head or clasp hands and simply maintain a respectful silence while the blessing is said.

Q: Someone lent me his handkerchief at a meeting recently; should I give it back?

A: Yes—but *only* after it's washed and ironed.

Q: When can I give or send someone flowers?

A: Almost anytime, for a good reason and for no reason at all. If you're sending flowers to someone in a hospital, check with the nursing staff first. Sometimes doctors forbid cut flowers, but allow plants. In intensive care and critical care, flowers and plants usually aren't allowed.

Q: I've been invited to play in a golf tournament at a local country club. I'm not a member, and I'm not sure what to wear. Suggestions?

A: When in doubt, call ahead and ask. Most clubs do have a dress code, and they'll be happy to share it with you. In general, it's probably better to pass on T-shirts without collars and with slogans (although polo shirts are fine). Some clubs require members to wear long pants for golf, and some have distinct preferences for what's worn on the tennis court. (White clothes with colored trim may be fine; neon colors may not be.) And of course, always remember to wear the proper shoe for the proper sport: spiked golf shoes, rubber-soled tennis shoes, rubber-soled shoes for the squash, basketball, and racquetball courts.

Q: My weekends are sacred, but they keep getting interrupted by religious proselytizers and kids selling magazines and candy! How can I politely turn them away?

A: Be firm: "Thank you, but I can't speak with you today. And I'm happy with my own religion, so I'd appreciate it if you don't stop by again." Let them know that now is inconvenient, but you also have no interest in later, either: "Thanks but I have all the magazine subscriptions I need. I don't want to order any more." Or "Thanks, but we don't eat much candy."

Q: Are phone salespeople allowed to call at any time? I've been interrupted at dinner, while I'm trying to put my kids to bed, and once at 7:30 A.M.

A: In some states, phone solicitations are limited to hours a court has determined are reasonable—9 A.M. to 7 P.M., for example. If you have an answering machine, let it pick up during dinner, bedtime stories, and other times you don't want to be inconvenienced. You might also answer the phone, tell the caller you have no interest, and ask him to take you off his phone list. In many states, tele-salespersons are legally obligated to comply.

Remember that there are lots of phone scams, too. Your con-antenna should go up if someone calls and informs you, out of the blue, that you've won something. The "free prize" you're usually awarded often has to be picked up in person—where you get the sales spiel you didn't get on the phone. Or that "free weekend" at the beach or casino has a fine-print clause that requires you to sit through a two-hour presentation on time-share vacation facilities . . . do you really want to do this?

Q: A new friend has invited me to her mosque for services, and I'd like to go, but I'm afraid of doing something wrong. How do I find out what's appropriate?

A: Ask your friend: "Kabilah, how should I dress on Sunday? Should my head be covered? What about my arms? Can I wear pants?" Your friend will be able to give you guidance. Some general rules:

Roman Catholic churches no longer require women to cover their heads before entering, although many do. It is still considered polite to cover your upper arms, even if you only use a shawl or sweater.

Muslim mosques require women to cover their heads (usually with a scarf veil) and wear long sleeves and ankle-length dresses. Pants may be worn under dresses or long tunics, but should not be worn by themselves.

Jewish women cover their heads for services. Conservative and Orthodox Jewish women wear dresses of "modest" length.

Q: When visiting another church, how do I know when to sit, stand, respond, etc.?

A: Look around you, and use the congregation as your guide. In some denominations, the church program or prayer book will actually tell you when to do this: "Prayer for the World read with pastor, audience stands."

Q: How can I tell how long I'm going to be in a service?

A: You can call and ask how long the average service takes.

Q: What do I say when . . .

. . . someone leaves a message on my machine that she's bringing five extra people to my space-tight party? "Oh, I'm so sorry you won't be joining us; I just don't have room for five extra people."

. . . someone drops by unannounced and I have things to do? "Jackie, you just caught us going out the door; Cydney has ballet in fifteen minutes, I'm sorry."

. . . someone eats my family's food at a BYOF picnic without being invited to? "We'd love to share, Darlene, but I only made enough for the four of us; I didn't know other people would be interested."

. . . my date shows up in jeans for a dinner party at my aunt's home? "Warren, did I forget to tell you this was a seventy-fifth-birthday party? Would you mind running home and changing? You know how older people are about being too casual."

Chapter 43

THINGS WE LOVE

- People who don't have a double standard of behavior for family and friends.
- People who send birthday cards on time.
- People who come bearing unexpected gifts ("I saw it and knew you'd love it!").
- Dinner guests who offer to help with the dishes. (We won't let them, but it's nice that they offered.)
- Folks who wave to kids on school buses.
- People who send handwritten notes of congratulations for accomplishments.
- Handmade and homemade gifts.
- Those who strive for excellence, not perfection.
- Special notepaper.
- "Pamper yourself" gifts.
- People who remember the foods you're allergic to (or detest) and don't serve them to you.
- Friends who send a note just to tell you how splendid the flowers were at your party.
- Guests who remember your favorite flowers and bring them.

- Weekend guests who adapt to the household rhythm, even when it's different from theirs.
- Houseguests who make up their beds.
- Those who use the "good silver" for no reason at all.
- Afternoon tea.
- Visitors who play with the children for a little while so the hosts can put the last-minute touches on dinner.
- Handmade gifts from children.
- Those who make new friends and cherish the old.
- Photographs that chronicle a period in time, or our culture.
- Scented soaps in the bathroom—especially the bathroom guests will be using.
- Black folks who patronize black businesses.
- Being given credit for good work within earshot of other people.
- People who stay home when they have a cold—instead of sharing it with the entire office or theater.
- Families who eat dinner together.
- Hostesses who put their guests at ease.
- Being told ahead of time who your fellow dinner guests will be (because you're curious, but wouldn't dream of being rude enough to ask).
- Men who still open doors for women. Women who let them.
- Hosts who remember to include a mixture of singles and couples and different age ranges in their gatherings.
- Cooking meals that can stretch, so an extra place can always be set for the last-minute guest.
- Videotaping oral histories from elder relatives, so you can compile a "living library" of your family's history.
- Library cards.
- Hats—for practical *and* aesthetic purposes.
- People who spend time in community service, through church, civic, or volunteer organizations. Or just on their own.
- Being told "good morning" by friendly strangers.
- Firm handshakes!
- Neighbors who look in on each other's homes while they're away on vacation.
- Being invited to share in a friend's success or joy.
- Eating out with people who don't quibble over the last nickel when it's time to split the bill.
- Someone who offers to help you do something she knows you hate—polishing the silver, washing the car, or cleaning out closets—because she knows the work will go faster with two tackling it.
- Listening to any church choir.
- People who feed a stranger's parking meter.

- Any random act of kindness.
- Men who wait as you exit the elevator.
- People who participate in their destiny by voting in local, state, and federal elections.
- Sealing wax.
- Children who look you in the eye and speak clearly.
- Children who look after their younger siblings.
- People who send friends a note just to say they think your daughter/son is terrific.
- Men who write thank-you notes. (Actually, *anyone* who writes thank-you notes.)
- Anyone who shares black history and achievements with young people.
- Men who send flowers (especially when they're your favorite) for no reason.
- Books as gifts.
- Bookplates.
- Women who value the company of other women.
- People who apologize before hanging up when they've reached the wrong number.
- Real handkerchiefs.
- Men with home training who treat their mothers, and all the women in their lives, with respect.
- Men who walk on the outside of the sidewalk, or in whatever position that most protects the woman.
- Hostesses who take care of the valet parking tip in advance.
- Men who meet you for dinner and take care of your valet parking without asking.

ENVELOPE WITH WAX SEAL, SEALING WAX, AND SEAL

- People who don't let others walk to their cars alone after dark, and wait to see that your car starts.
- Service workers who give honest estimates.
- Auto mechanics and plumbers who aren't condescending to women.
- People who offer to baby-sit for frazzled parents—even when they have nowhere to go.
- Friends and family members who respect the fact you're on a diet.
- Husbands who know you've had a rough day and have dinner and/or a bubble bath waiting for you when you get home.
- People who share from their garden.
- Friends who celebrate *(anything)* with champagne.
- Men who stand when women enter the room.
- Celebrities who "give back" to their community.
- People who remember where they came from.
- Anything personalized.
- Heirloom gifts from family members.
- Everyone who meets new people and treats them as they would like to be treated.
- Those who think big thoughts and cherish small treasures.
- People who donate a portion of their lottery winnings or other windfall to charity.
- Sports enthusiasts who wipe off exercise equipment when they've finished using it.
- People who freely, and with sincerity, give compliments.
- People who call just to say "hi" when you haven't heard from them in a long time.
- People who feel remiss about having forgotten a birthday, or haven't written in ages, and aren't afraid to be the one to renew the relationship.
- People who speak softly enough to allow you to hear yourself think.
- Folks who take responsibility for every area of their lives.
- People who really *listen* to you.
- People who entertain with ease.
- Fountain pens.
- Women who carry themselves as though their grandmothers were watching.
- People who celebrate life on a daily basis and don't save the good dishes, favorite sweaters, heirloom jewelry, or "company meals" for special occasions. Enjoy each day.
- Style and grace.

Chapter 44

DON'T YOU DARE!

♦♦♦

- Ask a person how much money he makes, what he paid for his home or car, or how much the wedding cost.
- Ask friends how much money, property, or heirlooms they inherited.
- Point your finger in someone's face or chest while you're talking (or arguing) with them.
- Inquire about a person's handicap or disability ("Hey, how'd you lose that finger?").
- Keep the extra money a clerk hands you when she makes a mistake in giving you change for your purchase.
- Accept any kind of terribly expensive gift from someone you are not married, engaged, or related to.
- Snap your fingers to get a waiter's attention.
- Answer the telephone, "Can I *axe* who's calling?"
- Tell your guests how much trouble or expense you've gone to in entertaining them.
- Switch place cards at a seated dinner.
- Forget to offer your seat to a person who is elderly, infirm, or pregnant.
- Stare at anyone who is handicapped.
- Push ahead of other customers waiting in line.

- Chew gum in public or snap or crack gum. (Better yet, don't chew gum at all.)
- Respond to an invitation by penciling in extra guests who haven't been invited.
- Scream at your spouse or child in front of others.
- Pass on gossip you know or suspect is untrue. In fact, don't pass on gossip at *all.*
- Slam doors.
- "Forget" to repay friends who've been kind enough to lend you money.
- Return things dirty or broken that you've borrowed.
- Have "selective recall" and keep borrowed items so long you start believing they're yours.
- Spit on the ground or out a car window.
- Throw trash anywhere but in a designated receptacle.
- Repeat anything that was told to you in confidence.
- Wipe off tableware in a restaurant or in anyone's home.
- Put your feet on anyone's table (including your own).
- Emphasize a point at dinner by waving your fork in someone's face.
- Cut up all your food before you begin to eat it (unless you're physically disabled).
- Talk through a prayer when you're asked to bow your head.
- Promise to do something you have no intention of doing.
- Try to ingratiate yourself with your supervisor by trashing a coworker. Or, if you're the boss, allow employees to get away with it.
- Take credit for another person's idea or suggestion.
- Tell anyone his illness or misfortune is his own fault, or God's retribution for some past sin.
- Yell out a window to anyone.
- Play your music loud enough to wake the dead—or your neighbor down the block.
- Honk your horn outside someone's home to signal your arrival to pick her up.
- Volunteer someone for an assignment without first checking to see if that person is interested and/or available.
- Tell people what you'd like to receive as a present, unless they've specifically *asked* you for suggestions.
- Perform professional services, such as catering, then tell others prior to the party what will be served. (We heard of a caterer who shared all the details of an upcoming wedding with everyone in earshot before they could experience it themselves.)
- Tell anyone how much your employer (hostess or company) paid for rentals, food, or any aspect of the party.
- Use profanity in public.

- Drink out of a bottle, can, or carton in someone's home. (Your host or hostess may offer you a single-serve can of your favorite beverage because everyone else is sitting outside in the yard drinking out of cans and bottles. If you're at the table—yours or someone else's—use a glass.)
- Wear rollers in your hair in public (not even when they're covered with a scarf). Ditto for shower caps and "do-rags."
- Smoke, or eat, on the street.
- Blow smoke in someone's face.

- Remove items from your teeth at the table. (And no, a toothpick is *not* "the black man's dessert.")
- Floss your teeth anywhere other than in the privacy of your own bathroom.
- Play with your food or silverware.
- Scrape and stack plates at the table. (Think about it: would you want a heap of garbage shoveled onto *your* plate while it's still in front of you?)
- Sabotage a friend or family member's diet just because you want company when you eat that chocolate cake.
- Peek in anyone's medicine cabinet. (We know it's tempting . . . but don't.)
- Ask anyone what they're taking medicine for, and what it is.
- Give someone else's telephone number out so you can receive calls while you're visiting (unless you check first to make sure it's okay).
- Tuck your napkin in your shirt or waistband. Grown-ups keep them on their laps.
- Network at a funeral. *(Please.)*
- Forget your mother's birthday. (Don't forget Dad's either.)
- Make long-distance calls on someone else's phone without prior permission and offering to pay for them.
- Go shopping barefoot. (Besides being a health and safety hazard, it's tacky.)
- Tell anyone about your partner's money troubles.
- Wear your underwear as outerwear.
- Be mean just for the sake of it.
- Go to dinner with friends, dutch treat, without any cash.
- Set your boyfriend/husband's car on fire.
- Drive around with suggestive "vanity plates" or bumper stickers.
- Wear suggestive, or vulgar, necklace charms.
- Call anyone that "b" word. Or that "n" word.
- Tell anyone how much you spent on her gift.
- Ask to charge something on someone else's credit card.
- Break wind in public, if you can help it. (Don't forget to apologize if you do.)
- Even *think* about being saddity.
- Put your business "in the street" on national television.
- Discuss family business with nonfamily members.
- Use someone else's name as an entrée without his knowledge.
- Sit in the front at a youth recital and get up and leave as soon as your child has performed.
- Borrow a car and return it on empty (even if you borrowed it on empty!).
- Comb your hair at the table.

- "Double-dip" at the buffet table with chips or other finger foods. (If you've bitten off of it, don't even *think* about redunking it!)
- Slurp when drinking from a mug or eating soup.
- Eat the insides out of the bread and leave the crust in the basket.
- Sit at the table licking *anything:* we don't care *what* the Colonel says.
- Refer to people as "parties" (the "party" of the first part, the other "parties," etc.).
- Ask for the ring back. (Especially if you broke off the relationship.)
- Give someone the same ring you used for the last fiancée.
- Stuff yourself into an outfit "2" sizes "2" small.
- Betray a sibling's trust.
- Feel a need to tell everyone how wonderful you are—if you're all that, we'll manage to figure it out.

Acknowledgments

Our names are on the front of this book, but we could not have written it without the assistance and guidance of many, many others. For that we wish to thank:

Our editor, Janet Hill, who saw the need for the original *Basic Black* and agrees that home training continues to be a necessary part of life.

Our agent, Faith Hampton Childs, who was tireless in advocating for a consistent look and feel to this second edition.

Deborah A. Porter, whose illustrations continue to reflect the mood and spirit of *Basic Black.*

Babes on Books, our literary sisters and support group.

Charlotte Hawkins Brown, whose early efforts blazed a trail before us.

The spirits of countless black women of style through the ages who have inspired us.

Ebony, Essence, and other black magazines that, since their first issues, have showcased black American families, values, culture, and accomplishments.

Our families.

From KGB: Thanks to Bruce W. Talamon, whose partnership and parenting and faith in my abilities allow me to juggle myriad balls, and to Jordan A. B. Talamon for being a child we're both proud to claim. To Pat Bates for being an excellent sounding board. And to my late father, Bernell H. Bates, who liked to point out that not doing the right thing is not an option. *From Karen Elyse:* Thanks to Don E. Freeman, whose love and support of my creative endeavors continue to be a source of inspiration. To my father, Elbert, my brother Paul, and my grandfathers, H. Claude Hudson and Paul R. Williams, whose quest for excellence is surpassed only by their leadership and generosity of spirit: thank you for being my touchstone when it comes to defining gentlemen. Home training at our house was, and continues to be, a shared experience.

Thanks to our mothers, Miriam G. Bates and Marilyn W. Hudson. And our grandmothers, Purry Dixon Grigsby, Florence Green Bates, Della Givens Williams, and Thomey T. Hudson, who remain with us in fond memory, for gently teaching us the principles of home training by daily example.

And thanks to our readers and countless others we've met in the past few years: your suggestions, questions, and observations were—and continue to be—tremendously helpful.

We are grateful to all of you.

Karen Grigsby Bates
Karen Elyse Hudson
Los Angeles 2005

Glossary

Aperitif An alcohol-based drink that is served before a meal, to whet the appetite.

Baccalaureate services Sermon usually given to a graduating class.

Bar mitzvah, bat mitzvah A coming-of-age ceremony for Jewish boys (bar mitzvah) and girls (bat mitzvah).

Beautillion A coming-of-age ceremony for young men in which each is presented to an assembly of guests. His escort is called a *belle.*

BYOB Bring Your Own Bottle.

BYOF Bring Your Own Food (usually used during a potluck gathering or a group event where participants are responsible for their own meals).

Concierge A hotel employee whose job involves the care and feeding of guests, including securing special services such as limousines, theater tickets, baby-sitters, etc.

Corkage The fee charged to uncork a bottle of wine; usually applied to wine bottles that are not ordered from the restaurant's cellar, but brought in by the diner.

Cotillion A coming-of-age ceremony for young women in which each girl is presented to an assembly of guests.

Debutante A young woman who is presented at a cotillion.

Digestif, digestive An alcoholic drink (such as a brandy, eau-de-vie, or cordial) traditionally served after dinner to aid digestion.

Eau-de-vie Highly potent clear brandy made from fermented fruit. Often served as a digestif.

Esquire An old-fashioned honorific applied to lawyers (e.g., Johnnie L. Cochran, Jr., Esq.). Is never used in conjunction with another honorific (e.g., *Mr.* Johnnie L. Cochran, Jr., Esq.), since two honorifics are considered overkill. Exception: ministers, who may be referred to as "Reverend," "Dr.," or both (the Reverend Dr. Martin Luther King, Jr.).

Faux pas Social mistake.

Gravy boat Vessel used for serving gravy and other sauces. Usually has at least one lip to accommodate pouring, or a gravy ladle.

Honorific Usually a prefix added to one's name to indicate gender, marital status, or office: *Mr.* Eddie Anderson, *Ms.* Jessye Norman, *The Hon.* Willie Brown, *His Excellency* James A. Joseph, etc.

Hors d'oeuvres Food that is served at a cocktail party or, increasingly, as the first course of a meal. Sometimes called canapés or appetizers.

Interment Burial.

Invocation A prayer given at the beginning of a gathering, service, or meeting.

Maître d' Short for maître d'hôtel. Headwaiter responsible for general oversight of the dining room in a hotel, restaurant, or club.

No-host bar A bar that charges for drinks. Typically offered anywhere *but* at a private party, where the host provides drinks and does not charge for them.

Per diem Daily expense allowance. ("We get a $40 per diem for breakfast, lunch, and dinner while we're on the road.")

Prix fixe A standard, or fixed, price, for a meal. Usually allows for choices within several categories (hors d'oeuvre, entrée, dessert) and is generally less expensive than a meal chosen à la carte, where a separate price is charged for each course.

Repast A meal that is offered to guests after a funeral or memorial service.

Saddity Stuck-up. Uppity. Snobbish.

Sommelier Wine steward. The person responsible for helping you to choose an appropriate wine for your meal. He may or may not serve the wine himself.

Trousseau A collection of domestic items (kitchenware, fine china, linens) that a single woman might accumulate in anticipation of her married life. Also refers to the bride's wedding-related wardrobe (honeymoon lingerie, a "going-away" suit, etc.).

Wine captain See *sommelier.*

You Tell Us . . .

Although we tried to give you the basics of home training in this book, space wouldn't allow us to include everything we wanted to. So:

- If there are things you'd like for us to include in future editions . . .
- If there are regional customs that differ from the ones we've described here that you think we should know about . . .
- If you have family traditions that you'd like to share . . .
- If we were wrong and your mother was right . . .
- Or if you have a dilemma or question involving home training . . .

. . . we'd love to hear from you! Please send your correspondence to:

The Two Karens
c/o Doubleday
1745 Broadway, 23rd Floor
New York, NY 10019

or e-mail us: the2karens@aol.com.

Thank you for your continued interest and support. We hope the information we've gathered in *The New Basic Black* has been helpful.

—Karen Grigsby Bates
Karen Elyse Hudson

"Racism is not an excuse to not do the best you can."

Arthur Ashe

Index

About the Authors

Karen Grigsby Bates is a correspondent for NPR's national news magazine *Day to Day*. For several years, she wrote for *Time* magazine and was a contributing columnist to the *Los Angeles Times* Op Ed page. Bates is the author of *Plain Brown Wrapper* and *Chosen People*, suspense novels featuring reporter-sleuth Alex Powell. She lives in Los Angeles with her husband and son.

Karen Elyse Hudson writes an advice column titled "Talk to Me" for the Wave Newspapers Group and is the author of a biography of her maternal grandfather, *Paul R. Williams, Architect: A Legacy of Style*, and a biography for young people, *The Will and The Way: Paul R. Williams, Architect*. She speaks extensively on etiquette, party planning, and architecture.

Deborah A. Porter is a freelance artist who also creates miniature needlepoint portraits depicting people of color from around the world.